Pat F. Booth

Indexing: The Manual of Good Practice

K · G · Saur München 2001

Die Deutsche Bibliothek – CIP-Einheitsaufnahme

Booth, Pat F. :
Indexing: the manual of good practice /
by Pat F. Booth. - München : Saur, 2001
ISBN 3-598-11536-9

Printed on acid-free paper

© K. G. Saur Verlag GmbH, München

Cover design by Amanda Barragry

Typesetting by Florence Production Ltd., Stoodleigh, Devon

Printed and Bound in Great Britain by Antony Rowe Ltd., Chippenham, Wiltshire
ISBN 3-598-11536-9

The Author

Pat F. Booth is a freelance indexer and trainer. She is a Registered Indexer (Society of Indexers) and a Chartered Librarian, with degrees in education and the social sciences. Before freelancing, she worked in libraries – mostly in industry – then taught information retrieval studies at a London college.

She is the editor of the second edition of the Society of Indexers' 'Training in indexing' open learning units and the author of 'Report writing: guidelines for information workers' 1991 2nd edn. Kings Ripton, Cambs: ELM Publications, and (with Mary L. South) of 'Information filing and finding' 1982 Kings Ripton, Cambs: ELM Publications.

Contents

Society of Indexers' Foreword

Indexing: the manual of good practice is at once a revelation for the potential or beginner indexer and a source of reference and revision – also of enlightenment – for the experienced practitioner.

Pat Booth's experience as librarian, indexer and teacher of indexing has given her a broad acquaintance with the sources of knowledge – literary, visual, audio and electronic – and of the ways in which enquirers seek for information and students stumble over instruction.

The would-be indexer is shown the uses of indexes and the indexing requirements of a document and then led into the practice of indexing, persuasively rather than dogmatically, because documents and readers are individuals and discussion and reference to others' opinions help to form the indexer's judgement.

'Making the index' is nevertheless a rigorous statement of the necessary steps: assessment of significance in choosing what to index, the presentation of names – of persons, corporate bodies, places, publications, objects and ideas – indication of their finding-places (locators) within the document and construction of the necessary cross-references that link words and subjects.

However excellent the individual entries, they do not make a satisfactory index without careful editing. Advice is given on harmonization of terminology, arrangement of entries and the solution of such niggling problems as those presented by characters that do not occur in the English alphabet, and on punctuation and layout, so that the completed index is clear, consistent and easy to use.

Certain forms of publication and certain subjects present problems peculiar to themselves. Serial publications, Images and sound recordings, Law, Medicine, Archaeology, Genealogy, Science and technology, Biography, and Literature for children are treated additionally and separately. Each form is analysed for its materials and readership and its peculiar indexing problems.

One may be a brilliant indexer but fail to organize one's time and one's financial affairs, or to make use of the technological help that is now available. What the author has learnt from her own experience, widened by reading and interchange of ideas with colleagues, has enabled her to include practical chapters on Management and Technology that discuss methods of working and record-keeping and the various devices and programs for saving time and repetition of effort. As elsewhere in the book, specific names and addresses are given where relevant.

Most lone workers benefit from the help and assurance conferred by membership of a craftsmen's guild, so the final chapter describes the aims and achievements of indexers' societies. It was at the request of the Society of Indexers, in pursuit of its constitutional aims of raising the standards of indexing and educating indexers, that Pat Booth wrote this book. Originally the Society had thought of up-dating Norman Knight's classic, *Indexing, the art of*, but that proved impracticable. There was no question of who best could now represent the Society in preparing a comprehensive and up-to-date British manual. Pat Booth herself acknowledges the help and support she has received from fellow-members of the Society of Indexers, and the Society's close involvement with the publication of her book. But *le style est l'homme même*. Pat Booth's writing is clear, straightforward and elegant. I think that no indexer could read her book without pleasure and profit.

Mary Piggott BA FLA
President of the Society of Indexers, 1995–1997
Carey Award for outstanding services to indexing, 2000

Preface

Many strands, woven together over several years, contributed to the idea of writing a book on indexing. A long-standing interest in enabling access to documentary information – at both the individual document level and the collection level – stemming from employment as a special (workplace) librarian and as a college lecturer in information retrieval studies, was one. Another, emerging from my work as a freelance indexer, was the recognition of the dependence of the usability of a text on the provision of a good index – that is to say an index that is worthy of the text, of the right size, accurately reflecting the coverage and treatment of the text, signalling its detailed content, and presented in a form suitable for the anticipated users. From contributing to, and editing, open learning materials for beginning indexers, and from tutoring courses for a variety of groups – trainee indexers, freelance indexers, in-house indexers, publishers' editorial staff responsible for commissioning indexes, and technical writers producing indexes to their own documents – came the realization that indexing has a very wide area of application and is carried out in many different kinds of organizations. Finally, the Society of Indexers expressed a wish for a wide-compassed text on indexing that would help to promote the best of practice, wherever indexing is done.

It is not my intention to establish new 'rules' for indexing. Published guidelines already exist. For certain situations there is quite clearly a 'best' – even a 'right' way; in others there are alternatives which, in their different contexts, may each be acceptable. I have indicated the 'best' ways, and have explained the alternatives so that indexers can consider them and make their own choices. Indexing is, after all, a thinking activity; it involves judgement and requires informed decisions to be made.

I acknowledge here the inspiration gained from past and present writers on indexing and from the many thought-provoking and productive conversations I have had with indexers, authors, editors, librarians, lecturers, and students. Contributors to the internet discussion groups for indexers have also – by revealing the technical topics that indexers at all stages of development and experience are interested in – sparked off some of the thoughts and ideas that found their way into the book.

I am grateful to the Society of Indexers' Publications Committee for its encouragement and support. Special thanks go to all the people (fellow indexers, family and friends) who, despite being very busy with their own work and commitments, read and commented on draft chapters or portions of chapters – Ken Bakewell, Judy Batchelor, Drusilla Calvert, Judy Coleman, Bo Cooper, Glennis Cooper, Yvonne Dixon, Jill Halliday, Christine Headley, Ann Kingdom, Cherry Lavell, Vanessa Longman, Beryl McKie, Betty Moys, Mary Piggott, Jan Ross, and Christine Shuttleworth. I am indebted, too, to Society members Hazel Bell, Barbara Britton, Laurence Errington, Jane Horton, Ann Hudson, Helen Litton, Anne McCarthy, Paul Nash, Richard Raper, Janet Shuter, Elizabeth Wallis, and Liza Weinkove, for providing me with information and discussing a host of technical points. Linda Hajdukiewicz and Kristin Susser at Bowker-Saur gave advice and guidance whenever it was needed. I greatly appreciate Jane Horton's acceptance of the job of creating the index.

Indexing is an activity that exercises practitioners' minds, extends their knowledge, stimulates their curiosity, requires them to marshal the skills and aptitudes of analysis, selection and representation – all with meticulous care. They need to be temperamentally suited to the work – anyone who is not is likely to regard it as overdemanding and unrewarding. I hope that the book will encourage all those who have what it takes to join the indexing community. For those already in the community – whether indexing is just a job or a way of life or a lifelong pilgrimage in search of perfection – I hope that it will be of some help.

I acknowledge with gratitude the permissions granted to reproduce extracts from published materials: Glennis Cooper for extracts from her *Electrical heritage: a guide and reference source* (1986) Kings Ripton, Cambs: ELM Publications; Bowker-Saur for extracts from *Abstracts in new technologies and engineering (ANTE)*; *British humanities index (BHI)*; and *Library & information science abstracts (LISA)*.

There are several lists in this book. Often a list is the best and clearest way of presenting detailed information. Anyone who does not like lists is free to skip them at the first reading and to consult them as and when the need arises.

Pat F. Booth

CHAPTER ONE

Indexes – purpose and uses

Myths about Indexes

- Only long texts need them
- They are not worth the money spent on them
- Books for children don't need them
- No-one bothers to use them
- A detailed contents list makes an index unnecessary
- Only printed textual documents need indexes
- Searching on the internet means we don't need them
- Full-text searching makes them unnecessary
- There is only one possible 'right' index for any document
- Fiction books never need indexes

Myths about Indexing

- Anyone can do it
- It's just making a list of names
- It can all be done entirely automatically by a computer
- It's just clerical work

- It's just picking important words out of the text
- It's boring and unsatisfying work

By the end of this book, the reader should be convinced that all of these are wrong and that there is much more to indexing (and indexers) than meets the eye. The reader will find that it helps to look at (even to read) as many indexes as possible (at home, at work) before, during and after reading this book. Opportunities to meet indexers, for discussion of practical points and working methods, and to find out about work chances and training, are available through the organizations mentioned in Chapter 12.

Introduction to Indexes and Indexing

Indexing is a vital activity that, nevertheless, often goes unnoticed. It is taken for granted by readers of a book that there is an index – usually, but not always, at the back – and that it will enable references to individual topics to be found. Users of libraries expect to be provided with a search tool that will help them to trace individual documents on a particular subject or by a certain writer, or having a given title. (The word 'document' is used throughout this book to denote any information-bearing item – such as a book, periodical article, report, image, audiotape, CD-ROM, or electronic file.) Researchers doing literature searches depend on the existence of indexes to periodicals (often cumulative, covering several years or volumes), and to collections of papers, reports and correspondence. Few index users, though, seem to be aware of how the index gets there, who creates it, and what is involved in its creation. Even those who work professionally with documents can realize – on meeting an indexer for the first time – that they have little knowledge of the techniques employed in the writing and production of an index, nor of what differentiates a good index from a bad one.

The words 'index' and 'indexing' have been used and continue to be used in a wide variety of fields and applications, as indicated by Knight (1979, Ch.1), Mulvany (1994, Ch.1) and Wellisch (1995, pp. 199–210). In this book, an 'index' refers to an organized (usually alphabetical) sequence of entries, each of which can lead a user to the desired information within a document, or to the required document within a collection. 'Indexing' is the process of creating – or, as some indexers prefer to say, compiling, or writing – the index. This book is mainly (but not wholly) concerned with whole-document indexing. The same principles apply whatever the type of document (book, periodical, encyclopaedia, collection of images, multimedia package, database), whatever the subject matter (arts, science and technology, social sciences, medical sciences) and whatever the target readership (students, research workers, professional practitioners, children, 'the general public'). In addition, each of these categories requires consideration of its special needs (vocabulary range, educational level, information-seeking skills, mode of use); the indexer must take care to formulate index entries suited to each individual document and to present them in the best format.

Some people assume that all indexes are (or could be) automatically generated, because the majority of texts and databases are now held on disk and so all references to a word can be identified and listed. Such 'word-counting' and 'mention-noting' methods are quite unsuitable for the majority of indexes. Indexing is not a mechanical word-spotting process. It involves intellectual activity – understanding and analysis of texts and their messages, selection of significant references to relevant topics, assembly of references, choice of suitable vocabulary for the representation of topics, and presentation in an accessible format. Headings in an index to a document do not consist solely of words appearing in its text, because part of the indexer's role is to supply additional headings that may be more familiar to certain index-users. This contrasts with a certain kind of concordance that lists in alphabetical order every word in a text and shows where each one occurs – such a listing is entirely dependent on the words themselves and is not concerned with the ideas behind them. Another kind of concordance, much used by researchers into language usage, lists individual words in their contexts (phrases and sentences) to show precisely how they are used in written and spoken discourse.

Levels of indexing

Indexing and information access are inextricably linked and can exist at different levels. At the finest (most detailed) level, as in whole-document (including 'back-of-the-book') indexing, it involves analysing and signalling the significant content of a single document (or a connected series of documents) and providing references to individual pages, paragraphs, columns or lines.

At the broadest level, it consists of selecting and providing access to basic identifying features of documents within a collection such as a library – e.g. names of authors, significant title words, series titles, and classification numbers or words representing the principal subject of each document – but not providing a detailed analysis of each part (page, section, frame) of each document. In libraries and other resource centres the creation of records describing the principal features of each document in the collection – author(s), title, edition, place of publication, date, extent (e.g. number of pages), series, standard number – is usually referred to as 'cataloguing'. These individual descriptions together make up the total record of stock (the catalogue) of the particular collection. Indexing then relates to providing access to these descriptions, by highlighting in a standard form the names of authors, document titles, series titles, and subject indicators. Subject indicators may be classification numbers or words and phrases (subject headings) normally selected from a schedule or standard listing. This enables the catalogue or database to answer questions such as 'Is there a document entitled *Child psychology for parents* in this collection?', 'Which books by Janet Frame are held here?' and 'What is there here on water purification?' This level of indexing is limited to showing the principal subject(s) of each document; it is sometimes called 'representational' indexing, because it aims only to represent the overall subject coverage and not to analyse at the 'microlevel'.

An intermediate level is sometimes practised in the indexing of periodical articles, for example by using a small number of significant words from article titles and from accompanying abstracts or the text. Because of the varying levels of indexing, the term 'indexing' itself can differ in meaning, according to the speaker or writer and the context of the discourse.

The necessity for indexes

Readers of this book – having been sufficiently interested to pick it up and start reading – probably need no convincing of the necessity of indexes. However, there are others, even some authors and editors, who – while agreeing that it might be a good idea to include indexes if there were time and resources available – do not regard them as essential components. It is no exaggeration to say that most documents benefit from the inclusion of an index and that the use of the majority of them is severely hampered by the omission of an index. Their value to literature, to study and research, and to information transmission and exchange, is incalculable.

Information and knowledge transmission

All documents are prepared for a purpose and contain a message or messages to be communicated to others – an individual, a group with a common interest, or the world at large. The originator (author) of a written document expresses thoughts, descriptions, and narratives in a suitable way so as to convey them to the intended readership. Publishers design and produce the finished version with the aim of appealing to that readership.

Everyone involved with the preparation and production of the document is, in one way or another, concerned with the promotion of the messages in it. The indexer's activity is an essential part of that process. Consider the ways in which different kinds of document are used. A report, for example, may be read rapidly from beginning to end by one user, who then wants to go back and check precisely what was said about a particular topic. Another user of the same report may not be too concerned with its main messages but needs to check whether there are any significant references to her special subject. Yet another only wants to check whether he, or his organization, is referred to by name. All these users can find answers to their questions more quickly if there is a good index.

Some students treat indexes as summaries or distillations of texts and read them through from A to Z to get an idea of the overall coverage and the significant themes. If the index entries as a whole appear to provide a good match with their current interests, or if there is a substantial 'bunch' of headings and subheadings relating to a specific relevant topic, then they can feel justified in spending time reading the main text or the relevant parts of it. If not, they can pass on to the next one.

The biography of a person living or recently deceased may be read straight through or used for checking of personal names, events and places. A textbook can be used, chapter by chapter, for learning, but is then likely to be referred to again and again for information on specific topics. An index provides an easy way of finding individual and multiple references to subjects, with – where relevant – indications of the major treatments and aspects of the subjects. The usefulness of the index continues for as long as the document itself is used, and its existence makes it more likely that the document will be used continually, because the information within it is accessible. It is amazing (and some would say disgraceful) that some lengthy texts are still being published without any indexes; the disservice done to the authors, and to the potential readers, is considerable; the usability of these texts is much diminished.

Large, complex texts obviously need indexes, but it is a mistake to assume that no short or small document does. The features of each individual document have to be taken into consideration. Imagine a ten-page booklet of instructions for the use and maintenance of a piece of equipment, presented in hierarchically numbered paragraphs (1, 1.1, 1.2, 1.2.1 and so on), with several diagrams and photographs. The print is small and dense. During the life of the equipment, many different users will need to consult the booklet to find out how to set up and adjust the machine, and how to identify the causes of faulty operation. A short index can provide immediate reference to the exact paragraph and save the user the annoyance of riffling to and fro – when already in a state of stress – trying to find the relevant information.

Indexes to documents, and to collections of documents, also provide a unique means for researchers and scholars to follow trails through literature, working backwards and forwards over many decades and tracing the ideas, events, activities, people and organizations relevant to the topic of interest. Where indexes are present – even though they differ in size, coverage, vocabulary and quality – they provide signposts for the scholar or researcher through a mass of literature whose treasures would have to be discovered by solid reading or by dipping in or by searching on the basis of a hunch.

Contents lists and indexes

It is common to meet producers of lengthy reports and manuals who are satisfied that a detailed contents list is sufficient to help the reader around the text. It is true that in a text divided into chapters with hierarchically numbered paragraphs or sections, a full contents list – or one showing perhaps the first and second levels of heading – is very helpful. This is not the point, however; the contents list and the index have entirely different (though complementary) purposes.

A contents list displays the overall coverage and structure of the text (in more or less detail and with a varying level of clarity), announcing the principal topic divisions of the text, in the order in which they appear, and thereby indicating the author's perspective on the subject. In an English-language document it is usually placed after the title page and before other preliminaries and the main text. In foreign-language documents – in French and Spanish publications, for example – they are sometimes placed after the main text rather than before it, and may be referred to as 'tables of contents' or 'indexes'.

Chapter titles shown in the contents list may be indicative of the general content of each chapter, but can be brief, or obscure, or jocular. Chapter subtitles similarly may reveal or conceal. However, even when the titles and subtitles are completely clear and meaningful, they give only a fraction of the total content because they are only overall indicators. In addition, a particular topic is frequently dealt with in more than one chapter – this is not easily discovered from the contents list.

An index, on the other hand, delves deep into the text, identifying and representing a wide variety of topics, bringing together the scattered references to topics, ordering them in sequence, analysing those with multiple references, and presenting them to the reader in a helpful order (usually, but not always, alphabetical). The following extracts show the difference clearly.

Contents list (extract)

I	Do's and don'ts	3
I.I	Before plugging in	3
I.2	Before switching on	3
I.3	During operation	4
I.4	Before switching off	5
I.5	After switching off	5

[etc. etc.]

Index (extract)

accessories   4, 25
action button   3, 4, 5
anti-splash guard   3
artificial lighting   3
attachments   3, 23
auxiliary pump   4
[etc. etc.]

An index is not dependent upon chapter and textual headings for its vocabulary. It includes not only words from the sentences of the text, but also synonyms that the user may employ to look up a topic referred to in the text by another word. Many such equivalent and overlapping words and phrases exist and instances can occur in any subject field – 'petrol' and 'gasoline', 'neonates' and 'newborns', 'taps' and 'faucets', 'felines' and '*Felidae*' and 'cat family', 'soups' and 'broths' and 'consommés', 'wind-surfing' and 'boardsailing' and 'sailboarding', for example. The index also contains cross-references to assist the user to search the index and uses typographical conventions (e.g. bold, italic) or other highlighting to indicate, for example, major references, illustrations, and definitions.

Only the index can give such fine representation of the total text, which is why some readers use the index as means of introduction to the text. It contains the essence of the text and reveals its coverage, enabling the reader to make a speedy decision about its relevance and usefulness for a particular purpose.

The distinction between contents lists and indexes is not helped by the practice of certain newspapers and internet web sites, which give a guide to their contents (not in alphabetical or other helpful order) but call it an index.

Applications of Indexing

Many of the descriptions and examples in this book relate to the indexing of printed materials, particularly the indexing of text, because that is one of the main areas of activity for indexers and because the principles and techniques of indexing can best be explained in that context. The same principles and techniques, however, apply to the indexing of any kind of document – with variations to allow for differences in physical form and the accessibility (to the user) of the information within them.

Who should care about indexes?

Experienced document users know all about the uses of indexes and many use them as the first port of call – either for a summary of content or for finding required information on a given topic. Too often, though, indexes are overlooked or ignored – why? Perhaps because – tucked away at the back of a book, for example – they are hidden from view and people are unaware of their existence. Alternatively, they sometimes appear intimidating – long strings of page references with unexplained typographical features (italic, bold), abbreviations and Latin words, or many levels of indented subentries. There may also be an element of 'unwillingness to ask directions' in some users, who feel that their intelligence alone should be sufficient to enable them to find what they want. For a practising indexer to observe someone hunting back and forth through the pages of a book and hoping in vain for the reference to turn up, is a frustrating experience. It seems that indexes need to be promoted and highlighted much more than at present, and that readers need to be introduced to them as early as possible so that they come to expect and demand indexes to all suitable documentary items.

Writers and editors involved with the preparation and production of documents for the commercial market presumably want the best for their 'progeny'; the reception and reputation of their publications is enhanced by the inclusion of a good index. Book reviews often (but not often enough) contain comments on the existence, content and quality of the indexes. People producing in-house company documentation – brochures, annual reports, pamphlets – can help to get the message across by providing indexes. Students – at school, at home, in university and college – can assist their learning and their preparation of assignments, projects, and theses, by exploiting indexes to all kinds of materials and to resource collections and also by indexing their own notes for easy use. Scholars and researchers can ensure that they search widely and comprehensively for material relevant to their fields of work by identifying and checking the relevant indexes.

Which kinds of document should be indexed?

Any document with informational content can be indexed, though not all need to be. Some documents 'speak for themselves' and need no explanation or interpretation; readers (users) then need no assistance via an index. A poster, for example, advertising a forthcoming event, usually provides all relevant information on the single side of a sheet. Everything is obvious and available to anyone who can read, so – apart from a contact address or number – nothing more is needed at the time (but see 'Change of use' below). Some documents are, in a sense, self-indexing –

a dictionary arranged in alphabetical order, for example. The user has a word in mind and looks it up in the alphabetical sequence to find the definition. It would be possible to include also an index to headwords (the words defined in the dictionary), indicating the page number on which each word can be found, but this is not usually considered necessary. Telephone directories and address lists are similarly arranged in indicative order – alphabetically by surname or organizational name. Very short documents may need no index because the content is simple, well structured and clearly laid out. A two-page report, for instance, that consists of short paragraphs with informative headings and plainly stated conclusions, could be very easy to scan and select from – an index would therefore be superfluous.

The most familiar index is probably the one in the back of a book. Most users of books know from an early age about the existence of such indexes, though fewer appear actually to use them as adults. The inclusion of indexes in factual books for children, to which some reputable publishers attach such importance, is clearly an important influence. Information skills teaching in schools, in which reference book indexes are used in practical exercises, is also important. Other early encounters with indexes can include using CD-ROM reference sources, and 'help' indexes with new software.

The existence of indexes is by no means confined to literary, educational and research spheres. Many people probably use them on a regular basis, without any conscious realization. Almost all activities in life involve, at some time or other, the use of an index.

For example:

Transport and travel: Train timetables, e.g. *High speed train and sleeper services* (FWT for the UK rail companies) – an alphabetical index at the front lists names of rail stations, followed by the number of the table in the booklet, e.g. Glasgow Central **1**, **3**, *14*. (Bold type indicates a service to London; light type a service to another destination, and italic type a sleeper service.) Street guides and atlases. Owners' handbooks for cars.

Shopping: Store guides – alphabetical lists of categories of goods and services, showing the floor or other location, e.g. Carpets – Floor 2; Restaurant – Mezzanine.

Entertainment: Catalogues of disks and tapes (arranged in categories, e.g. R & B, opera, rock, spoken word) with indexes of performers, composers, etc. Film and video guides (arranged in alphabetical order of film title), with indexes to directors and actors.

Home, leisure, hobbies and interests: Books, encyclopaedias and magazines dealing with individual interests: Cookery – indexes of names of dishes, types of meal, and food items. Gardening – indexes of plant names (common names and scientific/Latin names), plant families, plants for different purposes, and cultivation processes and problems. Antiques and collectables – indexes of furniture items, styles, periods, materials, artists, craftspeople, and manufacturers. Birdwatching – indexes of bird names (common names and scientific/Latin names) and habitats.

Directories and yearbooks: Phone directories. Organizational yearbooks, membership and service lists.

It is in the realms of literature, scholarship, research and study, however, that the need for indexes, and their value to knowledge transmission is particularly clearly highlighted. In the UK alone, the Publishers' Association [www.publishers.org.uk] estimates that over 108 000 book titles were published in 1999, of which around 55 000 were in the academic and professional categories (including science, technology and medicine), about 30 000 were adult non-fiction, around 9000 books for children, and about 4000 books for schools. Some of these thousands of titles were completely new, others were revised editions. Each time a book is to be published as a new edition, the index must be revised, too. The UK volume of *Willings press guide* (2000) contains more than 20 000 entries for newspapers, periodicals and other serial items. Various non-print items such as CD-ROMs, films and videos, audio materials and software also appear in large numbers. To this vast amount of published indexable material must be added the many documents not widely available – for example those produced in-house by companies and other organizations, for internal use or limited distribution.

Indexes are required not just to individual, discrete documents. Serials (e.g. periodicals and newspapers) need indexing by volume or by year; subsequently, cumulated indexes may be compiled covering, say, five years, ten years, and more. Some series of publications (e.g. official technical standards covering the safe handling and transport of a range of materials and substances) need an index to the series. Collections of disparate, unrelated documents, such as are found in libraries, resource centres, registries, office files, business archives, academic institutions, committees, public inquiries, medical centres, government departments, conferences, and personal collections, require indexes to their contents in order to be able to trace the documents relevant to certain topics. The value of the information contained in organizational records (older paper records and newer computerized ones) is now recognized within many organizations and they are taking steps to ensure that it can be accessed through the construction of good indexes. This can be done by trained indexers in-house or by contract to external freelance indexers.

Change of use

It is important to remember that documents can be subject to a change of use, and that the new use is likely to require a different kind of indexing. A poster announcing a rally or demonstration – or a concert, or a sporting event, or a competition – is likely not to have been indexed at all at the time of production. After the passage of time, however, posters can become part of an important archive, of value to social researchers, journalists, biographers, and others. It is then that they need indexing, in order that they can be traced by date, venue, people and organizations involved, subject field, and so on.

Other groups of unindexed documents that are subject to change of use and a need for indexing as they become historically interesting include: letters, diaries, notebooks, parish registers, business records, and the records of clubs, societies and associations.

Where indexes are used

Wherever there are documents, indexes are used – in the home, at the workplace, on the move. Obvious locations include libraries, travel agencies, shops, tourist information centres, hospitals, offices, finance houses, and factories. Access to electronically held information has extended the use of indexes, to enable enquirers to track down desired information.

How indexes are used

Indexers do not know as much as they would like to about the way in which readers use their indexes. Freelance indexers are, rightly, principally concerned about producing a good index by the agreed deadline; they hardly ever receive feedback from users once the index has been published and is in use. They are, of course, index users themselves and so know something of the ways in which they search and what they are searching for, but – because of their inside knowledge – do not experience the same problems as those who lack their knowledge and skill.

Librarians are conscious of the different information-seeking skills of the users of document collections, and know that some people require considerable help in finding and consulting catalogues and indexes, while others are competent enough to be left alone. The making of an index requires the indexer to consider who the likely users will be, and to make assumptions about their information skills, their familiarity with the subject of the text and its vocabulary, and the purpose for which they will be using the document. The lifespan of a document can be extensive and it may continue for many years (though perhaps being used for a different purpose).

Standards of document preparation

During their careers, indexers can expect to have to make indexes for all kinds of document, in terms of physical format and the quality of the text (or other information content).

Good indexing comes more easily if the original documents are prepared to a high standard. A document with a helpful structure (e.g. introduction, statement of purpose, exposition, development, conclusion), lucid writing, grammatical sentences, correct spelling and consistent presentation, all assist the indexer to identify the main themes and messages and to formulate suitable index entries. Documents that are prepared and edited in a careful, co-ordinated and professional way raise fewer problems for indexers than those that ramble or bounce from one topic to another and back again, which cite names and topics in several different ways, and that contain obvious factual errors. Guidance on the design and preparation of documents is widely available; indexers who also write and prepare their own texts can benefit from consulting some of the published items, such as Butcher (1992), University of Chicago Press (1993), and Schriver (1996).

'The Good Index': What Characterizes It

Simply, a good index provides straightforward, comprehensive and accurate access to required information, from the words and phrases used by the information searcher to the precise location (such as a page, paragraph, column, line, or image) within the document.

Intellectual and presentational features

The characteristics that identify a good index fall into two main categories: intellectual and presentational – summarized below and attended to in detail in Chapter 3 'What (and whether) to index', Chapter 4 'Forming the index entries' and Chapter 5 'Editing and presenting the index'.

Intellectual Features

- All the relevant text should be given suitable, balanced coverage in the index.
- All the significant references to topics likely to be of interest to the anticipated user should be represented by headings that:
  - are concise
  - are meaningful
  - are likely to be looked for by users (including synonymous terms that do not necessarily appear in the document)
  - lead to the correct place(s) in the document
- Cross-references should be included, where helpful, to link conceptually related terms.
- A clear introduction should explain (where necessary) coverage, arrangement and typographical conventions used.

Indexing is not merely a matter of spotting and listing the important words that appear in a text; nor is it a question of listing every mention of a topic. The indexer must understand the meaning of the text as a whole and of its parts. Each informative treatment of any significant topic must be represented by at least one heading in the index. Uninformative references ('mere mentions') are not normally indexed. For example, these extracts (from three imaginary texts) all refer to Marie Curie, but only one of them – the third – is worthy of indexing, because it contains information about her:

> In a career reminiscent of that of Marie Curie a hundred years earlier, Danielle's work resulted in significant advances in her scientific field and she died from the effects of her experiments.

> Family and friends teased her constantly about what she called her 'scientific work' in the greenhouse. Her younger brother would creep in when she was unaware, studying something intently with her toy microscope. 'Who do you think you are?' he would suddenly ask, making her jump and sometimes knock over the microscope, 'Marie Curie?'

> Pierre Curie gave up his own work to assist Marie in her researches. Together they isolated the elements polonium and radium and subsequently jointly received the Nobel Prize for Physics in 1903 with Antoine Henri Becquerel.

Judgement of significance and informative value requires the indexer to understand the message and purpose of the text. This judgement is, of course, subjective, which is why an index is an individual work. Two or more indexers making an index to the same text will produce different results because they judge significance at slightly different levels and because their usages of words and phrases differ. This does not imply that one of these indexes is superior to the other; they are just different.

The choice and formation of headings requires careful thought. Certainly most of the headings are likely to be words taken from the text being indexed, but many of them will require a change of form. It may be necessary to change from singular to plural, such as 'bus' to 'buses', or from verb to noun, like 'propagate' to 'propagation', or to add words to explain or modify, as in 'installations (art exhibits)' and 'installations (industrial equipment)'. The headings chosen are likely to fall into several different categories; not only proper names (such as people, organizations, places, and events), but words representing objects, qualities, substances, materials, attributes, and properties. The representation of abstract concepts – some of which may only be implied in a text, without being explicitly cited – is often a crucial aspect of the indexer's intellectual input.

Presentational Features

- Alphabetical order should be consistent within an index – there are different methods of arranging headings that consist of more than one word.
- Subheadings should be arranged in an order suitable for the purpose.
- Locators should be presented in a consistent form – there are different ways of showing a page range (a continuing sequence of text from one page to another).
- Overall layout, punctuation and style should be consistent, including the indention of subentries.
- Entries for the different letters of the alphabet (As, Bs) should be separated by spacing.

These features mostly concern the arrangement, layout and styling of the entries (headings and locators) on the page or on the screen. Some of them can be computer-assisted, but the indexer must be in control and aware of what the computer is doing. For example, alphabetical sorting is often performed automatically, but – because there are various ways of dealing with phrases containing spaces, signs and symbols, punctuation marks, and capital letters – the indexer must be able to decide the final arrangement. Similarly, there are different ways of laying out subheadings; each one may start on a new line, or alternatively may continue on the same line after suitable punctuation. The order in which subheadings are presented is also a matter of indexer choice and the computer can be instructed to follow one convention or another.

Number of sequences in an index

Examination of indexes in different documents will reveal that some comprise a single sequence, usually alphabetical A–Z, of headings of all kinds, while others consist of separate sequences for headings of different kinds. These are samples of supposed entries from three indexes in different fields:

Single sequence (in a book on banking):
    Adams, H.R.J. 46   *personal name*
    British Bankers' Association 92   *corporate name*
    Bank management 55   *title of a work*
    foreign currency translation 101   *'subject'*

Two sequences (in a gardening book):
    Blue-eyed Mary 12
    Chinese Lantern 45   }*popular, vernacular names*
    Evening Primrose 33
    New Zealand Burr 67
    Red Hot Poker 71

    Acaena 67
    Kniphofia 71
    Oenothera 33   }*scientific, Latin names*
    Omphalodes 12
    Physalis 45

Three sequences (in a law book):
    Elvington v Elmshire C.C. 231
    Felstead v Frimleigh 145   } *legal cases*
    Topham Spalding Ltd v Mather 301

    food hygiene regulations 134
    Inland Revenue: capital gains tax 111   } *'subjects'*
    intestacy 99

    Dangerous Dogs Act 1991   156
    Patents Act 1977   137   }   *statutes (legislation)*
    Timeshare Act 1992   255

It is wise to start from the premise that a single sequence is often better, because the user is not required to consider which kind of heading is to be looked up in which sequence – everything is together. Headings in the single sequence can – if thought helpful – be differentiated typographically, using italics or capitals, for example:

> *Dangerous Dogs Act 1991*   156
> ELVINGTON v ELMSHIRE C.C.   231
> FELSTEAD v FRIMLEIGH   145
> food hygiene regulations   134
> Inland Revenue: capital gains tax   111
> intestacy   99
> *Patents Act 1977*   137
> *Timeshare Act 1992*   255
> TOPHAM SPALDING LTD v MATHER   301

However, there are circumstances in which separate sequences may be desirable, for example a text having clearly defined categories of content that are likely to be searched for separately by particular kinds of user or for particular purposes. In some subject fields there may be a tradition of separating certain kinds of heading. In law, for example, it is common to provide a separate 'Table of Cases', which is in effect a separate index of legal case names (as 'Felstead v Frimleigh' above).

Similar situations can occur:

* in periodicals (journals) – 'letters' pages, advertisements, reviews, product listings
* in directories – company names, product names, goods and services categories
* in chemical texts – formulae starting with numerical elements
* in wide-ranging reference books – people, events, 'subjects' (abstract and concrete), dates
* in domestic handbooks – recipes, illnesses/ailments, DIY, legal matters
* in poetry collections – titles of poems, first lines, poets
* in large bibliographies – titles of publications, authors' names, topics of publications

The examples above are taken from (supposed) indexes in different subject fields, but – no matter what the subject area being indexed – the indexer and the client (or other person commissioning the index) need to decide at the start whether a single or multiple sequence is best for the document in question, taking account of the needs and expectations of the potential users.

Before deciding to make separate sequences of headings, the indexer should be certain that this arrangement will be the best for the user, remembering always that separation has the disadvantage of requiring the user to understand the distinction and to find the required sequence. As always, each case must be decided on its merits.

Index measurements

Beginning indexers often ask 'How long should an index be?' or 'How many index entries should you expect to make per page?', hoping for a 'text-to-index' formula to guide them. There is no single formula (number of pages, number of lines, number of entries, number of terms) that is applicable to all kinds of index, nor even for all book indexes. The answers to the questions are 'As long as it needs to be' and 'As many as are relevant'. An index should be worthy of the document to which it relates, providing a suitable search mechanism for readers and enquirers in relation to the expected use of the document.

Clearly, though, one can expect a lengthy document to require a larger index than a very short one would. An obvious mismatch would be a 2–page index to a 500–page medical textbook. The size and content of a book index should be influenced by the density of the text – not only the number and nature of the topics treated but also the incidence of indexable elements (topic treatments) per page. The density range is considerable. A children's fact book may have just one indexable element per page ('giraffes'), whereas a technical encyclopaedia may have twenty or more per page ('galaxies', 'Milky Way', 'Andromeda nebula', 'superclusters', 'radio telescopes', 'quasars', 'pulsars', 'black holes', 'radio astronomy', 'Cygnus', 'stars', 'Sirius', 'clusters', 'magnetic fields', 'starburst galaxies', 'Doppler effect', 'red shift', 'Hubble's Law', 'Crab nebula', and 'white dwarfs').

Mulvany (1994, pp. 63–67) quotes index sizes in terms of percentages – an index of 10 pages to a book of 200 pages being a 5 per cent index – and tabulates some categories of books with their typical index percentages, ranging from 2 per cent through to 15 per cent. Some indexes, particularly those that contain multiple sequences catering for different kinds of approach, may reach a considerably higher percentage.

Indexers are sometimes told that the publisher requires 'only a basic index'; it is not certain what this is intended to mean. It may simply mean 'short' (i.e. not many entries) perhaps because there is little space 'left over' for the index; or it may suggest that the headings themselves should be short (perhaps single words) and without subheadings. Alternatively, it may imply that only the most important topics and references need to be included – a dangerous principle, since this denies users potential access to important information just because it concerns a lesser topic or has only a few lines devoted to it in the text. To help to ensure a satisfactory index, the indexer should be permitted as much space as is needed for all the relevant entries, including cross-references to guide the user from one term to another. Books published commercially for the market, however, often do entail space (and therefore length) restrictions for the indexer; the situation is one that involves the indexer in careful judgements about what and what not to include and how best to present it.

One feature on which there is a general guideline is the maximum number of locators that may be included without either analysis into subheadings or typographical discrimination, in an entry. It is considered bad practice to follow a heading by a long string of locators (more than six or seven separate locators) without indicating (e.g. in bold) which is the primary one.

Categories of heading

For comprehensive access, an index needs to contain headings of all relevant kinds. A name-only index to a comprehensive history of France is likely to be inadequate, as it could allow access only by names of persons, places and events, e.g. 'Louis XV', 'Rouen', 'Somme', and 'St Barthélemy, massacre'; readers would not have direct access to subjects such as 'farming', 'university education', 'political parties', and 'music'.

The features of each document must be separately considered: the principal overall topic, the individual themes, the kind of treatment, the requirements of the users. It is usually apparent from a preliminary reading what kind of coverage and content exist. One document may consist of an investigation of an abstract concept such as 'beauty', with very few proper names – and even those may not be sufficiently significant to be selected as index headings. Another may concentrate on a group of individuals with brief details of their lives and very little discussion of abstract concepts, and no reference to events or places.

Vocabulary and style

The vocabulary, spelling and style of the index must be similar to that of the document. Differences between UK and US English practice must be observed. The relevant spellings of, for example, 'oestrogen' and 'estrogen', 'sulphur' and 'sulfur', must be followed as in the text. Where necessary, the indexer needs to add cross-references in order to help readers more used to another word or spelling and who may be unaware of the differences: 'sidewalks' *see* 'pavements', 'estrogen' *see* 'oestrogen'.

Specialist texts conventionally use the language of the practitioner, so in a medical text 'rubella' is more likely than 'German measles', therefore it should be the principal index heading. Again, a cross-reference should be supplied if the text may be referred to by some users who are thought likely to search under the other term – 'German measles' *see* 'rubella'.

The style of the index is also important – a serious, academic text requires an index of the same level of gravity, not containing snappy, jokey, or flippant entries.

The Thrills and Spills of Indexing

Indexing, like any other professional activity, has its high and low points. People contemplating it as an occupation, whether full-time or part-time, may wish to consider some of them.

The thrills

- Learning about new subjects, as well as about new branches and aspects of established subjects; the compilation of each index adds to the indexer's personal store of knowledge.
- Discovering and revealing valuable, previously unsuspected, information through the making of indexes to archival documents.
- Seeing a good index in print or on screen, with the indexer's own name at the head of it.
- Receiving a letter of appreciation from the author of a book that has been indexed.
- Reading a review that comments approvingly on the index.

- Winning an indexing award such as the Wheatley Medal.
- Being commissioned the second time by a client well pleased with an earlier index.
- Being recommended to a new client by an existing one.
- Recognition, by professional colleagues, of a good index.
- Keeping up with new technology.
- Making a living from regular, interesting work.

The spills

- Not quite meeting the deadline for an index, because of under-estimation of the time taken to do the work.
- Realizing that more knowledge of the subject is needed in order to produce a satisfactory index.
- Floundering through a poorly written text, trying to find out exactly what the author is saying, and what the messages are.
- Not being given enough page space for the appropriate size of index.
- Having to do a great deal of reference work, e.g. checking names in directories, because of inconsistencies in the text.
- Finding that the published index has not been printed as intended and as supplied – uneven indentions, misprints, locators out of sequence, incorrect turnover lines, omitted cross-references.
- Trying to complete several jobs at the same time, because of slip-page occurring elsewhere in the publishing schedule.
- Waiting for the next job enquiry.

References

Butcher, Judith (1992) *Copy-editing: the Cambridge handbook for editors, authors and publishers* 3rd edn. Cambridge: Cambridge University Press

Knight, G. Norman (1979) *Indexing, the art of: a guide to the indexing of books and periodicals*. London: George Allen & Unwin

Mulvany, Nancy C. (1994) *Indexing books*. Chicago: University of Chicago Press

Schriver, Karen A. (1997) *Dynamics in document design: creating text for readers*. New York: Wiley

University of Chicago Press (1993) *The Chicago manual of style* 14th edn. Chicago: University of Chicago Press

Wellisch, Hans H. (1995) *Indexing from A to Z* 2nd edn. New York: H.W. Wilson

Willings press guide (2000). Teddington, Middx: Hollis

CHAPTER TWO

Indexers

Indexers – Who Are They?

Indexing is not an activity normally practised in public and even when it is – as by an indexer using a laptop computer on a train – most people do not recognize it. The majority of indexers work on their own in their homes (if freelance) or at their workplaces (if employed), perhaps occasionally teaming up with other indexers on larger projects. Others are permanent members of indexing teams in publishing houses, involved in the production of indexes to those journals produced by the publisher. There are also indexers working in libraries and other knowledge resource centres who are responsible for the preparation of indexes to the various classes of materials held; they often combine that work with other library and information tasks such as cataloguing, enquiry handling and information retrieval. Similarly, indexers working in records management and archives may also be concerned with the acquisition, storage and conservation of the records. In any kind of corporate environment where there are large numbers of documents and databases, good indexers are essential to the smooth running of the organization.

For the indexers mentioned so far, indexing is a major component of their work. There are others whose principal task is the creation of documents – for example, authors of books for the commercial market, and technical writers preparing instruction manuals relating to equipment manufactured or supplied by their employers – but who are required also to compile indexes for them. Indexing is carried out, too, by the originators of non-text and non-print documents – such as photographers and sound recordists. A significant amount of indexing is also done on a voluntary basis by, for example, members of small societies and clubs who make a contribution in kind by indexing the minutes of committee meetings, pamphlets on special topics, collections of photographs, audiotapes, films and videos, and members' libraries. Lastly, anyone who has a medium-sized or large collection at home – of books, transparencies (slides), videos, posters, audiodisks or tapes – needs to compile an index of sorts. This kind of home-based, unpaid activity can be the catalyst that activates a potentially commercial indexer.

The work may be full-time or part-time. Many freelance indexers start off on a part-time basis – sometimes as a means of supplementing their income from employment in another job – and then, as they become better known or have more time available, develop into full-time working. They frequently do other work related to documents and information as well as indexing. For example:

- abstracting
- editing
- proofreading
- translating
- writing
- literary research
- lexicography
- bibliography compilation
- classification
- typesetting
- consultancy
- training
- database construction
- book reviewing
- historical research
- genealogy
- desktop publishing

- software development
- file conversion
- hypertext design
- picture research
- bookdealing

The related activities can be so varied that it is hard to say to which 'work world' indexers as a whole actually belong; publishing, literature, library and information management, information technology, communication, linguistics, and education – all are interconnected with indexing.

The reasons for first considering indexing as an occupation are diverse. Few people enter it as school-leavers or immediately after university or college education and it is not widely promoted as a career at that stage. The freelance indexer in particular can benefit from having had experience of the world at large and the time to amass a body of general knowledge. Some people are already aware of indexing through their work in publishing, libraries or information centres, and may subsequently decide to study and practise it. Indexing can suit home-based people who have part of their time allocated to other responsibilities – childcare, for instance; many people indexing full-time today started their activities in that way. Other people have turned to indexing after being made redundant or having retired early. For some indexers, their first experience was making an index to something they themselves, or a friend or colleague, had written; having tried it and liked it, they decided to continue.

So long as the necessary knowledge, aptitudes and motivations are present, and if it is realized that it is not the gentle, stress-free, 'easily fitted in with your normal daily programme' type of activity that some uninformed magazine and newspaper articles have suggested, indexing can offer an enjoyable and rewarding way of life.

Skills and aptitudes

'Indexing? Anyone can do it. A computer can do it.' These myths are easily dissolved. The ability and the desire to index are not possessed by all people – only some of them have the necessary fascination with words, the general and specialist knowledge, an interest in documents, the patience, and capacity for attention to detail. Computers help a great deal, by doing the 'chores', but humans do the clever work, not only creating the index but spotting errors (spelling, factual, typographical and so on) in the document.

To produce good indexes, and to practise successfully to a professional standard, an indexer needs:

- awareness and appreciation of documents
- ability to recognize the major and minor themes and 'authorial messages' in a document
- familiarity with types and styles of published index, as a user of documents
- good general knowledge (the basics of almost everything)
- up-to-date knowledge (not necessarily to an advanced level) of the subject fields in which it is intended to work
- fluency in the language of the documents to be indexed
- anticipation of the needs of users of the documents to be indexed
- knowledge of the vocabulary likely to be employed by users of the indexes
- impartiality and objectivity towards the subject of each document and the attitude taken by its author
- careful and methodical ways of working, to ensure consistency, balanced coverage and the minimum of error
- understanding of language structure and word formation
- wide vocabulary
- ability to spell correctly and to spot errors
- ability to pick out significant concepts in the documents (significant in relation to the entire content and to the likely users)
- ability to select the appropriate index terms for the concepts, together with synonyms and related terms
- ability to identify (and advise clients on) the most suitable kind(s) of index for the purpose
- knowledge of appropriate reference sources (both print and electronic), and ability to use them
- ability to present the index entries in an accurate and comprehensive sequence, indicate major references, distinguish text from illustrations, observe spelling and punctuation conventions, file in alphabetical (or other suitable) order, and structure index entries and subheadings
- knowledge of the documentary process (how documents come into

existence and are made accessible through publication)
- ability to work under pressure and to meet deadlines
- skill in using the necessary technology (keyboarding, word processing, using indexing software)
- skill in copy-preparation, checking and marking proofs and final copies

[Based on the list in Booth (1990),
Section 3: Knowledge and skills]

To operate as a going concern (as a freelance), an indexer needs business skills, the ability to communicate on a professional and cordial level with document originators, publishers, printers, and other clients (see Chapter 10: Managing the work for further information). Some freelances have started by getting small grants and going on start-up courses, acquiring some basic accounting skills, etc. Support and provision is constantly changing, and varies from area to area, but it is always worth checking to see what is available. Intending freelance indexers must also be prepared to work very hard indeed at times, in isolation, at unsocial hours, on more than one job at the same time.

Backgrounds and academic qualifications

The educational qualifications possessed by most indexers are – as is to be expected from the nature and demands of the work – high. Those employed within specialist companies, institutes and organizations are often graduates in the subject fields relevant to their employment, for example zoology, art history, economics, library and information science, or marine engineering. Freelance indexers come from a variety of backgrounds – some have previous experience (and qualifications) in libraries/ information centres, some in publishing, and others in fields as diverse as medicine, biology, teaching, law, engineering, chemistry, the armed services, computing, and the civil and foreign services. A survey of nearly 150 indexers, carried out in 1995 by Andrea Frame (1996, 1997), showed that they had, on average, two qualifications each. Those without formal qualifications have often acquired their knowledge through private study. All good indexers are likely to be voracious readers, collectors of facts, and hoarders of printed and other materials.

The appeal of the work

When asked what they like about their work, indexers use words such as 'stimulating', 'creative', 'challenging', 'cerebral', 'imaginative', and 'fun', and refer to the satisfaction of being in control of their own creative work, choosing and organizing the words and phrases, imposing order on them. In addition, indexing is almost always a learning process; from each document analysed, new ideas, new words, and new 'facts' are gleaned. Once learned, or their locations noted, they are available for future reference as part of the indexer's professional mental stock-in-trade and as an aid to other aspects of life. The social role is an attractive one, in which the indexer can be seen as 'opening the door' to information access – and thereby to knowledge and understanding – for some who may otherwise be excluded. Much indexing at the current time is done reactively – the indexer responding when someone makes a demand; a more proactive stance is desirable, with the indexer identifying specific indexing needs and offering solutions before they are requested.

Freelance indexers also have the freedom to choose the kind of jobs they want to do – or at least to turn down those they do not want. Some indexers enjoy doing a succession of short jobs, such as indexes to a series of moderately sized basic-level books, each one to be considered individually. Others prefer the challenge of making large indexes, as for a ten-year run of issues of a periodical, with an emphasis on continuity of vocabulary and style and, at the same time, provision of cross-references for alternative approaches.

Particular subject fields or disciplines have their individual appeal, too. Texts dealing with human lives, individual and collective, as in the fields of biography and history, are the preferred focus for some, while others like working with the precise technical vocabulary of law, science or technology. Medical literature can be fascinating, but is avoided by those who are easily convinced that they are suffering from whatever they are reading about. Suggestible indexers may also avoid indexing books about horrific crimes, serious transport accidents and great natural disasters.

The physical format of the document can also be a factor. Some indexers find aesthetic pleasure in working solely with text printed on paper, or with images and graphics (such as photographs or drawings), whereas others are more at ease with the immediacy of electronic formats.

Texts for different readerships have their devotees. Making indexes to books for children of different ages requires an ability to put oneself in the child's place as a reader; not every indexer can (or wishes to) do this. Similarly, the indexing of materials produced for use by EFL (English as a Foreign Language) students needs the indexer to think of the restricted approach of the student. On the other hand, many indexers also enjoy indexing the 'layperson's guide (idiot's guide)' type of publication intended as an introduction for adult readers.

There is pleasure for indexers in seeing their names credited at the top of their published indexes, acknowledged in authors' prefaces, or – more rarely, and perhaps only in major indexing works – emblazoned on title pages. Public recognition for the best work is signified by the various awards bestowed by professional indexing and publishing organizations (see Chapter 12: Professional organizations and interest groups). Feedback is not often received directly from index users, but there are frequently favourable mentions by reviewers – in literary magazines, and the review columns of periodicals and newspapers.

Knight (1979, Ch.13) provides examples of humour – both deliberate and unconscious – in indexing. The inclusion of deliberately humorous index headings is probably best left to those indexers who are indexing their own writings. Unconscious humour is most likely to amuse when an indexer comes across it in someone else's index; otherwise, it could be the embarrassing discovery of a double meaning or other gaffe, after the index has been published.

Authors and indexers

There are several kinds of relationship that can exist between indexers and authors. There are, indeed, situations where the indexer is the author. Some publishing contracts place the responsibility for supplying the index on the author of the text; the author then has the choice of compiling the index in person or of finding a professional indexer to do it. Another example is that of in-house writers employed by a company, whose job specification includes the preparation of manuals and other instructional literature (printed and on-screen); this usually includes responsibility for the production of the complete text of each document, including the index.

The question 'Who makes the better index, the author or a separate (preferably professional) indexer?' has been raised from time to time.

In one important respect, it misses the principal point, which is that whoever does the index should be someone who has knowledge of indexing principles and proficiency in indexing technique as well as knowing enough about the subject of the text. It is sometimes claimed that the author is the most suitable indexer, being the person most familiar with the aim, subject and content of the text. However, a separate indexer has not only the professional indexing expertise but also the advantage of being a new reader of the text and so is better able to anticipate the needs of potential users and therefore to formulate the index entries likely to be sought. Authors are often pleased, even eager, to rely on the services of an expert indexer, having put their all into the actual creation of the main text.

Naturally enough, when indexes are compiled by others the authors will be interested in the results (particularly when they are bearing the costs). In the case of commercially published documents, editors rather than authors are often responsible for commissioning the indexes (even when authors are paying) and so act as intermediaries between authors and indexers. Authors may supply lists of suggested terms for inclusion, or discuss by phone or email the general approach; on completion of the indexes, editors often send them to the authors for comment. Whatever the situation, the relationships between indexers, authors and publishers' editors are crucial (see Chapter 10: Managing the work).

Professional Knowledge

Indexing expertise has to be learned and developed, through the practice of understanding and interpretation of text, summarization and condensation, categorization, alphabetical sequencing, and logical ordering). The basics of this knowledge (which at this level means knowledge which is of value to everyone) are usually gained during the normal process of education and development – learning the order of the letters of the alphabet, acquiring a basic vocabulary, sorting items into categories according to likenesses, spelling, clause and sentence construction, forming words (singular/plural, verb/noun/adjective), and making summaries or précis. However, indexers need much more than just the basics; their business is words, therefore the importance of this kind of knowledge is intensified. Their vocabulary must be larger and they must know the terminology of the subjects in which they specialize. They must be aware of new words and new connotations, recognize equivalences and opposites (synonyms, quasi-synonyms, antonyms), understand explicit and implicit meanings, be fluent language users, and be able to identify the core elements in texts and to condense them into concise and meaningful words and phrases suitable as index headings.

The formation of index entries (headings with their relevant locators, such as page or paragraph numbers) is only the start of the process. The individual entries have to be moulded into an accessible, harmonious and informative whole, with a consistent style, linked and non-conflicting entries, cross-references to aid the user to find the relevant headings, indicators of the most important locators for a topic, and an explanation to the user. The finished product must then be presented in an attractive and easily consultable form. Mechanical aids can speed some of the 'chore' activities of sorting and presentation, but the essential intellectual input can come only from the indexer.

Training and qualifications in indexing

Indexing expertise – the actual technique of indexing – may be acquired in a variety of ways. Of indexers now practising, some have received formal training through a distance learning or in-house course. Others have studied privately, using books and journals on indexing, and yet others have learned by working with practising indexers, or being supervised or mentored by them, or by starting from scratch (sometimes from an early age) and learning as they go. The Society of Indexers (based in the UK) has a system of accreditation and registration, which assists indexers to establish and advertise their professional standing. The Society is, at the time of writing, considering a mentoring scheme, under which inexperienced indexers can be given advice, encouragement and supervised jobs.

Having been acquired, this technical knowledge must be kept up to date; over the years, indexing practices change (not just technologically) so that some styles and indicators are no longer widely used and acquire an old-fashioned look. New standards are formulated and published, and novel document formats appear which require different methods of indexing. The best combination for sustained proficiency in indexing is good training, wide experience, sharp intuition, and continuing contact with other indexers. In the absence of links with others in the profession, a freelance indexer – just like any other solitary, home-based worker – may not only fail to keep up with technical developments, but also remain unaware of stylistic changes and unwittingly develop eccentricities of practice.

Professional societies in many fields are now encouraging their members to involve themselves in a process of continuing professional development (CPD) and to keep records to show how they have done this. The Society of Indexers carried out an audit of current practice amongst its members in 1999, in relation to activities such as:

- attending conferences
- participating in workshops and seminars
- serving on professional committees
- attending local group meetings
- participating in online discussion groups
- engaging in distance learning
- doing private study
- teaching or lecturing on indexing
- coaching or mentoring or supervising less experienced indexers
- writing books, papers, reports etc.
- maintaining contacts with professional colleagues
- engaging in professional discussions with publishers
- subscribing to journals and online information services
- buying specialist books
- assisting the professional associations

It is also necessary to know about the world of publishing and communication, to be aware of the processes by which documents, of whatever kind, can be produced, and to know something of how – and for which purposes – documents in general and indexes in particular are used. Factual information relating to this last area – the use of documents and indexes – is the most difficult to discover, as it concerns individual, private, unreported, and often unconscious behaviour.

Some indexers oppose the idea of organized training and qualifications. They believe that a better way to become a good practitioner is to gain experience through studying indexes, preparing themselves by making private indexes to books published without indexes, taking on a few small jobs at first, then gradually extending themselves, always discussing the needs of individual texts with their authors and editors and then producing indexes that satisfy them – the indexer and the clients. On the other hand, other indexers know well that some authors and editors do not know very much about indexing and cannot judge the quality of an index; in those circumstances, it is the indexer who is the expert and who may need to explain the criteria and the techniques. It is not unknown for a perfectly good index to be criticized – even rejected – by an author, because it was not what was expected.

General Knowledge

This kind of knowledge relates to the world at large – current affairs, how things are run in one's own country, basic history and geography, and so forth. Some people have the habit of collecting 'facts' from an early age, and carry around in their heads such information as the names of the capital cities of the larger countries of the world, the dates of major events in the history of their own countries, and the names and achievements of famous persons in science, technology, the arts, politics, and other fields. They presumably remember the information because they find it inter-esting and so every new 'fact' that comes along is pigeonholed for future reference. To have a capacity for this kind of acquisition, storage and retrieval is valuable. It provides a background upon which the information presented in a document can be overlaid, helping the indexer to under-stand and interpret, check and verify, and then to produce suitable index headings.

To maintain a good standard of general knowledge, the indexer needs to keep in touch with day-to-day developments in current affairs, through whichever means are available – reading newspapers and jour-nals, listening to radio, watching TV, checking the internet. Many indexers work on their own, for example as freelances, and so have an increased risk – as do all freelances in whatever profession, trade or craft – of unwit-tingly getting out of date. One important aspect of being out of date is linguistic – the language of general social intercourse changes constantly, with new words, new expressions, new meanings; some of these novel-ties are, initially at least, slang terms and so their occurrence as indexable elements in texts may be limited, for a time, to linguistics or sociological texts. Words can also acquire new meanings. Two examples, from UK

English, show the change of meaning over the space of thirty years or so: a 'trannie' or 'tranny' in the 1970s was a transistorized radio, small and portable; in the 2000s it is a transvestite.

Special Subject Knowledge

Most book indexers are willing and able to index 'entry-level' texts in a wide range of subjects, but some specialist knowledge is required for the indexing of books above this stage. At that level it makes sense, therefore, for indexers to restrict themselves to those subjects of which they have experience and which they have studied in depth. In the 2000 edition of the Society of Indexers' *Indexers available* there are around 130 subject specialisms listed alphabetically, from 'accountancy and auditing' through 'materials science' to 'zoology' (see 'Specialist areas' in Chapter 10).

The knowledge required for more advanced indexing (above entry-level) may have been gained by formal study at an education or training institution, by practical experience, by private study, or by a mixture of all of these. Just as with professional and general knowledge, subject knowledge must be kept up to date – through, for example, membership of specialist bodies, reading new periodical articles and books, using news/discussion groups on the internet. Employed indexers who work full-time or part-time within specialist organizations have an advantage over freelance indexers in this respect; they are often in the midst of the developing subject, working with experts in the field, and with ready access to a library/information centre with all the relevant reference sources to hand either in printed form or available by computerized means. It is vital to keep up with new topics, names of new organizations, inventions, and new combinations of subjects (often interdisciplinary). Depending on the level of document to be indexed, it may not be essential – in fact it is often impossible – for the indexer thoroughly to understand every detail of the subject area. What is important is to recognize the changing vocabulary of the specialist subject and to keep in mind its current terminological pattern.

Neutrality of the Indexer

Every indexer comes to a document with a mental bundle of attitudes, beliefs, prejudices, received ideas, 'facts', general knowledge and 'conventional wisdom'. Much of this bundle is helpful in aiding understanding, interpretation and representation of the document content. Sometimes, with documents that are polemic in style, or that deal critically or controversially with a subject, indexers may have to cope with material that contrasts with their personal views. If there is a serious mismatch, with the indexer feeling so aggrieved by the content that the neutrality of the index is likely to be affected, the best course – in the case of a freelance indexer – is to decline the job.

It is not necessary for an indexer to be wholeheartedly in favour of everything within a document, but the index must reflect and represent the tone as well as the content. The indexer may experience distaste for some parts of the document, but this must not show through in the index. Although the index is a work in its own right, created by the indexer, and exhibiting the general and specialist knowledge and technical expertise of the indexer, it must not reveal the indexer's personal beliefs, attitudes or judgements.

The Indexer's Reference Sources

All indexers, whether freelance or employed, full-time or part-time, in whichever subject field, need at least a basic collection of reference sources – dictionaries, encyclopaedias, bibliographies and so on. Local libraries can be consulted for some of the material needed, but personal copies of some items are essential. Many reference sources, such as dictionaries and encyclopaedias, are available in CD-ROM form or on the internet – sometimes as well as in print. The minimum set suggested by the Society of Indexers for its members is:

- a dictionary of the English language
- a one-volume encyclopaedia
- an atlas
- a biographical dictionary
- a general handbook of facts such as *Whitaker's almanack* or *The world almanac and book of facts*

- a directory of publishers and other document originators, such as the *Writers' and artists' yearbook* (for a list of publishers, financial information for freelances, proof correction symbols)
- a textbook on index making
- a dictionary of abbreviations in the relevant subject field
- a thesaurus (list of subject headings) for the relevant subject field
- any other major reference sources in the relevant subject field
- British Standard ISO 999: 1996 *Recommendations for preparing indexes to books, periodicals and other documents* British Standards Institution

All these basic sources must be reputable and up to date, and should be replaced or supplemented by new editions as time goes by. Wise indexers keep (and collect) older editions – they are of great value when indexing documents relating to past events, people, and geographical areas. Much useful material is available via the internet, so indexers should aim to discover those web sites that are relevant to their work; only those which can be seen to be authoritative, however, should be relied upon for accurate information.

'How They Index'

It was mentioned in Chapter 1 that the results of the intellectual input of indexing (the index entries) vary from indexer to indexer. Indexers also differ in the ways in which they organize their work and proceed through the tasks involved in compilation and presentation. Each has to find an individual optimal method.

Descriptions written by six Registered Indexers of the Society of Indexers (Booth, 1996) showed how each one handled the making of an index in a different way. Of those book indexers who worked from printed page proofs, some liked to read quickly through and mark (for example with a highlighting pen) the words or phrases or sections that they regarded as likely indexable elements, then to go back to the beginning and start making their entries. Others scanned the text and indexed the more obvious elements (such as proper names) as they went; once through to the end, they then went back and indexed the non-name elements. Some made no marks on the proofs, but skimmed the text to get a general idea of the coverage, discourse and principal topics, then started to index in earnest. Some used a computer throughout, with a word-processing program, a database program or a dedicated indexing program; others started with written records, then keyed in the finished version. Working methods change and develop, with the advent of new equipment and software at affordable prices, so some indexers may now work entirely with on-screen documents, perhaps using embedding programs to mark words and to indicate the beginnings and ends of indexable elements, resulting in mechanically generated lists ready for elaboration and refinement by the indexers. (See Chapters 10: Managing the work and Chapter 11 Technology for detailed information.)

Who Should Not Be an Indexer?

Anyone may decide to take on work as an indexer – it is not a protected or officially registered occupation. Not everyone, though, is suited to the work. The idea of becoming a freelance indexer is sometimes provoked by newspaper or journal articles, radio and television programmes, 'new career' and 'restart' leaflets, and books on earning money from home. For some people who are reached in this way, it is a fruitful discovery and a life-changing opportunity. Anyone already having a background as a user of documents, whether in a formal or informal setting, plus good general and specialist knowledge, together with an interest in language and good written English skills, and who enjoys creative but meticulous work, should be able to develop into a good indexer. Sadly, some would-be indexers, attracted only by the (mistaken) thought that indexing is simple and that it can – when fitted into an already busy and stressed home regime – produce an easy and regular income, decide to take it up without first having considered whether they have the necessary knowledge, interest and aptitude. Their realization of inadequacy only arises after they start to study the subject, or attempt to compile an index, or when they do not meet the standard set by a training course, or – and it is hoped that things do not progress this far – when their offered index is rejected or criticized by the client.

Briefly, indexing is definitely not the job for someone who:

- is uninterested in ideas
- has little facility with the written and printed word
- has a low level of general knowledge
- cannot concentrate for long periods
- cannot spell
- works in a slapdash way
- cares little about grammar and good English usage
- never uses indexes to find information
- is reluctant to train and then keep up to date

References

Booth, Pat F. (1990) *Documents, authors, users, indexers* 2nd edn. Training in indexing Unit A. Sheffield: Society of Indexers

Booth, Pat F. (1996) (ed) How we index: six ways to work. *The Indexer*, **20**, 89–92

Frame, Andrea (1996) Indexers and publishers: their views on indexers and indexing. *The Indexer*, **20**, 58–64

Frame, Andrea (1997) Indexers and publishers: their views on indexers and indexing, part 2. *The Indexer*, **20**, 131–134

Knight, G. Norman (1979) *Indexing, the art of: a guide to the indexing of books and periodicals*. London: George Allen & Unwin

Further Reading

Mulvany, Nancy C. (1994) *Indexing books*. Chicago: University of Chicago Press (Chapter 2: The author and the index)

Wellisch, Hans H. (1995) *Indexing from A to Z* 2nd edn. New York: H.W. Wilson (pp. 31–41: Author-publisher-index relationships)

CHAPTER THREE

What (and whether) to index

The making of an index can be broken down into three main areas, loosely labelled 'selection of topics', 'formation of entries', and 'structure and layout'. This chapter and the following two chapters are concerned respectively with these areas.

The Indexer's Focus

The indexer's dilemma is in one respect the opposite of that of the writer. The writer looks at the blank page or screen and wonders how to fill it with meaningful, fluent and stimulating sentences. The indexer looks at the finished mass of text, consisting (depending on its documentary type) of foreword, preface, introduction, main chapters, individual sections and paragraphs, appendices, illustrations, tables, lists of references, and glossary, discerns a multitude of topics – including instances of proper names – and wonders how to distil it into a concise, comprehensive, user-friendly index that fits harmoniously with the text.

For trainee indexers the question 'how to start?', when faced with the first document to be indexed, is often the most perplexing of all. The matter can be considered in two parts: first, the physical, internal components of the document – not all of which are of equal importance when it comes to indexing; second, the conceptual content – the meaningful matter in the text, images, or sounds conveyed by the document.

Indexable Parts of Documents (Which to Index, Which to Ignore)

Most documents start with a prominent display of title and origin (provenance) information. Single printed text items contain title pages. Compact disks and audiocassettes have printed details on them. Films and videos have title frames. Electronic databases have title screens and internet web sites have home pages. The subsequent content varies according to the type of document. Some typical examples of print document contents are listed here:

A textbook:

- preliminaries (contents list, and all or some of the following: list of illustrations, list of tables, preface, foreword, acknowledgements, list of abbreviations) – usually numbered in small roman (iii, iv, v etc.)
- introduction (sometimes forming part of the preliminaries, sometimes a chapter in its own right)
- chapters of text, perhaps with footnotes or chapter notes and containing illustrations (e.g. halftones, diagrams)
- appendices
- glossary of specialist vocabulary used in the text
- bibliography (list of references)

A biography:

- preliminaries (as above)
- introduction
- chapters of text, with sections of photographs
- epilogue
- credits
- appendices
- notes

A single issue of a periodical:

- editorial
- feature articles, each with a short abstract (summary) at the beginning; some with illustrations
- general news items
- 'fillers' (quotations, aphorisms, etc.)
- membership news and announcements
- calendar of events
- historical snippets ('50 years ago' etc.)
- book reviews
- bibliographies
- product news and surveys
- letters to the editor
- advertisements

A loose-leaf multi-volume manual of financial information:

- foreword
- preface
- organization of the manual (its internal structure and how to keep it up to date)
- contents lists of all volumes
- list of abbreviations
- letter to subscribers
- customer record (for entry of dates and numbers of supplements received and incorporated)
- text divided into parts within each volume, each part into chapters, each chapter with its own contents list
- appendices to each volume (samples of financial statements, EU directives, lists of standards, codes of practice, etc.)

A dictionary of art:

- contents list
- preface
- text (containing one or two images per page), arranged alphabetically by name of artist, genre, movement, etc., interspersed with illustration sections each showing the art of a particular century
- acknowledgements

A book of poems by different poets:

- contents list
- introduction
- poems, arranged alphabetically by title
- glossary of unusual words occurring in the poems
- acknowledgements

A classic novel:

- contents list
- introduction by the present-day editor
- text, divided into chapters
- chapter notes by the present-day editor

A new novel:

- text, divided into chapters
- list of other works by the author

A computer users' manual:

- contents list
- introduction
- 'late breaking information' (addenda to the main text)
- text divided into chapters
- appendices
- glossary of terms

A training unit (manual) of a distance learning course:

- outline of the course
- contents list
- acknowledgements
- preface
- aims and objectives of the unit
- notes to trainees
- text, divided into chapters and numbered sections
- list of recommended reading

- self-administered test
- answers to the self-administered test

A bibliography of publications on a particular subject:

- contents list
- preface
- introduction
- guide to the classification used in the bibliography
- key to the numbers within each document entry
- the list of publications in subject classified order
- list of organizations related to the subject

A single issue of an abstracting journal:

- editor's notes
- contents list
- user guide
- list of journals abstracted
- abstracts (divided into subject groups)

An atlas:

- acknowledgements
- contents list
- foreword
- various lists and maps (world, regions, solar system)
- map projections
- list of symbols and abbreviations used on maps
- the main maps

A children's book:

- illustrated end papers
- contents list
- text on left-hand pages, illustrations on right-hand pages; no chapter divisions indicated, but each opening relating to a new topic
- illustrated end papers

A membership directory of an organization:

- advertisements
- contents list
- note from the chief executive
- mission statement of the organization
- outlines of departmental responsibilities and names of staff
- list of codes used to indicate members' occupational affiliations
- alphabetical list of corporate members
- occupational code list of corporate members
- alphabetical list of individual members
- occupational code list of individual members
- list of products and service categories
- categorized list of firms offering products and services (including advertisements)

A single-volume encyclopaedia:

- A-Z sequence of short paragraphs

Another single-volume encyclopaedia:

- subject-based chapters (science, music, history, etc.)
- maps

Minutes of a committee meeting:

- list of members present
- apologies received for absence
- confirmation/amendment of minutes of the last meeting
- matters arising from the minutes of the last meeting
- summary of discussion and actions on agenda items, in numerical order
- date, time and location of next meeting

A trade catalogue:

- order and delivery information
- contents list

- descriptions, illustrations and prices of products, arranged in broad categories
- fabric and colour guide
- order form

A travel guide to a foreign city:

- contents list
- map of the area
- basic information: when to go, how to get there, entry formalities, currency, sources of information, transport, where to stay, food and drink, what and where to avoid
- guide to the districts
- places to visit: galleries, museums, markets, restaurants, clubs, entertainments, parks and gardens
- historical and cultural background
- books to read for more (specialized) information
- essential words and phrases

The guideline on coverage in indexing standard BS ISO 999 (British Standards Institution, 1996, subclause 7.1.1) recommends that all matter in a document should normally be covered in the index. As well as the main body of text in a printed document, this could include the introduction, notes, addenda, illustrations, and appendices. Preliminary matter, such as the title page, dedication, and contents list, and additional features like chapter synopses are usually not indexed, but should always be checked for something unusual or important. The experienced indexer knows that each document must be separately considered, and that the coverage, form and content of the eventual index will be determined by the document's individual features and intended readership. The BS ISO 999 guideline is applicable in the majority of instances, but there are occasions when, for example, an introduction is brief or insubstantial in content and so would not be indexed, or where a chapter synopsis contains a significant 'fact' or reference that is not included in the main text and is therefore worth featuring in an index entry.

Glossaries

A text using specialist terms is likely to include a glossary containing definitions of the terms, for the benefit of readers not fully familiar with the subject. The glossary may appear either before or after the main text and its presence is normally indicated in the contents list. Each case of a glossary should be judged on its content and context. There is normally no need to index it under 'glossary' – it is a component of the text, not a topic. The terms in it, on the other hand, should be included in the index, with an indication that the reference is to a definition. Any glossary entry which is brief and gives no more detail than is present in the body of the text may be left unindexed. Publishers sometimes have their own house rules on inclusion and exclusion, but are receptive to indexers' opinions and advice on particular cases.

Illustrations

In the case of printed words in sentences on a page, it is a matter of indexing what is explicitly, and sometimes implicitly, expressed. Illustrations require special consideration. If illustrations and text are interdependent (one not being understandable without the other), then both require indexing. If the illustrations are the principal feature (as in a collection of photographs), then they form the main indexable component and there may be no need to index any of the text (though this will depend on its content and nature). If the illustrations are decorative, included to encourage the reader and 'lighten the burden' of reading, they may not need indexing. If, on the other hand, they can be considered 'works of art' in themselves, or if they are by a known artist, they should be indexed. Illustrations on endpapers (attached to the inside front and back covers of a book) should – if the editor has followed the practice recommended by Butcher (1992, pp. 79–80, section 4.0.2: Large illustrations) – have been repeated in the body of the book and so are to be indexed there. (See Chapter 7 Image and sound (audio) recording, for more information on illustrations.)

Notes

Supplementary, information is often provided in texts in the form of footnotes, endnotes (chapter notes) or marginal notes. The content of individual notes varies – even within a single piece of text – so each one has to be evaluated. A note providing a definition that does not appear elsewhere, or citing bibliographical information, or identifying someone not referred to in the main text, may pass the significance test and be worth indexing, whereas one making a flippant comment, or repeating something already covered, may not.

A topic that is explicitly referred to only in a chapter note, and not on the page on which the note number is given in the text, should be indexed only to the page on which the chapter note is given. To index it also to the page citing the note number would confuse the reader who is directed to it, but can find nothing apparently relevant.

Reading lists

Bibliographical references listed at the ends of chapters or articles, or gathered into a single list after the main text, are sometimes indexed, sometimes not. The nature, amount and value of this kind of content varies greatly from document to document and so its indexability has to be judged according to context. In certain fields, such as literature, science, technology, medicine, and history, the citation of works by earlier authors or by current workers in the field has significant research value; the need to trace and follow up these sources should therefore be satisfied through the indexes. (See also 'Authors' names and titles of works' below.)

Advertisements and publicity items

Advertisements and notices relating to current publications, products and events are common features of periodical issues (see Chapter 6: Serial publications). They appear less frequently in books and when they do occur usually contain information about similar publications produced by the publisher in question. In most cases, these items do not need to be indexed, but if they do, putting them in a separate sequence from the main index may be justified. Many years later, they may become of interest to people researching the history of advertising or of a particular company or society. In that case, an index focusing solely on those materials may be compiled specially for the purpose.

Indexable Content

Determining which 'physical' parts of the document should be indexed is easier than deciding exactly which elements (topics, names) to index within those parts. It is at this point that the beginning indexer needs to remember that indexing is not just a matter of picking out words from the text or naming objects in images and using those words as index headings. If it were, how easy (but how much less challenging and fascinating) it would be. Even those documents consisting entirely of lists of names with accompanying details (such as directories), and needing indexing to provide approaches from other nominal elements, require the indexer's judgement as to which form of name to use and which elements are most likely to be sought by users.

Identifying the indexable elements

Indexing is usually much more concerned with the meanings of words in combination, and with their relationships to other words, than with individual words as graphic or spoken items. Most documents, therefore, need to be looked through before indexing can start, so that the indexer can make a kind of mental map and summary of the content and structure as a whole. This does not necessarily mean making a lengthy study of each line of text or of the content of each image. The check can often be carried out briskly, perhaps by a scan of chapter and section headings, spot sampling of typical pages, or by reading through an introduction, statement of intent, the main arguments, and conclusion.

From this initial scan, the indexer can form a general impression of what – as a whole – the document is all about, what points are being made (what the gist and the messages are) and which kinds of topics (e.g. ideas, objects, people, organizations, places) are dealt with along the way. Then the detailed indexing work starts in earnest. It is a matter of deciding which topics are important in that particular context and whether the treatment they receive in the text is sufficiently informative to justify index headings. (See 'Significance' below.)

Individual indexers have their own ways of working and the situation is usually affected by the kind of document being indexed. Britton (1996) reports that she prefers to start indexing straight away (perhaps combining this with the initial scan) and so first of all she indexes the relevant names of people, events and places that she discovers. Then she makes a second trawl for the other (non-name) topics. The psychological advantages of this method are, first, that the names (having initial capital letters) are easily recognized within the text and, second, that the indexer feels quickly reassured that the job is under way and that the index is taking shape. When working from page proofs, some indexers mark up the indexable elements in the text as they read, and make marginal notes about cross-references, synonyms and so on; these markings suggest the raw material for their index entries.

Scrutiny of the content must, of course, be painstaking. The meaning and significance of each section of text – or, in the case of image and sound materials, of each image and set of sounds – needs to be appreciated and appraised in the context of the document as a whole. Context factors include:

- the subject focus of the whole document
- the level of vocabulary
- the intellectual treatment
- the author's or creator's intentions
- the characteristics of the expected readership or user group

All these should have a strong influence on the content and structure of the finished index. Freelance indexers who prepare indexes for commercial publishers are necessarily also influenced (sometimes to the detriment of the finished product) by economic factors such as:

- restrictions on the length of the index
- the time allowed for its preparation
- a client's unwillingness to pay for an adequate index

Words and Meanings

Indexers must always be conscious of the difference between topics (subjects, themes, concepts) and the words used to represent them. Every word conveys meaning, even when taken as an individual unit, but it is up to the indexer to discern the collectivity of meanings within the framework of each document being indexed and then to represent them by suitable headings. A word in a text may certainly be suitable to be used

– unchanged – to represent the concept as an index heading, but in many cases different word formations (nouns rather than verbal forms, for example) are required. For instance, a particular text may refer in different sections to 'measuring instruments', 'taking measurements' and 'linear measures'; these might all, finally, be indexed by the single term 'measurement' as a representation of the concept.

Significance

As indicated above, there are two aspects to significance, when it comes to identifying indexable elements. First, which topics are – in relation to the overall subject and context of the particular document – important enough to be indexed? Secondly, is what is said about each topic in the document important enough to be indexed? Only if the answer to both these questions is 'Yes', should the indexer go ahead and make an index heading for the topic.

For a topic merely to be mentioned is not sufficient for it to merit an appearance as, or within, an index heading. Only if something significant is said about it, some information of interest to the reader or user, should it be considered for representation. An 'index of mentions or occurrences' – more properly called a concordance – can have its uses as a work of reference, but is not a suitable form for most indexes. It is only too easy for the beginning indexer – intent on including everything that might be relevant – to pounce on easily identifiable items (such as people's names) and turn them into headings. These items can often, though, turn out to be 'false friends'. For example, the sentence from an imaginary novel:

> The singer's hair would have been described by John Milton – had he been alive to see it – as 'amber-dropping'.

would not normally be indexed under 'Milton, John'. The name certainly appears, and he is undoubtedly a major figure of English literature, but in this context it tells us nothing useful about Milton or his original use of the phrase 'amber-dropping'; it is just a literary allusion. It is rarely possible to say 'never' when it comes to indexing, though; if the text containing this sentence was all about the use of literary allusions in present-day writing, then the names of authors alluded to would be of great significance and therefore would feature as headings in the index.

The following extract (from a book on report writing), consisting of three hundred words, mentions several topics. In the context of the book as a whole, only four index entries are necessary.

ORAL AND WRITTEN COMMUNICATION

We transmit and receive information in several ways. The oral (spoken) and the written (using letters and numerals) methods are two of the most common. Each has specific advantages.

Oral communication has an immediacy and a personal touch which can be difficult to catch in the written method. This is because of:

- the physical senses (vision, hearing, touch) which can be used by speakers and listeners
- the range of tones, sound volume, expressions and speeds used to achieve attention, emphasise a point, create a diversion and so on

In addition, there is often (though not always) an informal and flexible setting, which lets the sender and the receiver interact with query and answer, comment and response.

Written communication lacks these characteristics but – perhaps because of its 'at a distance' presentation – has others which enhance it and can make it more effective:

- a more formal perspective, suggesting greater authority and trustworthiness
- a potentially permanent record, capable of extended life and of being read again and again
- extracts can be authentically quoted
- details can be checked
- suitability for reading at an individual's own best reading speed
- accessibility to a large readership (and thus to expert criticism)

The data included and the statements made are therefore more likely to be perceived as thought-out, valid and accurate.

When writing, bear in mind the advantages of the written method and try to exploit them to the full. At the same time, be aware of what may be lost by not being able to address your readers face to face. Try to compensate by introducing an element of immediacy and personal involvement, through the style, vocabulary and tone you use. What you are seeking is the written equivalent of grabbing someone by the shoulders and saying 'Just listen to this!'.

> [From Booth, Pat F. (1991) *Report writing: guidelines for information workers* 2nd edn. Kings Ripton, Cambs: ELM Publications]

The relevant index headings for this extract are:

communication, oral and written
oral communication
spoken (oral) communication
written communication

For novice indexers the assessment of significance can be bewildering. The temptation is to index everything possible, no matter how minor the treatment. Judgement of significance comes with practice, and can be helped by reading reputable indexes and checking back into the text from the headings, and by indexing (purely for practice and pleasure) as many documents of different kinds as possible. For a book indexer, the 'Introduction' or the first chapter, setting out the subject and the background, often gives strong indicators of topic significance and a summary of the book's content. Some indexers go back to the introductory text after they have indexed the rest of the book, to check that they have found all the important topics and to add entries for anything important that has not been dealt with elsewhere.

Even experienced indexers can have a problem with judging significance, particularly when dealing with lengthy texts encompassing a wide subject area and referring – sometimes fleetingly, but nevertheless interestingly – to topics from other fields. There is always the odd reference that hovers tantalizing over the boundary between 'significant' and 'less significant' and about which a decision must be made. A single reference to a topic, for example, that features early on in the text and is introductory in tone, but that is nowhere elaborated, could be significant to someone who has little knowledge of the subject but a well-known fact to someone familiar with the field.

An intriguing example appeared in a discussion on the online indexing discussion group Index-L concerning the indexability of some biblical references quoted in articles in a street newspaper. Opinions varied in the responses to the query; some respondents thought the biblical references not sufficiently significant – in that context – to be indexed at all, and others suggested broad headings such as 'biblical quotations' or 'biblical allusions', with or without subheadings for further detail. In another context, such as a book about the Bible, where the level of significance is very high, headings for individual chapter and verse references could, of course, be expected.

It may sometimes be advisable to check the level of significance with the author. Take the case of a paragraph, in a supposed political biography, describing in great detail a meeting held 'in the flat above Anna Smith's offices in Victoria Road. In this apartment, over a decade or more, many questionable activities were plotted and at least one box of incriminating documents was burned.' The indexer may not be able to tell from the text whether 'Anna Smith' is relevant or not, because there may be no direct reference to her involvement in the activities concerned, and she may have been mentioned only in passing. In this case only the author can confirm what was intended.

Categories of indexable element

It can be helpful for the indexer, when scrutinizing the document, to keep in mind the various categories that can be identified as indexable elements. This mental list can be used as a reference point from which to answer the question 'What am I looking for?'. Some texts are very dense – each page full of 'facts', ideas, thoughts, references to names – and can seem overwhelming to less experienced indexers. Having a prompt list of categories at hand can be a valuable aid to identifying the indexable items.

A comprehensive list of categories, adapted from Booth and Piggott (1995, Section 1.3.1: Categories of concepts) is given here, with examples added; most documents do not contain elements from all the categories, and some contain only one or two types. Further examples of categories that can occur in specialist subjects are given in Chapter 8: Subject specialisms.

- products, e.g. TV sets
- artefacts, e.g. oil paintings; vehicles
- conditions, e.g. happiness; illness
- qualities and attributes, e.g. generosity; transparency
- substances, e.g. calcium; water
- materials, e.g. aluminium (US aluminum)
- phenomena, e.g. rainbows; out-of-body experiences
- people, e.g. Shakespeare, William; engineers
- organizations, e.g. Organization of Oil-Producing Countries (OPEC); political parties
- animals, e.g. Bellerophon; cats; *Perissodactyla*

- parts, components and organs, e.g. cogs; limbs; brain
- structures, e.g. Forth Bridge; dams
- shapes and forms, e.g. circles; granules
- properties, e.g. malleability; brittleness
- actions, e.g. balancing; falling
- activities, e.g. swimming; housework
- aims, objectives and purposes, e.g. success; survival
- ideas and beliefs, e.g. humanism; Taoism
- areas of study and knowledge, e.g. philosophy; chemistry
- processes and techniques, e.g. smelting; recycling; intaglio
- objects of actions, operations and processes, e.g. waste products; workpieces
- agents of actions, operations and processes, e.g. industrial plant; artists' materials
- instruments and tools, e.g. clocks; steam hammers
- methods, e.g. Bates method; two-stage method
- styles, e.g. rococo; postmodern
- places, e.g. Rio de Janeiro; littoral zones
- dates, periods, e.g. 1745; Hanoverian period
- events, e.g. American War of Independence; literary festivals
- environments, e.g. *in vitro*; extraterrestrial
- characteristics, e.g. friendliness; insouciance
- aspects and viewpoints, e.g. political aspects; humanistic perspective

The examples given above may, of course, occur in a range of subject backgrounds and can therefore belong to different categories, dependent on the context. The categories can be divided into two main groups – entities (or concretes) and abstractions. Entities/concretes include, for example, tangibles such as materials, people, animals, and instruments and tools. Abstractions are non-tangibles like ideas, qualities, attributes, and processes. Some less experienced indexers feel that it is easier to identify the concretes in a document and are concerned that they may miss the abstractions or not know how to express them as headings. It is not necessary, though, for these indexers to keep asking themselves whether something is a concrete or an abstraction. The essential point is to recognize something that, in the context of that particular document, is indexable. This is done by:

- reading and understanding the broad sweep of the text, or examining the image or listening to the sound
- asking 'What is this about?' and 'If I direct users to it, will it tell them something either useful or interesting?'

Once an indexable element is identified, the next question is 'What should be the index heading for this?' (see Chapter 4: Forming the index entries).

Some documents are comparatively easy to index, because they contain readily recognizable items with fixed names or designations – such as manufactured products, botanical and zoological species, named people and organizations, geographical areas, and individual historical events. Other documents are largely concerned with abstract qualities, philosophical concepts, scientific principles, physical properties, or intellectual and academic activities – such as beauty, willpower, law of gravity, literary criticism, and Islamic studies. The perceived difficulty of indexing abstract elements, though, is likely to arise, not from the abstractness itself, but from the way in which the matter is presented in the document. Texts vary enormously as far as structure, style, complexity of vocabulary, and level of intellectual activity are concerned. A 'straightforward' text, which states plainly its coverage, propositions and conclusions in unambiguous, simple language, is normally easier to index – even if it deals with abstract concepts. By contrast, a text that focuses mainly on very common 'tangible' concepts, but is written with wry humour and contains many cultural or literary references, uses polysyllabic vocabulary and a convoluted style, can take more time and more thought.

Implicit Elements

Occasionally, a text may contain an allusion to something, or a description of it, without actually naming it. It does not happen frequently, but in this situation the indexer has first to recognize what is being implicitly referred to and then to make a suitable index heading for it. For example:

> His flamboyant lifestyle subsequently took a dive in the autumn when the country became involved in armed hostilities. There seemed no chance of recovery for him during the unfortunate events of the next few years. At one stage he found himself – unexpectedly and very much against his will – dispatched overseas. 'Exotic, yes!' he wrote

in his scrappy diary, 'But the heat drains my brain. And the clothes
– so rough, so unflattering, so demeaning! The very word 'uniform'
makes me shudder – we are nothing but a mass of cardboard cut-
outs, all alike. Help!' Amazingly, though, his enforced uprooting, and
what he always referred to as his 'battledress' experiences (though
he never saw combat), provided the spur and the foundation for his
later success as a cabaret entertainer. 'If it hadn't been for the armed
clash of nations' he admitted many years afterwards 'I would probably have died on the streets from self-indulgence long ago.'

This supposed extract relates to a wartime period and the significant effect of enforced military service on the career of the person in
question. The words 'war', 'military', 'army' and 'soldier' do not appear
in the text, but are likely to be suitable as first words in index headings
for the chapter in which the piece is featured. In the context of the whole
book, it would also be possible to identify the particular event and therefore to make an index heading for the name of the war, if deemed helpful.

Implicit references can also occur when examples or instances are
described without naming what they exemplify. In a history, say, when a
particular type of event has already been referred to in general (and
indexed), it can be relevant to index subsequent examples under the
heading for the type of event as well as under their own names. Alternatively, a *see also* cross-reference from the general heading to the specific
one(s) may sometimes be preferred.

What the indexer must never do is to look for hidden agendas or
to make implications, deductions or interpretations that are not clearly
evidenced in the text and intended by the author.

Proper names

The formation of name headings is dealt with in detail in Chapter 4:
Forming the index entries, but some cautions are relevant here.

Just because a proper name appears in a document, that does not
automatically mean that it must be included in the index; novice indexers
sometimes fall into this trap of total inclusion. Names are usually very easy
to spot because (in most cases) they start with capital letters. A proper
name, though, is just a special class of word, indicating a specific person,
group, event, place, or thing. For indexing purposes, it is subject to the
same 'significance test' as any other item; only if what is revealed about

it is sufficiently important, does it become worthy of indexing. As always, context is everything, and significance levels vary from subject to subject and from document to document. For an index to a biography, for example, the name of a person who is merely mentioned (e.g. 'She met Harrison only once, briefly, at a party; their paths never crossed again'), may nevertheless need to be indexed, because it is important for the reader to know the circumstances. It has been suggested, too, that the inclusion of all possible names in an index can boost sales of the book, because those included in it will be impelled to buy it.

Another common slip with the indexing of names is their automatic assembly into a 'names index' and their resulting exclusion from the so-called 'subject index'. A named person, just like a named organization, event, place, or object, can feature as a topic of discussion and therefore merit treatment as a 'subject'. In some cases, such as a bibliography listing many authors and the titles of their works, there may be justification for a sepa-rate sequence of authors' names (an 'author' index); in others, such as a directory of suppliers and services, a separate sequence of geographical locations (counties, provinces, towns, postcodes) may be useful as a 'place' index. In all cases, though, the indexer should consider the role of the proper names before deciding how to deal with them; a name treated as a subject may be handled differently from one used as the source of a quotation, and differently again from one that appears in a bibliographical citation. It is entirely proper for a name to appear in the 'author' sequence and the 'sub-ject' sequence, if the name appears in the text in different roles. A name mentioned only once in a text may or may not be worth indexing, depend-ing on context. If it is indexed, the addition of a modifying word or phrase, to indicate in what connection the name occurs, can be helpful.

Even when the names in a document relate to something significant, it still may not be necessary to index them specifically. A broader level of indexing may be more appropriate in certain contexts. For example, a book might contain, as well as text on the life of a particular artist, repro-ductions of a selection of her paintings, some of which are said to have been inspired by scenes in the plays of Shakespeare, others by episodes in the novels of Iris Murdoch, and the remainder by characters from popular television series. It may not be necessary, in this context, to index the names of the plays, novels, series, and characters; broad headings such as 'Shakespearean themes', 'Murdoch, Iris: themes from novels' and 'tele-vision series themes' may be sufficient.

Authors' Names and Titles of Works

Names of authors and titles of works cited within the main text, or as footnotes or chapter notes, often pose a problem for indexers, in terms of which (if any) to index. The references may be solely to the documents as sources, but can be descriptions or discussions of the features and merits of the works as subjects in their own right, as in a work of literary criticism.

The indexer needs to determine in each case, by discussion with the client, whether and how these references should be indexed. It is not possible to establish a single rule that applies to all cases – as always, each index must be judged within its context (the subject field, the level, the expected mode of use). Much depends on the purpose of the document, the number and type of references, and the space available for the index. Ideally, all cited authors should be indexed, to assist users who wish to trace references to their work, however small. Space restrictions often prevent this, and a common policy is to index only those authors whose writings or theories are discussed (not just mentioned) or who are major figures in the particular subject field.

In a bibliographically focused work or a scholarly or literary text, it is advisable to index in detail all the cited authors, because students and researchers may search for information by using the names of people known to be working in the subject field. Occasionally, citations can be ignored completely, particularly if only lightly mentioned and full bibliographical details are not given anywhere in the document.

There are several different (and entirely reputable) ways in which bibliographical references can be presented in text (British Standards Institution 1989, 1990; Butcher, 1992, Chapter 10 – Bibliographical references; University of Chicago Press, 1993, Chapter 15 –Documentation 1: Notes and bibliographies, and Chapter 16 – Documentation 2: Author-date citations and reference lists; Oxford University Press, 1983, pp. 50–54 – References to printed and manuscript sources). The form chosen affects the content of the related index entries. Indexers dealing with a range of customers and materials are likely to encounter all the methods – individual publishers, editors and writers have different preferences – and need to consider the effects each style may have on indexing need.

Authors' contributions

Some authors who have decided not to compile indexes to their own books still maintain an interest in their content – particularly when they are responsible for paying the indexers out of their advances from the publishers. They may send the indexers (directly or via the publishers) lists of words and phrases that they think important and relevant to the readership. A list like this can be helpful in providing information relating to the author's viewpoint, but it is not a finalized set of index headings. It can identify sought terms (terms that a reader may wish to look up), but it remains the indexer's responsibility to determine the level of significance of those concepts, as treated in the text, and to formulate the best possible headings for them. It is not unknown for an author to supply a list of 'index headings' and expect the indexer merely to add the locators – a request which a professional indexer would diplomatically decline. In the case of texts that are expected to be used by newcomers to the subject or by people in training, it is often easier for the indexer to understand the readers' problems and methods of searching than it is for the very experienced author. Where indexers are working directly for authors, rather than for their publishers, harmony and mutual respect are essential (see Chapter 10: Managing the work).

Headings in texts

Headings and subheadings used to break up texts into related sections and to announce the subject content of the next piece, can be helpful 'finding aids' for the user, whether reading the text from cover to cover, browsing through it or going into the text after having been directed there by the index. Sometimes – and only sometimes – they may provide words and phrases that can be used as headings in the index. Beginning indexers need to beware of snatching these text headings and subheadings without considering whether they accurately represent the subject of the section and whether they are useful as search terms. For example, in a book dealing with photography, one section of text may be divided as follows:

Section heading:	Infrared photography
1st paragraph heading:	Industrial uses
2nd paragraph heading:	Medical uses
3rd paragraph heading:	Other uses

The section heading and the first two paragraph headings might well be used as a basis for index headings:

infrared photography
industrial uses, infrared photography
medical uses, infrared photography

but it would be a mistake to put 'other uses, infrared photography' in the index, because no-one would use it to look for information. The other individual uses described in the subsection should each be indexed:

astronomical uses, infrared photography
forensic uses, infrared photography

Defined terms within texts

Individual words and phrases that are typographically emphasized in text – in italic or bold type, in capitals, in boxes, in colour, in reversed (e.g. black on white) type – to identify and define new topics, usually make good index headings, being words that will be looked for by users. Defined words that are not typographically highlighted are equally useful, but may be more difficult for the user to spot, particularly if they appear in the middle of a paragraph. In certain subjects, such as law, it is especially important to index definitions, interpretations and statements of meaning (see, in Chapter 8: Subject specialisms, the section on law).

Abstracts (summaries)

The main body of text in a report or a periodical article is often preceded by a short abstract summarizing the content. Its purpose is to give the reader a quick overview of the topic covered and the points made. Because there are different kinds of abstract – some indicate broadly what the text is about, others highlight important data and conclusions – and because they differ in length and form, their value as sources of indexable elements varies. They are always worth reading for ideas, but the main body of text remains the prime source. In some cases, however, periodical articles have to be indexed entirely from their abstracts (see 'Words and ideas from abstracts' in Chapter 6: Serial publications).

Captions

The captions (legends) to illustrations, tables and spreadsheets are usually indicative of the subject, but – being brief – do not necessarily provide all the information the indexer needs. Examination of the content of each illustration, table or spreadsheet is advisable.

'Sensitive' Content

As indicated in Chapter 2 (under 'Neutrality of the indexer'), indexers who feel uncomfortable about indexing a document because of its subject, or the way in which it is treated, should probably turn down the job. Some documents, while dealing with topics with which the indexer is at ease – or at least able to handle without difficulty – may still contain passages that include troubling ideas, descriptions or images that alienate the indexer. There are two temptations that the indexer should resist: the first is not to index such passages at all, the second to index them using headings implying criticism or condemnation. Despite the feelings that the content generates, the indexer should treat the material in the same way as the rest of the content; if it reaches the necessary level of significance, it should be included, and it should be represented by headings that reflect the attitude of the originator of the document. If factual errors are found, or dangerous or illegal practices recommended in the text, the indexer would be wise to make the publisher's editor (or other client) aware of these.

   In the formulation of headings, it is not for the indexer to show personal disapproval. The users of the document should draw their own conclusions from their reading of the text and make their own value judgements. For example, 'terrorists' in a text should be indexed as such and not as 'freedom fighters', a description of abbatoir procedures should not be indexed as 'cruelty to animals', nor should an account of a tycoon's multinational interests be indexed as 'capitalism, rampant' – unless the authors have described them in those terms. Cultural differences enter the picture here, too, so indexers need to bear in mind the background of the writer or creator of the document and the types of users for whom it is intended.

Revisions of Indexes

The need to revise an existing, completed, index can arise when:

- a book is republished, with the original text content, but in a different format and therefore with different pagination
- a book is updated, with some new content, and perhaps some old content removed – e.g. a revised, enlarged, or second (or later) edition
- a loose-leaf text is updated by the addition and removal of pages, paragraphs or sections; this may occur on a regular basis a few times per year
- indexes to individual volumes of a serial are merged into a single cumulated index

Revising an index is not the simple task that inexperienced indexers may expect it to be. Except in the case of the reformatting of an on-screen report that was indexed using embedded codes, where the codes automatically adjust the locators to show the new position, it is not just a matter of mechanically replacing one set of locators with another.

In a paperback version of a book previously issued in hardback, where the only change is the pagination, the index headings (the words) can usually be reused without amendment; the remainder of each entry (containing the locators) cannot be reused.

For an index to a revised edition of a book, it is often better (in terms of time and ease of working) to start afresh and make a completely new index than to attempt the pernickety tasks of addition, deletion and amendment of the entries in the earlier index. Changes to the text may include the addition, removal or repositioning of whole chapters and other sections of text and of illustrations. There are also likely to be new and changed bibliographical references. There may be more (or less) space available than before, allowing the index to be fuller or requiring it to be compressed or thinned down. Revision gives the indexer a chance to correct any errors that may have crept into the original index (during compilation or typesetting) and to have second thoughts about the form of words, the type and order of subheadings and so on. If there has been a long interval between the two editions, new words (general and special) will have come into usage and may therefore need to be added as main headings or in cross-references.

Some loose-leaf text for updating is supplied to the indexer in the form of red-lined copy showing the new material, the deleted words and passages and the changed paragraph numbers; this makes it possible to identify precisely which entries need attention. Increasingly, computer-edited formats are being provided, in which the changes may not be as obvious; the texts therefore need close and careful scrutiny. Failure to remove index entries for withdrawn material causes dissatisfaction and disillusionment among regular users of indexes to loose-leaf documents.

The merging of periodicals indexes, to form cumulations, requires much more than mere automatic amalgamation. All the headings need to be reconsidered, and many of the subheading sequences and cross-references reorganized (see Chapter 6: Serial publications for more information).

An earlier index can always be used as a checklist. Where the indexer has it on disk, a locator (page number) order file can be made, showing the entries for each page or paragraph of the earlier edition. An alphabetical list of the headings, with the earlier locators stripped off, can be used as a base for the new index. Other features of certain indexing programs (such as grouping of associated headings, and colour marking) can be used to assist the job.

Index Density (Depth of Indexing)

There is no rule of nature stating how many elements should be indexed, or how many index terms should be allocated, for any measure of text or any document – other than 'as many as it needs'. Often, individual indexing policies and space constraints for particular jobs impose restrictions on the number allowed – irksome for the indexer whose main aim is to provide an index worthy of the document. In the indexing of periodical articles, for example, it may be policy to allocate not more than three index terms for the subject content, plus one for the principal author. The same kind of limit is sometimes placed on indexes to abstracts and annotated bibliographies, which can have an obstructive effect on retrieval because each abstract – even if well executed – is already a much reduced version of the original text. The ceiling on the number of index terms therefore diminishes it further.

The experience of preparing indexes to several similar documents in the same subject field gives an indexer an indication of the number of entries likely to be generated from a single page (or screen). This figure does not necessarily apply to other kinds of document or levels of text or to other subject fields, so an indexer may wish to look at other published indexes and work out a rough guide for each type of indexing work to be done. Mulvany (1994 pp. 63–67) quotes examples of indexes to individual books with densities ranging from a mere 2 per cent to an impressive 54 per cent. A 5 per cent index – say 10 pages of index for 200 indexable pages of text – described as 'not exceptionally dense', could consist of around 5 to 6 entries for each indexable page. An indexer working with 'unexceptional' texts with different levels of writing may still find a range of from 2 to 20 entries per page. Dedicated indexing programs (see Chapter 11: Technology) can help by providing measurement data for individual indexes, which an indexer can analyse in order to obtain typical values for different subjects and levels.

References

Booth, Pat F. and Piggott, Mary (1995) *Choice and form of entries* 2nd edn. Training in indexing – Unit B. Sheffield: Society of Indexers

British Standards Institution (1989) Recommendations for references to published materials. BS 1629: 1989. London: British Standards Institution

British Standards Institution (1990) Recommendations for citing and referencing published material. BS 5605: 1990. London: British Standards Institution

British Standards Institution (1996) *Information and documentation – guidelines for the content, organization and presentation of indexes.* BS ISO 999: 1996. London: British Standards Institution

Britton, Barbara (1996) In: How we index: six ways to work, Pat F. Booth (ed) *The Indexer*, **20**, 90

Butcher, Judith (1992) *Copy-editing: the Cambridge handbook for editors, authors and publishers* 3rd edn. Cambridge: Cambridge University Press

Mulvany, Nancy C. (1994) *Indexing books*. Chicago: University of Chicago Press

Oxford University Press (1983) *Hart's rules for compositors and readers at the University Press, Oxford* 39th edn. Oxford: Oxford University Press

University of Chicago Press (1993) *The Chicago manual of style* 14th edn. Chicago: University of Chicago Press

Further Reading

Wellisch, Hans H. (1995) *Indexing from A to Z* 2nd edn. New York: H.W. Wilson. (pp. 137–138: Depth of indexing; pp. 210–213: Indexable matter)

CHAPTER FOUR

Forming the index entries

All the entries (headings with locators, and cross-references) that are made as an indexer proceeds through a text should be regarded as provisional. Once they are assembled into an alphabetical (or other relevant) sequence, they can be edited and organized and additional cross-references can be added. This chapter is concerned with the initial input of headings and locators. Chapter 5 explains the process of editing the entries and presenting the index in its final form.

Putting Ideas into Words – the Headings

Once the indexable elements have been identified (as described in Chapter 3), the indexer's next task is to construct suitable headings for them and to add the relevant locators. A 'suitable' heading is one that:

- starts with a sought term (a word or meaningful element that the typical user of the text can be expected to look up for that subject)
- is based on, or refers to, the terminology used in the text
- is meaningful and unambiguous
- is understandable by the average reader of the text

The headings are formed into complete entries by the addition of accurate locators or cross-references. Each entry aims to lead to useful information at the desired level of significance.

An indexer compiling an index with a space constraint on it, e.g. a publisher's specification of 'not more than 300 lines and no line longer than 38 characters (including spaces)', should take care not to index extravagantly in the early part of the text, otherwise all the available space may be used up before the index is complete.

Sometimes – but not as often as novice indexers probably expect – there is an exact match between a word or words in the text and in the required heading, in which case it is simply a matter of copying from the printed text or of inserting codes in electronic text. For example, the following passage happens to contain words and phrases that can be used as headings, without any changes:

> STAITE, William Edwards
>   1809 – 1854
>   In 1847 Staite patented an improved electric arc lamp powered by batteries, and exhibited it in many parts of the country during 1847–1854. In 1851 he tried to convince railway operators of the benefits of his new lighting system by installing it at Lime Street Station, Liverpool but the owners of the station, the North Western Railway, were not impressed. The Liverpool Dock Board however were sufficiently interested to install a lamp in a tower built on the dock wall, but for general use the lamp proved too expensive to be a commercial proposition.
>   [From: Cooper, Glennis (1986) (ed.) *Electrical heritage: a guide and reference source*. Kings Ripton, Cambs: ELM Publications. p. 135]

Headings for this piece, in the index, are:

> arc lamps
> Lime Street Station
> Liverpool Dock Board
> Staite, William Edwards

Because the personal name is already in reversed form (directory-style) in the text piece, it needs no amendment to become an index heading.

Most often the words in the text supply the basis of headings but require a little manipulation, addition, reduction, or other amendment, as in this passage (from the same source, p. 85):

> Boats were one of the first forms of transport to be electrically driven. In 1839, Jacobi, a Russian professor, fitted out a paddle-wheeled boat with a primitive battery constructed for the purpose and travelled for some distance along the River Neva near St Petersburg.

The personal name is augmented in the index as:
'Jacobi, Prof. M.'.

The index heading for a personal name usually uses the same words, but in a different order and with inserted punctuation, so that the family name (surname) becomes the entry element. It then matches the search term used by readers looking for information about the person.

Obviously, a document written in English requires an index in English, but some texts are produced in two languages – such as English and Welsh – or in several languages, as in publications of the European Union institutions. In such cases, an indexer may be involved in providing an index in more than one language. According to Hudon (1999) not all publishers perceive the need for multiple indexing; she reckons that indexers. too, must recognize that such texts need full analysis and processing. Of course, a straightforward, literal, translation of an index from one language into another will not do – the nuances and cultural references of each one must be revealed and incorporated.

If entries being constructed on a computer are to go into separate sequences (an authors' name index, a place index and a subject index, for example) they can be separately identified by a prefix as they are keyboarded, ensuring that each entry is filed in the relevant category; the prefixes can be rapidly removed once the index sequences are complete:

~a~Barker, Pat	[~a~ = author]
~p~Chingford, Essex	[~p~ = place]
~s~arable farming	[~s~ = subject]

Grammatical forms

In the majority of circumstances, the best grammatical form of word for a heading is the noun. Nouns may denote material (visible, tangible, or audible) items – engineers, horses, deciduous trees, capital cities, Isambard Kingdom Brunel, Bucephalus, Kuala Lumpur – or abstract forms (qualities, properties, activities) – strength, law, acceleration, consumerism, astronomy, snobbery, theft, harmonic motion, sport.

Most nouns referring to classes have singular and plural forms, indicating respectively one or more than one of the item referred to. Most plurals are formed by the simple addition of 's' or 'es', but others change internally. The effects on sort order (alphabetical arrangement) of singular/plural differences such as woman/women and mouse/mice must be borne in mind.

As a general rule in English-language indexes, the plural form should be used for nouns referring to countable items (about which the question can be asked 'How many . . . ?) and the singular form for non-countables (about which the question is 'How much . . . ?'). An exception to this is the use of the singular form in indexes to some kinds of scientific, technical and medical texts (encyclopaedias and defining dictionaries, for example), where 'echidna', 'bract', 'piston', 'heart' and 'femur' make more sense or are more appropriate than their plural forms. In the case of a one-member class, e.g. female British prime minister (at the time of writing there has been only one), the singular form should always be used.

In documents containing glossary or definitions sections, most defined terms are conventionally given in the singular form, whereas in the text they appear in singular or plural as required by the sense of the sentence. This variation need not bother the indexer; the choice of plural or singular for the index heading can be determined by the 'countable/non-countable' guideline, with the definition indicated as a subheading or by an abbreviation after the locator:

> epiphytes 47, 56
>   *definition* 5

or:

> epiphytes 47, 56
>   epiphyte *defined* 5

or:

> epiphytes 5*def*, 47, 56

Some indexers give both forms as headings:

epiphyte *defined* 33
epiphytes 47,56

but this separation of locators relating to the same concept can be confusing – particularly in a dense index where there are several similar headings – so this form should normally be avoided.

Nouns with plurals changed internally (not by just adding 's' or 'es') – such as goose/geese – may need the additional provision of either double entry ('goose' and 'geese') or cross-referencing ('goose *see* geese').

A few nouns have the same form for the singular and the plural, e.g. 'deer', whereas there are others that have different meanings in the singular and plural forms and so must not be used interchangeably, as for example:

law = the whole body of official rules governing a geographical or
    subject area
laws = the individual rules and regulations
ice = frozen water
ices = frozen desserts and confectionery

A particularly interesting case is 'fruit', which can have several meanings, concrete and abstract; for example, 'fruit' can signify a single edible specimen or a quantity of them, whereas 'fruits' can mean a collection of fruits or (in the abstract sense) the results of an action – 'the fruits of her hard work'. There are several other connotations, including biblical and slang terms, but these are less likely to occur in indexes.

In indexes in other languages, e.g. French and German, different conventions apply and the singular form of nouns is often used throughout.

Imperative forms of verbs (commanding the carrying out of actions) can also be necessary headings in technical contexts. In an index to a computer software manual, for example, the command functions can be entered as:

ACCEPT
COPY
DELETE

EDIT
INSERT

Gerunds (ending with -ing), formed from verbs but having the same function as nouns – can also make acceptable headings. Some indexers dislike and avoid them or limit their use to subheadings, but others consider them appropriate for use in technical documents such as operational manuals, because they reflect in a more active way the tasks to be done. In such a context, the headings 'measuring', 'deleting', 'testing', and 'cancelling' could be used instead of 'measurement', 'deletion', 'tests', and 'cancellation'.

Adjectives (words that assign characteristics to nouns) – 'heavy', 'economic', 'industrial', 'primary', for example – are not normally used alone as headings. They usually occur in association with nouns: 'heavy water', 'economic development', 'industrial decline', 'primary education'. One of the few contexts in which an adjective can be used on its own as a heading is in an index to a text on language usage, where a particular adjective (its use and misuse) is the subject of a passage of text. A similar exception applies to adverbs (words that assign characteristics to verbs) – 'literally', 'fully', 'hardly'.

Prepositions (words expressing relationships between two other words) – 'from', 'about', 'by' – are very useful within headings, but seldom form headings on their own (other than when individual prepositions are discussed as topics in their own right). A preposition is likely to be the entry element of a heading only if it is bound to another word in the heading, say by a hyphen:

> by-products
> in-car entertainment
> with-profits annuities

or if it is the first word in the title of a document:

> *To everlasting oblivion*

A more common use of prepositions is in subheadings, where they are included when necessary to prevent ambiguity (see 'Length and detail of headings' below).

Entry elements

Each heading must be, or begin with, a word or meaningful element which users are likely to look up (a sought term), otherwise its inclusion is a complete waste of time and space. Each of the following headings – whether a single word or several words – meets the criterion of 'sought-ness':

> democracy
> home, effect on educational achievement
> *Melursus ursinus*
> portfolio working
> Ziolkovsky, Konstantin Eduardovich

These headings do not, because they either begin with 'weak' words, or are too vague in meaning:

> avoiding infection
> effects of pollution on word processors
> miscellaneous proposals
> various uses
> why money is needed

Weak words, such as 'other', 'general' and 'assorted', are not usually suitable as entry terms in the index, because they are not what users will look for. There are some exceptions, for example where the words have strong and specific meanings in the subject field concerned – 'general elections' (politics), 'other ranks' (military affairs) – and where such a word begins a title of a work – *General linguistics* and *General Haig: butcher or war winner?*. Chapter and section headings such as 'About this book', 'Are you thinking straight?' and 'How to find happiness' should not be used as index headings, unless they are actual titles of documents.

Definite and indefinite articles ('the', 'a', and 'an') do not normally become entry elements; one exception is where an article is the first word in the first line of a poem:

> *Oxford companion to English literature, The* [Title of a book, under 'O']
> *'The wind doth blow today, my love'* [First line of a poem, under 'T']

(See 'First lines of poems' later in this chapter for more information.)

Whenever a heading of more than word is used, the indexer needs to consider whether another heading in reversed, permuted or adjusted form is also necessary, to allow a user to look for the topic using another word in the heading (or subheading):

> cultural deprivation
> deprivation, cultural
>
> television violence
> violence, on television
>
> poverty, result of unemployment
> unemployment, cause of poverty

Adapted forms like these are not always needed; their selection depends on the context. Taking the last example as a case in point – if the whole text is about unemployment, then 'unemployment' is not used as a heading in the index, except perhaps to indicate an official definition.

Most entry elements are words, but other possibilities are dates, alphanumeric codes (such as postcodes, classification numbers, product codes, and component numbers), single alphabetical characters (in assorted alphabets), and various kinds of signs and symbols. If any one of these is considered to be a sought term, it qualifies as an entry element:

> *2001: a space odyssey*
> RG7 1DX
> 681.443
> G241/234/45d
> *84 Charing Cross Road*

The positioning, in an alphabetical index sequence, of entries beginning with these non-alphabetical elements, is considered under 'Numerals in alphabetical sequences' in Chapter 5.

Length and detail of headings

The best heading is concise, comprehensible, unambiguous, and fitting to the topic and context. It should be as long as it needs to be, but no longer than is necessary. A short but well-constructed heading is perfectly able to convey in full the intended meaning.

Prepositions and articles (as indicated earlier), as well as conjunctions, are recommended for inclusion only when they are essential for meaning:

> education:
> > for management
> > management of
>
> fish and chips
> vehicles:
> > damage by
> > damage to

or when they are part of a proper name or the title of a work:

> Peter, *the Painter*
> *Ride the nightmare*

However, some indexers dislike the telegraphic style of headings that have been shorn of the connecting, function words, and prefer – particularly in literary contexts – the fluency of connected words as headings. It is, to a certain extent, a matter of personal taste and judgement, but when (as often happens) an index has to be fitted into a small space it is better to provide access through as many concise headings as possible than to supply a smaller number of headings of great eloquence.

Indexers sometimes worry that a simple, short heading may be uninformative, and so want to add an amplifying phrase. For example, 'Johnson, Amy' is a perfectly acceptable index heading, but an indexer might feel the need to take further information from the text and add 'English aviator' or even 'first woman solo flier, England to Australia'. If there is space available, a short qualifier can be included if thought necessary to distinguish one Amy Johnson from another, but the index should not attempt to précis the text. Indeed, if the only information in the text is that Amy Johnson was the first woman to fly solo from England to Australia, including this phrase in the index heading makes the index entry pointless – because the reader will gain no further information by going to the text page indicated.

Abbreviations can sometimes be used within headings, to keep them short and to avoid repetition of a commonly occurring element. In the index to a biography, for example, the name of the biographee can be represented by initials:

> Crosse, Imelda Pamela Susanna (sister of HC)

Similarly, in the index to a history of a group of companies, official names can be initialized:

> Bertram, Chris T, retirement from board of ICLZ
> Pascal, Jean, design of new logo for TGT

The use of such abbreviations should be explained in the introductory paragraph at the beginning of the index.

Word order in headings

Some beginning indexers, perhaps under the influence of consulting older classified-style indexes, sometimes suffer an attack of 'reversitis' when they start to formulate headings containing more than word. What should be entered as 'night-time meteorological phenomena' is wrongly converted to 'phenomena, meterological, night-time'. The guideline in indexing standard BS ISO 999 (British Standards Institution, 1996, subclause 7.2.2.4) recommends that multiword terms in common usage should be entered in direct form:

> primary education
> agricultural subsidies
> freedom of expression
> trial by jury

So long as the first word is one that users will look for, the direct form of entry is better. If the second and later words in the headings are also words that may be looked for, then additional (reversed) headings or cross-references can be made using those words as entry elements:

> education, primary
> subsidies, agricultural

expression, freedom of [preposition retained for clarity]
jury trials

Reversed headings are not made automatically for every multiword heading. The reversed heading 'education, primary' is not needed if education is the subject of the whole text; in that circumstance, 'education' would not normally appear as a heading at all – either on its own or as the first element. Headings such as 'National Front', 'sun in splendour' (a heraldic term) and 'chimney pots' would not be additionally entered in reversed form; their secondary elements are not (in those contexts) sought terms.

Capitalization

For clarity, enabling the user to distinguish one kind of heading from another, proper name headings should begin with a capital (upper-case) letter; all others should start with a small (lower-case) letter:

Eleanor of Aquitaine
elections
German shepherd dogs
germ warfare
Hobsbawm, Eric
House plants and cacti
humanism

This convention – which reflects the capitalization practice of the text, and so helps the reader to find the required passage – is recommended by the indexing standard BS ISO 999 (British Standards Institution, 1996, subclause 7.2.2.3) with the proviso that words from languages such as German, which customarily capitalize the first letter of nouns, are given in that style. Some publishers' house styles favour capitalization for the first letters of all headings, perhaps on grounds of consistency, but resulting in reduced lucidity and readability of the index.

There are differing practices for the use of capitals within titles of documents. The examples given in BS ISO 999 (subclause 7.3.4.2) follow the standard's overall guideline that capital letters are used only for proper names. Titles could therefore appear with an initial capital, as:

Through the looking-glass
European frozen food buyer
Not I, but the wind . . .

However, Butcher (1992, pp. 234–235) and the University of Chicago Press (1993, pp. 282–283) indicate the general use of initial capitals for all the principal words in titles:

Through the Looking-Glass
European Frozen Food Buyer
Not I, but the Wind . . .

At the time of writing, the latter style is probably preferred by the majority of publishers.

Spelling

The spelling of words in index headings should match the spelling in the text. Incorrect spellings noticed should be reported to the editor (or other responsible person) and the correct forms should be used in the index – except if they are deliberate misspellings forming the nub of the text: for example, if a child's version of a difficult word becomes a long-running family joke and part of its vocabulary, and is referred to at length in an autobiography.

Differences in English spelling, principally between the UK and North America, can require the indexer to make some fine judgements. A conference proceedings may contain papers written by contributors from several countries. A book may be written by a US author, and be published and indexed in the UK. Indexers should, as always, follow the usage of the text, but may be uncertain what to do if two or more spellings of the same word appear in papers by different authors. The wisest practice is to follow whichever is the majority usage of the text, if there is one; if there is not, then the practice of the main country of publication should be observed. If the effect of the differences is slight in terms of alphabetical placing of the headings:

colours, colors
defence, defense

enrolment, enrollment
fulfilment, fulfillment
travelling, traveling

then users more accustomed to the 'secondary' form are unlikely to be inconvenienced. If the differences are more significant:

oenology, enology
greywacke, graywacke
axemen, axmen

then either double entry or cross-referencing can be used to ensure that the entries will be found, regardless of the search terms used.

Indexers need to be aware of spelling differences not just in general vocabulary, but also in the subject fields in which they work. Reliance on spell-checkers and correction facilities of word processors to find errors in finished indexes and amend them can be hazardous if these international variations are not allowed for.

Punctuation in headings

Any punctuation in headings using words and phrases from the text must agree with that of the text – except if obviously incorrect, in which case the editor, author or other client should be informed. Punctuation practice is subject to a gradual process of change. The use of the hyphen in compound words (e.g. 'sky-writing') and between prefixes and word-stems (e.g. 'co-operation') is not universal, and there are periodic attempts to do away with the apostrophe in phrases such as 'miners' lamps' and 'worm's eye views'. The disappearance of hyphens and apostrophes from titles of annual publications such as directories and yearbooks has to be noted and copied by indexers. They may not always approve of the punctuation conventions of a text, but must replicate them in the index.

Words appearing in quotation marks in texts do not always need to retain them in the index headings. If the words in the text are within quotation marks only when the words are first introduced and not subsequently, the marks can be ignored. They should be kept only if they feature throughout the text, for example when the words are used with an idiosyncratic meaning or are nicknames.

Homographs

Word usage is full of traps for the unwary. Indexers – being natural word-smiths – are the most improbable people to fall into them, but they must take care to assist the users (who are sometimes less skilled). To use as a heading a single word in isolation can sometimes lead to ambiguity, particularly in an index that covers a wide range of subject fields. A common feature of the English language is the word with two or more meanings – or, more correctly, two or more words that look the same. There may be differences in pronunciation ('bows' – devices used by archers, tied loops of ribbon or string; 'bows' – the front ends of boats), but these are no help in distinguishing the printed words.

In indexes where there may be doubt about which meaning of a homograph is intended, or where both meanings are present, each relevant index heading needs to include a qualifier so that the meaning is clear:

>   fencing (materials for barriers)
>   fencing (swordplay)

Capitalization of the first letter of proper names is helpful in distinguishing meanings of some otherwise homographic terms:

>   Boxers   [for members of an early 20th century Chinese
>   secret society]
>   boxers   [for fighters]

Words denoting topics can also appear as proper names, or parts of proper names. The identity of some of them is clear from their form, but others may need qualifiers to distinguish them in sequences, as:

>   Berlin (Germany)
>   berlin (wool yarn)   [The order of these terms may vary.]
>   Berlin, Irving

and, as suggested by Batchelor (1999) – who makes the point that commas do not all represent the same relationship:

>   London, Jack
>   London, William

London (*UK capital city*)
    Central
    [etc.]
London Airport
London: an illustrated history
London, Midland and Scottish Railway

or:

London (*surname*)
    Jack
    William
  [etc.]

Some terms with similar meanings need careful discrimination in indexes. The word 'sheriff', for example, in England and Wales refers to the chief executive officer of the Crown in a county, in Scotland to a judge in a sheriff court, and in the United States to the chief law-enforcement officer in a county or town.

Synonyms

An indexer's knowledge and love of language can be tested to the utmost in thinking up all the possible terms that index users can employ in looking for the topics of interest. The prime indexing terms are normally based on words used in the text, but alternative approaches must be identified. The English language contains many synonymous and near-synonymous words and phrases (as well as some that are understood by some people to be synonymous, but that – strictly – are not).

A text on the growing of various crops that includes references to 'peanuts', may need to include the synonyms 'groundnuts', 'monkey nuts', and 'goober peas', as well as the botanical name '*Arachis hypogaea*', in the index. Other examples include:

sweets/candy
birds of prey/raptors
boxers/fighters/pugilists
clavicle/collarbone

> petrol stations/filling stations/gas stations/service stations
> ghosts/apparitions/wraiths/spirits/phantoms
> *Digitalis purpurea*/foxglove
> living wills/advance directives
> PSBR/public sector borrowing requirement
> TV/television
> manic depression/bipolar disorder

No indexer can be totally informed about every subject likely to feature in an index, so general knowledge often needs to be supplemented by reference to dictionaries and thesauri (particularly important for consistency in periodicals indexing), in order to ensure that all relevant words are provided as access points. These occurrences of alternative words are found in the usage of different nationalities, ethnic groups, socio-economic classes, age groups, professional practitioners, specialists, and academic communities. Language variations are noticeable, too, in texts aimed at differing levels of readership and in multi-author texts. They flourish also during the early stages of development or discussion of new subjects, before the vocabulary has 'settled down' and terms are fixed.

A slight difficulty can arise when an indexer realizes that terms are incorrectly used as synonyms in a text. Words that overlap in meaning, or that denote things in a broad/narrow or whole/part relationship, are sometimes loosely treated as synonyms: 'conifers', 'firs', 'pines', and 'evergreens', for example, have distinct definitions but are often confused by the layperson. A single manufacturer's trade name is sometimes inaccurately used to indicate the whole group of items, regardless of who made them: for example, 'hoovers', for vacuum cleaners of all makes (Hoover is a registered trade name and not, therefore, applicable to other makes). When these kinds of treatments occur, the indexer must help the index user by providing helpful headings, perhaps including qualifiers to make clear what is referred to in the text:

> vacuum cleaners ('hoovers')

Antonyms

Pairs of words that occur in the same text with opposite, or apparently opposite, meanings may at first sight both seem to merit treatment as separate headings with their own locators. Some opposites, though, are less opposite than others. Concepts like 'ferrous metals' and 'non-ferrous metals' are clearly two discrete 'either/or' categories, but notions such as 'health' and 'sickness', and 'morality' and 'immorality', can be seen as two ends of a continuum – with the possibility of intermediate positions ('fairly well', 'slightly immoral').

Decisions on the inclusion of headings depend therefore on the kind of relationship between them. Discrete categories referred to in the text should be separately indexed, with their own locators:

> ferrous metals 47–48, 63
> non-ferrous metals 49–51, 87–91

For terms on a continuum the most suitable treatment – depending on the emphasis, perspective and language of the text – may be to provide an entry (with the same locators) under each heading:

> health 33–67, 101, 104, 221
> sickness 33–67, 101, 104, 221

Where there are several locators to be included, requiring more than a single-line entry and perhaps a sequence of subheadings, and space is not available for two complete double entries, then the detail can be entered under one of the headings (whichever is the most suitable in the context) and a *see* cross-reference made from the other:

> health:
> > farmers 48–49
> > call centre workers 59–60
> > policewomen 35
> > shopworkers 54
> > teachers 45
> > teenagers 69–70
> sickness *see* health

Proper names

Indexers in some subject fields regard proper names (such as the names of authors cited in an advanced medical text, and of places referred to in a travel guide) as the easier items to deal with – they may be obvious in the text and simple to convert into the right form for headings. In other contexts, e.g. an encyclopaedia of art, quite the opposite situation pertains; names of people (historical or artistic figures, or of places throughout the world) have to be checked to ensure correct identification and headings have to be filled out in some detail.

People, places and events can be known by different names at various times and in different countries and cultures. Multi-element names, such as compound family names and names containing prefixes, and names that are sometimes abbreviated or become acronyms, can be looked for in more than one form. Indexers may have to rely heavily on authoritative reference sources for guidance in name presentation. Sources for the verification of names, which can be consulted on the internet, include the web sites of the British Library (www.bl.uk) and the Library of Congress catalogue (catalog.loc.gov)

Personal Names

Personal names feature in texts in a variety of forms, including:

- single names – Aristotle
- given names (forenames), or initials, and family names (surnames) – Dervla Murphy; A.N. Wilson
- given names, patronymics and family names – Mikhail Sergeevich Gorbachev (spellings of this name vary, because of different methods of transliteration; see 'Transliteration and romanization' later in this chapter)
- given names with identifying epithets or numbers – Peter the Wild Boy; Louis XIV
- nicknames – El Greco
- pseudonyms (aliases, assumed names, 'aka's, pen-names) – Saki; Barbara Vine

People's names should appear in an index in as full a form as is needed for identification in the context. It is not always necessary to give the name in its fullest possible form – for example, with all the given names or with long titles of honour or nobility. Often it is sufficient to use the name in the form given in the text, or, if the name appears in more than one form, in the most common, best-known or fullest form. If the other forms are very different from the chosen one, cross-references should be made from them.

Personal names in most English-language texts (and those in other modern European languages) are most frequently sought by looking for the family name, so the elements are reversed in index headings in order to place the family name first, usually followed by a comma, then the given name(s) or initial(s) – observing any peculiarities of capitalization and punctuation relevant to the person concerned:

Atwood, Margaret
Eliot, T.S.
Ihimaera, Witi
lang, k.d.
Liez, Jean-Luc
Smith, Stevie

On the other hand, names in the conventional Chinese form need no reversal for indexing purposes, as the family name always features first:

Jiang Zemin

The convention to reverse names of the 'given name, family name' type, for inclusion in directories and indexes, is so much taken for granted that it is hardly thought of as an intellectual task. When considering the automatic indexing of a text, though, it is obvious that these names cannot usually be grabbed for use, unaltered, in an index. Icelandic names are an exception to the reversal rule, being entered under the given name. The second element of these names is often a patronymic (derived from the father's or mother's name or that of an ancestor), not a surname:

Helgi Ágústsson
Jóhanna Sigurdardóttir

Many readers in other countries are unaware of this situation and therefore search for such names under the second part (the patronymic). Indexers have to decide, in the context of each index, whether to treat the occasional Icelandic name according to the national practice or to reverse it. Whichever decision is taken, a cross-reference from the other form is advisable.

Unreversed names may also be used in, for example, a firm's internal phone directory, where everyone is better known by given name and department:

Karen (Smith) *Sales* 1347
Kevin (Blue) *Internal Audit* 2461
Kevin (Sage) *Directorate* 2235
Kolya (Alexandrov) *Reception* 1762

In some indexes, such as those for scientific and technical periodicals and bibliographies, authors' names are sometimes given as surnames and initials only:

Meredith, T.
Quentin, H.M.
Stevens, J.

This gives a neater appearance, and occupies less space, but lessens the recognizability of the authors and can cause the entries for two people with the same surname and initials to be merged. Misleading information can also be given if 'Beth [full name Elizabeth] Anstruther' is abbreviated to 'Anstruther, B.', particularly if elsewhere in the text she is cited as 'Elizabeth'.

One of the problems of indexing personal names is that while there are strictly correct ways of entering them, governed by the customs of the relevant language, country or ethnic group, those ways are not known or understood by the majority of readers and writers. It is the responsibility of indexers to make informed decisions about the choice of entry element, to add cross-references or general directives from other sought elements and to explain the treatment of names in the introductory note (see 'Introductory note' in Chapter 5).

In cases of doubt, authoritative sources – general or specialized, according to the need – must be checked in order to find the correct form of entry. Broad general rules are given in indexing standard BS ISO 999 (British Standards Institution, 1996, subclause 7.3.1). Two more detailed, and very useful, sources on the customs and handling of names from different countries are *Names of persons* (International Federation of Library Associations and Institutions, 1996) and the *Anglo-American cataloguing rules* (AACR2) (Gorman and Winkler, 1988, Ch. 22). Both sources give reliable recommendations for headings intended for use in library and other catalogues. They are helpful to indexers for identifying the various elements of complex names and for determining under which element a name should be entered. Because much depends on the language of the person concerned (something that the indexer, the author and the reader may not know and may not be able easily to discover), the guidance given is not applicable to all indexing situations. Individual indexes need to be constructed in the best way for individual texts and are not intended – except in cumulative periodical indexes – to be consistent with each other. For example, in a list of bibliographical references, the indexer may sometimes have to reach a 'best for the situation' decision, using cross-references for possible alternative approaches.

The handling of personal names can be a thorny problem. It is always worth taking time to present them correctly, in order to avoid post-publication recriminations. Entering a name in an 'incorrect' form can cause irritation, even offence, to the named person and embarrassment to the author and indexer. On the other hand, entry in the 'correct' form may confuse the reader, so directions and explanations may be needed. Prior discussions with the author or the originator of the text may be necessary, and also the checking of reference sources. If there are many names to be included and checked, extra time needs to be allocated to the work (and the cost included in the fee charged).

Compound family names

When faced with a family name consisting of more than one element, the indexer may be unable to tell at first sight whether the second element is a 'middle' name (a second given name) or the first part of a compound family name. If it is known that the named person has a preference, or the name is found indexed in an authoritative source, that practice should be followed. Otherwise, the broad BS ISO 999 guideline is to enter under the first element, except where national or conventional usage suggests otherwise. The *Anglo-American cataloguing rules* (Gorman and Winkler, 1988, Rule 22.5C3) recommend that hyphenated names are entered under the first element:

Richard-Amato, Patricia A.
Robbe-Grillet, Alain

Many unhyphenated compounds, too, are entered under the first element:

> Vaughan Williams, Ursula
> Scott Wright, *Professor* Margaret
> Giscard d'Estaing, Valéry
> Ortega y Gasset, José

but practices differ from country to country and within countries. Reliable sources must be checked to ensure correct entry.

Some compound names seem to cause constant difficulty. For example, Arthur Conan Doyle (author of the Sherlock Holmes stories) should be entered under 'Doyle' (his own usage and that of the British Library catalogue), but (because he is often referred to as 'Conan Doyle') is frequently found under 'C' and not 'D'.

Names with separate prefixes
Family names that include articles and prepositions as separate prefixes should be treated according to the national practice of the named person, unless the person is resident in another country and has adopted the practice of that country. The *Anglo-American cataloguing rules* include a helpful list of languages and language groups (Gorman and Winkler, 1988, Rule 22.5D) with examples of names in each, and *Names of persons* (International Federation of Library Associations and Institutions, 1996) provides concise explanations and examples.

The capitalization of the first letters of prefixes varies, even between individuals in the same country. If the preferred practice of the person concerned is not known, it is probably better to capitalize the first letter, in consistency with the guideline that a proper name should normally begin with a capital letter.

Names with separate prefixes indicating family relationships are entered by the prefix in certain cases:

> O'Brien, Edna [Irish]
> Ní Chinnéide, Máire [Irish]
> Mac Néill, Séan [Irish]
> Ben Bella, Mohammed Ahmed [Arabic]
> Abu Tammam, Habib ibn Aus [Arabic]

and under the given name in others:

Dafydd ap Gwilym [Welsh]

Some general guidelines for certain groups of modern-style names are exemplified below.

N.B. Names from earlier periods may follow different conventions in the language or country concerned, so reputable reference sources should be checked in cases of doubt. It must be remembered that the bearer of a name may have an individual preference for its form of entry; this should always be followed if it can be ascertained. Some prefixes have an initial capital, some do not, but may all be capitalized in some indexes.

ENGLISH-SPEAKING COUNTRIES
Prefixes (normally foreign in origin) are used as entry elements:

de Paula, Clive
le Carré, John
de la Tour, Frances
du Sautoy, P.F.

DUTCH
Prefixes are not used as entry elements, except for 'ver':

Dijk, Wim van
Hoven, Johan van den
Koning, Jan de
Ver Boven, Daisy

AFRIKAANS
Unlike the Dutch names above, prefixes are used as entry elements:

Van der Merwe, C.J.
De Klerk, F.W.

FRENCH
Prefixes consisting of, or containing, articles are used as entry elements:

Le Goffic, Charles
La Serre, Jean Puget de

Du Fail, Noël
Des Roches, Madeleine

The prefix 'de' and its abbreviation 'd'' are not used as entry elements.

Gourmont, Rémy de
Aubigné, Agrippa d'

GERMAN
Articles and prepositions are not used as entry elements except when an article and preposition are combined:

Karajan, Herbert von
Decken, Frans von der
Vom Bruch, Rüdiger [vom = von dem]

ITALIAN
Prefixes are used as entry elements:

D'Annunzio, Gabriele
De Filippo, Eduardo
Di Stefano, Giuseppe
Della Casa, Anna

PORTUGUESE
Prefixes are not used as entry elements:

Melo, Eurico de
Costa, Jorge da
Santos, Luis dos

SPANISH
Prefixes are not used as entry elements, except for a definite article not accompanied by a preposition:

Vega, Ventura de la
Las Heras, Juan [article not accompanied by preposition]
Cervantes Saavedra, Miguel de
Rios, Manuel de los

NEW ZEALAND MAORI
Prefixed articles are used as entry elements:

Te Kanawa, *Dame* Kiri

A tantalizing situation for the indexer occurs when a personal name becomes attached to an idea, principle, object or process first proposed, invented or identified by that person; for example, the 'de Moivre theorem'. The French mathematician, who emigrated to England, should – according to the French convention – be entered as 'Moivre, Abraham de'. However, the topic associated with him is generally referred to in the subject field as the 'de Moivre theorem' and is likely to be looked for, in English-language indexes, under 'D', not 'M'. If the person is entered under 'M' and the theorem under 'D', this looks inconsistent; if both are entered under 'M' then they may not be found by the index user. Consistency can be achieved by putting both under 'de Moivre' – thus treating the personal name according to the English, rather than the French, convention – with a cross-reference from the other point.

Names with titles, epithets and dates
Many names referred to in texts are preceded or followed by titles or descriptive words. Some need to be retained in index headings, some do not. Such additions may usefully be italicized in order to indicate that they are neither given nor family names. For example, it is important for an index to distinguish between two people with the same surname, when one of them has the given name 'Earl' and the other has the aristocratic title 'Earl'.

Titles of address such as 'Mrs', 'Mr', 'Ms', 'Miss', 'Dr', and 'Rev', normally need to be included only when there is no given name, or if the person is customarily known by the title, or the profession of the person needs emphasis:

Gaskell, *Mrs*
Read, *Miss*
Smith, Colin
Smith, *Professor* Colin
Josephine, *Sister*, O.P.
Peter, *the Great*

The use of italics for titles distinguishes them from given names and family names. If preferred, the titles can instead be placed in parentheses.

In indexes to biographical texts, and others that include similar names, phrases are often added to show relationships to the main subject, and to distinguish people with the same name:

> Bland, Nora (stepmother of MT)
> Street, Margaret (schoolteacher)
> Street, Margaret (watercolourist)

Another way of distinguishing persons with the same name is to add dates of birth (and death, if appropriate):

> Quentin, Francis, *b.*1944
> Quentin, Francis, 1913–1988

Titles of honour and nobility, of which there are many in existence, can cause indexers some problems. Sometimes the full details are obvious from the text being indexed, but on other occasions the indexer may have to check authoritative sources to discover the correct title and formation. The full headings recommended in *Anglo-American cataloguing rules* (Gorman and Winkler, 1988, Rule 1.0D) for inclusion in library catalogue records are not usually relevant for use in 'routine' indexes, but they can be helpful for large biographical and encyclopaedic works. For example, Rule 22.16A3 gives the full heading for Prince Philip, the husband of the current British monarch, as: 'Philip, *Prince, consort of Elizabeth II, Queen of the United Kingdom*'. He is also sometimes referred to by the title 'Duke of Edinburgh'. Clearly, all this information is not needed for the majority of indexes, so the indexer has to select a concise form suitable for the text in hand – such as 'Philip, *Prince, Duke of Edinburgh*' if the text deals only with the United Kingdom.

Some British names with titles follow rules that are not part of common knowledge and if they are to be indexed it can be time-consuming to check the necessary background. For example, many titles of this kind are placed before the given name in an index entry:

> Dench, *Dame* Judi
> Richard, *Sir* Cliff
> Maitland, *Lady* Olga

but some should, according to aristocratic convention, be placed after the given name if the person concerned has a particular status – for example, 'Lady' if it denotes the wife of a knight or baronet:

> Gregory, Isabella Augusta, *Lady*

> Saints are usually entered under the given name:
> Hilda, *Saint* [or *St*]
> Hilary, *of Poitiers, Saint*

Irregular styles of name

Names should be presented in the styles preferred by their holders, even when they appear to contravene normal customs. For example, the initial letters in the names of writers 'e.e. cummings' and 'bell hooks' should not be capitalized.

Pseudonyms (aliases, assumed names, 'aka's, pen-names), initials

A writer or other person referred to by an assumed name or an initialized form throughout a text should usually be made accessible from both the names or forms of name. The exact treatment depends on the context, on the extent to which the two names are used in the text, and which (if either) of the two is better known. For example, in an index to a book about current British novelists and their works, or to a bibliography, references to Ruth Rendell could be made in a variety of forms – three possible alternatives are:

> Rendell, Ruth 34, 46, 57 *see also* Vine, Barbara
> Vine, Barbara 66, 79 *see also* Rendell, Ruth

or:

> Rendell, Ruth 34, 46, 57
>   writing as Barbara Vine 66, 79
> Vine, Barbara *see* Rendell, Ruth

or:

> Rendell, Ruth 34, 46, 57
>   *alias* Barbara Vine 66, 79
> Vine, Barbara (*alias* of Ruth Rendell) 66, 79

Where the real name of a person does not appear on his works, but is known, it can be included in the pseudonymous heading and a cross-reference:

> Belaney, Archie *see* Grey Owl
> Grey Owl (Archie Belaney)
> > *The adventures of Sajo and her beaver people* 45
> > *Pilgrims of the wild* 78
> > *Tales of an empty cabin* 82

Changes of personal name
People change their names for a variety of reasons. If the changes of name are mentioned in a text, they should obviously be reflected in the index; even if they are not referred to in the text, it may still be helpful to some users to include cross-references from the other names and to make the headings informative:

> Morris, James *see* Morris, Jan
> Morris, Jan (writing as James Morris until 1973)

Corporate (Organizational, Institutional) Names

All formally established organizations (societies, associations, companies, academic institutions, government departments) have official names, but many of them are frequently known by other – abbreviated, initialized, popular, or more convenient – names, such as 'BBC' for 'British Broadcasting Corporation'. The form of name used can vary from document to document – official names being used in directories and histories, other forms in memoirs and stories, perhaps. The indexer must always be aware that – even though an organization may be referred to by a single form of name in a text – readers looking for information may be using a variety of approaches. This does not necessarily imply that all possible forms of the name should be included as headings or cross-references in the index; it may be sufficient to include a statement in the introductory paragraph explaining the treatment of such names (see 'Introductory note' in Chapter 5).

An organization may be so well known by its initials or acronym that it can be acceptable to use that form as the heading. However, if there is the possibility of confusion for users of the index (because there are other organizations with the same initials, or because the initials are only understood within a particular subject specialism), then the initials should be followed by the full form in parentheses and a cross-reference (or double entry) given:

        BBC (British Broadcasting Corporation)
        British Broadcasting Corporation (BBC)

or:

        British Broadcasting Corporation *see* BBC

        National Institute for Clinical Excellence (NICE)
        NICE (National Institute for Clinical Excellence)

or:

        National Institute for Clinical Excellence *see* NICE

The decision whether to enter companies, government departments and so on under the direct form of name – University of Aberdeen; Institution of Electrical Engineers – has to be taken in context. Generally, it is better to enter all corporate names in the direct form – i.e. not inverted. The listing of universities in a consistent (and therefore helpful) way is complicated by the different word orders used in their official names – some starting with 'University', some with a place name, others with the name of a person or other designation – and with no indication of their location: University of Strathclyde; Brunel University; Open University; De Montfort University; University of Kent at Canterbury; University of Aberdeen. The indexer may, in one situation, consider it more useful to gather them (alphabetically) under a single topic heading:

      universities:
           Aberdeen
           Brunel
           De Montfort
           Kent
           Open
           Strathclyde

In another index, it may be better to enter them directly under their names, without any manipulation of the elements:

Brunel University
De Montfort University
Open University
University of Aberdeen
University of Kent at Canterbury
University of Strathclyde

However, it can sometimes be more useful in certain kinds of directory, or in indexes to texts oriented towards topics and places, or where there would otherwise be very long lists under elements like 'University of' or 'Society of', to provide inverted entries, as well as cross-references:

Architects, Royal Institute of British
Horological Institute, British
Psychical Research, Society of
Ulster, University of

In indexes that refer to government departments and official agencies from more than one jurisdiction (the territory within which a legal authority applies) or administrative area, the headings can be differentiated by being subordinated to the name of the relevant jurisdiction or area, as is widely practised in library catalogues:

Australia: Department of Resources and Energy
Canada: Department of Energy, Mines and Resources

If the text refers to the affairs of just one jurisdiction or area, there is no possibility of ambiguity and so the departmental names can be entered in direct form:

Department of Resources and Energy

or, if there are many departments, ministries and offices and it is thought that index users will not know the exact status of the one they want:

Resources and Energy, Department of

Subordinate units of larger bodies may be entered either under their own names – if they identify them adequately – or primarily under the names of the superordinate bodies to which they belong. As with the examples of jurisdictions shown above, the context of the index determines the chosen heading:

Center for Education Statistics

or:

Department of Education, Center for Education Statistics

with the approach from 'Center . . . ' provided for by a *see* cross-reference or a general directive.

A text may sometimes refer to the head of a department, or to the government minister responsible, rather than to the department itself: '. . . a recent statement by the Data Protection Commissioner . . . ' (rather than the Office of the Data Protection Commissioner). Unless the reference is to the individual in question – something personal about him or her or something concerning one particular head as opposed to another – it is better to treat the department and its head as one and the same, using either double entry or a *see* cross-reference, depending on the circumstances:

Data Protection Commissioner, Office
Office of the Data Protection Commissioner

or:

Data Protection Commissioner, *see* Office of the Data Protection
     Commissioner
Office of the Data Protection Commissioner

In this case, cross-references may be made from the names of the individual departments and agencies, or a note can be included in the introductory statement to explain how such names are treated.

Changes of corporate name
Changes of name are frequent, as companies merge, government departments change their areas of responsibility, academic establishments alter their status, professional societies and institutions modernize, and so on. Earlier and later forms of name may need to be included, either as double

entries or as cross-references, depending on the relevant information in the document and the needs of the index. For example:

> Liverpool John Moores University (formerly Liverpool Polytechnic)
> Liverpool Polytechnic *see* Liverpool John Moores University

Place Names

Names of places (from continents to individual settlements and parts of settlements, from mountains and deserts to oceans, as well as other parts of the universe) feature commonly in indexes. They are usually easy to spot when explicitly referred to in texts, less so when alluded to indirectly: 'They set up a new operation in the jewellery quarter of a city in the English Midlands . . .' – most likely to be Birmingham, which could be confirmed elsewhere in the text; 'Our stay in the 'rose-red city half as old as time' was not the spiritual experience we had hoped for . . .' – Petra in Jordan, as referred to in the poem *Petra* by Dean Burgen. As indicated under 'Implicit references' in Chapter 3, the indexer must only make such additional entries when the facts are certain – no entry should ever be made on the basis of supposition or guesswork. The headings would, of course, need to include the actual words from the text:

> Birmingham, jewellery quarter
> Petra (Jordan), 'rose-red city'

Situations like this can be a good test of general knowledge and of using reference sources.

Many places are known by different names in other countries – Munich/München, Cologne/Köln – or have twin forms within bilingual countries – Bruxelles/Brussel (as well as the anglicized form Brussels); Nova Scotia/Nouvelle-Écosse. A particular problem arises when a place name is commonly anglicized but its eponymous physical feature is not, e.g. the city of Moscow (in Russian, Moskva) and the river Moskva, on which it stands.

Names with more than one element can be tricky, particularly when the first part is an article or a preposition: Le Havre, Oporto, Los Angeles. Indexing standard BS ISO 999 (British Standards Institution, 1996, subclause 7.3.3.2) recommends that such articles and prepositions are retained in names of which they form integral parts, and that filing order for such names should follow local usage. (See Chapter 5 for more on filing order.) Where the words are not a part of the name, they are left out of the heading: 'Lake District' not 'The Lake District'. Names with elements indicating relative location, size or importance (West Wittering, East Wittering; High Hesket, Low Hesket; Great Tew, Little Tew) are sometimes all entered in direct form, sometimes all reversed, according to the nature of the index. The introductory note to the index should specify which policy has been applied (see 'Introductory note' in Chapter 5).

Places with identical names need to be sufficiently distinguished from each other, if found in the same index:

Newport (Isle of Wight)
Newport (Shropshire)   [In an index covering the UK only]

Newport (Quebec, Canada)
Newport (Mayo, Ireland)   [In an index covering the world]
Newport (Isle of Wight, UK)
Newport (Shropshire, UK)
Newport (Rhode Island, USA)

Luxembourg (city)
Luxembourg (country)

Gulf States (Persian Gulf)
Gulf States (US)

When 'The Gulf' is referred to without qualification, its meaning must be ascertained from the rest of the text. It may relate to the Persian (or Arabian) Gulf, the Gulf of Carpentaria (Australia), the Hauraki Gulf (New Zealand), or the Gulf of Mexico (US), for example.

Named topographical features usually require a qualifier to clarify their identity, unless it is obvious from the context and the users can be expected to know what is intended:

Ellen (river)
Roseberry Topping (hill)

Punctuation and spacing in names should follow that used officially by the place concerned:

> Henley-on-Thames
> Ashton-in-Makerfield
> Ashton upon Mersey

Changes of place name

Places (countries, cities and towns, regions, counties) are subject to changes of name, usually for political, administrative or cultural reasons. As usual, the context of the work being indexed must determine whether cross-references are needed to help the index user, or whether additional information should be included after a heading. The principal name headings that go into an index should be those used in the text, but it may be relevant to include cross-references from former or later names. Much depends on the circumstances, for example the period of time during which the situation described in the text occurs:

> Ekaterinburg (known as Sverdlovsk 1924–1992)
> Sverdlovsk *see* Ekaterinburg
> Yekaterinburg *see* Ekaterinburg [alternative transliteration]
>
> Bombay *see* Mumbai
> Mumbai (formerly Bombay)

Apart from official name changes like those shown above, there are sometimes changes in the way in which people refer to areas outside their own countries. For example, the area often referred to by people in the UK as 'the Gulf' has been known as 'the Persian Gulf' and also 'the Arabian Gulf'. All three forms must be accessible for as long as they remain current or in the literature.

Changes in the punctuation, capitalization and spacing of names also occur from time to time; for example, Heathrow (the site of the main airport for London) was formerly Heath Row. At the time of writing there is discussion about a completely new name for the airport; if this comes about, indexers will need to provide cross-references for some time to come.

Further information on place names is given in Chapter 8: Subject specialisms, in the section on archaeology.

Names of Individual Things

The proper names of individual objects and occurrences, when used as headings, may need qualifiers to identify them clearly:

> Canberra (ship)
> Concorde (aeroplane) [N. American ... (airplane)]
> Grizelda (cat)
> Jarrow Crusade (1936)
> Koh-i-noor (diamond) [or: Kohinoor, Kohinor, Kohinur]
> Skylon (structure, Festival of Britain, 1951)
> Skylab (US space station)

Titles of works (documents)

These may be titles of books and periodicals, paintings, musical compositions, or any other individually named works. In indexes they are usually given in italics or distinguished in some other way. As much other information as is needed – creator, type of document, date, place of publication – may be added to clarify their identity, usually in parentheses:

> *Fresh carpet* (Ivor Cutler) [Given name and surname of author]
> *Lament for Tadhg Cronin's children* (Michael Hartnett)
> *Dressing up for the carnival* (Shields) [Surname of author]
> *Harry Potter and the prisoner of Azkaban* (Rowling)
> *End of the affair, The* (novel) [Category of work]
> *End of the affair, The* (film)
> *Spectator, The* (London, UK) [Place of publication]
> *Spectator, The* (Hamilton, Ontario, Canada)

Initial articles ('A', 'An' and 'The') in titles are often transposed to the end (as for *The Spectator* above), so that the first significant word is positioned at the beginning of the entry. This form is recommended by indexing standard BS ISO 999 (British Standards Institution, 1996, subclause 7.3.4.2), and neatly ensures that readers can run their eyes straight down the left edge of the list in order to find what they are looking for. It does, though, make the individual title heading look clumsy, so some indexers prefer the untransposed form ('*The Spectator*'), in which 'The' – though present in its proper place – must be ignored in filing. The individual heading then looks normal, but the apparent inclusion under 'S' of what looks like a 'T' heading can give the sequence an irregular and untidy appearance.

It is usual to capitalize the first letter of the entry word in a transposed title (as for *End of the affair, The*). As mentioned above under 'Capitalization', the indexing standard BS ISO 999: 1996 gives titles with no capitals within (except for proper names and in words in languages requiring them). The use of lower-case throughout a title is by no means universally practised, so the house style of the publisher should be followed. In its examples (which are illustrative, not prescriptive), the indexing standard (subclause 7.3.4.2) uses a lower-case letter for the entry word as well, which would give:

> *end of the affair, The*

This is visually unattractive to some indexers and readers, but unexceptional to others.

Some older books with long titles are better known by the secondary part, or by a shorter form of the title, and so are normally referred to by that part. For example, *The posthumous papers of the Pickwick Club* is conventionally known as *The Pickwick Papers*, giving the usual heading *Pickwick Papers, The*.

Works that are internationally well known, or that have appeared in several different versions (such as a book, a film, and a TV series), are frequently known under several different titles, or have individual parts known under their own names. In order to bring them together, they can be entered under a single uniform title (often the best-known, or authorized title). They include some sacred works such as the Bible and its parts. Unless the whole text is about the Bible – in which case the individual books are indexed directly under their own names – the parts are conventionally all entered under the uniform heading, followed by the details of the parts:

> Bible. N.T. Revelation [i.e. the book of Revelation in the
>   New Testament]

Detailed guidance on the listing of parts of sacred scriptures is given in *Anglo-American cataloguing rules* (Gorman and Winkler, 1988, Rules

25.17–25.18) and can be helpful for indexers dealing with references to many different parts of such documents, but that depth of analysis is not usually relevant for indexes containing just a few references. Where this kind of collecting together is done in an index, it should be explained in the introductory statement, or cross-references made from the names of the individual parts.

Musical items are frequently known by more than one name – Beethoven's string quartet in E flat (opus 74), for example, which is also known as the *Harp quartet*. Both 'official' and nicknames or descriptive names must be accessible.

When dealing with titles in languages with which they are not familiar, indexers should check with an authoritative source to ensure that they enter the titles in the correct form. It is essential to recognize which initial words are articles (so that they can be transposed or at least ignored in the filing order), and to know which capital letters must be retained:

> *Fledermaus, Die* [German: feminine 'the']
> *Ballo in Maschera, Un* [Italian: masculine 'a']
> *Tennis, Le* [French: masculine 'the']

First lines of poems

Indexes of the first lines of poems are common in books of poetry, because they are the principal means of identification used by readers – sometimes remembered more easily than the actual titles of the poems. The main feature of first line headings is that (unlike the titles of works) all initial articles are retained and are used as entry words:

> 'A frog he would a-wooing go' [under A]
> 'The old grey hearse goes rolling by' [under T]

An interesting point arises if such a first line also acts as the poem's title. On the one hand, the article should be used as the entry word (because it is the first element of the first line), while on the other it should be ignored (even transposed to the end) because it is the first word of the title of a work. In this situation, it is best to use the article as the entry word for both the headings – the 'first line' rule taking precedence over the 'title' one.

Transliteration and romanization

Texts frequently contain names and other terms that have been transliterated (converted from another alphabetic system, such as Cyrillic) or romanized (adapted from a non-alphabetic writing system, e.g. Chinese). Because there is not a one-to-one match between the letters or characters of the various systems, a variety of methods has developed for presenting these terms. The indexer does not have to select a method – that will already have been done by the author – and so should reproduce the words exactly as they appear in the text. If there is a chance that the users of the index may be searching for the words in significantly different forms – particularly if the other forms start with different letters, for example – then cross-references need to be added. Indexers producing cumulated indexes encompassing a long span of years may find that different methods have been used during that time and so will need to select one form of each term (probably the latest) for the main heading. Well-known changes of name presentation include: Beijing (China), formerly shown as Peking; the Russian composer Tchaikovsky, sometimes transliterated as Chaikovskii; and the Libyan head of state, variously given as Gadafy, Gadhafi, Qadhafi, among other forms. Other terms that may be encountered include 'tsar', 'czar', and 'tzar', 'khus-khus' and 'cuscus', and 'suslik' and 'souslik'.

Accents and modified letters

Accented and otherwise modified letters, whether they affect pronunciation or not, should be reproduced in the index exactly as in the text:

> Grünewald, Isaak
> Légion étrangère
> Hôtel des Invalides
> *Herr Mueller*

A name that is sometimes presented with a modified letter, an accent, an umlaut or a diaeresis and sometimes without (or in an expanded version) needs to be presented in one form in any single index.

Qualifiers

As emphasized earlier, headings should be concise. This does not imply a succession of bare, single words without context or amplification. Any heading may be qualified, as shown already in several examples, by a word, phrase, date or other indicator – in parentheses – in order to establish its identity:

> pipes (musical instruments)
> pipes (tobacco smoking equipment)
> pipes (tubes)

Subheadings

To indicate the particular aspects of a topic referred to by various locators, additional words can be added after the heading:

> computers, use in rural areas 77, 79, 91

> building design: national parks 195–196

> information technology:
>   and rural change 18–20
>   and deskilling 34

Subheadings, like headings, should be no longer than is necessary to convey the required meaning; articles, conjunctions and prepositions should be included only when necessary to prevent ambiguity. The use of 'and', linking two concepts, is a useful device – so long as it is limited to the specific meaning 'in relation to'. Its misuse, in situations where another word or phrase (such as 'with', 'after', 'influence of') would have been better, has led some people to regard it as too vague to be useful. An alternative, occasionally seen, is '*irt*' ('in relation to'), but this takes up as much space as 'and' and needs explanation in the introductory note, so would seem to have no advantage.

A succession of subheadings accumulated against a single heading is arranged as a sequence, if they cannot reasonably be merged into a single phrase:

cars:
> licensing 43–44
> ownership and use 38, 162
> parking restrictions 182, 193
> registration 56

or:

> cars: licensing 43–44; ownership and use 38, 162; parking
> restrictions 182, 193; registration 56

The decision whether or not to add subheadings must always be taken in context. The type of text and kind of expected user may not require the additional information. If there is limited space for the index (often the case in published books), there may be no room for subheading sequences. There is certainly no need to provide a subheading that summarizes or reproduces a piece of text. The index should lead to the text; it is not its function to replace the text or to report it.

The choice of wording of subheadings needs care. Each subheading should be concise, unambiguous and well-suited to the heading to which it is attached. Where – in a biographical text, for example – subheadings are required under personal name headings, sensitivity and awareness are needed, particularly when the persons referred to are still living. Most such texts will have been read by the publishers' libel lawyers and the necessary adjustments made; an indexer should therefore take care that the headings and subheadings constructed represent only what is contained in the text and do not imply something that (although suspected by the indexer) is not explicit:

> Browne-Greene, Q.Z., behaviour towards Grey-Black, Y.Y

may be more satisfactory and objective than:

> Browne-Greene, Q.Z., humiliation of Grey-Black, Y.Y.

Indexes of authors' names sometimes require subheadings showing the titles of individual works:

> Fairfax, T.H.Z.
>> *Hungry in Hedgeby* 121
>> *Scorching spring* 234
>> *Watersend Farm* 46

The punctuation, grouping and layout of subheadings is described under 'Subheading layouts' in Chapter 5.

Indicating the Position – the Locators

The locations of pieces of text (images, sounds, etc.) are indicated by the numbers (sometimes letters, or a combination of both) of the physical units on or in which they appear. These may refer to pages, paragraphs, columns, lines, volumes, parts, items, dates, files, sides, or any unit that can be represented by a known position in a sequence.

Headings and locators should be clearly separated by spacing, and perhaps punctuation, the style being consistent throughout an index. Indexing standard BS ISO 999 (British Standards Institution, 1996, subclause 7.4.5) suggests either two spaces, or a comma and a space, or some other unambiguous punctuation mark. In many cases a single space or two spaces, with no punctuation, will be sufficient to present a clearly understood entry. Simple punctuation can be useful in indexes where many headings end in numerals (and so may be mistaken for locators) and in those where the locators are mixtures of letters and numerals:

> string quartets 48
> long-distance lorry drivers 77
> ringed plovers, 34
> Voyager 2: 98
> *Finance Act 1999*: 89
> Schedule D: C4/213a

Where there is more than one locator for a heading, they are arranged in ascending numerical order, or alphabetical order, whichever is relevant:

> warehousing 7, 55, 119
> emergency shelters A/13, C/45, L/91

A string of six or more undifferentiated locators is usually considered unhelpful. This can be avoided by highlighting the principal references, indicating special matter, removing references of minor significance, or analysing into subheadings (see 'Long strings of locators' in Chapter 5 for details of these techniques).

Page ranges

When a topic is treated continuously (without interruption) over more than one page or other unit, the full extent of the range is shown, using the numbers of the first and last pages:

> Cape Verde Islands 18–25
> Asperger's syndrome 83–89

Indexing standard BS ISO 999 (British Standards Institution (1996) subclause 7.4.3.1) recommends the fullest possible form of number, for maximum clarity:

> *Viburnum tinus* 15–16, 34–35, 160–166

With ranges in which the initial number is the same, a reduced (squashed, elided, minimal) form is often preferred by publishers (56–9 instead of 56–59). Styles of reduction vary, so an indexer may need to produce different forms according to the jobs in hand.

In *Hart's rules* (Oxford University Press, 1983, p.19) the least number of figures possible is specified, except for the 'tens' and 'hundreds' sequences:

> 5–10, 33–4, 103–4, 310–14, 404–13

The *Chicago manual of style* (University of Chicago Press, 1993, paragraph 8.69) uses the full style for numbers less than 100 and for 100 and multiples of 100:

> 6–11, 33–34, 200–207, 1000–1007

then for 101 through to 109 (in multiples of 100):

> 103–4, 404–13, 1001–5

and for 110 through to 199 (in multiples of 100);

> 122–24, 354–412, 1245–48

The indication of page ranges can be a problem when applying embedded indexing methods to electronic texts, because some systems record only the number of the first page of the range. This is not at all helpful to the user of the index.

Because of the way in which printed books have to be put together, continuous treatment of a topic is sometimes 'interrupted' by an interposed illustration relating to another topic. If such an illustration takes up a whole page (say p. 23 in the middle of a range) the indexer is left wondering how to show this 'almost continuous, but not quite' situation. Some indexers ignore the interruption and give the full page range:

21–27

Others give the separate parts:

21–22, 24–27

which is more specific but does not indicate that the text is continuous. So far, there is no 'official' recommendation for this circumstance, but individual indexers may devise their own ways of indicating. For example, these have been suggested:

21/24–27

or:

21–22 & 24–27

or:

21/27

or:

21--27

The first two methods are better, because they show how many pages are involved and cite their exact numbers. The other two methods remain vague as to exactly which pages, or even how many pages, are involved. Any of these methods used must be explained in the introductory note (see 'Introductory note' in Chapter 5).

The abbreviations '*ff*' and '*et seq*' – meaning 'and the following pages' – are imprecise and not meaningful to many index users, and so should not be used.

Intermittent treatment within consecutive pages

Very often, a topic is dealt with on several consecutive pages, not continuously but interspersed with passages on other topics. If the treatments are all significant, and therefore worth indexing, the individual locators should be shown, separated by commas:

humanism 231, 232, 233

This should not be converted to '231–233', which implies a page range with continuous treatment, as described above.

The use of '*passim*' after a page range, meaning 'scattered throughout the pages indicated', and found in older indexes, is specified as 'not recommended' by indexing standard BS ISO 999 (British Standards Institution, 1996, subclause 7.4.3.2). It is not readily understood by present-day readers and has at times been employed as a lazy and inadequate alternative to the formation of subheadings. However, when properly used, it was a valuable indicator of references which were not of major importance and not suitable for analysis into subheadings, but which could be useful to someone researching a subject and needing to glance at them in case they provided interesting snippets of information. Some indexers would welcome a contemporary equivalent, in shorter form – perhaps, for example:

113–23dis [dispersed or distributed]

or:

67–74sep [separate]

or:

81–89*var* [*various*]

or:

127 . . . 135

Such forms should be strictly reserved for the specific circumstances described above and should never be employed as a short cut or instead of providing subheadings. Their use must be explained in the introductory note.

Indication of illustrations and other material

It is helpful to readers to indicate locations where illustrations, tables and other special material can be found. Conventional methods for this are by the use of italics, abbreviations, or square brackets:

> dermatitis 45, *46*
> Norfolk pine 101–102, 278illus
> rotary engine 47, 48*fig*
> Victoria Falls, Zimbabwe 49i
> respiratory diseases in UK regions 87, 88t [t = table]
> Alibhai-Brown, Yasmin [126], 131 [square brackets indicating
>   a photograph]

If the context seems to require it, locators for illustrations can be given in a separate sequence after the locators for text:

> Gobelin tapestries 35, 141–150; *143, 149, 166*

When text and a related illustration appear on the same page, the indexer has a choice between several forms, some more informative than others. Three of the possibilities are:

> Flatiron Building, New York 46 [page number without distinction]

or:

> Flatiron Building, New York *46* [page number italicized]

or:

> Flatiron Building, New York 46, *46* [page number repeated, the
>   second one italicized]

Caption Information

Captions to illustrations sometimes include indexable elements that do not refer directly to the illustration itself. In this case it would be misleading either to give the locator in italics (or whatever other style has been chosen for illustrations), or to show it in plain type as though a text page. The indexer must present it in a unique form, perhaps using an abbreviation, and explain the form in the introductory note. For example:

> 118c
> 431*cap*

Complex locators

Indexes to multivolume books and to serials such as newspapers and periodicals require not just page numbers, but also volume numbers or dates or both, and so can become lengthy. The punctuation and typographic styling of such locators varies from publication to publication, but must be consistent within one index (and should be explained in the introductory note):

> Trailles, P.P.P.
> > 'Facing the north wind: Trailles' trial.' 1999, v6 (1) Jan 67–74
>
> Belldone, W.Y.
> > 'The feeding and nesting habits of birds in suburban gardens in East Hertfordshire' J Nat Soc Herts (1937) **8** 90–96
>
> rescue archaeology 3:14–15
>
> toxic substance transport regulations: **5** 149–152, **8** 56–59
>
> prisoners, rehabilitation 85 Apr 2000 34–40

Where more than one locator from a single volume is referred to, the volume number may be repeated, for clarity, where space permits:

> digital television 1.3–4, 1.16–18 [clearer than 1.3–4, 16–18]

though much depends on the final presentation of the index – the style and size of type, for example. The main concern is that page numbers should not be mistaken for volume numbers.

Accuracy in presentation of locators

The purpose of the locator is to direct the user to the precise page (paragraph, column, line, image, etc.) where the wanted matter appears, so it is essential that the number is given correctly. Indexers who are entering their headings and locators via keyboards therefore need to take great care not to transpose, omit or add numerals (or letters). As each locator is keyed in, it should be visually checked on the screen. If an embedded system is used, where tags or markers are inserted into the text (on screen) of the document itself, the locators are automatically added to headings (as long as the document remains within the same word-processor or dtp system) and so should be correct. Even so, it is worth checking that page ranges are suitably and consistently presented and that the system has not converted separate but consecutive locators (8, 9, 10, 11) into ranges (8–11) – these two styles have different meanings, as explained above.

Temporary locators

When temporary locators have been used in the compilation of the index – because the indexer has worked from the original typescript or manu-script, or from individually paged chapters, rather than the final typeset page proofs – extra care is needed to ensure that they are all removed and the new ones correctly substituted (see 'Locators for unknown or changed pagination' in Chapter 11).

Locators for multilingual texts

Texts containing versions of the text in different languages need indexes in those languages (as indicated at the beginning of this chapter). Because of the varying lengths of the text – some languages have a longer average word and sentence length than others – the locators relating to any passage of text are likely to differ from version to version. The locators in the index for, say, the English version cannot be automatically copied for use in the French version. It is essential, therefore, that each index contains only the locators relevant for that version.

'Brainteasers'

There is a cluster of odd locator problems that can worry indexers, and for which standard guidelines do not provide solutions. Because there are no widely accepted recommendations for them, they should be quickly resolved in the way most suited for the index in question, with explana-tion (if needed) in the introductory paragraph. They include:

Treatment and Analysis of Large Divisions of Text

Opinions differ about making a subheading analysis of a large section of text (e.g. a chapter) when the whole page range is already indicated after the heading, and the analysed terms are already headings in their own right:

> Afrode-Drayge equipment 230–80
>> agricultural use 230–45
>> educational models 271–80
>> forensic use 246–70
> agriculture, Afrode-Drayge equipment 230–45
> educational models, Afrode-Drayge equipment 271–80
> forensic use, Afrode-Drayge equipment 246–70

The alternative is to provide the heading with the full page range only (with no subheadings), and to give the other terms (as before) as headings in their own right:

> Afrode-Drayge equipment 230–80
> agriculture, Afrode-Drayge equipment 230–45
> educational models, Afrode-Drayge equipment 271–80
> forensic use, Afrode-Drayge equipment 246–70

Views on this matter are strongly held. Some indexers regard the 'heading with duplicated subheadings' pattern as bad practice, as did Knight (1979, p. 54), because the subheadings merely point to locators that are already stated against the heading. Others stress its helpfulness to users, because it indicates both the complete extent of page coverage and the sectional content of the very large chunk of text. The most important point is that any sought terms must be accessible as headings, not just hidden away as subheadings and therefore possibly not found.

Locators in Hierarchical Headings

In relation to the analysis problem described above, indexers sometimes wonder how to deal with subheading locators, when some come within the page range given for the superordinate heading and some do not. In this case, each subheading must be followed by all its relevant locators. For example, having made these entries (to file under A, C, D and G):

    animals 6–19
    cats 12–13, 25
    dogs 9–11, 37, 39, 56–7
    gerbils 14, 23

an indexer decides not to add this simple cross-reference:

    animals 6–19 (*see also* cats; dogs; gerbils)

but instead to list the individual animals as subheadings, as well as headings in their own right (the double entry method). All the relevant subheading locators must be given – those within the overall page range and those outside it:

    animals 6–19
            cats 12–13, 25
            dogs 9–11, 37, 39, 56–7
            gerbils 14, 23
    cats 12–13, 25
    dogs 9–11, 37, 39, 56–7
    gerbils 14, 23

If there is space available, this double entry method can be accommodated.

Awkwardly Placed Text

Texts are not always presented in the most helpful way for the indexer – this is no-one's fault, but just a result of dividing the text into pages. A well laid-out text should not contain 'widows' (short lines at the top of pages), and most commercial editors take care not to include them.

A typical problem, bothersome to beginners and experienced indexers alike, is the indexable text that starts at the bottom of a page (perhaps even just the last line on a recto (right-hand page), continues right through the next page and ends a few lines from the top of the page after that. If presented as, say, 121–123, it can give the impression that three whole pages are devoted to the subject, when in fact little more than one pageful is involved; also, a user looking for the passage will obviously start at the top of page 121 and have to scan through to find the start of the piece. If given as 122–123 (where the bulk of the passage is located, users then have to turn back a page to see the first sentence or so. Either way, there is a slight inconvenience to the user, but it is not usually a major difficulty.

A similar situation arises when the treatment of a subject starts on one page, but is not explicitly named – i.e. the text does not use the indexable word or phrase – until a little way down the second page. As before, the worst case is a piece that runs from a recto page to a verso. For example, a person may be described initially on page 45 as 'a sinister figure – who was to have an adverse influence on my career – appeared unexpectedly at the reception'; the text relating to this person continues on to page 46, but the person is not named (the writer wishing to build up the tension) until page 47. Indexing this accurately is difficult, but the indexer must try. There seem to be two possibilities. The first is to give only the page on which the name appears, trusting the intelligence of the reader to discover that the previous text is also relevant: Smythe-Jones-Browne, M. 47. The second is to give the whole page range, but to include the descriptive phrase in the heading, so that the reader will know what to look for: Smythe-Jones-Browne, M. ('sinister figure') 45–47.

Another example is the splitting of a personal name, with the first element of the name at the end of one page and the second at the beginning of the next. Good editorial practice should ensure that this does not happen.

Large-format books with very dense text, perhaps presented in two or more columns – certain encyclopaedias, for example – sometimes label the quarters of the page 'a, b, c, d' in the outer margin or number the columns or lines. Indexers can then use these indicators to show more clearly the relevant position of the indexed item:

earthquakes 914c [page 914, section c]
Tractarianism 235/1/52 [page 235, column 1, line 52]

Topics Referred to, in Separated Pieces of Text, More Than Once on a Page

A topic may be significantly referred to more than once on a page – perhaps in the first paragraph and the last paragraph. The most common practice is just to give the locator in the normal way and to leave it to the reader to discover (or not) that there is more than one relevant passage on the page. To be more helpful, the indexer can add an indicator to the page number (with an explanation in the introductory paragraph to the index):

> 69[2]
> 133^2

In older indexes, the Latin forms for 'twice' and 'thrice' can be found, but are not now recommended, as the words are not widely understood:

> 38bis
> 89ter

References to a Topic in the Body of the Text and in a Footnote on the Same Page

A topic may be treated on a page in the main text and also in a footnote on the same page. Indexers are sometimes uncertain whether to include both as locators: 167, 167n. The matter can be decided by asking whether readers are alerted to the footnote by reading the appropriate piece of text. If they are, there is no need to add the second locator; if they are not, because the footnote is contained in a later piece of text which does not explicitly refer to the topic in question, then the locator with the footnote should be added.

Page Ranges that Include Chapter Notes

If a page range in an entry includes the final page where there are relevant chapter notes (not footnotes, but numbered notes at the end of a chapter), there is usually no need to include specific locators for the notes:

> transcendental meditation 26–39 [not 26–39, 39n1–4)

Misnumbering of Pages, Paragraphs or Items of Text

In texts where the numbering of pages, paragraphs or items is not done automatically, there is sometimes an uncorrectable error in the numbering or lettering. This happens occasionally in the numbering of committee minutes; each minute has a number, but the minute writer may mistakenly allocate the same number to two minutes (perhaps the last minute of one meeting and the first of the next meeting). By the time the annual batch of minutes reaches the indexer, the various quarterly copies have long ago been dispatched to committee members and it is too late to make changes. A similar condition occurs from time to time with periodical issues, when volume numbers, part numbers and dates are wrongly printed on covers and at the bottom of pages. Another example is the duplication of figure or table numbers. In these situations, the indexer must make the best of a bad job, and add a suitable identifying character or abbreviation to the duplicate locator:

> awards 99/14, 99/81
> donations 99/5, 99/14#

The meaning of such characters must be explained in the introductory note.

Cross-References

Cross-references are not essential in every index, but the majority of indexes benefit from their inclusion. Their purpose is to guide the user to other headings in the index. They can provide access for users who look up terms similar in meaning to those used in entries with locators – someone who looks up 'low-pressure areas' may be directed to look for the equivalent term 'depressions' because that is the term used in that particular index. They can also suggest additional terms that may be of interest to the user, because they are conceptually related – a user who has already found a reference by looking up the term 'white-collar crime' in a certain index can be told that other related references may be found under 'fraud'.

Without cross-references, the burden is on the user to think of all possible terms under which relevant information could be entered; with suitable knowledge of the subject, this may not be too much of a problem, but otherwise the user may have to read right through the index.

Cross-references use the forms *see* and *see also* (or in thesauri, *use* and *BT*, *NT* and *RT* – broader, narrower and related terms) and are always made in the context of a particular index, so they differ widely from index to index. This is quite different from the cross-references produced for library catalogues, which generally follow a standard pattern, following the hierarchy of whichever classification scheme or subject headings list is in use. Some cross-references necessary in indexes may seem strange at first sight, but are entirely apt in the context. A certain filing system once contained the *see* cross-reference 'anthrax *see* politics' – because a particular document dealt with an aspect of the use of the anthrax bacterium which had political implications.

It is claimed that some users (particularly children) do not understand the instructions *see* and *see also*, and alternatives such as *look at*, *search using* and *look under* have been suggested as alternatives. However, *see* and *see also* are very widely used and can be explained, if necessary, in the introductory note. (See 'Cross-references' in Chapter 9 'Literature for chidren'.)

See cross-references

Several examples of the use of *see* cross-references have been given in the earlier sections of this chapter. Language is rich in synonyms, near-synonyms and overlapping terms, so there is usually a possibility of someone trying to look for the topic using a term other than the one used throughout the text.

Also known, when featuring in a thesaurus used for indexing and retrieval, as a *use*-reference, a *see* cross-reference guides the user to a 'preferred' term (or terms) in an index, e.g. from an initialized or abbreviated form of name, or short form of a topic term, to the full form (or vice versa):

> British Broadcasting Corporation *see* BBC
> EBM *see* evidence-based medicine
> WTO *see* World Trade Organization

from a synonym or near-synonym to its equivalent:

neckties *see* ties

from one spelling form to another:

tires USE tyres

from a real name to a pseudonym (or vice versa):

Cornwell, David *see* le Carré, John

from one name to a later (or earlier) name:

Wedgwood Benn, Anthony *see* Benn, Tony

or from a broader to a narrower term (or terms), a narrower to a broader term, or from one related term to another:

fleas *see* infestations
pollution *see* industrial effluents; sewage outfalls; vehicle exhaust
    gases

A 'preferred' term in a particular index is one that is listed with locators against it. 'Preferred' does not indicate that it is an approved term to
be used in all indexes. It is 'preferred' only in the context of that particular index; in another index, it may be the 'non-preferred' term from
which a 'see' cross-reference is made. The choice (as explained earlier in
this chapter) is always made on the basis of the vocabulary used in the
document being indexed.

See cross-references can be made from subheadings (and lower
levels) to headings:

brownfield sites:
    hypermarkets
    industrial contamination *see* pollution

or to subheadings (one or more), sub-subheadings and so on:

Mexico *see* agriculture, Mexico; *maquiladora*; migration, Latin
    America

The use of *see under* has been favoured by some indexers, as an alternative way of referring to a number of subheadings that all contain the word in question:

> unemployment *see under* financial services; manufacturing;
>   rural areas

This method produces a shorter entry, but is not as clear as the fuller style

> unemployment *see* financial services, unemployment;
>   manufacturing, unemployment; rural areas, unemployment

See cross-references can also be made from one subheading to another in the same sequence. This is only necessary when there are many subheadings and the two in question are so far apart that the index user might miss the chosen term:

> forestry
>   economics
>   education *see* training *below* [or *see* . . . training]
>   [etc., etc., etc.,]
>   taxation
>   training

A *see* cross-reference is sometimes made, where space is restricted and the preferred term's entry is lengthy, as an alternative to providing double entries, but there is little point in making a *see* cross-reference if it leads only to a single-line entry, as no space is saved.

Normally, 'see' cross-references do not contain locators; they point from one word or phrase to another. Some indexers do include them when they are indexing multiple authors of periodical articles:

> Doe, J.D. *see* Smith, A.B. and Doe, J.D., 109–115

For further information on author cross-references, see 'Multiple authorship' in Chapter 6: Serial publications.

The equivalence of terms is judged in the context of the content being indexed. In one index it may be appropriate to say 'weather *see* climate' – the terms are overlapping, not exactly equivalent, but may both serve to represent the topic in a general way; in another index the two terms may both need to appear as full headings with their own locators, because in that context they have technically different meanings.

'See *also*' cross-references

These inform the user about other terms in the index that are conceptually related and so may be of interest. A conceptual relationship between terms may be one of several types, including 'genus and species' (seabirds/albatrosses), 'whole and part' (computers/screens), 'class and individual' (musicians/Evelyn Glennie), and 'occasional' instances (wasps/pests, advertising/newspapers). In a thesaurus, relationships are indicated by BT (broader terms), NT (narrower terms) and RT (related terms).

Unlike *see* cross-references, the first term cited in a *see also* cross-reference is always followed by at least one locator. The locator in the entry for the term to which the user is directed must be different from the one given for the original term (otherwise there is no point in the *see also* instruction):

> eels 89–91
>> *see also* Sargasso Sea
> Sargasso Sea 118, 224

The cross-reference to 'Sargasso Sea' above would be given only if the text on those pages contained information relevant to eels. In another context, it might be appropriate to have:

> eels 124
>> *see also* food fish
> food fish 47, 49, 67
>> *see also* eels; sardines; tuna

and in another:

> eels 56–62
>> *see also* migration, fish

migration, fish 231, 423, 515
    see also eels; salmon

Like a *see* cross-reference, a *see also* cross-reference can refer to a subheading or lower level:

    edible plants 67–90 *see also* fungi: edible

The use of *see also under* has been used as a shorter, but less clear, way of referring to a subheading:

    folk songs 114 *see also under* Celtic music; country and western;
        Hungary; nursery rhymes

    See also cross-references between names are used to alert users to the possibility of other spellings of similar-sounding names, for example in directories:

    Bachelor *see also* Batchelor
    Beecham *see also* Beauchamp

and to indicate earlier or later headings where more information can be found:

    Leicestershire County Council 67–70, 88, 101 *see also* Rutland
        County Council
    Rutland County Council 134–135 *see also* Leicestershire County
        Council

    See also cross-references between broader and narrower terms are most often needed to refer from the broader to the narrower (the general to the specific):

    noble gases 56 *see also* argon; neon; xenon

but the context of an index sometimes requires a reference from the narrower to the broader:

> fountains 13, 33 *see also* water features

The reference from 'noble gases' here indicates that information specific to the individual gases named can be found on various other pages. The reference from 'fountains' signifies that the section on water features contains information that is applicable to all kinds of water feature, including fountains (while not specifically identifying them).

Older indexes have sometimes included the direction *q.v.* (an abbreviation of the Latin *quod vide*, meaning 'which see'), as an alternative to *see also* in entries where different locators are to be found under the headings:

> Stalingrad 115–116 (later Volgograd, *q.v.*)
> Volgograd 45–6 (formerly Stalingrad, *q.v.*)

This is a neat construction but, as it is not widely understood, is best avoided.

General directives

See and *see also* cross-references are also used to give directions to classes of topics, using various forms of words, as in:

> fruit *see names of individual fruit*

This indicates that there is nothing on fruit in general, but that information is given on particular types of fruit. This kind of direction is suitable if the index user can be expected to know the names of fruits to look up – otherwise all the featured fruits should be listed in a normal *see* cross-reference. It can be helpful to give one example in a general directive, to show the user the type of entry to look for:

> bird migration 221–224 (*see also specific birds, e.g.* swallows)
> metal fatigue 134–136 (*see also specific metals, e.g.* steel)
> spa towns *see names of countries*, e.g. Belgium: spas

Checking cross-reference connections

Cross-references can be made at any time during the compilation of the index. The need for some will be obvious to the indexer from the start – either because synonymous terms, different forms and related terms appear intermingled in the text, or because the indexer's knowledge of the subject suggests alternative words that users may employ to search for certain topics. Others can only be added at the editing stage, when the make-up and structure of the whole index is clear; at this stage, too, the cross-references already made must be reviewed to ensure that they are still appropriate.

Failure to check cross-references in the final index can result in highly visible errors:

'Blind' see Cross-References

> SIC *see* Standard Industrial Classification
> social factors 90–93 *see also* environment

Error = the entries 'Standard Industrial Classification' and 'environment' are missing.

'Circular' see Cross-References

> holiday industry *see* tourism
> tourism *see* holiday industry

Error = there are no locators at either heading.

'Serial' see Cross-References

> automobiles *see* cars
> cars *see* motor vehicles
> motor vehicles 77, 85, 94

Error = the first cross-reference leads to another cross-reference, not to the preferred term.

Duplicated Locators with see also Cross-References

> oil prices 234–235, 331, 334 (*see also* spot market)
> spot market 234–235, 331, 334 (*see also* oil prices)

Error = where the cross-references are not required, because both headings have the same locators.

Location of cross-references

See cross-references are filed in the normal alphabetical sequence of entries:

> savings ratio 312–314
> scam economy *see* black economy
> scatter diagrams 442
> share ownership:
> >   privatization *see* deregulation
> >   tax position *see* taxes

See also cross-references are usually most helpful when placed after the locator(s) of the heading or subheading from which they refer:

> farming 13, 16, 18 *see also* Common Agricultural Policy
> leisure centres:
> >   inner-city 34, 38
> >   rural 69, 70–71
> >   suburban 43, 57
> >   *see also* sports clubs
>
> clothing:
> >   indoor 68, 69
> >   outdoor 116, 119 *see also* waterproofing

Where there is a great deal of information assembled after the heading (a long sequence of subheadings, for example), it may be better to present the *see also* cross-reference in parentheses immediately after the heading, giving the reader the chance to consider straight away whether the related terms might be more useful:

castles (*see also* châteaux; forts; keeps; towers) 112–113
    Berkshire 123
    Gwynedd 147
    Kent 136
    [etc.]

Where several terms are cited in the *see also* cross-reference, they are usually given in alphabetical order, separated by semicolons, as in the example above.

Preparation for Editing

The editing process, described in the next chapter, is not sharply separated from the selection and formation of entries. Many, probably most, indexers do at least a small amount of editing as they go, making sure that each new entry is free of errors and that it matches the general style of those already made.

    Each indexer develops a preferred method of working – some like to input all their raw entries as quickly as possible without pausing to check or revise anything – perhaps inserting query marks to indicate things to check later. They then look at the index as a whole, working carefully through it to harmonize the headings, adding reversed or permuted headings, constructing subheadings, adding cross-references, ensuring consistency of style and so on. Others like to proceed more slowly and keep an eye on the structure of the index as it grows; when they see that subheadings are becoming necessary for any heading – because many locators are being allocated to it, or because several different aspects of the topic are being identified – they group the locators accordingly by appending suitable words or phrases. They check anomalies in the presentation of names and variations in spelling and capitalization when they arise, and add alternative headings (reversed or permuted) and cross-references as soon as they identify the need. This preliminary 'on the hoof' editing does not cancel out the need for final editing – some needed amendments only become evident when the index is looked at in its entirety – but it divides the work into stages.

    If certain differences in style have already been decided on, they can be incorporated as soon as the indexer starts to input the entries. For example, in an index that contains multiple kinds of heading, one kind of which needs to be extra-clearly identified, all the relevant headings can be completely capitalized or emboldened, in order to make them instantly visible:

> airlines 45–46
> ALEXANDRIA (Egypt) 128
> antiques, export 236
> AUCKLAND (New Zealand) 98
>
> Essendon, Maria Eliza 78
> **Essex** 34
> Essex, Florence 56
> **Exeter** (Devon) 88

It is important to remember that perfection is often not achievable in the formation of index entries – to observe consistency in one feature can cause inconsistency with regard to another, and to follow a technically correct guideline can result in something that looks odd in a particular index. A pragmatic approach, treating the text with respect and making access as simple as possible for the user, is the best.

References

Batchelor, Judy (1999) Homograph arrangement. *The Indexer*, **21**, 189

British Standards Institution (1996) *Information and documentation – guidelines for the content, organization and presentation of indexes.* BS ISO 999: 1996. London: British Standards Institution

Butcher, Judith (1992) *Copy-editing: the Cambridge handbook for editors, authors and publishers* 3rd edn. Cambridge: Cambridge University Press

Gorman, Michael and Winkler, Paul W. (1988) (eds) *Anglo-American cataloguing rules* 2nd edn. 1988 revision. Chicago: American Library Association; Ottawa: Canadian Library Association; London: Library Association Publishing

Hudon, Michèle (1999) Accessing documents and information in a world without frontiers. *The Indexer*, **21**, 156–159

International Federation of Library Associations and Institutions (1996) *Names of persons: national usages for entry in catalogues* 4th edn. Munich: K.G. Saur

Knight, G. Norman (1979) *Indexing, the art of: a guide to the indexing of books and periodicals*. London: Allen & Unwin

Oxford University Press (1983) *Hart's rules for compositors and readers at the University Press, Oxford* 39th edn. Oxford: Oxford University Press

University of Chicago Press (1993) *The Chicago manual of style* 14th edn. Chicago: University of Chicago Press

Further Reading

Mulvany, Nancy C. (1994) *Indexing books*. Chicago: University of Chicago Press (Chapter 4: Structure of entries)

National Council on Archives (1997) *Rules for the construction of personal, place and corporate names*. National Council on Archives

Wellisch, Hans H. (1995) *Indexing from A to Z* 2nd edn. New York: H.W. Wilson (pp. 228–231: Terminology and synonym control; pp. 276–292: Locators)

CHAPTER FIVE

Editing and presenting the index

The Need for Editing and Presentation

In its entirety, the finished index must provide balanced and relevant coverage of the document's significant themes and messages, enable access by all likely terms (through the use of double entry or cross-references), be clearly laid out – with well-structured subheading sequences (if needed), be preceded by an apposite explanation, and meet the specification agreed with the client. Individual entries may require editing, and the index needs also to be looked at as a whole, to ensure consistency of form and structure and the elimination of errors.

Good presentation influences the readability and use of the index. It should be easy for readers to find the headings they are looking for and to understand them unambiguously, to spot the references most likely to be of interest to them, and to find their way around. Presentational aspects are normally already in the indexer's mind during input and so some features can be incorporated from the start – capitalization and punctuation, and the indication of major references and illustrations, for example. Final presentation – spacing and layout, additional styling, and preparation for the chosen form of copy (paper, disk, email file, camera-ready) – can only be given attention when the individual entries and the overall structure are in place.

Timing of editing

Editing usually starts during the input stage, if only to correct a miskeyed word, add the occasional synonymous heading, insert the odd subheading or cross-reference, or tailor the entries to the client's house style. Once all the raw entries have been made, conclusive editing can begin to attend to subheading sequences, doubtful spellings, and addition of further information to add contextual or distinguishing detail to headings. A further bout of editing may be necessary even after the supposedly final index has been supplied to a client, if queries are raised or very late changes to the text are made. Additionally, when typeset proofs of the index are checked, there may be extra amendments to be made.

It is important to keep under tight control the time spent on editing. It is only too easy to go on refining the index, having second thoughts, and weighing up one possibility against another. Every job should have its budgeted time and – except when an index is being prepared as a labour of love or personal dedication, when perfection is more important than time – a pragmatic view must be taken. A sloppy, carelessly compiled index is never acceptable. The aim is to produce the best possible work under the prevailing circumstances – which include the cost of time.

Whether the index is edited entirely on screen or, initially, on a printout from which the amendments are then keyed in, depends on the indexer's preferred method of working. Printing out and marking a hard copy takes extra time, but it is easier to scan a printout, flip back and forth to compare entries, see where improvements and corrections are needed, make notes, and keep track of amendments made. The work can be done comfortably on a flat surface, using a coloured pen, then all the changes can be made on screen.

The last possible opportunity for editing an index for a printed document is during the checking of the index page proofs – which some indexers prefer to do themselves rather than leaving it to publishers' staff (see 'Proofreading the index' later in this chapter).

Amount of editing

The amount of editing to be done depends on several factors.

The Quality of the Input

As indicated under 'How they index' in Chapter 2, some indexers prefer to work at speed, entering headings exactly as they appear in the text or suggest themselves to the indexer's mind, adding only the most obvious cross-references, not stopping to correct conspicuous errors (transposed letters, for example), and not checking that they have entered the locators accurately. Others favour taking time to ensure that each new entry 'fits in' with what has gone before, is correctly spelled, that locators are accurately given, and that cross-references are added whenever they can be seen to be needed. If more time is spent during the input stage, less is required for editing – it is a matter of personal choice.

The Length and Complexity of the Entries

An index containing many multiple-word headings, or headings with several subheadings (and maybe sub-subheadings), or featuring complicated locators, needs more editing time than one consisting of single-word headings with no subheadings and with simple locators.

The Number of Queries Noted by the Indexer during Input

Indexers frequently notice errors and variations in spelling in the text. Rather than spend time querying them individually with the author, editor or client each time one arises during input, it makes sense to batch them and deal with them all during editing.

The Incidence of Special Characters in the Entries

Some characters required for inclusion in headings – such as mathematical symbols, accented letters, and Greek, Cyrillic or Arabic characters – may not be available on the indexer's keyboard. Others may be available on the keyboard and visible on the screen but not reproduce correctly when the computer file is transferred to another system (at the publisher's or printer's workplace). The positions of special characters that are not available on the keyboard can be marked during input by using other keyboard characters, so that they can be converted or noted during editing. If there are many such special codings or markings, more editing time is needed.

The Number of Entries in the Index

The longer the index, the longer it takes to edit – not only because of the proportions, but also because it can be more difficult to spot inconsistencies between entries in different parts of the index and to remedy them.

A Mismatch Between the Length of the Index and the Space Available for it

An indexer is often aware from the start that a limited amount of space (so many pages or lines) is available for the index, and so can aim to keep entries short and to index only the most significant topics and references. Nevertheless, the index may still turn out to be too long. If it is not possible to make more space available or to print in a smaller size than originally intended, the indexer is faced with the vexing and time-consuming job of reducing or removing entries. It can also happen that the index is too short in comparison with the allocated space. (See 'Making the index shorter or longer' later in this chapter.)

Style Requirements

Most required features of capitalization and punctuation, italicization and emboldening can be incorporated at the input stage, but others must wait until all the entries have been made and sorted. For example, emboldening the locators for the major references in entries can only be done when all the relevant locators have been entered. In addition, some clients may require additional, sometimes unusual, styling – lines, boxes, dots, outlining, for example.

The Degree of Autonomy of the Indexer

The indexer is usually entirely responsible for decisions on the content and formation of the entries; the editor (client) needs only to ensure that the submitted index meets the agreed specification and fits into the space allocated to it. On other occasions, the index supplied by the indexer is subject to approval by the editor and/or the author of the text. Any suggestions they make – for addition and removal of entries, or changes of wording, for example – should (as professional etiquette requires) be referred back to the indexer for consideration and comment.

The Time Available

At times, regrettably, the very tight schedules within which some indexes are prepared do not allow for thorough editing. In such cases, indexers must attempt to monitor their input and make adjustments to it as they work. A final read-through – however brisk – is essential, so that any glaring inconsistencies and errors can be remedied. Indexers generally have a very low degree of tolerance of errors, and occasionally they need to make their clients equally aware that time for inspection and 'pulling into shape' is necessary.

The Process by Which the Index is to be Produced

The physical forms in which index copy is prepared vary according to the requirements of the client (see Chapter 10: Managing the work). An index file prepared using a dedicated indexing program or a word-processing program, for subsequent typesetting by the client or another firm, can be sent by email or through the post on a floppy disk. Indexers often send a hard (paper) copy as well. Some publishers' editors no longer require a hard copy, but if one is supplied, it provides the client and the typesetter with a clear view of the complete index and its intended layout, and also allows the indexer to add notes concerning accents, unusual characters, or other features to which the typesetter needs to be alerted. The indexer's responsibility for all types of copy is to ensure that the content of the individual entries is accurate, that subheadings are clearly and consistently indicated, and that the alphabetical (or other) order of the entries is correct. The page dimensions and the type font and size used in a typeset document are almost always different from those used by the indexer, and the index is likely to be set in at least two columns per page.

An indexer with suitable software may sometimes be required to produce a camera-ready copy of an index – a 'master' copy that is perfect in every particular, in high-quality professional print, perhaps in double-column format, and requiring no further attention (apart, maybe, from the addition of a number to each page) before it is reproduced as part of the published document. Considerable care – and therefore additional time

– is needed for the preparation of this kind of copy, particularly if there are subheading sequences that may be broken by ends of columns or pages and so require continuation statements.

In-house writers producing documents on dtp (desktop publishing) systems may compile their own indexes using embedded codes placed in the text (see Chapter 11: Technology). These systems generate raw indexes from the words that have been coded in the text. Editing is still needed to harmonize word-forms, add cross-references, construct suitable subheadings, and deal with broken sequences of subheadings. The individual locators should be accurate and so should need no checking, as they are 'automatically' linked to the relevant text. However, some systems cite only the first page number in a page range ('34' instead of '34–40') and so the ranges may have to be added during editing.

The Indexer's Responsibility for Proofreading the Index

This stage of editing takes place later, after the index has been printed. It is best done by the indexer, but is often dealt with by clients' editorial staff (see 'Proofreading the index' later in this chapter).

What May Need to be Done

The tasks involve both visual and mental checking, which can be carried out simultaneously.

Spelling errors and literals

Any indexing process that relies on human input via a keyboard carries the risk of errors – characters that are transposed, omitted, duplicated or wrongly capitalized, incorrect spacing and punctuation, and the rest. The best thing is to take care when inputting so that no errors are made in the first place, but if they are made they must be corrected during the editing stage. Apart from giving the impression that the indexer is an ignoramus, they can result in misunderstanding, misfiling and misinformation. Some errors are so obvious that they jump off the page or screen at the first glance. Others, such as an error in one word that has made another (meaningful) word – 'conversation' instead of 'conservation', 'Nolan' instead of 'Bolan' – are only found by character-by-character reading of the headings, while keeping in mind the context of the index. For 'public areas' to appear as 'pubic areas', or 'dwellings' as 'swellings', may be amusing to read about here, but can be an embarrassment or worse for the indexer.

Similar characters are sometimes wrongly keyed – the numeral '0' and the capital letter 'O', for example. In such cases, a computer-sorted index will misplace the entry.

Careful keyboard work during input should ensure that very few errors are introduced, but indexers working when tired or in a hurry run the risk of keying in an occasional wrong character or transposing two characters. Actual spelling errors should occur rarely, as no-one who is not an exemplary speller should be in the business of indexing.

Spelling checkers (included in most word-processing programs) are valued by some indexers as an aid to the detection of mistypings. The stock of words can be augmented by the indexer, so that a customized list of the words likely to occur in the indexer's work can be established. They cannot detect errors of the kind exemplified above (where a mistake makes another real word) or tolerate unusual names, and because they lag behind the living language, they may indicate as errors some words which are, in fact, acceptable.

Multiple word-forms, synonymous and near-synonymous terms

In the raw index, references to a single topic may be scattered under different word-forms – 'measuring' and 'measurement', 'mice' and 'mouse' – or under two or more synonymous or near-synonymous terms – 'industry' and 'manufacturing' and 'production'. If the relevant references are left as they are, dispersed under more than one heading, the index user is likely to be confused about precise meanings and may also miss relevant information. For each topic, therefore, there should be just one word-form – the noun form 'measurement' or the gerund form 'measuring', the plural form 'mice' or the singular form 'mouse', depending on the context. Other forms may require *see* cross-references.

Alternative approaches

Information on any topic should be accessible from all the words likely to be looked for. All the words in a multi-word heading therefore need to be considered as possible additional entry words: 'cirrus clouds' may need to be entered also under 'clouds, cirrus' and 'agriculture, France' as 'France, agriculture'. With some programs, a simple keyboard command can reverse ('flip') headings with modifiers, such as 'agriculture, France', to produce 'France, agriculture', and so both the direct and reversed forms are frequently made at the input stage. Alternatively, the direct heading can be quickly marked for later attention during editing.

Longer headings may need more than one alternative approach: 'political cartoons, effect on general elections' may also require entry under 'cartoons, political . . .', 'general elections . . .', and 'elections, general. . . .' Additional entries like these do not necessarily need to be keyed in completely; with an indexing program it may be possible to pull down (or 'yank') elements of an existing heading, as well as its locators, in order to make up a new one. As with the reversal technique mentioned above, this is sometimes done at the input stage, while the train of thought is fresh (see Chapter 11: Technology).

If the author of the text has provided a suggested list of words for inclusion in the index, this should be checked in case it provides alternative headings. Thesauri, dictionaries and other indexes can also be used to supply alternatives.

Some indexing (subject headings) systems, used for example for subject indexing in library catalogues and for uniform indexing of periodical articles, employ rotation or manipulation of multiword headings in order to provide access from all likely points:

Cantilever tubes
    Decommissioning – Platforms – Offshore
      production: 1561
Decommissioning
    Platforms – Offshore production: 1561
Mild steel
    Cantilever tubes – Decommissioning -
      Platforms – Offshore production: 1561
Offshore production: 1561

Platforms
>   Offshore production: 1561
Safety
>   Transverse loading – Mild steel – Cantilever
>>   tubes – Decommissioning – Platforms -
>>   Offshore production: 1561
Transverse loading
>   Mild steel – Cantilever tubes -
>>   Decommissioning – Platforms – Offshore
>>   production: 1561
>>>   [From *Abstracts in new technologies and engineering*
>>>   (1999) **3** (1) (Bowker-Saur)]

Another method of providing alternative approaches is to use cross-references. The choice depends on the kind of index, the importance of each individual approach, and the space available for the index (see 'Suitable cross-references' below).

Balance of coverage

When examined as a whole, the index may be seen to be uneven in its coverage of the various parts of the text. This is not just a matter of equal numbers of entries – some parts of the text may be densely populated with topics and so, quite properly, generate more entries than other parts. Rather, it is a question of ensuring that each part of the text is given fit treatment in the index and that no important topic or reference has been missed out. If the author of the text has supplied a suggested list of terms or keywords, this can be used as a checklist. A file of headings arranged in locator number order (a 'page-number-order' file) – as can be produced by a dedicated indexing program – shows up which pages or units have been heavily indexed and which more lightly; this is not necessarily an indicator of unbalanced coverage, but it can reveal passages that require more attention.

No hint of the indexer's prejudices or opinions should be detectable in the headings themselves or in the amount of attention given to any part of the text (see 'Neutrality of the indexer' in Chapter 2).

Suitable cross-references

Provisional cross-references (*see* and *see also*) are often added during input, but very few of them can be regarded as final until they have been checked in the light of the whole index structure. It is not possible, either, to see which additional cross-references are necessary until the full index exists.

Frequently there is a choice to be made between double entry (where all the relevant locators are entered under both headings) and a *see* cross-reference from the non-preferred term to the preferred term (see 'Cross-references' in Chapter 4). Where space is restricted, the use of a single-line *see* cross-reference, instead of a heading with a sequence of subheadings occupying several lines, may be necessary. In another situation, word usage in the text may decide the issue – some indexed articles may refer to 'roundabouts', some to 'merry-go-rounds', some to 'carousels' and others to 'rides', making it advisable to give a full entry under all the terms.

It is essential to check that all cross-references work as intended – they must all lead to headings that exist in the index and that are followed by locators (see 'Checking cross-reference connections' in Chapter 4). Dedicated indexing programs normally have an automatic checking facility that indicates cross-reference errors (see Chapter 11: Technology).

Overlong headings

Short – but not cryptic – headings are usually better. Long headings take the user more time to read through, occupy more space, and can obscure their meanings. Book publishers tend to set indexes in lines of 37–40 characters (including spaces and punctuation). It may help to bear in mind this general measure at the input stage, but it is not always possible immediately to think of the most succinct phrase and so a temporary, wordier, one is used. During editing, longer headings can be reduced (by the removal of unnecessary prepositions, for example) or rephrased.

The necessary length of an entry is not, of course, restricted by the line length used in setting the index. Any entry longer than the specified number of characters will turn over to the next line, indented. The longer the heading and the more locators that follow it, the more likely it is that a turnover line will be needed.

Accuracy and completeness of locators

Any input made via a keyboard runs the risk of including an occasional error. Checking at the time of input – making sure that the fingers have obeyed the mind and not transposed or omitted any characters – should minimize the problem, but may not altogether remove it. Also, when using an indexing program with a facility to repeat – by a single command – the locator from the previous entry, the indexer may be lulled into 'repeat mode' and forget to change to the new locator when moving to the following page or numbered paragraph. This is not a problem when using text processing or dtp programs, as any index terms generated will have their locators automatically attached.

Complex locators containing, for example, volume and part numbers and dates, or consisting of combinations of numerals (arabic and roman) or of numerals and letters, need inspecting to ensure that they are complete and comprehensible. The introductory note to the index may need to explain their form. Ideally, all locators should be checked at the edit stage, but schedules do not always allow sufficient time for this. A file in locator number order (a 'page-number-order file') from an indexing program is a help in checking locator accuracy.

Page ranges must be given in consistent form, either full (123–124), slightly reduced (123–24) or minimal (123–4). Styles for dealing with numbers in the 'tens' and 'hundreds' sequences vary (see 'Page ranges' in Chapter 4).

The length of the dash between the two numbers must be consistent within an index. The 'en-dash' (longer than a hyphen) is often indicated by a double dash in typescript and word-processed copy:

Christmas trees 45--46

Long strings of locators

A long string of undifferentiated locators after a heading can be an obstacle to the reader, because it gives no indication of relative importance nor of the aspects discussed. Some index users may give up the search after checking the first few; others may persevere, but not find anything of real interest until they reach the last one.

Views differ about the 'reasonable' length of a string. In most situations a string containing six or seven undifferentiated locators is unlikely to deter the user. Longer strings can usually be avoided by one or more of the following techniques:

- removal of any locator which, when the reference is compared with the others, is less important
- indication, in italic type or by an abbreviation, of any locator referring solely to an illustration, note, definition, appendix, bibliographical reference, etc.; this gives the user some basis for selection:

    condensation *13*, *16*, 17–18, 23*n*, 45, 77, 92, 116*def*

    and, more helpfully, they can be moved to the end of the string:

    condensation 17–18, 45, 77, 92; *13*, *16*, 23*n*, 116*def*

- highlighting, for example in bold type, of any locator leading to major information or a particularly significant point:

    traffic management 89, **112–114**, 191, 201–204, 241, 319, 424, 511, 513

- analysis of locators under subheadings referring to particular aspects or relationships:

    traffic management 112–114
        Belfast 511
        Birmingham 89, 201–204, 424
        Cardiff 241
        Glasgow 319, 513
        Stevenage 89
        Wolverhampton 191

When analysing into subheadings, any locators leading to major information on the subject as a whole are retained alongside the (main) heading, as in the 'traffic management' example above. All the other locators, relating to specific issues or connections, are entered under subheadings. There must be no 'leftover' locators. The use of a final subheading labelled 'others' or 'other references' or 'mentioned' – bringing together disparate, unallocated locators – is occasionally seen, but gives the subheading an unfinished appearance and is of little help to users.

Retention of Long Strings

In certain specific cases, long strings may be expedient or unavoidable. One example is the listing of locators relating to the authors referred to in some bibliographical works, where the entry is merely required to show whereabouts in the text a particular author has been cited. There may be no one reference that is more important than the others and there may be no advantage in analysing under subheadings.

Another is the indexing of documents intended for use by readers who need or want to be informed of every single reference to the subjects of interest to them. These documents include, on the one hand, scholarly works for academics and researchers which contain numerous indexable elements and many references, and on the other, popular 'coffee-table' books and annuals consisting of copious illustrations relating to a limited number of topics. In both cases, the readers want to be referred to everything on their chosen subject, no matter what the context and regardless of the amount or type of information given. No distinction between locators is therefore needed. Researchers using the indexes to scholarly works could actually be hampered by the provision of subheadings based on the indexers' perceptions of the thematic patterns, because they need to make their own analyses of the materials.

Thirdly, long strings at subheading or sub-subheading (or lower) level may be unavoidable, if a topic has been analysed to the lowest possible relevant level in the context of a particular index. If the locators at that level cannot be thinned down or distinguished on grounds of significance or of difference in type of information, there is no alternative but to list them all.

Ambiguous and imprecise headings

Some headings, when looked at within the whole index, can be seen to require clarification, qualification or modification in order to make their meanings and aspects explicit. A single-word heading may have more than one meaning; if it is not absolutely clear which meaning is relevant in a particular index, a word or phrase should be added, or the heading amended: 'alcohol', for example, may sometimes need to be presented as 'alcohol (fuel)', sometimes as 'alcoholic drinks' and sometimes as 'alcohol abuse'. A personal name shared by several people is likely to need an addition – and will definitely do so if more than one of them features in the text: 'Hunter, John (naval captain)', 'Hunter, John (surgeon)'.

There are also occasions when it is necessary to divide up a group of locators referring to a person and the eponymous theories expounded by the person: 'Marx, Karl' [the person] and 'Marxism' [the ideology].

'Catch-all words'

Headings beginning with the same word are sometimes unintentionally arranged in unsuitable ways – particularly if initial capital letters are used for all terms, not just for proper names. This can happen with some indexing programs, if the headings are incorrectly punctuated at the input stage, causing unwanted separation of terms and odd-looking subheading sequences. The headings 'fish and chip shops', 'fish farming', 'fish, tropical', 'fish eagles', 'Fish, Michael', and Fish Trade Authority should be arranged as:

> Fish, Michael
> fish, tropical
> fish and chip shops
> fish eagles
> fish farming
> Fish Trade Authority

and not as:

> Fish
> > and chip shops
> > eagles
> > farming
> > Michael
> > Trade Authority
> > tropical

Sequences like the following should, of course, never be seen:

> home
> > -grown vegetables
> > helps
> > -lessness

> ownership
> -sickness
> -workers

'Headings starting with the same term', later in this chapter, gives guidance on arrangement.

Inconsistent subheadings

It is helpful to the user if similar forms of words are used in subheadings that deal with comparable aspects. A subheading sequence is better phrased as:

> politics
>> effect on culture
>> effect on education
>> effect on sport

rather than:

> politics
>> and culture
>> cause of problems in education
>> sport, and

Dubious headings

If there remain any doubts about the validity or accuracy of any heading – the correct usage of words in the context, the precise meanings of words, the accuracy of spelling, the correct forms of names – they must be cleared up at the editing stage. Outstanding queries that cannot be resolved from reference materials may need to be referred back to the editor or client.

Alphabetical order adjustments

The need to check and edit alphabetical order may not arise if the index consists of straightforward, single-word headings with no punctuation, no subheadings, and no accented letters or special characters. In most indexes, though, the alphabetization of headings and subheadings throws up at least one or two points that require thought and decision-making. Alphabetical order is not in all situations the clear-cut system that it is thought to be (see 'Alphabetical arrangement' later in this chapter). It is always necessary to check indexes that have been sorted automatically by indexing and other programs – they have different ways of handling signs such as hyphens, apostrophes and other punctuation marks, and also of sorting subheadings, and may not be able to deal at all with special characters.

Subheading order

The order within each sequence of subheadings may need revision at the editing stage; the subheadings as originally entered may be precise and comprehensible but – when looked at together – may appear haphazard. The order of subheadings does not have to be the same throughout the whole of an index. Arrangements may sometimes need explanation in the introductory note, but if they have been well chosen for the purpose the reader should be able to consult them comfortably and without guidance.

Whichever arrangement is chosen, any subheading terms that are likely themselves to be looked up by an index user must, of course, also be included as headings in their own right:

brussels sprouts
    harvesting
      pests and diseases
diseases, brussels sprouts
harvesting, brussels sprouts
pests, brussels sprouts

Alphabetical

This is often the 'default' mode of arrangement and is often entirely acceptable. However, with subheadings containing prepositions, articles, conjunctions, or other function words, it is important to decide whether the alphabetical arrangement is to take account of these 'little' words:

plays:
>
> by children
> by prisoners
> by Russian writers
> by Swedish writers
> for children
> for two actors
> in Spanish
> with music

or whether they should be ignored in filing:

plays:
>
> by children
> for children
> with music
> by prisoners
> by Russian writers
> in Spanish
> by Swedish writers
> for two actors

In this case the first arrangement is better, because the prepositions enable useful subcategories to be seen – plays suitable for particular groups, plays in particular languages, plays by particular kinds of individuals.

In the next example, alphabetization by the significant word in each subheading may be better, because the function words, although important for meaning, have less significance than in the previous example:

economies of scale:
>
> through advertising
> at Almoode-Fuller Ltd
> as barriers to entry
> in oligopoly
> effect on productivity
> in transport management

The decision whether to ignore or to recognize function words must be made in relation to the context. Dedicated indexing programs usually have options for the recognition and non-recognition of these words and may allow an indexer to specify which words should be ignored.

Chronological or Progressive

Subheadings representing actions, processes and events that have a fixed order should usually observe that order:

> festivals:
> > January
> > February
> > March
> > April
> > etc.

and not be listed alphabetically (April, February . . .).

Similarly with date and other numeric forms:

> fashions:
> > 17th century
> > 18th century
> > 19th century

and not as though spelled out ('eighteenth century' . . .).

The following sequence of simple subheadings follows the order of events, rather than the alphabet:

> potatoes
> > planting
> > pests and diseases
> > harvesting
> > storage
> > freezing
> > cooking

If other vegetables appear in the index, the same pattern of subheadings can be used for each.

In biography indexing, the use of chronological subheadings for the major stages or events of a life ('birth', ' marriage', 'divorce', 'death') can be much more suitable than an alphabetical arrangement that places them in apparently random order.

Grouped, Systematic, Classified, Hierarchical

It can sometimes be helpful to divide the subheadings into logical groups suitable for the context, thus turning them into sub-subheadings:

```
government policy:
        external relations
                defence 102–104
                foreign affairs 106–108
                overseas aid 91–92
                trade 71–73
        internal affairs
                agriculture 46–47
                arts 121–122
                education 27–29
                environment 84–85
                health 31–33
                housing 35–36
                industry 65–66
                regional development 116–117
                science 119–120
                social security 37–39
                transport 98–100
```

rather than just a single alphabetical list of subheadings from 'agriculture' through to 'transport'. Logical grouping is not always straightforward – it can be argued that 'defence' has as much to do with 'internal affairs' as it has with 'external relations', for example.

```
    birds:
            resident
                    breeding patterns 89
                    populations 33
                    protection measures 45
```

winter visitors
  arrival dates 72
  routes from summer sites 81
migrant
  losses en route 82
  sightings, Isle of Wight 75

rather than a series of multiword subheadings like 'breeding patterns of resident birds', 'indigenous bird populations' 'protection of native birds' and so on.

Canonical (Authoritative, Standard)

In a particular subject field, there is often a generally expected or well-known order in which items are listed, in which case it should be used in a subheading sequence. The books of the Bible, for example, are conventionally grouped in a fixed order.

By Locator

It can occasionally be more useful to have the subheadings arranged in locator number order, either ascending or descending. Locators in ascending order (15, 23, 35, 69, 112) match the treatment of the topics in the text and so sometimes reflect the chronology of events. In documents which are being frequently updated by additional matter at the end, or by supplements, locators in descending order (512, 501, 468, 334, 261), can be useful to readers who need to consult the latest information first.

Combined

Usually the same arrangement is used throughout a subheading sequence, but in certain circumstances subheadings can be arranged in two groups having different arrangements. For example, in the index to the history of an industry, the first group of subheadings under a certain company's name, referring to the founding and development of the company, could be arranged in chronological order (which may happen also to be ascending page number order). The second group, referring to named products of the company, could be in alphabetical order:

> Graystowe & Trione Ltd:
>> startup 69
>> first factory 71
>> factory extension 73
>> move to Pennydown Moor 76
>> overseas branches 81, 90
>> 'Minovel' 73
>> 'Nelspin 34' 80
>> 'Revi-go' 78
>> 'Yelzo ZB' 80
>> 'Wizzyroto' 72

If the same arrangement is used for all companies in the index, the user is provided with a recognizable pattern.

Alphabetical Arrangement

The most common arrangement for headings and subheadings is alphabetical – a system known and understood by the majority of the reading public and information users. Finding the desired heading in an A-Z sequence of single words is straightforward enough. However, when headings contain more than one word and so include spacing, and perhaps punctuation, the situation is more complicated.

Put simply, the central question is: should 'acid rain' go before or after 'acidification'? The word-by-word ('nothing before something') method of alphabetizing, which gives a value to the spaces between words so that the shorter word precedes the longer, requires:

> acid rain
> acidification

The letter-by-letter ('all-through') method ignores spaces between words and so puts 'acidification' first, because 'i' comes before 'r' in the alphabet.

The difference between the two arrangements, for a given sequence of headings, may be slight or substantial, depending on the form and number of headings. In a lengthy sequence, the difference can be noticeable:

Word-by-word:

West Bank
West-by-northwest
West Coast jazz
West End
West Hartlepool
West Indies
West Lothian
West Midlands
West of England
West Point
West Side story
Westacott
Westbourne
Westbury on Trym
Wester Mandally
Westerlies
western hemisphere
Westfalen
Westinghouse brake system
Westman Islands
Westmeath
Westminster
Westmorland
Weston-super-Mare
Westward ho!

Letter-by-letter:

Westacott
West Bank
Westbourne

Westbury on Trym
West-by-northwest
West Coast jazz
West End
Westerlies
Wester Mandally
western hemisphere
Westfalen
West Hartlepool
West Indies
Westinghouse brake system
West Lothian
Westman Islands
Westmeath
West Midlands
Westminster
Westmorland
West of England
Weston-super-Mare
West Point
West Side story
Westward ho!

Both methods are valid, reputable and widely used; neither of them is inherently superior to the other. Some publishers have a preference for (or tradition of) word-by-word, some favour letter-by-letter, and others leave it to the discretion of the indexer. The decision for any index cannot usually be made confidently until all the entries exist in at least the raw form. A comparison of the results of the two methods may show that one is distinctly better than the other, for that particular index. Dedicated indexing programs usually have a facility to re-sort rapidly, so that the two arrangements can easily be compared. The automatic sorting done by some word-processing programs does not always give the desired outcome, so indexers using them need to check the results and possibly make some adjustments.

Whichever method is selected for a particular index, it should produce headings suitably positioned in relation to each other and sequences which are intelligible to the user. Whether the user is conscious of the arrangement is not the main matter. If sought headings can be found without racking of brains or studious deliberation, then that is what is required. Most index users are probably unaware that there are two possible systems. Someone who 'naturally' uses letter-by-letter order – often without knowing it – may not recognize what is going on in a lengthy word-by-word sequence, not find the sought heading and so conclude that there is no relevant information. An equally 'natural' word-by-word person can have a similar experience. An index in which the entries would be very differently arranged by the other method should contain an explanation of the arrangement used. General directives can also be included in the index sequence, guiding the user from the expected placing to the correct position.

Although the indexing standard BS ISO 999 (British Standards Institution, 1996, subclause 8.2) proposes that the word-by-word method should be used – while recognizing that the letter-by-letter system may be needed to continue an existing index – it seems unlikely that there will be conformity to a single system, because both have their good points.

Word-by-word order gives a neater look to the sequence and so may make it easier for the eye to run down the list, from shorter entry word to longer. It can also keep together multipart headings that are related – which, as Mulvany (1994, p. 126) points out – can be particularly helpful in legal and medical indexes. In this sequence, for example, the words which begin with 'liver' or 'Liver', but which are unrelated to the liver, are listed after the related terms:

> liver extract
> liver fluke infection
> liver surgery
> liver tumours
> Livermore Valley
> Liverpool
> livery stables

In letter-by-letter order, 'Liverpool' and 'Livermore Valley' would come in the middle of the 'liver' group and so split the sequence of related terms.

Letter-by-letter can be better for terms that appear with varying spacing and punctuation – such as place names in older documents, personal names in different presentations, and newly coined phrases of which a single authoritative form has not yet been determined – and also for terms which users may be uncertain about:

> Heath Row
> Heathrow
>
> Falconsmith, Anna
> Falcon-Smith, T. F.
> Falcon Smith, Wilhelm
>
> e-mail
> email
>
> South End Gardens
> Southend Terrace
> South Gate Avenue
> Southgate Rise
> South Green Lane

In word-by-word order, in which spaces and sometimes hyphens are given filing values, the relative positions of these terms could be quite different.

Proper names (apart from those with variable punctuation and spacing, as above) are normally more happily filed in word-by-word order:

> Robb, Selina G.
> Robbe, Margaret
> Robbell, Charlie
> Robben, F.G.
> Robbie, T. Wallace
> Robbin, V.W.
> Robbins, C.
> Robbo, Toni

Letter-by-letter order, if applied right through the names, would arrange them thus:

Robbell, Charlie
Robbe, Margaret
Robben, F.G.
Robbie, T. Wallace
Robbins, C.
Robbin, V.W.
Robbo, Toni
Robb, Selina G.

This sequence is not helpful to users, who would normally expect to find the name 'Robb' before 'Robbell', 'Robben' and so on. It is best, therefore, even when using letter-by-letter order for all other (non-name) terms, to file names by the word-by-word system, observing the comma as a natural break point.

Even when one or other order has been chosen and the headings sorted accordingly, it is still necessary to check for any irregular placings. These may sometimes be caused by punctuation signs (see 'Punctuation marks: their effect on order' later in this chapter). Another source of occasional difficulty is the allocation of inappropriate filing values by a program's automatic sort, as when headings starting with capital (upper-case) letters are placed in a separate sequence from those beginning with small (lower-case) letters, or when alphabetical characters such as 'x', 'i', 'v' and 'm' (and their upper-case forms) are mistakenly sorted as roman numerals.

Headings starting with the same term

The indexing standard BS ISO 999 (British Standards Institution, 1996, subclause 8.5) proposes that headings that begin with the same term should be filed in this order:

- the term with or without subheadings
- the term with a qualifier
- the term as the first element of a longer term (in which the usual rules of alphabetization apply)

This gives a sequence such as:

flowers
    garden
    wild
Flowers (film)
Flowers and Frills Partnership
flowers of sulphur

Identical headings usually need qualifiers to distinguish them, and so the added punctuation can be given relative filing values, to achieve the required order (BS ISO 999, subclause 8.1). For example, in a reversed personal or corporate name the natural break made by the comma can be used to give the name headings precedence over a document title heading, if that is the order required:

flowers
    garden
    wild
Flowers, Tabitha
Flowers, W.G. Ltd
Flowers (film)
Flowers and Frills Partnership
flowers of sulphur

Some indexes contain long sequences of 'same first element' (sometimes identical) headings of different kinds – personal names, corporate names, geographical names, titles of documents, and 'subject' words – some having subheadings or qualifiers. There is no fixed, universally accepted rule that one type of heading must come before another. If the sorting of these headings is left to a computer – as sometimes happens – the result can be unhelpful; computer sorting operates by recognizing characters (including punctuation), not kinds of heading, and may therefore mix the different types in a way which makes no sense to the index user. It is up to the indexer to decide the best order for the purpose and, by the use of punctuation, qualifiers, typestyle and capitalization, to distinguish the headings from each other and to group them suitably for each index.

Initial articles

A definite or indefinite article – 'the', 'a' and 'an' – at the beginning of a heading is usually ignored in filing, and sometimes transposed to the end of the heading, but there are some important exceptions.

A place name that starts with an article should be filed according to the custom of the country, so in some cases the article becomes the entry word and in others it does not:

> **L**
> La Rochelle
> Long Mynd, The
> Los Alamos

The first line of a poem starting with an article should be filed under the article (see 'First lines of poems' in Chapter 4):

> **T**
> That's my last Duchess, painted on the wall
> The little love-god, lying once asleep
> There is nothing to remember in me

Indexing practice may differ from country to country. An explanation of the treatment of articles can be included in the introductory note, or the appropriate general directive(s) can be included in the index.

'Mac', 'Mc' and 'M'

The arrangement of names beginning with these elements is much debated. The principal choice is between treating them all as though spelled 'Mac', which is helpful to index users searching for a person by name, but who don't know which spelling is correct in that particular case:

> McAndrew, G.
> MacCarthy, M.
> McCarthy, O.
> MacDonald, F.
> McDonald, T.
> M'Pherson, E.

and, on the other hand, arranging them exactly as spelled, so that they are in strict alphabetical order:

> MacCarthy, M.
> MacDonald, F.
> McAndrew, G.
> McCarthy, O.
> McDonald, T.
> M'Pherson, E.

The problem concerning the choice of arrangement arises from the fact that in some countries the existence of the various forms of 'Mac' as name elements is very well known and understood and so interfiling is helpful, even essential. Elsewhere, index users may be unfamiliar with the situation, be bewildered by the absence of alphabetical order and not find what they want. Another problem is that there are names which – although containing the same letters – are not in the 'Mac' tradition ('Mace' and 'Machin', for example) and which therefore look odd if interfiled in a single 'Mac' sequence.

Indexing standard BS ISO 999 (British Standards Institution, 1996, subclause 7.3.6) recommends that contractions should be filed as given, not as if spelled out. However, British Telecom's phone books (one of which is in almost every household in the UK) treat all the forms as 'Mac' and also interfile 'Mace' and 'Machin' in the 'Mac' sequence.

The indexer's choice between the two arrangements must be based on the kind of index and the likely knowledge and needs of its users. Within the UK at least, the treatment of all forms as 'Mac' has much to commend it. Where there is the possibility of confusion, the method chosen should be explained in the introductory note. A general directive can also be placed in the index at the appropriate point, e.g.:

> **M**
> Mabbs, A.M.
> Mabey, P.
> Mabon, T.
> *Mac: Names beginning with 'M', 'Mc' or 'Mac' are all filed as though spelled Mac*
> McAlpine, W.

MacDonald, Y.
McEwen, D.

'Saint'

This element appears as the first element in many proper names – persons, places and organizations – and in various forms: Saint, St, Ste, S and so on.

As with 'Mac' above, the treatment of these forms varies. There is general agreement that an individual saint should appear under personal name:

Teresa *of Avila*, *Saint*

but surnames, names of places and so on can be either interfiled or separated into sequences according to form. Context should normally determine the choice, but – as with the various forms of 'Mac' – users do not always know whether the person or place or organization uses the full form or a contraction, so interfiling is often a convenient solution. On the other hand, the guideline in BS ISO 999 (referred to above), proposing that contractions should be filed as given and not spelled out, does ensure strict alphabetical order and does not require the user to know that 'Ste' is the short form of 'Sainte', or 'S' of 'San' or 'Santa'.

Abbreviations

The filing of abbreviations is sometimes influenced by local, cultural, or technical conventions, but in general (and excluding the abbreviated forms of 'Mac' and 'Saint' dealt with above) treating them as given (as though they were words) seems most helpful. Cross-references or general directives may be needed in the index, and perhaps also an explanation in the introductory note.

Ampersand

The ampersand sign '&', most often seen in company name headings, can either be filed as though spelled out as 'and' (or its equivalent in another language, when relevant):

Green and Brown
Green & Smith
Green and Wilkins

or given a filing value, perhaps to take precedence over alphabetical characters:

Jones & Fielding
Jones & Patel
Jones and Bonnard
Jones and McCarthy

Some directories ignore the ampersand in filing, but this is not recommended – it is, after all, an integral part of the company name.

'Broken' order

The strict rules of alphabetical order are sometimes broken, but only when this is in the best interests of users, as in the cases of 'Mac' and 'Saint' forms, described above. Another example concerns the large numbers of organizations called 'Institute of . . .', 'Institute for . . .', 'Institution of . . .' or 'Institution for. . . .' People looking for information about a particular one do not always know the correct form, so if an index of names is in precise alphabetical order, the searcher may have to toil through as many as four sequences to find the required name. This can be avoided by merging the headings into a single sequence:

Institute of Administrative Management
Institute for Animal Health
Institution of Electrical Engineers
Institute of Engineers and Shipbuilders in Scotland

'Society of' and 'Society for' and other similar headings can be treated in the same way. This imposition of 'broken order' can be criticized for not observing a strictly correct order, but – in the right context – it can be helpful. If used, it needs to be explained in the introductory note and perhaps also (concisely) at the beginning of the 'Institut . . . ' sequence in the index.

Prefixes

Alphabetical prefixes are taken into account in filing when they are integral parts of subject terms, such as:

A
A-team, The

B
B-movies

D
D-notices

but are usually ignored as the primary elements in filing when they are the first elements of chemical terms (in Roman, Greek or other characters – sometimes italicized):

B
cis-but-2-ene [not under 'C']

C
E-cadherin [not under 'E']
β-carotene [not under 'B']

For further information on prefixes and on infixes in medical and chemical terms, see 'Medicine' and 'Science and technology' in Chapter 8: Subject specialisms. Subject knowledge and up-to-date reference sources are essential for the indexer who has regularly to handle such terms.

Diacritics and special characters

Whether these affect filing or not depends on the convention of the language or country. In English-language indexes accented letters are normally interfiled with the unaccented equivalents:

eating habits
élites
empathy

Jarman, Derek
Järnefelt, Armas
Jarre, Jean-Michel

festivals
Fête des Fous
Feydeau, Georges

Kubrick, Stanley
Kühne, Wilhelm
Kurchatov, Igor V

Management today
Mañana
Manders, G N T

Names sometimes occur in variant forms – Kühne and Kuehne, for example; this can be confusing for a user who tries to find a reference after having heard the name but not having seen it written. A cross-reference or general directive may be made in the index, or a reminder about variant forms (with an example) can be included in the introductory note.

In contexts in which it is particularly helpful to separate foreign words from English words, any headings beginning with accented letters may be placed separately, either in a single sequence or in alphabetical chunks following the 'ordinary' letter sequences.

In classical texts the digraphs 'ae' and 'oe' are sometimes printed as the ligatures 'æ' and 'œ'. When this occurs, the published index should reproduce the characters in the same way. If the indexer is unable to produce them correctly, a code may be inserted at the appropriate place and the hard copy marked up, or a note supplied, to show the typesetter exactly what is required.

Some other languages have different rules to deal with special characters or groups of characters. Any indexer compiling indexes with a large foreign-language component should find out whether any such rules apply. For example, Robertson (1995) provides examples of some German indexes in which words beginning with the letters 'Sch' and 'St' are filed in two separate sequences after the main 'S' sequence. In Spanish, words beginning with 'ch' conventionally file in a separate sequence, after all other words beginning with 'c' and before those beginning with 'd'. Readers not familiar with the conventions of other languages are likely to be confused, so in indexes for them it is more helpful to interfile any occasional heading (putting 'ch . . . ' in the 'c' sequence, for example). Alternatively, to use the correct linguistic arrangements, together with an explanation in the introductory note and a general directive in the index, may be considered more educative.

Numerals in alphabetical sequences

Numerals can feature in index headings in various positions – '2003 Committee', '*2001: a space odyssey*', '*Room 101*', '314A/H widgets', '*100 day report*', and so on. How each set is treated depends on the position in the heading, the number of other similar headings, the kind of document being indexed, and the expectations of the users.

Numerals as First (or Only) Elements

Headings (and subheadings) beginning with numerals, or consisting entirely of numerals, can be handled in several ways. The context should determine which is best.

Interfiled, as though spelled out
This is most suitable for the occasional heading that belongs to the same category as other (fully alphabetical) headings, as in an index to titles of documents:

> *Thirty Russian folk-songs*
> *33 Victoria Street* [as though 'Thirty-three . . . ']
> *Three men in a boat*
> *Three yellow jerseys*
> 2003 Committee [as though 'Two . . . ']

> *Twyford Down*
> *Tyrone Guthrie: a biography*

An occasional problem with filing numerals as though spelled out is that some can be differently spoken (and therefore spelled). For example, 1050 can be either 'One thousand and fifty' and so filed under 'O', or 'A thousand and fifty' or 'Ten fifty' and so filed under 'T'. A cross-reference or general directive may at times be needed.

Separate numeric sequence. either before or after the alphabetical list
If numeric headings represent members of a distinct series, carrying most meaning when they are seen together, it is advisable to list them in a separate sequence outside the alphabetical one. If the numeric sequence is short in comparison with the alphabetical one, or if the numeric headings are likely to be more frequently consulted than the alphabetical ones, the sequence is better placed before the A-Z list, so that it is easily seen. The numerals are usually best filed in ascending order:

> 1984 Political Fiction Prize
> 1990 Festival of Music
> 1996 Living Sculpture Award
> 1999 Poetry Competition
> 2000 Millennium Urban Park Grant
> 2001 Space Fiction Prize
>
> A
> art deco
> artisan workshops
> [etc.]

Initial numerals ignored
Numerals at the beginning of chemical names are usually passed over as the primary element in filing, so that the name files under the first alphabetical character:

> M
> 2-methylbut-2-ene

N
1–nitronaphthalene

(See 'Science and technology' in Chapter 8 for more information on chemical headings.)

Numerals as Elements Within Headings

Numerals inside chemical names in chemical and biological texts are usually ignored in filing (except if needed to distinguish homographs):

I
indole-5-butyric acid
indole-3-carbinol

Numerals within other (non-chemical) headings should be treated according to context – either filed as though spelled out:

class consciousness
class 5 activity
class structure
Committee of London Clearing Bankers
Committee of 100 for Tibet [As though 'One hundred']
Committee of Permanent Representatives

or in numerical order:

Type 3 projects
Type 4 projects
Type 5 projects

George I
George II
George III
George IV
George V
George VI

motorways:
    AIM
    M3
    M4
    M62
    delays through roadworks
    signage
    speed restrictions

Punctuation marks: their effects on order

In some situations, punctuation marks in headings need have no effect on filing order. They must be retained in headings for whichever grammatical or stylistic purposes they serve, but they can be ignored for filing purposes:

'its and misses on the range
It's time to go
Its 'Tu-whit, tu-whoo' was heard again

O, from what power hast thou this powerful might
O me! what eyes hath love put in my head
O! What shade is this?
O, wild West Wind, thou breath of Autumn's being

Because word formations vary and because the word-by-word and letter-by-letter methods can produce different arrangements, punctuation values should be established for a given index. In a word-by-word index, for example, hyphens in family names may be better treated as equal to spaces:

Caulfielde-Henderson, J.J.   {variable forms
Caulfielde Henderson, P.Y.   {of same
Caulfielde-Henderson, S.   {name

but in another word-by-word index, for certain 'subject' words, it can make more sense to give hyphens a null filing value and so ignore them:

cookery
cooperage
co-operatives
coordinated projects
co-respondent shoes

prepared meals
pre-prandial drinks
prescribed drugs

The apostrophe (as in *It's spring again* and *Gardeners' World*) may be regarded as insignificant and therefore is usually ignored in filing (but not omitted from the heading). In the world at large, it is often misplaced and sometimes left out; some think it is in danger of dropping out of use altogether, so ignoring it in the arrangement of indexes may be the wiser practice.

Other punctuation signs may be given relative filing values when they are used to indicate structural features of headings, and therefore can influence order if the indexer so wishes. The comma in reversed personal names – 'Russo, Maria' – provides a natural break point and so can be used to ensure that all 'Russo' personal name headings are grouped together, subdivided alphabetically by given names or initials. Parentheses used to enclose qualifiers, as in 'Catatonia (band)', can be given a value to make the heading file before or after other similar ('catatonia') headings. Dedicated indexing programs usually provide the means of sorting according to the desired values.

Presentation and Layout

Even though the production of the final printed and published version of the index may be in the hands of the publisher and the typesetter, its appearance is certainly influenced by the quality of the copy supplied by the indexer. The judicious use of capitalization, punctuation, typestyling (italic and bold), indention, and spacing, are some of the features that can help to ensure that the finished index looks as though it has been put together by a professional. The copy – whether recorded on paper or disk or prepared for electronic dispatch – should have on it, or be accompanied by, any further information that the publisher and typesetter need. The format of a disk file also influences how the data will be reproduced (see Chapter 11: Technology).

It helps if the indexer can leave an interval between completing the index copy and sending it to the customer. Leaving it aside for a while, to work on another job or to attend to other (non-indexing) commitments, makes it easier to return to it with a fresh mind and eye – errors not previously noticed are spotted and ideas for improvements can occur. Experienced indexers get to know how an index is likely to look when printed as part of the published document, and so are able to make a few final adjustments. The copy should be looked at overall and quickly read through. It should be neat, distinct, uncrowded and unambiguous, with the pages of hard copy (if provided) numbered, and any notes to editor or typesetter – concerning, for example, the addition of special characters – clearly presented.

Capitalization

The first letters of proper names are normally capitalized (see 'Capitalization' in Chapter 4).

Occasionally an index is seen in which the whole of the first heading (or its first word) in each letter sequence – As, Bs and so on – is capitalized. This is just a style feature and has no informative value to the index users – in fact, it may distract or confuse, being thought to have some special meaning. It is better to present all entries consistently, without intrusive and unnecessary styling, leaving a linespace between each letter sequence.

Another variation is the capitalization of all 'primary' ('main') headings, with subheadings in lower-case type. This form can help where there are long sequences of subheadings and perhaps sub-subheadings, by making very clear the extent of each heading sequence. On finding a sequence that continues from column to column, or from page to page, users can tell – from the case (upper or lower) of the type – whether they are in a 'main' heading or subheading sequence. It is still necessary, though, to include continuation statements (see 'Continued statements' below) for page turnovers. The disadvantage of this kind of capitalization is that it is no longer possible to distinguish proper names in headings. It is often better to differentiate headings by using bold type than by capitalizing them throughout.

Small capitals are occasionally used to distinguish particular categories of heading. They may not be reproducible by the indexer's printer and so the style requirement must be carefully marked for the typesetter.

Subheading layout

It is essential that subheadings are clearly distinguishable from the headings to which they are subordinate, and – in turn – from any sub-subheadings that follow them. Subordination can be signified in either of two ways – setting out and running on. The set-out method gives a clearer display and can accommodate many levels of subheading; the run-on form takes up less space but is limited in the number of subheading levels it can handle. Some publishers specify which form they prefer, but others leave it to the indexer, in which case it is usually better to provide copy in set-out form because the structure of the index is clearer.

Where there is only a single subheading (really a modifier), it should always be run on:

> fairs 34
> festivals, musical 56
> fiestas 77

and not:

> fairs 34
> festivals:
>   musical 56
> fiestas 77

Setting Out

In this layout, each subheading (wherever there is more than one) starts a new line, with indention being used to show subordination, and any further levels of subheading are progressively and evenly indented. There is no limit to the number of levels that can be set out (apart from the width of the page or screen).

income:
    average:
        Ireland 221
        United Kingdom 200
    disposable 34–35
    earned 46–47
        from self-employment 88
    national 101–102
    taxable 52
        basic rate 145
        higher rate 146
    unearned 48–49
        from investment 136
            in shares 147
            in savings accounts 148

The use of a colon to follow a heading that has no locators listed against it, as in the example above, is not universal. It is favoured by some indexers and editors because it 'announces' the subheadings below and also shows that there is nothing missing from the line – if there is just a blank space it can lead to suspicions that something is missing.

Running On

This method has subheadings continuing on the same line, with punctuation indicating subordination. When the line is full, it turns over to the next line, which is indented by one space. Only two levels of subheading can be accommodated if the subheadings are run on directly after the heading:

income: average (Ireland 221; United
  Kingdom 200); disposable 34–35; earned
  46–47 (from self- employment 88);
  national 101–102; taxable 52 (basic
  rate 145; higher rate 146); unearned 48–
  49 (from investment 136, 147, 148)

A combination of set-out subheadings and run-on sub-subheadings can incorporate a further level:

income:
          average: Ireland 221; United Kingdom, 200
          disposable 34–35
          earned 46–47: from self-employment 88
          national 101–102
          taxable 52: basic rate 145; higher rate 146
          unearned 48–49: from investment 136 (in shares 147;
              in savings accounts 148)

If subheadings which were intended to be run on are subsequently set out – perhaps because extra space is available – the punctuation (semicolons in the example above) must, of course, be removed.

Turnover lines (continuation lines)

Unless the copy being prepared is camera-ready, or the exact line measurement in the finished version is known, an indexer cannot usually tell for certain whether, or where, a long entry will need to turn over to the next line. In a set-out layout, a turnover line must not look as though it is a subentry, so it must be indented further than a subentry. The BS ISO 999 guideline (British Standards Institution, 1996, subclause 9.1.2.4) is that a turnover should be indented more deeply than the deepest subheading in the index (in printer's terms, one 'em' deeper):

diagrams 92
        computer-generated 234
  graphs and charts 87
  illustrations (*see also* art reproductions;
        holograms; laser displays)
  maps 104

Spacing

Spacing should be consistent in any one index, in order to make plain the structure of the entries, the relationship between headings and subheadings, and the separation of the letter sequences (A, B, C and so on).

Between Heading and First Locator

A clear space should be evident between each heading and its first locator, with or without punctuation. As indicated under 'Indicating the position – the locators' in Chapter 4, the indexing standard BS ISO 999 (British Standards Institution, 1996, subclause 7.4.5) recommends either a comma plus a space, or two spaces, or some other unambiguous punctuation mark. Dedicated indexing programs usually have a number of options for spacing and punctuation, so the style can easily be changed – by a simple command – before printing out; the indexer does not have to amend each entry one by one.

Some indexes are presented with the locators justified right (aligned to the right-hand margin). In this case, the space between headings and locators varies according to the length of each heading and the number of its locators. These spaces are sometimes filled with rows of leader dots – a style regarded by some indexers as messy and a waste of ink:

technical economies of scale 48–56
turnround times..13, 27, 41, 70

Between Letter Sequences – As, Bs, Cs . . .

A linespace after each alphabetical letter sequence makes it clear where the new letter starts and so is a good finding aid for the user:

Alaska
[etc.]
Australia

Bahrein
[etc.]
Brazil

Cambodia
[etc.]

Any hard (paper) copy in which a letter sequence ends at the bottom of a page should be marked to show that a linespace is necessary; the linespace will, of course, be present on the accompanying disk or emailed copy, but the visual reminder may be helpful to the typesetter.

Display letters (header letters)
As well as a linespace, a displayed letter can be placed at the beginning of each letter sequence, if thought useful in the context and if space is available. It is particularly recommended in indexes intended for children or for people unused to finding information in alphabetical lists.

> **M**
> Minotaur
> [etc.]
> molluscs
>
> **N**
> Nineveh
> [etc.]

Between Locators

Individual locators are usually separated by a comma or another unambiguous punctuation mark, plus a space for easier legibility:

> market segments 26, 41, 75, 89
>
> import duties 147.2.3; 221.4; 312.1.1

Between Run-on Subheadings

Punctuation used to separate run-on subheadings is followed by a space, so that the subheadings are clearly distinguishable from each other:

> driveways: brick paving 35; concrete 56; gravel 42

Between Target Terms in Cross-References

When multiple terms are cited in cross-references, the punctuation mark separating them should be followed by a space:

footpaths 119–120 *see also* bridle paths; green
        lanes; rights of way

Typestyling

Italic type is customarily used for foreign words, document titles and scientific Latin and Greek words:

singing competitions
son et lumière
soul music
Sound of music, The

weevils
Wesmaelius quadrifasciatus
wireworms

and also for locators, or indicators added to locators, that point to special kinds of information, such as illustrations and glossary entries:

handwriting styles 14, *15–18*
uncials 216*gl* [or 216*g* or 216*G*]

The purpose of bold type, which should not be used unnecessarily, is usually either to draw the reader's eye to the principal reference(s) in a string of locators:

classroom discussion 9, 23, **45–46**, 54–55, 77, 91, 123–124

or to distinguish volume numbers from part or page numbers:

planning appeals **62** 43–44

or to highlight a particular category of heading:

local education authorities 23–26
London College of Fashion 69

London School of Economics and Political Science 77
lottery funding 39

Dedicated indexing programs can add codes for italicization and emboldening, ensuring that the characters will be correctly reproduced in the finished version. Hard copy (if required) should be clearly marked to show where these styles are required. The conventional way of indicating them to typesetters is underlining for italics:

> singing competitions
> son et lumière
> soul music
> Sound of music, The

> handwriting styles 14, 15–18
> uncials 216gl

and wavy lining for bold:

> classroom discussion 9, 23, 45–46, 54–55, 77, 91, 123–124

> planning appeals 62 43–44

> local education authorities 23–26
> London College of Fashion 69
> London School of Economics and Political Science 77
> lottery funding 39

If required, italic and bold can be indicated together:

> earthquake damage 46, *56*, **92–93**, *110*, *114*, 139, *146*

marked up on hard copy as:

> earthquake damage 46, 56, 92–93, 110, 114, 139, 146

Any wavy lining required on hard copy has usually to be added by hand; if the disk file is correctly coded to show bold type, and the bold print on the hard copy is clearly visible as such, manual wavy lining is rarely necessary.

Accented letters and special characters

Some computer programs and printers reproduce some accents and special characters without difficulty, but others do not. During output, indexers need to keep a close eye on all accents and special characters. Before dispatching the index, they must be clearly marked and explained, to ensure that they appear correctly in the published index. Some common requirements are:

é [acute]
è [grave]
ê [circumflex]
ç [cedilla]
ä [umlaut, diaeresis]
ñ [tilde]
α [Greek alpha]
β [Greek beta]

Introductory note

The introductory note usually needs to explain only one or two features and so takes up just a few lines. In the case of a large multisequence index with complicated locators, many abbreviations and typographic indicators, several paragraphs of explanation and guidance may be necessary.

The note should contain any information that the user requires in order to understand the content, function and structure of the index. One or more of the following features may be dealt with:

- the coverage (which parts of the text are covered by the index and which not)
- the order of entries, if not entirely obvious (including any 'broken' order, as for 'Institute' and 'Institution' and for 'Mac' and 'Saint' forms)
- the make-up of complex locators (e.g. date, volume, part and page)

- the use of typestyles such as italic and bold (e.g. to indicate illustrations, or locators for major references)
- the special use of capitals (e.g. small capitals for a category of heading)
- the use of abbreviations in headings (e.g. (N) for news items)
- the use of abbreviations with locators (e.g. *fig* for figures, *n* for notes)
- the treatment of multi-element names (such as names with prefixes)
- the existence of variant forms and spellings of names (e.g. Philips and Phillips, De La Cour and Delacour)
- the omission or transposition of definite and indefinite articles ('the', 'a', 'an')
- the purpose of cross-references (*see* and *see also*)

There is no 'model note' that is applicable to all indexes, not only because each index has its own set of characteristics, but also because indexers have different ways of presenting information in entries – using their favoured typestyles, abbreviations and other indicators. Each introductory note must therefore have its own customized text explaining whichever features the indexer considers need clarification.

The following eight examples of complete notes from different kinds of index give some indications of possible length and content:

- References are to page numbers, except where otherwise specified, (e.g. figure (Fig.) number). Glossary definitions are shown by 'G' after the page number.

- Entries are in word-by-word order, which takes account of the spaces and hyphens between words; so 'natural resources' precedes 'naturalism'.
  Locators followed by *n* indicate chapter note numbers: 134*n*1.

- Company, departmental and other organizational names are entered in their direct or official form, e.g. Department of Employment, Transport and the Regions [under D]; T.C. Jones Ltd [under T]. Place names such as 'North Yorkshire', 'Greater Manchester' and 'Upper Heyford' are entered under the second part of the name – 'Yorkshire, North'.
  References are to entry number and column letter: 241c.

- Volume numbers, shown in bold, are followed by month (abbreviated) and page numbers: **65** Apr 29–34.
  Titles of articles are shown in single quotation marks.
  Numerals in headings are arranged as though spelled out, e.g. '4–minute warning' is filed as if 'Four-minute warning'.

- References are to year and minute numbers: 00/34 is minute 34 of 2000. Some minutes from the July 19 meeting were given the wrong numbers, resulting in some duplicate numbers for the April 20 and July 19 meetings. The duplicate numbers for the July meeting are indicated by '#' after the number: 00/13#.
  Annexes are shown by A after the reference: 00/55A.

- The index covers the Introduction, Chapters 1 to 14 and the Appendix.
  Titles of books are italicized: *Searchlight on Spain*. Titles beginning with 'A', 'An' and 'The' are entered under the next word: *Anatomy of Peace, The*.
  Personal names are entered according to their national or cultural customs; most Western names are therefore placed under family name (surname). Customs vary for multiple-element names (such as names with prefixes), so if one of these is not where you expect to find it, look for it under another element.

- The topics in the book are alphabetically arranged in the index, so look for 'space travel' under S, and for 'global warming' under G. The number shown after the word you have looked up is the number of the page where you will find the information you want.
  Sometimes, instead of a page number, you may find a cross-reference telling you which other word or words to look at. Example: If you look for 'sun', you will find the cross-reference 'see solar system'. If you now look for 'solar system', you will find several page numbers to look up.
  If you don't find either the word you want or a cross-reference, try looking at another word that means more or less the same, or is closely connected. Example: If you look for 'Moon probes' you won't find it; try 'space probes' and you will find the page references there.

● Subject index entries are made for the terms that appear as subject headings in the main Abstracts Section. They lead to abstract numbers of the individual articles abstracted. In addition, there are thesaural references from synonyms; from broad to narrower terms; and between related terms. [From *British humanities index* (1999) (1) 253 (Bowker-Saur)]

The last example listed above is the note at the head of the subject index. The detailed user guide at the front of *British humanities index* gives much more information on the structure and use of this index:

It is an alphabetical sequence and allows you to find highly specific terms and then locate the abstract number(s) which have used these terms. To illustrate, [. . .] using abstract 11240, if you look in the Subject Index for the terms 'Spain' or 'Bilbao' or 'Guggenheim Museum' you will see that these terms appear in bold print, followed by a colon and space, and then by abstract numbers including 11240. In the case of 'Spain' you will also see the term 'Art gallery buildings' appearing before the abstract number, since that term preceded 'Spain' in the subject string. The subject index also provides additional leads to terms not appearing in the subject string over the abstract. For example, at 'Gehry, Frank' there is a lead to abstract 11240.

The Subject Index also has entries which do not lead to abstract numbers but instead to other terms. For instance, if you look in Issue 3 at 'Business archives', you see on the next lines 'narrower term Account books'. This indicates that you should now look at 'Account books' and if you do so you will find abstract number 15279. Similarly, if you look at 'Catastrophes' you will be referred to another term 'Disasters': the Subject Index says 'Catastrophes see Disasters'. In this case 'Disasters' is not a narrower (i.e. more specific) term but is instead the term we have preferred to use rather than 'Catastrophes'. Lastly there are terms like 'Occupational health' where there is no abstract in this particular issue [. . .], but we do use the term when appropriate; and at 'Occupational health' there is a reference 'See also Occupational safety' which refers you to 'Occupational Safety', where you will find an abstract number.' [The relevant entries from the index are shown in boxes after this statement in the user guide.]

Indexers should always provide introductory notes whenever they judge them necessary, and emphasize to clients that an introduction is an integral and essential part of an index, without which the reader may not fully understand it or how to make the best use of it. The status of the introductory note can be established if it is mentioned in the index specification agreed by the indexer and the client at the start of the work. If an introductory note is supplied but not used by the client, the indexer should take the matter up with the client and ensure that future copy will be treated in the professional way it deserves.

The indexer's name

Writers of texts, or their publishers, may sometimes publicly recognize the work of indexers, by including their names in the acknowledgements or elsewhere. More frequently, there is no mention. The indexing standard BS ISO 999 (British Standards Institution, 1996, subclause 6.4.4) recommends that indexers should be given the opportunity to be named in the document. Indexers who wish to be so credited should ensure that this is agreed in the contract for the work and should make certain that they see and approve the 'ready for printing' version of the index after it has passed through the final processing by editors and typesetters.

Not all indexers do wish to be credited, sometimes out of unjustified modesty, but more often because in the past they have discovered too late that the pagination of a book was altered after the index was produced, with the result that the published index contained incorrect locators. It also happens that an index itself is altered after it has left the indexer – entries added, entries removed, separate locators merged, for example, and all without consultation. The results can – entirely without justification – make the indexer appear careless and unprofessional, even incompetent. Indexers who assert moral rights in their indexes (see 'Moral rights' in Chapter 10) should be better protected against this situation.

Making the index shorter or longer

Tiresome, and time-consuming, tasks for the indexer are the reduction and expansion of indexes; they are not required frequently, but it is as well to be prepared for the event.

Reduction

Reduction is sometimes necessary because:

- extra matter is added to the document at a late stage (foreword, illustrations, appendices, for example), and so uses up some of the space allocated to the index
- the index contains more entries than anticipated or includes many sequences of set-out subheadings, which use up the space available

Sometimes the problem can be resolved by making alterations to the setting of the index, such as:

- resetting in smaller type, or in columns (or more columns)
- printing subheadings in run-on form instead of set-out
- removing punctuation between each heading and its first locator
- removing display (header) letters from the beginnings of letter sequences
- using the minimal form for page ranges instead of the full form
- placing *see also* cross-references on the same line as the heading from which they refer, not on a new line

Other solutions require the indexer to make changes to content. If absolutely necessary, but at the cost of downgrading the information content, and therefore the quality, of the index, one or more of these steps can be taken:

- shortening entries that turn over
- removing subheadings, shifting all the locators to the heading, and emboldening the principal one(s)
- removing some *see* and *see also* cross-references
- removing less significant locators
- removing less significant headings

The alteration or removal of any entry may have repercussions on other entries, including cross-references, so it must be painstakingly done.

Expansion

Expansion may be required because:

- the text of the document is shorter than expected and there is extra space available
- the index may turn out to have fewer entries, or less detailed entries, than anticipated
- the client proposes more in-depth treatment, or the inclusion of parts of the document that were previously unindexed

Potential actions involving reformatting include:

- printing subheadings in set-out form instead of run-on
- adding punctuation between each heading and its first locator
- using the full form for page ranges instead of the minimal (squashed) form
- inserting display (header) letters at the beginnings of letter sequences
- resetting in large type or in a single column rather than in double columns

It is much better, though, for the indexer to take the opportunity to improve the information content and structure of the index, by:

- analysing strings of locators into subheadings
- using double (multiple) entries instead of *see* cross-references
- adding *see* and *see also* cross-references
- adding headings for less significant topics
- adding locators for less significant references
- placing *see also* cross-references on a new line, instead of continuing on the same line as the heading they follow

Proofreading the index

Typeset indexes need to be proofread to ensure that the structure and layout of the index is as the indexer intended and that no errors have crept in since the copy left the indexer's hands. Sometimes – for speed and convenience – proofs are checked in-house by publishers' staff. It is better for indexers to take on this responsibility, and some insist on this, including it in their contracts with clients (See Chapter 10: Managing the work). It is the last chance for the indexer to check that everything is as it should be in terms of layout and styling of the entries (evenly indented subheadings, consistent use of italic and bold), that an introductory note is positioned at the head of the index, and that any necessary 'continued' statements are included.

Occasional 'hiccups' at this stage include:

- subheadings not indented
- turnover lines going back to the left margin
- turnover lines indented as though subheadings
- superfluous punctuation (e.g. semicolons) remaining when subheadings prepared for run-on form have been subsequently changed to set-out style
- italic or bold type in the wrong place
- bold type (for 'major reference') for a locator when it is the only one in the entry
- headings shifted to the subheading position

'Continued' Statements

It is only when the final printing is reached that it is known whether 'continued' statements are needed. Before then, any amendment to the index, however small, can shift a line or two from one column or one page to the next.

If possible, the breaking up of related sequences should be avoided – and editors and typesetters usually try to achieve this – but it is often inevitable in an index with many subheading sequences. The best that the indexer can do is constantly to emphasize the necessity for 'continued' statements whenever it seems that they may be required. If they are not provided, index users may miss useful entries or be confused by carried-over subheadings.

Conventionally, the 'continued' statement is placed at the top of the carried-over column. The heading that is being continued should be included:

    land use (*continued*)
            recreational 67
            residential 45

and similarly for a subheading:

    population
            distribution (*continued*)
                    Indonesia 8
                    Japan 23

In the case of a sequence that is broken at the bottom of a recto (right-hand page) it may also be helpful to indicate there that the sequence carries on overleaf, particularly when the last subheading on the recto begins with a letter towards the end of the alphabet – otherwise the reader may assume that the sequence ends there and so miss what is on the following page:

    traffic congestion
            inner cities 89
            rural areas 101
            tollroads 67
            (*continued*)

'The look'

Freelance indexers do not often have the opportunity to determine the published 'realization' of their work, but they should aim always to dispatch high-quality content in good order, and to take an interest in its subsequent handling and production. Any indexer who feels that the appearance of the published version does not match the quality of the index supplied should let the publisher know, and make sure that the matter is resolved before doing any further work for the firm concerned (see 'Keeping the relationship sweet' in Chapter 10).

References

British Standards Institution (1996) *Information and documentation – guidelines for the content, organization and presentation of indexes.* BS ISO 999:1996. London: British Standards Institution

Mulvany, Nancy C. (1994) *Indexing books.* Chicago: University of Chicago Press

Robertson, Michael (1995) Foreign concepts: indexing and indexes on the Continent. *The Indexer,* **19,** 160–172

Further Reading

Butcher, Judith (1992) *Copy-editing: the Cambridge handbook for editors, authors and publishers* 3rd edn. Cambridge: Cambridge University Press (pp. 3–28: Typescripts: hard, electronic, camera-ready; pp. 195–201: Style within the entry)

University of Chicago Press (1993) *The Chicago manual of style* 14th edn. Chicago: University of Chicago Press (Chapter 17: Indexes)

Wellisch, Hans H. (1995) *Indexing from A to Z* 2nd edn. New York: H.W. Wilson (pp. 155–167: Editing: the 21 steps)

CHAPTER SIX

Serial publications

Working with Serials

The indexing of serial publications can provide regular and fascinating work for many freelance and in-house indexers, sometimes continuing over extended periods of time. It is a fruitful sector for proactive indexers seeking to increase their field of work; at any time there are numerous periodical titles published without indexes and – unlike books – periodicals can have their indexes produced after publication of the relevant issues (sometimes many years after). Yearbooks and directories of any reasonable size are almost useless without good indexes, and there are many now in publication that could do with improvement. Committees, councils, boards, and other permanent groups that have regular meetings, produce minutes or records of their deliberations, decisions and actions, which should be (but often are not) indexed. Enterprising indexers who take the initiative and manage to convince editors and publishers of the value of indexes – by the volume, by the year, and perhaps cumulative – may secure dependable sustained work for many years.

Some indexers who deal only with book indexes tend to view periodical indexing as a lesser art because it does not always involve the minute, line-by-line analysis and detailed representation that they practise. This is to misjudge the situation. The compilation of effective, well-styled indexes to periodicals requires good understanding and up-to-date knowledge of the subject, and the ability to identify the principal messages, form suitable headings, subheadings and locators, and to arrange and lay out the completed entries – just as for indexes to books. All indexers should have a wide knowledge of the world and its ways, but indexers of newspapers and general magazines perhaps need to be especially well-rounded human beings, with a wider and more up-to-date knowledge than most – because any topic at all may appear and require indexing. Specialist knowledge is of course vital for indexing serials in academic, professional and special-interest fields.

The main differences appear in the level of indexing – which can vary from serial to serial – the diverse types of content to be covered by the index and to be differentiated within it, the continuity of approach, the monitoring of specialist vocabulary change (and the consequent need for considerable cross-referencing) and the fact that – as long as the serial continues to be published – the job is never really finished. The following of threads, from issue to issue or volume to volume, dealing with inventions and discoveries and their development, and the blossoming of new words necessary to describe and discuss them, can make for an exciting and testing kind of indexing that is often denied the book indexer. Periodicals indexers compiling cumulations for journals for which they have previously prepared individual annual or volume indexes have to risk finding their earlier injudicious entries coming back to haunt them, but – unlike book indexers completing an index once and for all – they have a chance for improvement the second time around. Another difference, applicable to some (but by no means all) periodicals is that the finished index may not be produced until some time after publication of the issues to which it relates, giving – in theory at least – more time for the indexer to consider and refine the index content and presentation. It is also possible for a serial to be indexed twice, currently – either at or close to the date of publication – and retrospectively (possibly much later), in order to cover material not previously included or to reflect more closely the needs of a new group of users (social or historical researchers, for example).

The usefulness and physical life of the individual issues of some serials (daily newspapers and monthly consumer-oriented magazines, for instance) may appear to be short-term, but in countries with effective legal deposit regulations permanent files of all published titles are retained. The British Library, for example, is a major repository of copyright deposit material, having the right to receive one copy of every publication distributed in the UK or the Republic of Ireland. Legal deposit rights are also held by the Bodleian Library in Oxford, Cambridge University Library, the National Library of Scotland, the National Library of Wales, and Trinity College in Dublin. Indexes, whether compiled in-house by the publishers, by specialist commercial agencies or by individual freelance indexers, make possible the extensive use of serial resources for many years after their original publication.

What is a Serial Publication?

A serial is any publication that appears under the same title in consecutive parts (each part distinguished by date or number) and that is expected to continue. Newspapers, periodicals, journals, and magazines are therefore regarded as serials. Other kinds of document that can be included are annual reports, minutes of permanent committees, yearbooks, and regularly produced directories – though individually they can also be identified as single documents in their own right. A multipart work of which the parts are published simultaneously or consecutively, but which is complete once the intended parts are published, is not a serial. Each published serial is uniquely identified by an International Standard Serial Number (ISSN) – for example, the Society of Indexers' periodical *The Indexer* is ISSN 0019–4131.

The range of serial publications is wide, covering a myriad of subjects. *Ulrichs international periodicals directory* (2000) lists around 158 000 serials from around the world. In *Willings press guide* (2000) 20 000 entries are featured for the UK. Some serials, particularly those reporting developments in scientific, technological and medical fields, are usually indexed in detail with provision for access by several different kinds of heading (subject, author's name, product, formula, for example). Others, such as popular magazines to be found in newsagents' (US: newsdealers) displays, often lack indexes of any kind – though they usually have at least a contents list.

No attempt is made here to make fine distinctions between 'the journal', 'the periodical' and 'the magazine'. The idea (floated by some) that a magazine must be much lower down the scale than a journal is negated by the existence of *Philosophical magazine* – a primary journal for physicists, which has been in publication since 1798. Librarians tend to call them all 'periodicals' or 'journals' – regardless of type. Some people reserve the designation 'journals' for the organs of societies, associations and institutions.

As well as being materials that can be (and need to be) indexed, serials constitute valuable funds of information that indexers themselves use as reference sources in the process of indexing other documents.

Serial Types and Their Characteristics

The categories identified below are characterized from the indexer's perspective and provide a general overview. Others (librarians, publishers, journalists) would group them differently, according to their needs and practices. The groups are not necessarily mutually exclusive; the interests and targets of certain titles within each category frequently overlap.

Newspapers

The frequency of publication varies from title to title, some appearing every day, some every weekday in the evening, others weekly. Their subject coverage can be extensive and they may have many types of content. Although reflecting current events and intended to be read principally on the day of publication, with most copies being discarded very soon after, they nevertheless provide a fascinating and valuable record, which becomes a rich source of material for historians, social commentators, writers, and researchers of many kinds. Few are provided with integral indexes at the time of publication – what is featured under the heading 'Index' in some of the broadsheets is often just a selective contents list giving a quick guide to regular items ('TV and radio 20; Crossword 33; Weather 32; Money 25').

Some of the major papers compile in-house indexes, or have indexes compiled by specialist firms, for publication (and in some cases, online consultation), so that anyone can search the issues of past years. In many cases, though, there are no indexes, and much material – including valuable 'actuality' items such as eye-witness accounts, interviews, and photographs, cannot be quickly located. Newspapers at all levels are increasingly become available online, with frequent updating. Indexing this fluid kind of material offers a challenge to indexers who are used to working with 'fixed' editions.

National

These are usually published daily, on weekdays (including Saturdays), or weekly (on Sundays) – for example, in the UK *The Guardian*, *The Mirror*, *The Scotsman*, *The Sunday Telegraph*, and *Wales on Sunday*; and in Ireland *The Irish Times* and *The Sunday Independent*. There may be more than one edition per day, with headlines and front page items, in particular, changing in line with breaking news, and content may also vary in editions published for sale in different geographical areas. Compilers of indexes may need to distinguish these variants, or there may be one edition that is regarded by the publisher as definitive.

Broadsheet (large format) papers typically consist of at least two separate sections, the main part devoted to current news (home and international), analysis, comment, and correspondence; other sections may cover the arts and media, sport, finance, education, computers, society, and so forth, perhaps allocating each subject area to a particular day of the week. The content can include text, tables (numerical and other data displayed in columns) and illustrative matter – halftones (reproductions of photographs) in black and white or in colour, and line illustrations (cartoons, graphs, maps, diagrams). Tabloid (smaller format) papers may also have more than one section. The news and comment element normally consists of much less text than do the broadsheets, and contains more photographic illustration.

Regional

These may – depending on the country of publication and the territory covered (state, province, or other intermediate area) – be equivalent to national newspapers, but with emphasis on events in the geographical area concerned and on the effects on that area of national and international events. Frequency may be daily or weekly and the content is a mixture of text and illustration, the proportion varying from paper to paper. Examples include: in the UK, the (London) *Evening Standard*, the *Yorkshire Post*, the *Belfast Telegraph*, the *Aberdeen Evening Express*, and the *South Wales Argus*; in Ireland, the (Dublin) *Evening Herald* and the (Cork) *Evening Echo*.

Local

These are usually published in and for a smaller geographical area – a town and its surrounding administrative district, for example. Some – such as the daily (often evening) ones – give the main national stories as front page news, and then concentrate on matters of local interest. Others, more often published weekly, report any local effects of national happenings and policy decisions, but otherwise cover community concerns and events including local controversies, housing and planning, transport, entertainment, crimes and court cases, births, deaths, marriages, and celebrations of all kinds. They often feature items of local historical relevance. There are usually many illustrations and several pages given over to advertisements, often divided into subject sections – property (real estate), motoring, trades and services, items for sale and wanted, pets, personal columns, and so on. Examples include: in the UK, the *Worthing Herald*, the *Derbyshire Times*, the *Forres Gazette*, and the *Coleraine Times*; and in the Republic of Ireland, the *Galway Advertiser* and the *Clare Champion*.

In addition to those published on a 'for sale' basis – some of which are of very long standing – there are also some titles that are delivered free to households or distributed in the street and that are financed by advertising. Their information value as newspapers varies considerably, but even those with meagre news coverage can have worth as social documents.

Smaller, voluntary 'newspapers' exist too, for example in the UK at parish level. They may be small in size, irregular in frequency, and variable in newsworthiness, but nevertheless provide a record of local events and concerns. Indexes to them are rare, and not usually compiled on a commercial basis, but they can be valuable as information sources for local history groups and other researchers.

Academic and learned journals

These normally focus on the study of a particular subject field or discipline, or of one of its branches. Some learned and academic bodies publish certain titles themselves; others delegate publication and distribution to commercial publishers, who may handle many titles on behalf of several institutions. From time to time, a society or department decides to change publisher; in that case, any freelance indexer who has been supplying indexing services to the original publisher will probably have to negotiate a fresh contract with the new publisher, once its identity is discovered. Regrettably, indexers are not always kept fully informed, by the societies and companies concerned, about this kind of change.

Academic and learned journals customarily contain longer articles reporting research in progress, work completed, state-of-the-art reports, and correspondence relating to previously published articles. They may focus on a subject field in general (such as *New scientist*), or on a particular branch (for example *International journal of food science & technology*), or on one of the institutions that exist to promote study, research and understanding of a specific substance, process or property (like the *Proceedings of the Royal Microscopical Society*). The articles are authoritative, having in most cases been subjected to refereeing or peer review (close scrutiny by people of equal or superior standing in the relevant field) before acceptance. Bibliographical content may be of special importance in these journals, featuring either as a source of authority – quoted within or at the end of an article or as an individual literature survey, perhaps with annotations – to enable readers to follow the inception and development of a given topic of interest.

Many subjects are catered for by an assortment of periodical titles, variously aimed at a specific group of practitioners, or at workers in a given environment or having a particular long-term aim. Some of these titles overlap – in interests and readership – with some of the professional journals described in the next section. In these kinds of journal, access by subject indexes is often regarded as the principal concern, but author indexes are of importance, too, because they enable the output of given authors (including smaller items like letters to the editor) to be traced – perhaps over several years, through a number of volumes. Some of the titles have been published continuously over several decades (even over more than a hundred years). They have become valuable resources for research and investigation – in which context the compilation and cumulation of good indexes is crucial.

Professional and trade journals

One group of these reflects the needs and concerns of the practitioners of a certain profession, trade, industry, craft or service – architects, plumbers, school teachers, clergy, economists, business people, librarians and information managers, hairdressers, dog breeders, fashion retailers, caterers, photographers, and economists, for example. Another group consists of titles produced mainly by individual manufacturing or service companies, for internal distribution; they typically provide news and features about company matters, new products, events, and staff members. A third group, also produced (or at least generated) by individual companies, includes technical reviews and product bulletins – often of high quality in terms of production and design – aimed at publicizing the companies' activities and progress to the outside world.

Most commercial and socio-economic activities give rise to at least one periodical title devoted to the interests of their practitioners, and some have many – for example the medical and health care professions. They concern themselves with matters affecting the members of the activity and its related areas, reflect their opinions, provide technical specialist information and news, promote and report on relevant events, new products, legal points, research results, and much else. Their coverage often overlaps, in terms of topics, but the style and perspective of the presentation – and the amount of detail provided – vary according to the intended readership. Some have a very high proportion of one kind of content – advertisements perhaps, tabular financial data, details of new laws and regulations, photographs, or news and stories of passing interest.

The frequency of publication varies considerably from title to title. Some are regular – usually weekly or monthly – others irregular, appearing only when the need arises. Many are indexable and can thus become worthwhile sources later on (in addition to their value while current).

Consumer and special-interest magazines

The number of titles in this group – even just in the UK – is enormous, mirroring the myriad interests, passions and hobbies occurring in the population, as well as the many groups identified in society by age, gender, ethnicity, physical and mental state, and attitude. Many of these periodicals are intended for immediate reading and, once the next issue has appeared, are discarded. Devotees of a particular title, though, are likely to retain back issues or to pull out useful pages for their personal files (and perhaps even compile a rudimentary index for their own use). Public libraries may hold stocks, for a certain time, of a few of those most in demand. Subjects represented include computers, horseriding, birdwatching, knitting, motorcycles, lifestyles of the rich and famous, and all kinds of indoor and outdoor sport and recreational activity.

Despite the apparent transience of some of the titles, magazines of this kind frequently require indexing – not necessarily at the time of their first use, but later, when they have existed long enough to become of interest to students of the subject or the period. Whether the theme is cookery, gardening, football, adventure holidays, jazz, rambling, political satire, or sex, the content can be suitably indexed for the benefit of the researcher.

Literary magazines

This group could be regarded as belonging to the 'special-interest' category described above, but is different in that the emphasis in the content is on literary ideas and published works. Much space may be occupied by book reviews and by analytical commentaries on the *oeuvres* of chosen authors. A great deal of the input may be provided by well-known writers. Feature articles, correspondence, diaries of events (such as literary festivals), notifications of medal winners, and advertisements, are also likely to appear. As a source of information in later years, they can have equal value with academic journals, particularly as their content is highly indexable.

Indexing and abstracting journals

These secondary serials provide access to descriptions (citations) or abstracts of primary publications (including the contents of serials). Some are based on a particular subject field, others on a certain type of publication, others on works published within a geographical area. The arrangement of the contents varies; some have the descriptions and abstracts in subject classified order, others list them chronologically, others alphabetically by author or title. The indexes therefore provide for alternative access, as relevant. Styles of bibliographical citation (the ways in which the titles, authors, dates, publishers and so on are presented) vary – some using the Harvard (name and date) system, others their own house styles, some full of detail, others much abbreviated. This affects how they need to appear in indexes.

Committee minutes

The records of the meetings of committees, councils, working groups, boards, and panels are a valuable resource concerning decisions, plans, proposals, and actions. Members of the various bodies come and go, following appointment, election, retirement, and resignation, and often there is little continuity and no reliable 'corporate memory'. The provision of indexes to the minutes can greatly enhance the organizational efficiency and dependability of these groups, enabling previous discussions and their conclusions to be identified, actions to be followed through, and consistent policy decisions to be made.

Yearbooks, regular directories, annual reports

Annuals and other 'self-contained' publications produced on a regular basis have a dual existence. They are serials in the sense that they are intended to be continued indefinitely, but each individual edition is similar to a 'one-off' publication with its own exclusive index. Although a particular edition may only be used on a single occasion by some readers, for whom the index need bear no relation to the indexes of other editions, regular users consulting successive volumes need continuity – particularly as the type of content tends to appear under the same, or similar, chapter and section headings from edition to edition. The index vocabulary therefore needs to be consistent for topics that appear regularly, while incorporating changes in terminology and adding cross-references from old to new terms in order to assist searchers following a topic over several editions.

Directory-type publications, particularly large ones with many text entries, sometimes benefit from the division of index headings into separate sequences. The kinds of sequence required depend primarily on the arrangement of the text entries. A trade directory giving details of companies, arranged alphabetically by company name, could have one index sequence for product and service types, another for geographical location – by county, state, city, town or postcode – and a third for brand names. An index of company names may also be considered necessary, but if the text entries are clear and if running heads show the first and last names on each page, then finding a particular company may be easy without an index. Whatever the decision regarding a name index, it should not be forgotten that company names containing more than one element can cause confusion for searchers – whether 'Chris Paterson Ltd' is under 'C' or 'P', for example – so that cross-referencing is necessary in the name index if there is one, or otherwise in the appropriate places between the directory entries themselves. The treatment of names beginning with 'Mac', 'St' and similar forms also needs attention. (See 'Corporate names' in Chapter 4 and 'Alphabetical arrangement' in Chapter 5.)

Annual reports – whether from companies, charitable bodies, societies, associations, government agencies, local administrative authorities, or clubs – represent the official records of achievement and progress of the organizations concerned. Despite their importance and – sometimes – their legal status, most do not have indexes; members, shareholders, supporters, local tax payers, and other interested parties, therefore frequently have no easy way of finding the page, paragraph or subsection that contains the nugget they seek. If a local club's report runs to no more than a few small pages, no great harm may be done by the lack of an index. For company reports, though – combined as they often are with the annual accounts, and consisting perhaps of a hundred or more A4 pages with pictures, graphs, and tables, the deficiency is serious. Headings that are statutorily or customarily required to be used in the presentation of annual accounts are often matched by comment under those or similar headings in other parts of the report, so anyone wishing to read through all the relevant information needs to be directed to them via an index, which brings together the scattered references and may also indicate the various forms of information presentation – table, graph, chart, and so on. Consistency of index vocabulary from report to report makes searching over successive years more reliable, but new terms must be introduced from time to time – sometimes to reflect additional coverage in line with changed legal requirements – and so effective cross-referencing is crucial.

Extracts

Selections and Collections

Selected articles from periodicals are often reprinted in collections – as gift-type annuals, for example, or one-off *The best of . . .* collections. A single collection can be treated like a book, but if regular or successive volumes are published without intended end, the title becomes a serial in its own right. Can the same index entries be used for the serial and for the collection? It depends; each must be viewed in its context. If the collection is itself a serial, the same factors apply as for the original journal in terms of the use of a standard vocabulary. In a collection (whether a book or a serial), the provision of an author index may be more important than in the original – the fact that the articles have been selected can give the identity of the writers increased importance.

Cuttings, Offprints and Tear-outs

Libraries, resource centres, companies, and individuals sometimes maintain organized collections of cuttings (clippings), offprints and tear-outs from newspapers and magazines, on subjects of particular interest to them. The scope of the collections differs according to the concerns of the collectors, so each is likely to have its own set of index terms, focused on the needs and requirements of its user group.

Formats

Electronic

Ashcroft and Langdon (1999) report an annual rate of increase of around 30 per cent in the number of electronic journals, with more than 7000 titles currently available. These figures include journals on the internet or CD-ROM or provided by other electronic means. In the academic and research fields in particular, there has been a noticeable increase in the number of periodical titles being published in electronic form as well as, or instead of, in print. For some titles, the electronic content exactly matches that of the printed version, but for others the provision may be of selected articles only or just a contents list. A smaller number (usually known as e-journals) are available only online. Some titles make the full articles freely available on the internet, whereas some provide abstracts for free consultation, and others are available only to subscribers or after online registration with the producers.

Electronic provision is continuing to develop, and offers interesting possibilities for the exchange of information in scientific, technical and medical fields. The journal content can consist of the very latest research findings, news of planned projects, questions and answers, debates on topical matters, and several other forms. Serious articles in printed journals are normally subjected to a refereeing process before publication, so that unreliable and false material can be identified and rejected. With electronic journals, it is possible to have a visible system of review, with original articles being provisionally displayed, so that comments from fellow-workers in the field can be added; authors may then amend the articles before making them available in their final, permanent, versions.

The economics of journal publishing will determine the ratio of printed to electronic forms. In scientific, technological and medical fields in particular, e-journals can speed up the reporting and reviewing of research, to the benefit of all concerned. Discussion of new papers can take place more quickly, with the possibility of comment from a wider range of workers in the field than with the printed version. Nevertheless, most periodicals are likely to continue for some time to be published on paper – perhaps until environmental influences severely reduce world supplies of paper or until electronic communications equipment and the means of access become overwhelmingly cheap and attractive to both mass and specialized markets. Publishers may increasingly decide to economize by no longer producing printed indexes and directing searchers instead to the online versions of their periodicals, which can be searched in various ways.

Indexes may be provided that are similar to the printed versions, but without locators such as page numbers – searchers have just to 'click' on a heading (whether author or subject) in the index, for the relevant article or item to be displayed on the screen. Another approach is to use full-text searching by significant words (keywords), although using unrefined natural language for searching has pitfalls: the occurrence of words having the same spelling but different meanings (printers – people and firms who print; equipment for printing), the existence of more than one word to represent a particular concept (panthers; pumas; mountain lions) and variant spellings (oesophagus; esophagus). Large subject-oriented databases containing articles from different journals can similarly be searched by title word and text word. Indexers could play a more active role in the design of databases like these, by supplying advice on the most effective methods of providing access for various kinds of user.

The factors affecting the indexing of electronic media in general are dealt with in Chapter 11: Technology. As far as serials are concerned, the indexing needs of users are the same, regardless of the physical format of the materials. The difference lies principally in the provision of rapid access from multiple entry points (for example in full-text searching). The indexes to web sites containing the texts of periodicals vary in form. In some, the user has first to select the periodical title from a list of items produced by the same publisher and is then shown a list of year dates from which to choose. Picking a date produces a list of individual issue dates or numbers, and subsequently the contents list of the chosen issue. In others a letter of the alphabet is selected, giving a list of titles starting with that letter; selecting a title gives successively year dates, issues and contents, as just described. Author and keyword searches are often possible, either by calling up a list and browsing through it or by entering the name or word in a 'dialogue box' and commanding a search.

Audiovisual

Some magazines, newsletters and bulletins appear solely in audio form, or on film or video, designed often for groups with particular listening or viewing difficulties. The index needs of users of these serials are equal to those of people consulting printed materials. (See Chapter 7: Images and sound (audio) recordings.)

Why is Indexing a Serial Any Different from Indexing a Book?

The content

The indexer of a standard book normally considers the text as a cohesive whole and so identifies its aims and conclusions, interprets and analyses the discourse, notes the arguments and points of discussion, follows the threads (themes, subthemes) throughout, and indexes the significant references. The indexer of a typical issue of a periodical is faced with a collection of discrete items, probably covering different topics within the overall subject addressed by the periodical and comprising a variety of forms – the mixture depending upon the nature of the periodical (academic journal, company newsletter, committee meeting record, daily newspaper).

The forms can include: feature articles, some of which may have more than one author (sometimes several, even many, authors); news items; letters to the editor; pictures (colour, and black and white);

diagrams; cartoons; book reviews; state-of-the-art reports; obituaries; notices; advertisements; jokes; extracts from earlier issues ('50 years ago this month'); editorials; and several more. Some classes of items appear as regular features, others are occasional or once-only pieces. Although most content is subject to a level of editorial control and harmonization, articles within a single issue may be written in several different styles. Within a particular subject field, periodicals vary in their use of vocabulary – some being aimed at professionals, and others at laypeople.

One of the first decisions to be made, when starting on the index to a new journal, or one that has not been indexed before, concerns which items to represent in the index and which to leave out. This is something for the indexer to discuss with others having an interest in the finished product – the editor, the editorial board of the learned society, the publisher, and (if possible, though this is rare) intended users of the index. For some titles, it will be obvious that the main articles should be indexed by author and principal topic(s) – and that content of transient interest (diary of forthcoming events, advertisements by suppliers of goods and services, lists of new members, for example) can be ignored. For others, the distinction may be less clear. Correspondence, for instance ('Letters to the editor', 'You write'), is usually worth indexing if it relates to feature articles in previous issues or to topical matters affecting the profession, because it provides the reader with relevant supplementary information. On the other hand, if it is merely a succession of amusing anecdotes and badinage, and therefore not likely to be consulted at a later date, it is not relevant for indexing. The absolute minimum access that should be provided for a periodical is usually by author and title.

Currency

Information published in periodicals is often much more up to date than book material – and this is even more the case with e-journals. The preparation time for an article is usually considerably shorter than that for a book and – particularly in a frequently published title – the production time is shorter, too.

In academic and research fields, periodicals have long been the most important medium of information exchange and of comment and challenge by peers. Reputable journals of this kind require submitted articles to be read and privately commented on by (perhaps two) other workers in the particular subject field, before they agree to publish. This peer review is carried out in order to attempt to present original information, and to prevent fraudulent or unreliable work being reported. Pressure to publish, for reasons of career advancement or 'the rush to be first', has occasionally caused problems for some titles, so that corrections and revisions (and sometimes withdrawals) have had to be included in later issues. It is, of course, essential that these corrections and revisions are indexed, and their status usually needs to be specially indicated in the headings or locators, so that they are not taken to be less important references. The indexer needs not only to match up the scattered references (one of the regular purposes of an index) but to formulate headings and subheadings that show the sequence of events.

Page Format

Whereas books typically consist of continuous text covering whole pages that are gathered into chapters, intended to be perused from start to finish, the disparate pieces making up a periodical – which can be read in any order – are frequently arranged in column format. This type of presentation is most common in newspapers, the broadsheet type having perhaps eight columns across a page. The indexer therefore has to provide locators that contain more than just page numbers, so that the user can be directed to a specific portion of the page (see 'Locators' later in this chapter).

Long-term value

Some periodicals are short-lived because they are launched on a tide of optimism when there seems to be a good market for a title reflecting a trend that turns out, after all, to be ephemeral. Others may fail after a brave attempt to cater for the needs of a particular interest group that, economically, is too small to support continued publication. Inadequate forward planning, insufficient capital resources, inexperience, low quality of content, a surplus of competitive titles, scarcity of firms prepared to pay for advertising space, and sheer bad luck, also account for the demise of individual titles.

Given the right circumstances, nonetheless, a title can remain in publication for many years; the first issue of *Philosophical transactions of the Royal Society*, for example, was published in 1665 and the title is still being published. A publication of this kind is invaluable to scholars and researchers within the relevant subject field, allowing them to trace details of events and reports of progress, identify trends, collect opinions, and follow developing themes from year to year, from decade to decade, and even from century to century.

The periodical publishing industry is vulnerable not just to economic changes but to social and political trends. As a result, periodicals expand, shrink, merge, split, change title, adjust their frequency of issue, and shift their subject coverage. This can make for an interesting (and sometimes uncertain) life for the indexer, who may have to compete for the retention of responsibility for an index or to submit a proposal for incorporating, into an existing index, the index of another title that has been taken over.

The indexability of a periodical, however, need not be influenced by its length of life. Many titles that had only a brief existence contain valuable resource material of interest to students of the literature of the subject. They should not be overlooked in this context, but – because they are no longer published and so have no-one commercially interested in them – it is easy for them to be ignored and then forgotten. Indexers looking for work could benefit by identifying suitable defunct titles for indexing and then seeking out possible publishers (not necessarily in the commercial publishing field) with whom to co-operate. It may be possible to consider indexing more than one title in a combined index, focusing on a particular subject area; indexes like this, enabling easy access to the contents of several journals, make useful research tools, saving researchers' time and providing a means of comparing and contrasting subject coverage and treatment. If the original publishers are still in existence, they are obviously the first port of call, but if not, others may be interested – copyright requirements permitting. Present usage and future usage both need to be considered.

Levels of subject indexing

This is the area in which periodical and book indexing can differ most. Book indexers aim to represent in fine detail the whole subject content, looking at individual pages, paragraphs and sentences, and including headings containing words that may not appear in the text but that are likely to be sought by index users. Indexers of periodicals tend towards general representation or summarization of each article, perhaps indexing the overall subject and a small number of topics (four or five, say, or up to ten) – sometimes referred to, particularly in electronic media, as 'metadata' or 'metatopics'. Indexing of this kind, characterized by less detailed representation of the topics in an article, can resemble the subject indexing (classification) of items for a library catalogue. The indexer can require great skill to denote the whole significance of a complete article within a small set of index headings.

Some publishers – even those of 'serious' periodicals – provide no subject index, including instead merely an index of article titles alphabetically arranged according to the first (significant) word of each title. This is of little use to someone searching for subject information, as few users have in mind the exact title of an article when they are searching for information on a topic. At best, they are browsing lists. Typically, an entry starts with the first non-article word (which may or may not be a significant word), then the author's name, then the locator. Such indexes can complement a proper subject index, but by no means do they replace it. Another variation on this is to use the article title as a subheading to a chosen keyword (or keywords) – an improvement, but again, not as helpful as it could be.

In the indexing of any kind of document, the best practice is to provide a heading that represents the topic most directly, so that users can depend on finding what they need at the point of look-up, not having to consider under which broader heading the topic may be included. An item on comets should be indexed as 'comets' rather than just as 'solar system' or 'solar system: comets', for example. An index consisting of a succession of 'classified' heading sequences, in which sought terms are listed merely as subheadings under broader headings – with no possibility of direct look-up, is unhelpful to the user and should be avoided.

Title Words

Sometimes the index terms are taken directly from the title of the article; this can be satisfactory, but only when the title is truly and comprehensively indicative of the content and message, as may be the case with articles in scientific and medical journals. The quality of an index may otherwise be poor because the essence of the articles is not captured and valuable information relating to topics featured within the articles is ignored. Titles are often poor indicators of content and are certainly not always to be taken literally – an article about crimes in international banking and finance, bearing the title 'Laundering and whitewashing around the world' would not be helpfully indexed by using the two principal keywords from the title. Title length can vary according to the ideas of the author and editor and the house style of the publication; short titles can sometimes be uninformative, concealing the identity of interesting topics covered. As in any form of indexing, sole reliance on the words appearing in any part of the text (word-spotting) is usually unsatisfactory.

Whole titles are sometimes used as a basis for indexes, with the words manipulated on an automatic basis. The process enables all significant words – defined as any words not included in the 'stop list' – to feature as index terms. The 'stop list' normally consists of function words such as 'the', 'a', 'by', 'with' and 'for'. The resulting lists can be displayed in different forms, the best known of which are KWIC (KeyWord In Context) and KWOC (KeyWord Out of Context). In the KWIC form, the titles are usually rotated around a central 'search' column, with locators (such as dates and pages) ending the entry:

	Canning lines for soft drinks	Oct. 41–4
Canning lines for soft	**drinks**	Oct. 41–4
Canning	**lines** for soft drinks	Oct. 41–4
Canning lines for	**soft** drinks	Oct. 41–4

Long titles have to be arranged around the central column:

emissions from	**construction** sites in England. Gas	Jul. 88–9

The KWOC form is similar, but with the index term displayed in a column at the left of each entry, followed by the whole title and the locator(s). Both forms sometimes present the whole title in capital letters, or may capitalize only the index term column. The use of unaltered title words in keyword indexes raises the risk of separating references to articles on the same subject, but written by different authors using variant spellings ('oedema', 'edema') or different words ('breeze blocks', 'cinder blocks') or different word-forms ('mouse', 'mice'). There may also be confusion because terms that look the same, but that have different meanings, are interfiled ('grease-repellent *paper*'; 'Response to H J Smith's *paper* on pesticide safety'. Additionally, if an enquirer is searching by using a synonymous term not used in any title, nothing is found, because there are no helpful cross-references. Indexes constructed on this basis are still in use and can be effective as long as the searcher is familiar with the subject and its terminology and so knows all the terms under which relevant information might be found.

Periodicals in which the articles are presented in unambiguous technical terms, with highly indicative titles and comprehensive abstracts – appearing most often in the fields of science, medicine and technology – are more suited to these basic methods than are those in which imaginative, literary language is used.

Words and Ideas from Abstracts

Another source of indexing terms for an article can be its abstract, which is sometimes positioned at the head of the article or as an introduction to it. Before using such terms, the indexer must be certain that the abstract is of good quality and suitable length, and competently written, so that it accurately conveys the substance of the article. Different kinds of abstract can provide different words for index headings; an 'indicative' abstract provides a description of what is contained in the article, whereas an 'informative' abstract summarizes the information given. The principal danger of relying on abstracts as generators of index terms is that (unless the indexer is also the abstractor, which is sometimes the case) the indexing is done 'at second hand' rather than directly from the original. However, because the indexer is no longer relying just on words appearing in titles, there is the opportunity to add as headings any relevant sought terms that do not feature in the text.

Words and Ideas from the Text at Large

This method can give even better representation because the article as a whole is scrutinized. In practice, it often means that the indexer reads the article selectively, concentrating perhaps on the introduction, in which the aims of the work and the background are described, the method or operation and the outcome (what actually happened, what was observed and what conclusions were drawn).

Words from Thesauri and Other Vocabulary Lists

Control and continuity of vocabulary from year to year can be assisted by the use of a standard vocabulary such as a thesaurus of terms covering the relevant subject field. There is then no doubt as to which term, and which spelling of the term, should be used for indexing a particular topic. So long as the thesaurus is kept up to date by the addition of new topics and the insertion of necessary cross-references, it will continue to reflect the current and past coverage of the periodical. Some thesauri show against each term the date when it was first used (or the bibliographical source from which it was taken); an obsolete or 'no longer preferred' term has the date when its 'recommended' status was removed in the thesaurus, and the term(s) by which it has been replaced.

If a thesaurus or subject headings list is used, it is helpful to provide some user information about it, so that the selection criteria and structure of the index terms are understood. For example, the user guide in *Library & information science abstracts* states, in relation to the Subject Index:

> Every abstract in *LISA* is indexed with a general term taken from the *LISA* thesaurus, to which qualifying terms are added to increase the specificity of the string. In this case 'Library staff' is the general term to which 'Training' and 'Internet' are added to describe the main subject of the article. The index is then compiled from these subject strings using the chain indexing method. [Examples].
>
> The Subject Index also has entries, from the *LISA* thesaurus, which do not lead to abstract numbers but instead to other terms. For instance, if you look at 'Publishing', you see on the next lines 'narrower term Electronic publishing'. This indicates that you should now look at 'Electronic publishing' where you may find abstract numbers for abstracts on this more specific topic.
>
> [From *Library and information science abstracts*
> 1998 (9) (Bowker-Saur)]

Authority files
Even if no pre-existing list is used as a source of indexing terms, it is wise to build up an authority file, adding each new index heading to it; in this way, the indexer (and any colleagues or successors) has a record of terms already used and so can ensure that they are always employed in the same form and that new similar headings follow the same pattern. Any names

that are included in the index should also be entered in the authority file, with cross-references from any other form in which they might be sought by users.

Authors' Keywords

Authors of articles are sometimes asked to supply a small number (say up to five) keywords for each article, for use in the subject index. Although words provided from this source can be helpful to the indexer, they cannot be relied on as the sole basis for an index. Authors may not be sufficiently conversant with indexing techniques and therefore may tend to 'word-spot' or to suggest unsuitable word-forms. The indexer must ensure that each article is indexed consistently and adequately, with the inclusion of cross-references to link related terms, variant spellings, different words for the same topic. The finished product should be co-ordinated and harmonious.

Classification and Coding

It is also possible to index periodical articles using a system of coding or classification, in which topics are represented not by words but by alphabetical or numerical codes (or a combination of both). The system may be one of the well-known and internationally used ones such as the Dewey Decimal Classification (DDC), the Universal Decimal Classification (UDC) and the Library of Congress Classification (LC), or a unique system tailored to the subject coverage and vocabulary of the journal in question and to the precise needs of its readers. Using such a system, the indexer must identify the indexable topics (at the appropriate level) and convert them into the class numbers or codes that most suitably represent them – as is done for books and other materials being entered in library catalogues. Because the class numbers and codes from the widely used systems are internationally understood, they can be used in indexing and abstracting services to bring together articles in different languages and from assorted countries. In the Dewey Decimal Classification, for example, the class number 370 represents the concept 'education', whatever the language of the writer or reader.

Complex entries

Forming sets of entries (headings plus locators) for some types of periodical article can be more complicated than for books.

Authors' Names

As with any kind of name index, it may be necessary to choose the form of name to be used for authors who are cited in different ways – such as full given and family names, best-known given name and family name, and initials and family name – and to provide *see* cross-references from other forms (see 'Personal names' in Chapter 4). Some indexes reproduce the authors' names as fully as they appear at the head of the articles, but in others space considerations may determine that initials, rather than first names, are used and so the indexer must find some way of distinguishing two or more authors with the same name. In cumulated indexes both these aspects of name treatment gain particular importance. Cumulations also have to take account of any changes of name that occur during the working life of an author.

It is not usually necessary to include academic or occupational titles or positions, or institutional affiliations, in index headings, except possibly in cases where two people with the same name need to be distinguished. There are frequent instances of similar names occurring in articles – Smith, T., Smith, T.A., Smith, Terry A, and so on. The indexer should not assume that these are the same person or attempt to guess which is which. Unless the situation is incontrovertibly clear from other evidence, the indexer should refer the query to the person with editorial responsibility.

Multiple authorship of articles is common in scientific journals, as when all the members of a research team are attributed; in a few cases, over a hundred names have been reported. Entries in the author index for such articles can take one of several forms (see 'Multiple authorship' later in this chapter).

Other Names

Names of people other than the authors of articles – such as book reviewers – feature in indexes to some periodicals. Corporate names and brand names of products may also be included. If they appear in the same sequence as the authors, their role should be distinguished in some way. This can be done, for example, by typographical style:

Triesman, J. on Smith's *History of Cairo* 245

or by a modifier or subheading:

MacDonald, M.H., reviews by 56, 92, 141

or by abbreviation:

Jones, T.H.(R) 136, 179 [R = reviewer]

'Subjects'

Headings for subjects of articles are sometimes necessarily lengthy, particularly if they employ the article title, or a summary of it, or a structured chain of keywords representing it:

Crops – Genetically modified organisms – Safety – Public opinion – International trade – European Union
[From *British humanities index* (1999) (1) (Bowker-Saur)]

In cumulations, long sequences of subheadings can develop, which will almost certainly need editing and reducing before final sorting (see 'Subheading sequences' below).

Headings are presented in various styles, using bold and italic as well as capitalization and abbreviations, to distinguish them from the other parts of the entry. Styling differs from index to index, but must be consistent within any one index:

PUBLISHING
Academic textbook writing (Evans, T.F.E.) 98
Samizdat in the Soviet Union (Ivanova, K.L.) 43

INTERIOR DESIGN Restaurant and hairdressing salon interiors (N) (1998) **61** Apr 67 [N = News item]

monetary policy
  Bank of England has second thoughts (N) Feb. 286 [N = news item]
  Urban renewal: the effect of government policies, 1985–95 Jun. 234–57

Locators

Locators can be intricate when they need to include indicators of different kinds of content (to be helpful to the user), or bibliographical citations (as in the case of an index to a group of periodicals within a particular subject field, or to publications related in some other way). Clarity of presentation is vital and the system should be explained in the introductory note. Prefixes and suffixes can be added to locators, to indicate the kind of item:

window frames A101, F213
thermal imaging 56(A), 96 (E), 112–15(F), 192(R)
[A = advertisement, E = editorial, F = feature, R = book review]

Entries in some periodical indexes give only the number of the page on which the article starts. This gives the index user no help in distinguishing a longer (potentially more informative) article from a briefer note; the indexer should ensure that the page range is given in entries relating to the subjects of whole articles and also to their authors. This indication is also important for information searchers wishing to request copies of articles – they need to be able to specify the numbers of the pages they require. Entries for topics that are dealt with only on certain pages within the articles should be accompanied only by their relevant page numbers, not by the whole page range (see 'Indicating the position – the locators' in Chapter 4).

Some items in periodicals include the authors' names only at the end. The author entry should still include the numbers of all the pages, not just the last one on which the name is presented.

Entries for authors responsible for many articles may contain long strings of numbers. Sometimes this is acceptable, and index users may be content to work right through the string, checking each article in turn for information. It is more helpful to distinguish the different references by

the subject of the article (perhaps grouping the references by subject), or
by its title, or to give abbreviations to show the types of article:

Moran, M.
Additives in baby food 34–35
Dieting hazards 145
Eating disorders in adolescence 46–57
Food safety in restaurants 224–225
[etc.]

Barry, J.I.
articles 67–8, 91–3, 145–67, 220–20, 342–4, 355–6
correspondence 23, 35, 45, 389, 413
reviews 13, 29, 42, 55

Powell, M.J. 11–15(A), 22(R), 35(L), 45–47(A) [etc.]
[A = article, L = letter, R = review}

If the index is just for one volume and the page numbers are continuous throughout the volume (starting at 1 in the first issue and finishing at
1241 with the last, for example), the locator need consist only of the page
numbers. It can be useful, though, for the index user to be told the date,
month or part number as well, particularly if the issues of the periodical are
loose (not bound together in an annual volume). If, perhaps for space reasons, individual issue details cannot be included, the page allocation for each
issue can be indicated at the head of the index, with the introductory note:

1–90 January
91–180 February
181–276 March
[etc.]

For an index to a periodical of which each issue starts afresh at page
1 – such as a newspaper or a popular magazine – dates or issue numbers
are essential. Additionally, in the case of newspapers, because of the size
of the pages, page numbers may not be sufficiently precise for the location of an item, so column data is often added to show the exact position
on the page.

Boston Symphony Orchestra 24 July 14b   [page 14, column b]

The locators in a cumulated index to a single journal (covering, say, five years) must include sufficient date and volume information to guide the user to the correct component:

DNA testing (2000) 29(3): 70–71   [year, volume, part, pages]

In an index to an abstracting or indexing journal, in which each abstract or description has a unique number, that number may be used as a locator:

Drugs: 1707–1714
Ducati 996 racing motor cycles: 1268
                    [From *Abstracts in new technologies and engineering*
                                    (1999) **3** (1)(Bowker-Saur)]

Also in abstracting and indexing journals (depending on the internal arrangement of the content), bibliographical citations – sometimes very abbreviated – may appear as locators:

tax planning IBFL **10** (12) 1992 172–3
[IBFL = *International Banking and Financial Law*]

It is helpful if the indexer can make use of the journal's own database of bibliographical citations for the journal's articles, so that it is not necessary to keyboard the data separately as part of the input process. The citations can then be used as locators, or as subentries – depending on the nature and needs of the index – and the authors' names can form the basis of the author index. Alternatively, the citations can sometimes be freely downloaded from another database (so long as copyright conditions allow).

Subheading Sequences

The index to just a single volume of a periodical may well be lengthy, given the need to provide user access to several different types of heading and subheading. A cumulated index is likely to consist – in its raw, unedited state – of merged entries with long strings of locators and with subheadings that are similar but not identical.

Subheading sequences must be broken up or distinguished in some way so that the user can more easily select the relevant items. The best ways of doing this are to organize the locators into related clusters using group subheadings:

> nuclear power stations:
> India **98**: 34–5, 91–5; **99**: 314, 424; **00**: 56–7, 78–80
> [year in bold]
> United Kingdom **98**: 41–2, 89–90; **99**: 223–4, 301–2;
> **00**: 12–15
> [etc.]

or to list each locator separately with its own subheading:

> graduates:
> female, career choice 16(1) Apr 76–77
> recruitment by finance industry 17(3) Oct 156–157
> [etc.]

or to use the article titles (which may provide greater specificity because the exact words are used, but at the same time have the disadvantage that items on a similar aspect may be widely separated in the subheading sequence):

> museums:
> Life under the Tudors: the Mary Rose Museum May 99
> 16–20
> Museum documentation and information management Oct
> 97 34–5
> New galleries for old: refurbishment at Newtown Dec 98
> 67–8
> Odd objects: using the internet Jan 97 3–4
> Salvage and treasure at the Mary Rose Museum Feb 98 22–3

It is also common practice to list as subheadings the titles of reviewed books, under the heading 'Book reviews', and – similarly – the titles of articles belonging to a series under the heading for the series. This approach is useful, as it brings scattered references under a sought heading, but it should not be the only approach to the titles.

Cross-references

The use of cross-references (*see* and *see also*) in periodical indexes follows the same rules as for indexing any other kind of document (see 'Cross-references' in Chapter 4), but – because of some special characteristics of periodical articles – additional conventions for the formation of the complete entries are sometimes needed.

Multiple authorship

The circumstance of multiple authorship in academic and learned journals is a case in point. For an article with (say) four authors it is advisable to provide access from the family names of all the authors. There are various ways of dealing with this. Before deciding on the most suitable method, the indexer and editor need to consider the kinds of enquiry for which the author index will be used. Some users will wish to look for a known article by a known author or authors. Others will want to search for all work, or the latest work, in which a particular individual has been involved.

It should also be noted that – depending on the ethos of the particular group of authors – the authors' names may be given in order of rank within their employing organizations, in alphabetical order of family name, or in order of the size or importance of their contribution to the article. The first-named author may therefore be the principal author from a bibliographical standpoint, but not necessarily as far as the subject community is concerned. It is common, too, for a sequence of articles reporting progress on a project, and all written by the same authors, each to be published with the authors' names given in a different order. In this case, it is essential for all the names to be accessible through the index – not concealed by the use of 'and others' or '*et al*'.

The situation is often neatly handled by giving full details under the name of the first-named author, and having *see* cross-references from the names of the other authors. Exact formations can differ, according to taste and house style. For example:

Entries under individual authors' names, with no indication of which is named first on the article or of the title of the article:

Higgins, J. 139
Morris, A. 139
Potter, M. 139
Selby, C. 139

Full author/title entry under the first-named author. Cross-references (containing all authors' names) from each co-author:

> Higgins, J. *see* Morris, A., Higgins, J., Potter, M. and Selby, C.
> Morris, A., Higgins, J., Potter, M. and Selby, C. Heavy metal soil analysis 139–43
> Potter, M. *see* Morris, A., Higgins, J., Potter, M. and Selby, C.
> Selby, C. *see* Morris, A., Higgins, J., Potter, M. and Selby, C.

Full author/title entry under the first-named author. Cross-references (using 'and others' or '*et al*') from each co-author:

> Higgins, J. *see* Morris, A. and others [or *et al*]
> Morris, A., Higgins, J., Potter, M. and Selby, C., Heavy metal soil analysis 139–43
> Potter, M. *see* Morris, A. and others [or *et al*]
> Selby, C. *see* Morris, A. and others [or *et al*]

As above, but with locators after each cross-reference:

> Higgins, J. *see* Morris, A. and others [or *et al*] 139–43
> Morris, A., Higgins, J., Potter, M. and Selby, C., Heavy metal soil analysis 139–43
> Potter, M. *see* Morris, A. and others [or *et al*] 139–43
> Selby, C. *see* Morris, A. and others [or *et al*] 139–43

Abbreviated author/title entry under the first-named author. Cross-references (using 'and others' or '*et al*') from each co-author:

> Higgins, J. *see* Morris, A. and others [or *et al*]
> Morris, A. and others [or *et al*] Heavy metal soil analysis 139–43
> Potter, M. *see* Morris, A. and others [or *et al*]
> Selby, C. *see* Morris, A. and others [or *et al*]

As above, but with locators after each cross-reference:

> Higgins, J. *see* Morris, A. and others [or *et al*] 139–43
> Morris, A. and others [or *et al*] Heavy metal soil analysis 139–43

> Potter, M. *see* Morris, A. and others [or *et al*] 139–43
> Selby, C. *see* Morris, A. and others [or *et al*] 139–43

Full details could conceivably be given against each participating author (multiple entry), but this enlarges the index without being a great deal more helpful, and can appear messy and confusing. It often happens that a team of workers publishes several articles one after the other, as the project progresses. To give each author's name a full entry for every article may make for a cumbersome index, particularly if it is a cumulated index for several volumes. In this case, it may be adequate to put the full entry under the first author (adding 'and others' or '*et al*') and to make *see* cross-references from the others. If it is necessary to distinguish the articles from each other in the *see* cross-references, each cross-reference is followed by the locator for the article.

It is most helpful (and more equitable) to give the full complement of authors' names, at least in the entry under the first-named author, rather than to summarize as 'and others' or '*et al*'. The 'secondary' authors have an equal right and need to be traceable through indexes, and index users need as much information as possible in order to be able to distinguish one set of authors from another. The use of 'and others', rather than the Latin *et al*, is to be preferred – being more readily understood. Nevertheless, for subject fields in which *et al* is widely known, the Latin phrase has the advantage of being shorter – often an important consideration in indexing for publication in print.

Related topics
The enormous variety of topics, aspects of topics and links between topics that are treated in periodical articles requires the indexer to be adept at supplying informative cross-references. Some quite correct, but very brief, cross-references may seem odd at first sight:

> children *see also* building materials
> sin *see* shopping
> soldiers *see also* fashion

Where cross-references are necessary between topics that have no obvious connection, it is helpful to extend the headings to show the link:

children *see also* building materials, toxic effects
sin *see* shopping, moral aspects

Index sequences and arrangements

There is a choice to be made, for any periodical, between providing separate index sequences for different types of content, and integrating them into a single sequence (to enable quick look-up) often with indicative subheadings, e.g. Review.
Heading and sequence types include:

Author-title
Name (all kinds)
Subject
Bibliographical
Product
Advertisers
Reviews

and may give index sets such as:

Author index; subject and name index; source index
Author index; subject index; source index
Name index; subject index
Author index; subject index
Subject index; author index; case index; legislation index; book
    review index
Products index; advertisers index

The relative importance of the index sequences needs consideration. There may be no need for an author index, if most of the articles are written by members of staff of the serial – they may not be known, or it may depend on the type of article (but see also 'Extracts' earlier in this chapter).
Separate sequences require the intending index user to proceed in two stages; first to decide which kind of heading is to be searched for, then to look it up in the right sequence. This may well suit the informed, information-skilled user, who is familiar with the vocabulary and the house style

of the periodical, who understands clearly the distinction between the sequences and who perhaps uses one particular sequence more than any other. It is less satisfactory for people less used to consulting indexes, who expect just to look something up in 'the' index, without having to stop to consider which kind of heading their enquiry falls under. They may also be slightly confused by the fact that a heading may appear in more than one sequence. The name of a person, for example, may quite correctly be included in both the 'author' sequence (as the writer of an article in the periodical) and also in the 'subject' sequence (because she, or her work in her special field, is discussed in an article written by someone else). If there is a sequence called a 'name index' there can be uncertainty whether 'works by' and 'works about' a person should all go into it.

Almost all indexes require an introductory note (see 'Introductory note' below) to explain them. Indexes containing separate sequences have a special need for explanation, to indicate the number and nature of the sequences and to show which should be consulted for a particular enquiry.

Frequency and Position of Index

It is comparatively rare to find a periodical that has an index in each issue; if there is an index, it may be to that issue alone or it may cumulate throughout the year or volume. Usually, though, readers have to rely on the contents list as a finding aid. Some titles that appear monthly have interim indexes every quarter or half-year, culminating with the annual index. From the user's point of view, an index in each issue would be helpful, as contents lists give only a broad indication of the subject. Indexers can perhaps persuade editors and publishers to remedy this lack of access.

An index may be produced annually or for each volume; volumes and years sometimes coincide, but there is great variation between titles, with some having more than one volume per year and others having volumes that span more than a year. The physical embodiment of annual indexes also varies. Some are produced as separate pamphlet-type publications that can be filed or bound in with the year's or volume's issues; others are printed as part of the final issue of the year or volume, and – less usefully – some are printed as part of the first (or a later) issue of the following year or volume. Indexers taking on the compilation of indexes to periodicals need to discuss the timing of index publication and to plan their schedule of work carefully. An index that is to appear in the final issue must include index headings for the contents of that issue, so the indexer must be able to work very quickly in the last stages in order to produce the final index for incorporation.

In a multisequence index (authors, subjects, products, for example) the most important sequence – if it is possible to identify one – should be placed first. The subject sequence is often judged to be the principal one, but each case must be decided in context, taking into account the needs of particular reader groups and the purposes for which the index is most likely to be used. The final order is usually at the discretion of the editor, but the indexer's advice can be valuable.

Order Within the Index

Alphabetical arrangement is dealt with in detail in Chapter 5 and all that is said there applies equally to periodicals. When compiling the first index to a new periodical, the indexer should compare the results of both methods (word-by-word and letter-by-letter), to discover whether one gives a more helpful arrangement than the other. If there is little advantage either way, the guideline in BS ISO 999 (British Standards Institution, 1996, subclause 8.2) – to use the word-by-word method – should be followed. If the periodical is produced by an organization that has a house style for all its publications, this is likely to impose one of the methods on the indexer; if the result is inferior, the indexer should notify the editor of the disadvantages for the users, and hope to induce a change of mind.

Two alphabetical matters in particular may cause concern to indexers of periodicals. One is the handling of subheadings, which can sometimes be long and contain 'non-significant' words (see 'Subheading sequences' earlier in this chapter). The other, relevant in particular to medical and scientific literature, is the treatment of prefixes in chemical, pharmaceutical and biological names (see 'Prefixes' in Chapter 5, and 'Medicine' and 'Science and technology' in Chapter 8).

Introductory note

Most indexes need an introduction for the user (see 'Introductory note' in Chapter 5), but for periodical indexes they can be crucial in explaining the structure and display to the intending user. If the index is a single sequence, containing different kinds of headings and subheadings that are distinguished from each other typographically, and including locators that are more complex than just sets of page numbers or that have abbreviations attached to them, it is essential to explain the use of type, the form of the locators, and the meanings of the abbreviations.

Cumulations

The compilation of cumulative periodical indexes demands far more than just merging the annual or volume indexes. Mere amalgamation of such pre-existing indexes is likely to result in:

- headings and subheadings that are similar but not identical
- headings and subheadings containing outdated terms
- long strings of undifferentiated locators in some entries
- mixed subheading sequences
- insufficient cross-references and others that are incomplete
- abbreviations, directions and styles of presentation that do not observe current practice (if the cumulation includes indexes compiled decades ago)

These features are not in themselves indicative of the varying quality of the earlier indexes; they reflect changes in vocabulary and in indexing styles that have taken place over the relevant period of time, during which the indexing policy for the journal may also have changed in terms of what is covered and in what detail. If there have been successive indexers during that time – and particularly if there was no written practice guide nor any record of indexing decisions – there are likely to be differences in their individual styles and practices, which will need harmonization.

Some indexers would prefer to start afresh, when faced with a collection of dissimilar annual indexes compiled by other people, in order to ensure consistency of coverage, approach and presentation. Others would rather use the available entries as a raw database on which to work and to concentrate on refining and remodelling them. Whichever method is employed, a policy must be agreed on coverage (which kind of content is to be included and which excluded), how the subject headings are to be constructed (freely taken from the text, taken from a standard vocabulary, using manipulated titles), the forms of personal name to be used (full, initials), the nature of the locators, the indication of content type (illustrations, bibliographical data), and the alphabetical (or other) order of entries and subentries.

An indexer who is compiling annual indexes and, at the same time, feeding the entries into a cumulation for later publication, can maintain a measure of control over the vocabulary, ensuring as much consistency as possible and using the ongoing cumulation as a source of headings and cross-references. Final editing of the cumulation is still essential, but the amendments are reduced in number.

Working Arrangements

Because of the continuing nature of periodicals indexing, with indexers sometimes working over extended periods, the relationship between the indexer and the client can become closer than applies to a book indexer doing various one-off jobs. Periodicals indexers are more likely to be involved in providing advice leading to policy decisions affecting the content and compilation of indexes – including the development of a house style for indexes – and may be regarded by clients as important semi-permanent members of the editorial team.

Working out and providing estimates for periodicals indexing jobs can be more difficult than for book indexes, because the amount of work is harder to predict. Detailed discussions need to take place, so that the indexer can gain a clear idea of coverage, level of indexing, amount of text, presentation, styling, and the amount of data (such as bibliographical citations) that can be supplied direct from the client's own electronic base. Any changes of editor – and of publisher – can have effects on policies relating to the index; at such times the indexer has a particular responsibility to maintain continuity of approach.

Some periodicals indexing is done on a co-operative basis, with indexers (freelance or in-house) working together and dividing up the work between them – perhaps by content type. This can work well, so long as each member of the team understands and observes the ground rules and there is the opportunity and atmosphere for exchange of information and discussion of tricky points. There can also be co-operation in the cumulation of indexes, with the work being split on the basis of date, content type, or subject. The Wheatley Medal – awarded each year by the Society of Indexers and the Library Association for an outstanding index published in the United Kingdom – was won in 1995 by Ruth Richardson and Robert Thorne (1994) for *'The Builder' illustrations index 1843–1883*.

References

Ashcroft, Linda and Langdon, Colin (1999) The case for electronic journals. *Library Association Record*, **101**, 706–707

British Standards Institution (1996) *Information and documentation – guidelines for the content, organization and presentation of indexes*. BS ISO 999: 1996. London: British Standards Institution

Richardson, Ruth and Thorne, Robert (1994) *'The Builder' illustrations index 1843–1883*. London: The Builder Group and Hutton and Rostron in association with the Institute of Historical Research

Ulrich's international periodicals directory (2000). New York: Bowker

Willings press guide (2000). Teddington, Middx: Hollis

Further Reading

Beare, Geraldine (1999) *Indexing newspapers, magazines and other periodicals*. Occasional papers on indexing: no. 4. Sheffield: Society of Indexers

Blake, Doreen, Clarke, Michèle, McCarthy, Anne, and Morrison, June (1995). *Indexing the medical and biological sciences*. Occasional papers on indexing, no. 3. Sheffield: Society of Indexers (Ch.4: Journals)

Wellisch, Hans H. (1995) *Indexing from A to Z* 2nd edn. New York: H.W. Wilson (pp. 347–354: Periodicals)

CHAPTER SEVEN

Images and sound (audio) recordings

Indexability and Indexing Needs

Images and sounds are just as suitable for indexing as are portions of text. The extent to which they are indexed depends on their nature and purpose and on any relationship to a text with which they may be associated. The purposes for which image and audio materials (sometimes referred to loosely as non-book, non-print, non-text, or audiovisual materials) are used may be educational, artistic, documentary, instructional, and recreational.

The indexing of illustrations and sound materials that accompany – in a supporting role – the content of textbooks, reports, manuals, guides, and periodical articles, is normally straightforward. Because they supplement the text and are not the primary conveyors of information, it is often sufficient to italicize the relevant locator or to add a suitable abbreviation in order to signify that there is a relevant illustration on page 227 or an example on Side A, Band 3 of a certain disk (see 'Indicating the position – the locators' in Chapter 4). This by no means belittles the quality of the items, but recognizes that in the context of a particular document, they play a subsidiary part.

This chapter is principally concerned with images and sound materials – and combinations of the two – that are significant in their own right. Most aspects of human life and activity are portrayed in them, so their importance as sources of information requires that they are well indexed (see Jacobs (1999) on images). The role of the indexer is therefore to analyse and represent the content in some detail, as with the text of a book, and not just to indicate their location in relation to text. Some indexers start to develop their image-indexing and audio-indexing skills when their own collections of family photographs and recordings – built up over several years and perhaps added to by succeeding generations – become too large for easy retrieval. Some may be stimulated to create their own thesauri or classification schemes for the purpose.

It can happen that illustrations that were originally seen as secondary to the text in which they were published, and that were indexed only as relevant to particular sections of the text, are extracted at a later date – sometimes decades later – and published as a collection having its own more detailed index. Alternatively, a comprehensive index may be published on its own (without the illustrations), giving the precise locations so that users can easily locate a desired image in the original document; one example of this 'after-the-fact' type of index is the illustrations index to the journal *The Builder* (Richardson and Thorne, 1994), which was awarded the Wheatley Medal.

Some materials contain both images and sounds, each medium supporting the other but at the same time being itself important. A piece of archive film showing well-known political figures of the 1930s may be interesting not only because of their physical appearances, what they are doing, and the background against which they are shown, but also on account of the sound of their voices, their accents and modes of speech and what they are saying. Materials like this, which may have been very lightly indexed – if indexed at all – at the time of production, can be extremely rich in indexable elements by the time they reach the archival stage. There may also be associated, but separate, text items, in which case the texts play the secondary part – a series of posters advertising a film, and the press reviews following its premiere, for example, or a leaflet listing the contents of a language tuition tape. Images are commonly accompanied by text in captions and annotations, but the images are the primary feature.

The materials are widely distributed among organizations of many different kinds (all of which are potential sources of work for the indexer):

- museums
- public libraries
- film archives
- film libraries
- press agencies
- photo agencies
- stock shot libraries
- sound archives
- historical centres
- manufacturing companies
- service providers
- newspaper libraries
- learned societies
- professional associations
- workplace libraries
- broadcasting organizations
- film companies
- film distributors
- photographers
- university departments
- schools
- entertainment organizations

Individuals, too, have collections – sometimes large – of slides, prints, videos, audiotapes and CDs.

Some collections are enormous; national museums and galleries, newspaper libraries, broadcasting organizations, manufacturing company archives, and commercial photolibraries, for example, may hold millions, some of which date back to the earliest days of photography, cinematography and sound recording. Exhibitions and displays, catalogues, descriptive and themed publications give an indication of the range of subjects covered by some of the repositories open to the public. Indexers considering working in the field can find it helpful to study these and observe the detail in which the items can be described and indexed.

Many formats exist, from the latest forms of electronic record, to materials that are no longer made and which are so fragile or unstable that they can only be handled under controlled conditions. Many older individual items and collections exist in private and public hands, and constitute a very valuable archive resource – accessible only through good and often very detailed indexing; some remain unindexed and so offer an opportunity for present-day indexers.

User needs vary according to the collection of materials. Images are required for inclusion in:

- published books and periodicals
- TV and radio programmes
- films
- displays and exhibitions
- government information campaigns
- educational materials
- advertisements
- corporate internal reports
- manufacturers' catalogues
- art films and videos
- training materials

Sound items similarly have a range of uses in broadcasting, education, research, advertising, historical and social research, the arts, musicology, training, entertainment, and leisure.

Groups of images and sound recordings are often created or collected because they relate to a common theme – rivers of Scotland, nuclear power generation, the Bauhaus school of architecture, wedding music of Eastern Europe – or perhaps are examples of particular materials or types – Victorian lantern slides on religious and social themes, or old dictating machine disk recordings of Northumbrian folk tales and songs. Each image or sound item, or group of items, can be of interest from many different aspects – subject, date, location, creator or originator, publisher or producer, type of item (single black and white photograph, set of colour slides, video, CD-ROM, audiocassette), and its associations with events or people or organizations. User needs can reflect any one of these or any combination of them, so cataloguing and indexing should aim to ensure the provision of multiple access points. Guidance on compiling catalogue records (descriptions) for images and sound recordings is given in the *Anglo-American cataloguing rules (AACR2)* (Gorman and Winkler, 1988, Chapters 3, 6, 7 and 8).

This chapter concentrates on the indexing of subject content and thematic associations, for which a multifaceted approach is often needed. The 'what, where and when' of an image (many vehicles on a busy section of the M6 motorway near Lancaster, on a Saturday in June 2000) or of an audiotape (sheep being herded down from the summer pasture in Provence, France, 1985) can often easily be set down in words – but to go on to specify what that scene and those sounds symbolize ('pollution' or 'freedom to travel'; 'rural idyll' or 'the lonely life of the shepherd') or what kind of mood they represent (gloom or contentment) is more difficult. The overall indexing guideline, that user needs should determine the type and detail of indexing, still applies, but individual images and sound recordings can be used for several purposes – some of them very different from those for which they were created. The interpretation of images and sounds is also affected by the culture, experience, background, mood, age, and attitudes of the viewer and listener.

The size of a commercially published book-type index is often restricted by the space available for it, forcing the indexer to limit the number of entries and to rely on cross-references rather than detailed double entries. This is particularly unfortunate when images and sound materials are involved. For effective and speedy retrieval, each of these items may require many index terms, each representing a separate topic. In addition, users often need immediate results at the first look-up, not wishing (or having time) to follow up several cross-references. Indexes for use within an organization, therefore, should be able to incorporate as many terms as are needed and employ multiple entry rather than cross-references.

A particularly wide, and sometimes specialized, knowledge is needed for the indexing of images and sounds, particularly in historical and archival collections. The ability to recognize background scenes and sounds can be crucial in clarifying a date, location, or situation. The indexer may need to allow time for consideration, along with the client or colleagues, of the level and detail required and to decide which is the most suitable for the task in hand. Much depends on what can be expected of the users – not only the kinds of enquiry they make and the range of topics of interest, but their levels of knowledge and searching skills, and whether they are willing to spend time browsing through a selection of items. Schroeder (1998a), in the context of a corporate manufacturer's archive, specifies three types of necessary knowledge – professional (indexing theory and technique), subject (departmental procedures and product information) and client needs (priorities; cultural, historical, political and emotional perspectives).

There is currently a high level of interest in image retrieval methods among people from different fields of activity – multimedia technologists, information retrieval specialists, image collection managers, indexers, and others. Recent conferences in the UK on 'The challenge of image retrieval' have included sessions on image metadata and content-based image retrieval (Frost, 1999). Research into the use of non-verbal methods – such as shape-matching – and into speech-recognition techniques for the retrieval of extracts from sound recordings, has been described by Cawkell (1998), Enser (1995), and Lancaster (1998, Ch.13). These methods are interesting, but outside the scope of this book, which is concerned with the kind of indexing practised by most working indexers, who are reliant on the informed and imaginative use of words. However, any opportunities for indexers and researchers to work together are worth exploring with enthusiasm.

Sequences

The existence of a multiplicity of types of heading in image and sound indexes may justify the placing of entries into separate sequences. The index to the illustrations in *The Builder* magazine, by Richardson and Thorne (1994), contains six sequences (all explained in a user guide to the index): year, page number, type of illustration; title of illustration; names of people associated with the subjects of the illustrations; places; subjects (using the enriched keyword system of the Royal Institute of British Architects (RIBA); observations and comments. Multiple sequences are also presented in *The Gilbert and Sullivan photofinder: an index to published illustrations of Savoy Opera* (Dixon, 1995) – names of performers, names of characters, names of operas, names of people associated with the Savoy Opera and names of some places associated with the productions.

Typical sequences for moving image indexes could be: names of people (anyone involved with the creation, production and performance of the film or video – director, producer, actors, screenplay writer, camera personnel, make-up artists, costumiers, musicians, etc.); titles of films, videos, and TV programmes; genres; subjects; locations; dates. Sound materials require a similar mix of headings for creative, performing and production personnel, locations and dates, genres and subjects.

Vocabulary control

The importance of strict vocabulary control in image and sound indexing is underlined by Jacobs (1999). The immense range of topics that may be represented in a large image collection – literally anything under the sun, and around it, and of it – together with the assortment of needs for images, make it essential to index consistently and not to scatter references to a topic under different headings. Apart from the general lists and schemes, covering all topics, used in libraries – Dewey Decimal Classification, Universal Decimal Classification, Library of Congress Classification and Subject Headings, for example – there are specialist thesauri and schemes covering certain subject fields. These include the *Art and architecture thesaurus* (Petersen, 1994), the *Thesaurus for graphic materials* (Library of Congress, 1995), TELCLASS (Evans, 1987), and Iconclass (Waal, 1973–1985). A specialist collection with unique coverage, content and requirements may be best indexed with a thesaurus especially developed for its needs; a case in point is described by the Shoah Visual History Foundation and Crystal (1998).

Images – Categorization and Features

Images are commonly divided into two categories: still and moving. Certain items from different categories can be closely related – a still (a single shot) taken from a film, for example. They can be modern or archival – a film showing an eye operation in progress, using the latest surgical technique, or a glass negative of a very early eye operation.

Images now being added to collections are frequently in digital form – CD (compact disk) and DVD (digital video disk, or digital versatile disk), for example – and some items from existing stocks have been digitized. The process of conversion of some older materials will continue, but many valuable items are likely to remain in their original form, and previously unknown private collections are discovered from time to time. Indexers will need, therefore, to continue to work with a range of image materials.

Certain features may be easily identified and recorded in catalogue descriptions of images – and can be used as index terms as required – title or caption, name of photographer, and the date, for example, and physical features such as the size or extent, and format. If an image has no title or caption, the indexer may have to create one. In some cases it may be sufficient, for the purposes of the collection or the publication, to index very simply from the information provided with the image. In other cases, more detailed analysis of content may be necessary, looking not just at the principal character or item but also at others playing secondary roles and at the background. Then there is the question of what the image could be said to represent and what mental associations it might stimulate; this could be relevant if the image might be wanted as an illustration in a book, or for display in a themed exhibition, or as a background to an advertisement.

Descriptions of these aspects of pictorial subject indexing, by Enser (1995), Jacobs (1999) and Lancaster (1998, Ch.13), all refer to the three approaches suggested by Panofsky (1955): pre-iconography (the main subject matter and the kinds of things, people and places shown), iconography (the secondary subject matter and the individually named things, people, places and events) and iconology (what the image means). Meaning in images is of course also influenced by features such as colour, contrast, background, light and shade, angle, juxtaposition, as well the subjectivity of viewers and the conditions in which the images are viewed. Schroeder (1998b) describes a layered approach to indexing images in the media archives of a large manufacturing corporation. The object layer represents the objects appearing in the image, ranked according to importance. The style layer concerns the purpose for which the image was created (documentary, advertising, engineering testing, for example). The implication layer relates to the point of the image, its uniqueness and information value, the reason why someone would wish to look at it.

Some indexes employ co-ordinated headings, in which all the subject (and some form) elements are combined in a single heading: Wales, farms, sheep, landscape, winter, black and white print; markets, flowers, Amsterdam, dawn, colour transparency. This kind of heading provides a very informative summary of content, but requires an agreed citation order for the various elements (people, objects, activity, place, time/season, background, for example) and also needs either multiple entry (using rotated forms of the heading) or cross-references leading from those elements cited second, third and so on.

Still images

Still images include:

- photographs (single items and collections; prints, negatives, transparencies, slides)
- art works (original paintings, drawings, cartoons, caricatures, prints)
- reproductions of art works (prints, halftones; details from works of art)
- designs
- overhead projection (OHP) sheets
- technical drawings (diagrams, flowcharts))
- architectural plans
- maps (relief, political, administrative, military, meteorological)
- charts (aeronautical, celestial, nautical)
- satellite images
- pictorial catalogues
- advertisement illustrations
- book cover and magazine cover illustrations
- clip art and click art
- x-ray images (medical, forensic, archaeological, art research and conservation)
- halftones (printed reproductions of photographs in books, serials and other publications)
- lantern slides
- artists' impressions

Some images are typically the work of individuals, others the result of collective or co-operative work. Computer-aided design is frequently employed for the preparation of technical drawings and is also used by some artists in the creation of art works. Names of originators and designers (individual and corporate) may need to be indexed. Storage media for images range from paper through film, glass, and microform (film and fiche), to CD-ROM, and online and other digitized forms. The electronic methods not only have the capacity to hold very large numbers of images, but can enable keyword searching in titles, captions and other elements of descriptive records.

Individual items are normally identified by, at least, a caption, which may provide a minimum of information or much detail. A posed photograph of a group of people, for example, may be identified only as 'Class 5, Dimsietown School, 1967' or may be accompanied by a numbered key-list of names of all the pupils, the teachers, the exact date, and the name of the photographer or studio. A collection of slides may just be labelled 'Liverpool in the 1950s' or may have, for each slide, details of the scene, the building, the people, the event, the exact date and time of day, as well as a note of the kind of film and the apertures and speeds relating to each shot.

Halftones used to accompany text in printed publications often have only brief information attached to them, aimed at indicating their relevance to a particular section of text. Sometimes they are placed individually or in small groups throughout a book, sometimes all collected in one section. An image may be used with different captions (sometimes conveying dissimilar messages or moods) in more than one publication or even in the same publication; this is because 'library pictures' used by the published and broadcast media can be differently interpreted and so can be used and reused effectively – but they can pose a dilemma for an indexer. Books that consist mainly of photographs concentrating on a single theme, with explanatory and commenting text – such as *Another way of telling* by Berger and Mohr (1982), which features many photographs about the lives of mountain peasants in France but which is also concerned with the ambiguity of photographs and the meaning of appearances – may require equal indexing coverage for the images and the text.

Still image collections may be complemented by sound recordings (of interviews, reminiscences, spoken extracts from press reports of the time) and original documentation. The descriptive cataloguing of such collections should make clear what each 'package' consists of, and the indexer should ensure that the materials are consistently indexed and that the user can see which kind of material is referred to in a particular index entry.

Some terms appearing in the descriptive records of images may be used as index terms:

- names of artists, photographers, designers, illustrators
- original and translated titles (*La Gioconda/Mona Lisa*)
- dates of production

- periods, schools, movements, and styles (High Renaissance, mannerism)
- genres (portrait, landscape)
- materials and media (oil on canvas, Bromesko)
- sizes
- photographic, printing and reproduction process (daguerreotype, lithograph)
- places of publication
- colour and type (black and white, colour, sepia, tinted; positive, negative)
- names of people or organizations involved in production, publication, distribution
- special effects (solarized, bas-relief, 'pen and ink')
- angle, perspective (aerial, wide-angle)

From the point of view of subject content, examination of an image may reveal several indexable items. Recognizing them all and judging their significance demands visual and imaginative dexterity. Approaches like those of Panofsky and Schroeder, described above, can help indexers – perhaps in consultation with their colleagues or clients – to determine the requisite detail and treatment for a particular indexing project. The question of what to index on any occasion, and in how much detail, is influenced by the purpose of the collection and the kinds of information need presented by the users. A painting of a ship at sea could be described as '19th century sailing ship' or 'four-masted steel barque, leaving Port Lincoln (Australia), with a cargo of grain, 1891'; the name of the ship, if known, would also become an indexable element. If automated keyword searching is possible, it is obviously more helpful for images to have detailed captions. It is important also to identify the messages that an image can convey (with or without added words as caption). For example, an uncaptioned photograph of a man and woman sitting opposite each other at a table in a barely furnished room, an unshaded light bulb overhead, faces slightly turned away from the camera; this could perhaps be an interrogation, a scene of poverty, an attempt at patching up a relationship, or a waiting room (a waiting room for what?).

User requests for still images may be expressed solely in terms of the subject, but commonly they reflect a combination of physical features and subject interest. The subject may be expressed generically – 'what is there on temples in Southeast Asia?' – or specifically, by name – 'is there a picture of Kek Lok Si Temple, Penang, Malaysia?'. The level and amount of indexing is always determined by the nature of the collection and the needs of the users, but may need to be sufficiently detailed to retrieve images like these:

- a typical Rocky Mountains landscape in summer
- six cartoons, by different cartoonists, showing the US President of the time
- an aerial colour photograph of Sydney Harbour Bridge and Opera House
- ten drawings of scenes from the same London street, one for each decade of the twentieth century
- a view, from below, of the inside of the dome of Liverpool Town Hall
- a black and white close-up of a mosquito biting a hairy human arm
- an x-ray view of a human stomach containing a leftover surgical instrument
- a profile of a giraffe's head and neck
- an exploded diagram of a lawnmower, showing how it should be assembled
- a solarized print of a boy's grinning face
- a bird of prey rising from a river with a fish in its beak
- a satellite image (in natural colour) of Mount Egmont, New Zealand
- a selection of images with prominent red features (anything: flowers, scarves, sunsets, fruit, confectionery, balloons, umbrellas, flames, paint, clowns' noses, racing cars, jockeys' colours, fish, autumn leaves, fireworks . . .)
- 'aiming high' (e.g. a rock-climber halfway up a vertical rock face)
- two pictures, by a courtroom artist, of a judge and jury

Commercial collections, from which images are licensed for use in publications, exhibitions, advertisements and the like, often produce catalogues illustrating a representative selection of their images. The catalogue sections reflect the current interests and demands of their customers, and so the broad categories may change from time to time. Some typical category headings, which might supply index terms, are:

- lifestyles: singles, couples and groups out and about, spending money, having a good time
- celebrations: Christmas, weddings, birthdays
- homes and families: home interiors; children, babies, several generations
- culture, customs and tradition
- education and training
- fitness and sport
- business, finance and commerce
- industry, science and technology
- entertainment: theatre, cinema, concerts
- architecture and construction
- transport
- environment and pollution
- abstracts: symbolization of success, teamwork, happiness, challenge, retirement . . .
- universe: the world, maps, space
- health, medical care, social welfare
- beauty and glamour
- holidays and leisure
- crime and antisocial actions
- travel: abroad and exotic
- backgrounds: skies, unspecified landscapes, patterns and decorations
- agriculture, horticulture, flowers and fruit
- wildlife
- personalities: portraits, groups
- reportage

Locators for Still Images

The type of locator used in an index depends on the formats of the images, where they are located and how they are kept. Whole-page halftone illustrations in books sometimes bear page numbers in the same sequence as the text; alternatively, they may have separate numbers (such as plate numbers, perhaps in roman numerals). Figures (whether whole-page or part-page) are usually numbered in sequence throughout the book as well as having normal page numbers; in this case, the page numbers are usually used as locators, but figure numbers can be added for clarity if necessary. (See 'Indicating the position – the locators' in Chapter 4.)

Loose images in collections may be stored in boxes, vertical or hanging files, wallets, drawers, or cabinets. Electronically stored images may also be identified by individual numbers and codes. If each image is allocated a running number (accession number) or a code representing its subject group, date, container or position, these numbers and codes can be used as locators:

carnivals 144, 1046, 2345, 3392

dawn 551.59/13

ammonites 99–143, 99–254, 99–678, 99–1123, 00–23, 00–56

effervescence 14/3, 17/5, 19/2, 19/3, 23/6–23/10

Baltimore, Maryland US: 445, 679, 998

Moving images

Moving images occur in a variety of genres, including:

- feature films and programmes
- documentaries (film and TV)
- newsreels and news programmes
- cartoons and animations
- art films
- drama performances
- music performances
- comedy performances
- scratch videos (mixes of short clips, usually with soundtrack)
- training materials
- advertising and promotional materials
- educational materials
- tourist and travel materials
- home movies and videos
- corporate films and videos (product-centred)

The images may be held on film (in various sizes and formats, with and without sound), on videotape (in many sizes and formats), on disk (CD-ROM, DVD), and in online digital files. A film's soundtrack may be either recorded on the film or produced as a separate tape. In video-recordings, the sound is integrated with the images. Most of the moving image materials created are professionally made and their production can require large numbers of people, involved in a range of specialist activities – producers, directors, actors, technicians, designers, reporters, and so on. Valuable material worthy of preservation can also come from amateur and home films and videos, containing unusual – even unique – opportunistic shots that were missed by the professionals and that may be important for news and archive purposes. Individual images can be extracted and may then become of interest as still images. Similarly, short unused sequences (stock shots) may be removed and used for a quite different purpose.

Whole films, videos and disks usually come complete with titles and other identifying information. Catalogue records (descriptions) may need to be very detailed in order to to be of help to potential users, who cannot easily scan the materials themselves. Each record should incorporate as much information about the film 'package' as is relevant for the kind of use expected. Typical elements are:

- title: there may be several variants – provisional (working) title, final title, translated title (of foreign-language version), series title
- duration/extent: footage and/or timing
- shotlist: summary/description of shots, with timings, types of shot
- types of material and components of the 'package': formats and sizes, print/negative
- soundtrack details
- colouration: colour/black and white
- originators and contributors: directors, producers, screenplay writers, actors, speakers (e.g. for voice-overs), musical performers, camera personnel, production staff, composers, musical directors
- production studio, company
- distributor
- dates: filming, completion, release
- language of dialogue
- subtitling

- target or most suitable audience
- official classification
- related items, such as a TV programme about the making of the film in question, or trailers for it
- accession number or code, identifying the item in the collection

Some films and videos have a continuous subject, theme or plot throughout – 'urban foxes in Britain', 'handling conflict at work', 'winter holidays in Alberta', 'the life and music of Arnold Bax'. These may be easier and quicker to index than materials such as newsreels and magazine programme compilations that contain several sections on different topics, related only by being in the news on a particular day; for example, a single programme could deal with floods in Orissa (India), the abolition of the House of Lords, a flu epidemic in Western Europe, a government plan for social housing in inner cities, the death of a well-known character actor, and a rugby championship final.

Just as the retrieval needs of users vary from collection to collection, so the kind of indexing required may differ. Apart from simple enquiries based on title, producer, actor, director and so on – many of which can be satisfied by searches on the terms included in the relevant part of the catalogue description – there are several levels of subject enquiry. Subject requests may relate to a single straightforward theme or to an abstract concept, or to a combination of topic and physical characteristic of the image. The particular responsibility of the indexer is the representation of content, but physical features frequently form an essential part of enquiries for visual material:

- news film shot amidst the crowds at the opening up of the Berlin Wall, 1989
- close-up sequence of a lengthy surgical operation in progress
- amateur video of a group of children (3 to 5 years old) making a sandcastle on a beach, happily at first, then ending in tears; what the children say must be clearly audible
- training video on health and safety at work (no longer than 10 minutes), for office use, with Welsh language dialogue
- any recent film or video of a tornado moving towards and through a township (exterior shots)
- extracts from a performance of John Adams's opera *Nixon in China*

- black and white film of chair-bodgers at work in the Chiltern beech-woods in the 1930s
- time-lapse film of an apple tree bursting into blossom and forming fruit
- aerial film of the Grand Canyon (US)
- natural history films on bird migration between Britain and Africa
- appearances, in various TV comedies, of a now-demolished building
- three censored scenes from British films of the 1950s
- documentary on the use of heavy horses in working situations, e.g. timber hauling in forests
- cartoon film on the theme of forgiveness, for use in schools

The catalogues of commercial collections, which provide stock shots and films for use in a range of settings, sometimes group their holdings into broad categories similar to those described earlier for still images.

Wilkie (1999) points out that digitization (using DVD-ROM, for example) can reduce the time taken and the amount of detail required in descriptive cataloguing, but that the indexing requirements remain the same. Indexers working with these media can leave the automatic search to look for shots, angles and other physical features, and can concentrate on enhancing accessibility to the images through the intellectual approach of subject indexing. As with still images, objective and subjective content are both important, and the approaches of Panofsky and Schroeder (referred to above) may help in the recognition of different levels of indexable element, including abstract concepts.

Locators for Moving Images

As with still images, the ways in which the moving image materials are stored and catalogued determine the kinds of locator used. Individual items may be numbered for identification and may be coded according to format, subject, position in a sequence, or sector of film or disk.

Sound Materials – Categorization and Features

Sound materials may be of interest on their own (for individual sounds, compilations of sounds representing subject themes, artistic performances and so on) or as integral parts of audiovisual materials (such as film sound-tracks and tape/slide presentations). The sound component of an audio-visual may be extracted and become of interest in its own right. As with images, the subject content can range far and wide.

The main formats are disk and tape, of which there are several kinds, many no longer in production, with some older items existing on cylin-ders and in special-purpose formats such as piano rolls. The development of disk and tape is continuing, and many sound collections therefore consist of several forms and sizes of both. As with images, conversion and remas-tering of older formats is being carried out, but many earlier items are retained – sometimes because of their intrinsic value, sometimes because the cost of conversion is not considered worthwhile. Indexers in this field may therefore need to work with open reel (reel-to-reel) tape, cassettes, cartridges, and disks of several types (shellac, vinyl, CD), sizes and speeds (78, 45, 33⅓ rev/min).

Some collections hold only professionally recorded items, but others have mixtures of professional and amateur recordings. The recordings may have been gathered in the course of research projects, or produced for broadcasting, for use by the visually impaired, for commercial purposes (sale or hire), for educational use, for industrial training, as a personal hobby, or for family reasons.

Sound genres include:

- news
- documentaries
- drama, poetry and prose readings
- comedy programmes, quizzes
- talks, speeches, interviews
- discussions, phone-ins
- audiobooks and stories
- commentaries (sport, state occasions . . .)
- current affairs analysis
- language tuition (foreign language learning)
- musical performances: live shows and concerts (pop, light, jazz, clas-sical, etc.)
- musical performances: studio recordings (ditto)
- wildlife programmes
- religious services and events

- children's programmes
- sound effects

As with images, the catalogue records relating to sound items usually contain a number of indexable elements:

- author
- composer
- speakers: presenter, reporter, commentator, interviewee
- conductor
- performers (individual and group)
- production personnel
- titles: whole works and extracts (original and translated); series
- content sequence and identity of sounds
- opus number
- extent: running time
- catalogue number
- dates of recording and production
- location: where recorded
- type of recording
- recording company
- types of sound material
- language of dialogue
- target or most suitable audience
- accompanying and related items (text documents, films)
- accession number or identifying code

The indexer's role, dependent – as always – on the type of collection and its purpose, is to ensure that the full potential of the materials is revealed by suitable indexing so that enquirers can find what they want without having to toil through hours of disk and tape. The multilevel approach, referred to earlier for images, can be applied equally to sound items – so that the specific, generic, locational, and symbolic aspects are all recognized. A particular importance attaches to the indexing of sound materials in that they are especially relevant to those users with visual impairments. It is also relevant to note that a certain kind of material can be of use to different categories of user; for example, audiobooks (books on tape cassette) are widely used by the visually impaired as an alternative to reading, but are also valued by sighted people on the move (out jogging, in vehicles), by language students, and by teachers working with pupils (adults and children) having difficulty in learning to read.

User needs encompass many subjects, forms and technical features. The combination of full descriptive cataloguing and detailed subject indexing helps to find audio materials relevant to specifications such as these:

- summer, deep in the country (no cars, no people)
- composer Elizabeth Maconchy, talking about her music
- street sounds of Dublin in the 1930s
- the dialect of Cumbrian shepherds
- news items from successive bulletins illustrating the breaking, development and climax of a named political scandal
- religious choral music recorded in a church in St Petersburg, Russia
- a high-pitched, intermittent whistle
- samples from radio programmes made over 60 years by a (named) broadcaster who has just died (for a tribute programme)
- four contrasting renditions of 'Summertime' (by George Gershwin) – two female, two male
- the repertoire of calls made by the curlew (*Numenius arquata*)
- a self-study Japanese course, for business travellers
- a selection of minimalist music, for use as a background to an art exhibition

Locators for sound materials

The form and style of locators is determined by the way in which the sound items are catalogued and stored. As with images, they may be held in a variety of containers. Individual sound items can be numbered, coded and grouped by subject or format, according to the nature and needs of the collection. When several items of different formats make up a package, they may be individually numbered or may be referred to by the overall number of the package, with an additional code representing the format of the item. Discrete items following in sequence on a disk or tape can be referred to by their position:

storms at sea 1130 track 4; 2355 track 2 [item, track]

balalaika ensembles 99/14 Side 1 (7); 00/34 Side 1 (3) [date, item, side, track]

Temminck's stint (*Calidris temminckii*) 598.3/12 B:5   [class/item side:track]

References

Berger, John and Mohr, Jean (1982) *Another way of telling*. London: Writers and Readers Publishing Cooperative Society

Cawkell, Tony (1998) Checking research progress on 'image retrieval by shape-matching' using the Web of Science. *Aslib proceedings*, **50**, 27–31

Dixon, Geoffrey (1995) *The Gilbert and Sullivan photofinder: an index to published illustrations of Savoy Opera*. Ayr: Rhosearn Press

Enser, P.G.B. (1995) Pictorial information retrieval. *Journal of documentation*, **51**, 126–170

Evans, A. (1987) TELCLASS: a structural approach to TV classification. *Audiovisual librarian*, **13**, 215–216

Frost, Cath (1999) The challenge of image retrieval. *Managing information*, **6**, 47–48

Gorman, Michael and Winkler, Paul W. (1988) (eds) *Anglo-American cataloguing rules* 2nd edn., 1988 revision. Chicago: American Library Association; Ottawa: Canadian Library Association; London: Library Association Publishing

Jacobs, Christine (1999) If a picture is worth a thousand words, then. . . . *The Indexer*, **21**, 119–121

Lancaster, F.W. (1998) *Indexing and abstracting in theory and practice* 2nd edn. London: Library Association Publishing

Library of Congress, Prints and Photographs Division (1995) *Thesaurus for graphic materials*. Washington, D.C.: Library of Congress, Cataloging Distribution Service

Panofsky, Erwin (1955) *Meaning in the visual arts: papers in and on art history*. Garden City, NY: Doubleday Anchor

Petersen, Toni (1994) *Art & architecture thesaurus* 2nd edn. Oxford: Oxford University Press

Richardson, Ruth and Thorne, Robert (1994) *'The Builder' illustrations index 1843–1883.* London: Builder Group and Hutton and Rostron in association with the Institute of Historical Research

Schroeder, Kimberly A. (1998a) Indexing training and workflow on large digitization projects. *The Indexer,* **21,** 67–69

Schroeder, Kimberly A. (1998b) Layered indexing of images. *The Indexer,* **21,** 11–14

Shoah Visual History Foundation in cooperation with Mary Crystal (1998) Survivors of the Shoah Visual History Foundation: an introduction to its indexing methodology. *The Indexer,* **21,** 85–89

Waal, H. van de (1973–1985) *Iconclass: an iconographic classification system.* Completed and edited by L.D. Couprie with R.H. Fuchs, E. Tholen. Amsterdam: North-Holland. 17 volumes

Wilkie, Chris (1999) *Managing film and video collections.* Aslib know how guides. London: Aslib

Further Reading

Beare, Geraldine (1999) *Indexing newspapers, magazines and other periodicals.* Occasional papers on indexing: No.4. Sheffield: Society of Indexers (pp. 20–21: Indexing of non-text material; p. 39: Advertising and illustration; p. 41: Sound and moving-image indexes)

Eakins, John P. and Graham, Margaret E. (1999) *Content-based image retrieval: a report to the JISC Technology Applications Programme.* Newcastle-upon-Tyne: University of Northumbria, Institute for Image Data Research. [The full report is available on the internet at: www.unn.ac.uk/iidr/research/cbir/report.html]

Harper, D.J. and Eakins, J.P. (1999) (eds) *CIR-99: the challenge of image retrieval: papers presented at 2nd UK Conference on Image Retrieval, Newcastle-upon-Tyne, February 1999.* Electronic Workshops in Computing Series. Swindon: British Computing Society [Information about the May 2000 conference is available on the internet at: www.unn.ac.uk/iidr/cir/cir.html]

Wellisch, Hans H. (1995) *Indexing from A to Z* 2nd edn. New York: H.W. Wilson (pp. 332–343: Nonprint materials)

CHAPTER EIGHT

Subject specialisms

Indexing is indexing, whatever the subject, and the core techniques set out in Chapters 3, 4 and 5 are broadly applicable to all fields. This chapter aims to highlight what is different, important or unusual about index making in some specialist areas, and to identify some useful sources of information.

'Generality and Speciality'

A distinction is sometimes drawn between indexing for 'the general reader' and indexing for 'the specialist', but this contrast is too crude. There are levels of generality and speciality, therefore almost any well-trained indexer with wide general knowledge can index in a less familiar field up to a certain point. Some subjects, though, arise from a huge corpus of special-ized study, feature a unique and complex terminology, and have their own characteristic modes of index use; to index them at anything above the most basic level of document requires relevant understanding and experience.

The qualifications for advanced indexing in specialist areas are twofold and of equal importance: competence in indexing techniques, and knowledge of the subject. Possession of a degree or diploma, or practice in a profession, or a passionate interest in a subject, does not alone bestow the ability to make a good index, but provides an excellent background from which to acquire a knowledge of indexing technique.

Freelance indexers are usually willing to accept commissions in a wide range of subject areas, at least for texts at a basic level. Their education, work experience, social and domestic life, and organizational memberships, as well as their general knowledge of current affairs, enable them to tackle work of this order. For indexers who do not wish to freelance, there are opportunities for employment with publishers of current-awareness lists, with compilers of online databases, and in specialist libraries and resource centres. In its schedule of recommended practice (printed in the annual directory *Indexers available*), the Society of Indexers (see Chapter 12: Professional organizations and interest groups) states that indexers should 'compile indexes to a text on a specialist subject only with adequate knowledge of the specialism and competence to deal with the intellectual level of the text under consideration'. Indexing a text that is above the most basic requires knowledge of the conceptual framework of the subject, familiarity with its terminology, and understanding of the gist and purpose of the particular text. It is not sufficient to rely on picking up significant-looking words from the text, transposing section and paragraph headings into index headings, and depending on specialist dictionaries for meanings of words.

Advanced-level texts often introduce new terms, usually for new concepts, discoveries, revised ideas, or inventions, but sometimes as replacements for older ones. Technical terms made up of several elements, some of which may be numerical characters or letters from non-Roman alphabets, need to be entered correctly (in the form and order in which readers expect to find them) in the index. Words that have everyday meanings when found in newspapers or used in conversation can have quite different and very specific meanings in technical texts. Any indexer tempted to 'have a go', without expert assistance, at a higher-level text in an unfamiliar subject field runs the risk of floundering, being revealed as ignorant, and having payment withheld by a dissatisfied customer. However, experienced indexers find that their long-standing publisher clients tend to place many of their index commissions with them, regardless of subject, because they are confident of a good job being done. Indexing at this level can be testing, but – and this is what many indexers love about the work – it gives the opportunity to learn even more.

Keeping up to date with the specialist subjects is essential. Science, technology and medicine have a rapid rate of development, contemporary culture is kaleidoscopic, and the arts constantly evolve new forms, styles and trends. Knowledge must be actively maintained by the most suitable means, such as reading periodicals and newspapers, belonging to societies and attending their meetings and events, acquiring new editions of dictionaries and other reference sources, and monitoring and consulting internet web sites.

Readership

The indexer must be clear about the readership for which the document is intended – informed layperson or professional practitioner, for example. This enables predictions to be made about how the index will be used, the kinds of topics, and the ways in which they will be searched for, from which the indexer can determine a suitable level of indexing.

Indexable Content

The main text of a document is usually the indexer's prime focus and it is thoroughly mined for indexable elements (see 'Indexable content' in Chapter 3). Documents in specialized fields frequently include additional components, such as glossaries, notes (footnotes, chapter notes), bibliographies and reading lists, tables, and illustrations of various kinds. These can be excellent suppliers of indexable elements and so should always be examined. Some indexers find preliminary consultations with authors or editors useful, ensuring that all concerned in the index are in general agreement about its coverage and the needs of its potential users.

Number of Sequences

Some specialist fields conventionally feature multisequence indexes, rather than a single sequence containing all categories of entry (see 'Number of sequences in an index' in Chapter 1). This can sometimes be justified as a way of breaking up a long and complex index containing very different kinds of heading. It can also be helpful in those cases where the majority of index users are only interested in one kind of heading (such as personal names).

Form and Detail of Entries

The specialized terminology of fast-developing and many-faceted fields can give rise to multipart index headings and lengthy sequences of subheadings. New words and phrases must be fitted into the terminological pattern of the subject in question. Every heading must be presented in a form which is sought by users (see Chapter 4: Forming the index entries). Different sets of vocabulary (popular and professional, UK English and North American English, for example) may need to be catered for in some indexes – requiring decisions to be made on whether double entry (even multiple entry) or cross-referencing is more suitable in the context.

The use of standard vocabulary lists, such as thesauri, classification schemes, and subject headings lists, is a feature of specialized fields, particularly for current-awareness publications such as indexing and abstracting journals. The advantages of these lists are that they enable the subjects of documents to be indexed in a consistent way – a topic is always indexed by the same term, no matter how it is referred to in the indexed document – and that cross-references from synonyms and to related terms are supplied by the lists. Even if the lists are not used as sources of headings, indexers can find them helpful for definitions and for clarifying the conceptual pattern and terminological relationships of the subject.

A simple page number may not always be the most suitable locator. Some texts in specialized fields have hierarchical paragraph numbers, or lettered sections, or columns, as well as page numbers. Some have numbered illustrations, tables, appendices, or supplements, all of which may be indexable. A current-awareness publication that covers recently published documents may need to refer to periodical articles in a highly compressed form. The locator type chosen must be clear to the user and should provide the most specific reference possible to the piece of text (see 'Indicating the position – the locators' in Chapter 4 and 'Locators' in Chapter 6).

Specialist Areas

The extensive range of subject areas within which indexers currently work, and to which they contribute, is indicated in *Indexers available* (Society of Indexers), the 2000 edition of which identifies around 130 subject specialisms:

accountancy and
    auditing
advertising and
    marketing
agriculture
allied health
animals
anthropology
antiques and
    collecting
archaeology
architecture and
    architectural
    history
art and art history
astronomy and space
    sciences
aviation and aviation
    history
beekeeping
biochemistry
biographies and
    memoirs
biological sciences
biotechnology
botany
broadcasting
building and built
    environment
buses
business studies

cartography
chemistry
child development
children's books
civil engineering
classical studies
complementary
    therapies
computer science and
    IT
consumer affairs
co-operative
    movement
countries and regions
crafts
criminology
current affairs
dance and ballet
development studies
earth sciences
ecology
economics
education
electrical and
    electronic
    engineering
employment and
    trade unions
engineering
environmental studies
European studies

fashion and style
film and film studies
finance
folklore
food and drink
food science and
    technology
gardening
gay and lesbian
    studies
gender studies
genealogy and family
    history
general arts and
    humanities
genetics
geography
geology
government and local
    government
health and safety
history
home maintenance
    and DIY
human rights
industrial archaeology
information science
    and management
interior design
international relations
Islamic studies

landscape design
law
life sciences
linguistics
literary theory
literature
local history
management and
   administration
Marxism
materials science
mathematics
mechanical
   engineering
media studies
medicine
meteorology
microbiology
military and defence
   studies
molecular biology
motor sports
mountaineering and
   rock climbing
museum studies
music

natural history
naval and nautical
   studies
new age
nursing and midwifery
nutrition and dietetics
oceanography
ornithology
personnel and human
   resources
   management
pharmacology
philosophy
photography
physical sciences
physics
politics and political
   history
psychiatry
psychology
psychopharmacology
psychotherapy and
   counselling
publishing
religion and theology
science (general and

popular)
social work and social
   services
sociology and social
   sciences
soil science
sports and games
sports science and
   medicine
statistics
sustainable
   development
taxation
technology
telecommunications
textiles
theatre
trade and industry
training and
   development
transport
travel and travel
   literature
veterinary science
welfare rights
women's studies

Specialist subject groups have been formed within some of the indexing societies, giving members the opportunity to exchange information and discuss problems particular to their fields (see Chapter 12: Professional organizations and interest groups for indexers).

Some features of six subject areas, in which there is a great deal of indexing work being done or needing to be done, are summarized in this chapter – law, medicine, archaeology, genealogy and family history, science and technology, and biography. These areas have been selected for their particular characteristics and differences, not on grounds of importance or value. Literature for children is dealt with in Chapter 9 and serials (periodicals) in Chapter 6.

Law

Law is a fruitful sector for suitably qualified indexers. Its many branches reflect its application to every aspect of life. It has generated, and continues to generate, enormous quantities of documents – many of them lengthy and complex. The quality of its practice relies heavily on indexes for trustworthy and comprehensive access to information.

Just as some legal practitioners work in selected branches of the subject – employment law or criminal law, for example – so do some indexers. Because laws differ from country to country, and sometimes vary between states, provinces and regions within sovereign countries, subject knowledge may not be easily transferable and care needs to be taken to confirm the meanings of legal terms that appear in the law of more than one jurisdiction. What is legal under one jurisdiction may be illegal in another. An action referred to by one term in country A may be denoted by another in country B, and a word that has the same written form may have entirely different meanings in region X and region Y. The indexer needs to have reliable reference sources at hand, in case clarification is required while working.

Materials and readership

The indexable materials of law – some published, some unpublished, include:

- textbooks, at a variety of levels (for practitioners, for students, for the layperson)
- periodicals
- statutes (acts): individual and collected (including annotated versions) and their secondary (enabling) legislation (the statutory instruments, regulations, rules, orders and other documents that enable the statutes to be implemented); existing statutes are sometimes revised, amended, consolidated, or repealed by later legislation
- reference works, including loose-leaf services and CD-ROMs
- current-awareness services (indexes and abstracts)
- proceedings of government enquiries
- internet web sites of law materials
- proclamations

Depending on the type of document, the information contained may need to be accessed, for different purposes, by one or more categories of legal personnel and by others involved in legal processes – barristers, solicitors, legal clerks, judges, magistrates, advocates, legal advisers, attorneys, litigants, members of Parliament, civil servants, prosecution service staff, procurators fiscal, ombudsmen's staff, local authority officials and councillors, Citizens' Advice Bureaux staff, legal librarians, social researchers, and others. Members of some of these groups obviously possess superior knowledge of the law and have greater familiarity with legal terminology than those in other groups. Compilation of any index should, therefore, never be undertaken without first establishing the purpose and probable user group of the document in hand.

One noteworthy characteristic of law-related documents is that older material is frequently as relevant as newly published items. Certain acts that were passed many decades (even several centuries) ago are still in force, and ancient legal cases that established important precedents are cited in relation to current situations. This means that older indexes remain in use and also that there is the need for consolidated indexes that provide access to related materials published over a wide stretch of time.

Indexable content

Law-related documents can vary considerably in content, form, style of presentation, physical format, and purpose. Some may contain – in addition to the principal text – glossaries, bibliographies, facsimiles of older legal documents, lists, and extracts from statutes, perhaps presented in appendices. The main text may feature footnotes or chapter notes – sometimes lengthy and packed with significant information. Clusters of documents relating to the current law of a particular subject – landlord and tenant, f or example – frequently appear in loose-leaf form, with regular amendments (which require indexing) to ensure that the collection is up to date.

Legal works sometimes have detailed contents lists, containing not only chapter headings but also the headings of sections and subsections. This is clearly helpful to the reader who wishes to establish the general coverage and structure of the text. It is sometimes suggested that the existence of a full contents list dispenses with the need for a comprehensive index. This is a misguided idea, as the contents list and the index have different purposes (see 'Contents lists and indexes' in Chapter 1).

Number of sequences

The long history of law and the enduring relevance of its documents have resulted in the creation of certain traditions and conventions in legal indexing. One of these – currently followed – is the division of indexes into separate sequences according to the type of heading, so that it is common to find that a textbook dealing with a particular branch of law contains a subject index, an index of cases (usually titled 'table of cases' or 'list of cases'), an index of statutes ('table of statutes', 'list of statutes') and sometimes an index of secondary legislation. These tables are often placed towards the beginning of a book, but may be positioned towards the end, just before the main index. In a serial publication that indexes articles from periodicals, there may be separate sequences for subjects of articles, authors of articles, legal cases, titles of statutes and other documents, and titles of publications reviewed. Although, generally, it can be argued that a single-sequence index is easier for the user, separate sequences can be justified in the case of indexes that are accessed by different groups for very different kinds of information, and that would – if merged – be very long and cumbersome.

Language

One feature of legal texts is the use of highly specialized language, including many Latin and Old French words and phrases, such as:

> Anton Piller orders
> estoppel
> feu duty
> *ultra vires*
> writ *ne exeat regno*

Some of these terms (sometimes known as 'terms of art') have no, or little, meaning outside the legal profession and may appear – to an uninformed indexer – to need reversal or a change of order or spelling, for inclusion in an index. However, terms of this kind should normally be used unaltered as headings. For example, *ultra vires* is a term in its own right and is not required in reversed form. An understanding of legal terms and their relationships is essential. Because the language of law is not the language of everyday use, indexers need to take great care when converting text terms into headings. There may be unusual (but entirely correct) spellings and word-forms, and uses of capitalization and type that should be followed as in the text. Simplified versions of documents, intended for the layperson, are usually written in 'plain English', and so may be suitable for indexing by non-specialists.

A text using a large specialized vocabulary normally includes many definitions of terms. These may appear in a glossary section or be scattered throughout the text, each term being explained when it first occurs. Definitions form an important set of indexable elements and so should always be included in the index, each term featuring as a heading – perhaps with the qualifier 'definition' or 'defined', or with the locator emphasized in some way. Some indexers also include 'definitions' as a heading, with all the defined terms listed alphabetically as subheadings; this is helpful to users who want to check the meanings of all the new legal terms introduced in a text or the specific interpretations – in a new context – of existing terms.

Some words have multiple meanings in legal contexts and need to be differentiated by the addition of qualifying terms. For example, a 'charge' may be an accusation, a price or fee, or a financial liability or debt. Singular and plural forms of nouns may have different meanings (Moys 1993), such as 'cost' (the price paid) and 'costs' (the legal expenses of a case), so it is sometimes necessary to include both as headings.

'Classified' and 'direct' headings

One older method of arranging headings in legal indexes is to group them under a limited number of broad headings reflecting traditional divisions of the subject, with the constituent topics displayed in sequences of increasingly indented subheadings. This 'classified' style of arrangement shows the hierarchical relationships within the broad subject, which can be helpful. However, it also has the seriously negative effect of making some sought terms difficult to locate, because they do not appear as headings in the main alphabetical sequence but rather as subheadings, or sub-subheadings (or even further levels) to a broader heading. Combing the list of subheadings and sub-subheadings for a specific topic can be frustrating and time-consuming, particularly for users not familiar with the terminological pattern of the subject.

The purpose of any index is to lead the enquirer to the place(s) in the document where all the needed information can be found. It is not the role of a legal index either to state the law or to provide a structured summary of it. Any term that is likely to be sought in its own right should be entered first of all as a heading, not concealed by being included only as a subheading. For example, enquirers wanting information about 'the proper plaintiff principle' or 'professional secrecy' should be able to find these sought terms as headings in the P section of the index:

> professional secrecy 94, 132
> proper plaintiff principle 56–57

It is not at all helpful, as sometimes happens, to have them listed only as subheadings or sub-subheadings (as here in the M and S sections):

> minority shareholder:
> > proper plaintiff principle 56–57
>
> securities:
> > admission of securities
> > > professional secrecy 91, 132

The best practice is to include every sought topic as a heading and, where appropriate, also as a subheading or sub-subheading, making different user approaches possible. A subheading sequence under a single heading, like this:

> disclosure
> > accounting policies
> > pension costs
> > remuneration
> > > auditors'
> > > employees'
> > > trustees'
> > [etc.]

should, therefore, be complemented by headings like these (which derive from the subheadings above):

> accounting policies, disclosure
> auditors' remuneration, disclosure
> employees' remuneration, disclosure
> pension costs, disclosure
> remuneration, disclosure
>> auditors'
>> employees'
>> trustees'
> trustees' remuneration, disclosure

If this double/multiple entry produces long subheading sequences for which there is insufficient space, the alternative is to use *see* cross-references (see '*See* cross-references' in Chapter 4).

Fullness (length) of headings

Single-word headings are undoubtedly clear and concise (see 'Length and detail of headings' in Chapter 4), but for many legal indexes it would sometimes be impossible to express the required concepts as single words; additional words conveying contextual information are frequently required, full multiword legal phrases may need to be included, and the detail of the topic may be extensive. Long headings can, therefore, be acceptable and proper, so long as they express the topics concisely and unambiguously.

Subheading sequences (such as those shown above) are a necessity in many legal indexes, providing essential analysis and detail (see 'Subheadings' in Chapter 4 and 'Subheading order' in Chapter 5). Two levels of subheading (i.e. subheading and sub-subheading) can normally be easily grasped by users, but if there are further levels – and particularly if the headings are lengthy – the resulting layout can be difficult to follow, especially when the sequence continues from column to column or page to page. The exclusion or inclusion of function words needs care; if excluding a word like 'to', 'for', or 'by' could give a subheading more than one possible meaning, then it should be retained. Function words can also influence the arrangement of subheadings (see 'Arrangement of entries' below).

Proper names

The names that commonly need to appear as headings – apart from names of people, places and organizations, which occur in almost all fields – are:

- titles of statutes and secondary legislation
- names of legal cases
- names of courts

Names of countries or other jurisdictions need to be included when an index refers to the legislation of more than one legislative area (see 'Places of jurisdiction' below).

When abbreviations occur in texts, representing the names of statutes and the names of well-known organizations, both the full form and the abbreviated form should normally appear in the index – either as two complete entries or as one entry and a cross-reference, depending on the number of locators involved (see 'Cross-references' in Chapter 4).

Statutes

There are conventions concerning the way in which statutes and other legislation are referred to in texts and in tables of statutes. Often an indexer is able to copy the names exactly as they appear in the text, but must still watch out for references using other forms. Lengthy titles are often abbreviated or reduced to a short form in texts, as well as in the workplace, for ease of reference – PUSWA for the Public Utilities Street Works Act, for example. Sometimes an individual title may be known in various forms in different places. To avoid a scatter of information under different headings, the indexer must select one form of the title against which to list all the references.

Dates are an indispensable component of headings for legislation. The date is part of the unique identity of each item and must always be included. In the UK, for example, a new Finance Act is passed each year, its title distinguished only by the year date. With automatic sorting, care is needed to ensure that dates are treated as integral parts of headings, and not sorted as locators:

Disability Discrimination Act 1999   106, 117

or:

> Disability Discrimination Act (1999) 106, 117

Regnal years were used for older Acts:

> 1 Victoria [i.e. 1837]

Individual parts of statutes are often referred to, using abbreviations such as 's.' for 'section' and 'Sch.' for 'schedule'. Items of secondary legislation, such as statutory instruments, are usually identified by number as well as by date, so all must be included. House styles of presentation vary. For example:

> S.I. 1982 No. 1707 or SI 1982/1707 or SI 1982 no.1707

Cases

Headings that consist of the names of legal cases are presented in conventional formats (with house style variations), depending on the type of case, and may require a cross-reference from the name cited second (where the case concerns a plaintiff and a defendant). The date of the case is part of the heading. If a few case headings appear in a general book index, the date is often given in parentheses:

> Department of the Environment v Royal Insurance plc (1987)
> Hughes v Smallwood (1890)
> R. v Highbury Corner Metropolitan Stipendiary Magistrate ex
>   parte Di Matteo (1991)
> Manurewa Transport Ltd (Re) (1971)

In a law book, though, specific meanings attach to the style of bracket (square or round) used around the dates. Each case is conventionally followed by an abbreviated reference to the series in which a report of the case appears:

> Tower Boot Co Ltd v Jones [1995] IRLR 529

and the abbreviations are explained at the head of the table:

IRLR Industrial Relations Law Reports

Square brackets around the date indicate that the source series is organized in yearly volumes, round brackets that volume numbers do not run concurrently with the years.

Courts

The names of courts should normally be given in their official form:

> Court of Appeal
> High Court
> International Court of Justice

If an index contains names of courts from more than one jurisdiction, the names of the jurisdictions should be included:

> Federal Court of Canada
> Supreme Court of Trinidad and Tobago

or, if grouping by jurisdiction is required:

> Canada: Federal Court
> Trinidad and Tobago: Supreme Court

Places of Jurisdiction

The names of countries and regions governed by particular jurisdictions should be clearly identified in the indexer's mind. Laws and regulations exist in the UK at local authority level (by-laws) and at national level (acts, statutory instruments, etc.). Acts and regulations may apply to the whole of the UK or to one or more of its constituent parts (England, Wales, Scotland, Northern Ireland). It is therefore important to use the correct jurisdiction name. Loose usage (in social discourse, in the media, and in sources outside the UK, for example) often obscures the difference between the United Kingdom, Britain and England. European Union law also applies to the UK and frequently requires inclusion in tables of statutes. Several countries – such as Canada, Australia, and the US – have legislatures at provincial or state level as well as at the national level. For some Commonwealth countries, the Privy Council in the United Kingdom is the final court of appeal. When using an index, the reader should be left in no doubt about the coverage of the index as a whole and of the individual headings.

Keyword indexing

The extraction of (unaltered) keywords from texts, to stand as index headings, can be effective for certain kinds of legal indexes – current-awareness services, for example. They are suitable for professional users who are completely familiar with the specialist vocabulary and who are sufficiently information-skilled to know that they may need to look up more than one term to find references to the desired topic. Services that aim to cover more than one legal jurisdiction may need to add cross-references, and to add qualifiers to headings in order to clarify their contexts; even in the UK, the law of any subject may be contained in separate legislative documents relating to England and Wales, Scotland, Northern Ireland, and the European Union, using different terms to represent the same topics.

Thesauri and classification schemes

Another approach to the representation of topics (other than statutes, cases and other 'proper name' elements) is to use terms taken from standard lists such as thesauri and classification schemes, such as Moys (2000) and Miskin (1999). These are particularly useful for representing the overall or principal subjects of books, periodical articles and other documents, in regular indexing and abstracting publications. Efficiency of searching is aided by the consistent use of terms from the list. One term is always used for a subject, however that subject is referred to in the text of different documents – so 'prisons' may always be assigned as a heading even though some texts refer to 'jails' and others to 'gaols'.

Choice of locators

For many textbooks the normal use of page numbers as locators is suitable. By contrast, in books that analyse, interpret or comment on specific statutes, the chapters are likely to be laid out in numbered paragraphs –

the first part of the number being the chapter number (10.1, 10.1.1, 10.1.2, 10.2 and so on). Documents in loose-leaf form and books that are frequently revised may also use the numbered paragraph form. In these cases, using the paragraph numbers as locators is much more helpful; as the text of the document is revised – additional paragraphs inserted, some removed, others extended – the relevant entries can be added to the index or removed from it without large parts of the index being affected.

Locators in indexes to multivolume and loose-leaf publications can be lengthy, containing volume numbers, chapter numbers or section letters, as well as paragraph or page numbers – also sometimes supplementary page numbers in small roman type. The aim should be to express them as concisely as possible, while maintaining the necessary clarity and not confusing the index user:

> market value **H**:4.151(iii) [Part H, chapter 4, paragraph 151,
>   supplementary page iii]

Indexes to individual statutes or to collections of statutory legislation frequently need to include references to particular sections, subsections and schedules; the locators should follow the form in which the extracts appear in the text of the statute:

> constructive dismissal   s.22(31)

The name (or an abbreviation of the name) of the statute must be included if the index refers to more than one statute:

> parental leave   Employment Relations Act 1999 s.7, Sch.4(I)

Arrangement of entries

As in most fields of indexing, the choice of word-by-word or letter-by-letter order (see 'Alphabetical arrangement' in Chapter 5) can considerably affect the usefulness of the index. Mulvany (1994, pp. 126–127) suggests that word-by-word alphabetizing may be the best way of keeping together groups of related multipart terms, and notes that legal indexes frequently use this method.

The arrangement of subheadings that start with necessary function words (such as articles, and prepositions) needs scrutiny. Often a function word, even though appearing in the heading, can be ignored in the filing order:

> disclosure:
>> to accountants
>> to Customs
>> to Inland Revenue
>> by journalists

In other situations, though, the function words are particularly significant in law and so should be given filing value (not ignored) because they provide a more satisfactory order in the context:

> offences:
>> against children
>> against public morals
>> by juveniles
>> by women
>> in England
>> in Wales
>> involving alcohol
>> involving motor vehicles

References

Miskin, Christine (1999) *A legal thesaurus*. Mytholmroyd, West Yorkshire: Legal Information Resources

Moys, Elizabeth M. (1993) (ed.) *Indexing legal materials*. Occasional papers on indexing: no.2. Sheffield: Society of Indexers

Moys, E.M. (2000) *Moys' classification and thesaurus for legal materials* 4th edn. East Grinstead: Bowker-Saur [in press].

Mulvany, Nancy C. (1994) *Indexing books*. Chicago: University of Chicago Press

Further Reading

French, Derek (1996) *How to cite legal authorities*. London: Blackstone Press

Moys, Elizabeth M. (1997) Classified v. specific indexing: a re-examination in principle. *The Indexer*, **20**, 135–136, 153–155

Wellisch, Hans H. (1995) *Indexing from A to Z* 2nd edn. New York: H.W. Wilson (pp. 258–268: Legal texts)

Medicine

This is another fertile area for indexers with sufficient knowledge (though those who are unable to read about a disorder without being certain that they are suffering from it may need to be selective about the jobs they accept).

Materials and readership

The annual output of medical documentation is substantial and varied:

- textbooks
- reference materials (printed, CD-ROM and online): encyclopaedias, pharmacopoeias
- periodicals: institutional journals, subject reviews, abstracting and indexing publications
- government and other official records
- research reports
- manufacturers' trade publications
- equipment manuals
- practice guides
- proceedings of conferences and symposia
- information/advice leaflets and newsletters from support groups
- films and videos for teaching and training
- online reference sources and other services
- medical practice and departmental records

Historical aspects of medicine and personal recollections relating to medical matters also appear in memoirs, diaries, and biographies.

Materials are published at many levels, for different readerships – medical researchers, consultants, clinicians, general practitioners (family doctors), teachers, undergraduate and postgraduate students, nurses, midwives, physiotherapists, chiropodists/podiatrists, optometrists/opticians, complementary therapists, administrators, medical and social historians, athletes and sportspeople, the elderly, parents, adolescents, children, members of ethnic groups, livestock farmers, and veterinarians. Some texts produced for ethnic groups in the UK appear in languages other than English (Hindi, Urdu, Greek, Turkish, and Chinese, for example), some of which use non-Roman characters.

The mode of use in this field is largely referential. Documents are not always read right through from beginning to end, but dipped into, and checked for information relevant to a topical question. Wyman (1999), in a survey of reviews of medical indexes, concluded that the essential elements for a high-quality medical index were accuracy, thorough analysis (subheadings and cross-references), completeness and comprehensiveness, and usability. To exemplify the importance of indexes in urgent situations, she quotes an extract from a review of a book on medical intensive care; the reviewer highly commends the index, having used it as a rapid reference source during two weeks while covering an intensive care unit.

The indexer's knowledge should be suitable for the text in hand. Indexers tempted to take on medical texts outside their normal speciality, or beyond their level of clear understanding, should recognize that in making the index they may unwittingly conceal important information or even gravely mislead the index users. Further advances by others in the field can be promoted by the provision of access to the information through a clear, accurate and well-constructed index, but will be hindered by a poor one. A book containing advice on general health and fitness, using everyday language, is not likely to pose problems for any good indexer. A collection of articles in a medical research journal, describing the development and trialling of a new drug and its potential for the treatment of Parkinson's disease, on the other hand, needs suitable knowledge of pharmaceuticals and of the disease. Few indexers can match the knowledge and experience of the authors of advanced documents, so anyone indexing at that level must be able to grasp new concepts and quickly become familiar with the latest terminology. A good stock of reference materials is essential, and consultation with the author or editor may be necessary in order to clarify precise meanings and synonymous terms.

Indexable content

Most indexable material is in the form of printed text, but illustrations (photographs, diagrams, charts) and tables feature significantly and are sometimes the prime carriers of information. Footnotes and chapter notes can also be important.

Number of sequences

For a book index, a single sequence of terms is frequently satisfactory. Where there are several kinds of heading and where some users may be primarily interested in only one kind, it may be advisable to provide separate sequences. A book that describes medicines commonly prescribed for various disorders, for example, may have one sequence for the illnesses and another for the generic and proprietary (brand, trademark) names of the drugs. A book on healthy living, aimed at the general public and including recipes for daily meals, could usefully place the recipes in a separate sequence, for quick reference.

Language

Being a field in which innovation and development are actively pursued on a worldwide basis and in which very large numbers of people and organizations are involved – health professionals, support staff, national and local governments, manufacturers, service providers, charitable organizations, voluntary workers, and patients – medicine has a wide-ranging and constantly expanding terminology. A particular feature is that a variety of terms can be used to represent a certain topic. A formal term or its abbreviation may be used in medical literature and records and by health professionals, and another in everyday parlance by laypeople (some equivalents being more precise than others):

    trachea = windpipe
    TSH = thyroid-stimulating hormone
    myopia = short sight
    heart attack = myocardial infarction = MI = coronary thrombosis
        = cardiac infarction

In addition, there is often more than one way of referring to a disorder, according to whether the noun form of the organ or part is cited first or whether the adjectival form (often from a Latin root) is used:

    chest *or* thoracic . . .

In multi-author documents such as conference proceedings consisting of texts by contributors from more than one country, different words may be used for the same concept, or at least the spellings may vary:

    oesophagitis [UK] = esophagitis [US]

Pharmaceutical drugs, apart from sometimes being known by different brand names in different countries, also have generic names and are classified into categories of drug:

    Ceporex = cephalexin = an antibiotic
    Timoptol = timolol = a beta-blocker

There are many examples of terms that resemble each other, differing only by a few characters; they must not be confused when they are encountered in the same text:

    sulphadiazine [In US: sulfa . . .]
    sulphadimidine
    sulphanilamide
    sulphasalazine

Glossary terms and terms defined in a text are important elements in this literature and should always be included in the index, with an indication that the reference is to a definition (such as a subheading '*definition*', or a suitable abbreviation after the locator). While the general rule in indexing is that countable items should be given in the plural as headings (see 'Grammatical forms' in Chapter 4), the singular form – 'leg', 'eye', 'shoulder' – is often more suitable in medical indexing, where each part of the body is viewed as an item in itself.

Some medical terms are very long, so particular care is needed in transcription:

renin-angiotension-aldosterone system
hypertrophic obstructive cardiomyopathy

Omitting one of the words or syllables, or transposing two characters, can cause a sought entry to be overlooked and may change the
meaning of the term. With compound terms such as these, the indexer
should decide (and can only do this with sufficient knowledge of the
subject) whether double or triple entry or cross-referencing is required
under the second and third elements of the term.

Alternative approaches via synonyms and short forms should not be
forgotten. Users can search for information using different words, some
of which may not appear at all in the text but which should be included
in the index:

birth *see* childbirth
parturition *see* childbirth
feedback *see* biofeedback
salpingo-oophorectomy *see* oophorectomy

It is not necessary to make cross-references from all possible
synonyms – there is no need for an indexer to ransack dictionaries and
thesauri every time an index is under construction. All that is needed is
to include any synonym which the users of that particular index might
employ as a search term. In the examples given above, for instance, 'parturition' is unlikely to be looked for in a general, plain-English guide to
women's health and so the cross-reference would not be made.

Numerals, Greek letters and Latin prefixes commonly occur:

5–fluorouracil cream
cis-platinum chemotherapy

They must always appear in headings, but – depending on the nature
of the term – are sometimes ignored in the alphabetical arrangement.
Following the guideline in BS ISO 999 (British Standards Institution, 1996,
subclause 8.3(c)), '5–fluorouracil cream' would be filed as though 'fluorouracil. . . .' Normal practice is to file '*cis*-platinum' as though 'platinum';
this practice would, of course, separate '*cis*-platinum' (under P) and the
drug 'cisplatin' (under C), so may require cross-references. Reliable

medical and pharmaceutical reference sources should be checked to ensure that the current conventions for presenting such terms are followed (see 'Prefixes' in Chapter 5 and 'Arrangement of entries' in the 'Science and technology' section later in this chapter).

Changes in Terminology and Punctuation

Over a period of time, as more becomes known about the nature and causes of existing diseases, the ways in which they are classified change, and some disease terms fall out of use and are replaced by others:

St Vitus's dance = Sydenham's chorea = chorea minor

Anyone doing cumulative indexing – such as amalgamating thirty years of annual indexes to a journal, or indexing older medical literature, or working on historical records relating to military campaigns or social surveys, will need to provide access via both modern and earlier terms, using either double/multiple entry or cross-references.

Other terms may change only in their use of punctuation, particularly those consisting of several parts. These differing forms require harmonization, so that terms like these are presented in one form only:

non insulin-dependent diabetes
non-insulin-dependent diabetes
noninsulin-dependent diabetes

'Classified' and 'direct' headings

As in any field of indexing, the aim should be to provide headings in the form in which most users will look for them. In the past, some indexes have tended to group topics under broad headings – so that information on tracheitis can only be located by first looking up 'respiratory system', tracing the subheading 'disorders' and then the sub-subheading 'tracheitis'. Rapid location of needed information may be impeded if topics can only be discovered in this way, particularly when there are several levels of subheading. Any term that is likely to be sought by an index user should feature as a heading in its own right. If thought relevant, it can also be included as a subheading to a broader heading, or included with a *see also* reference.

Subheadings are very often necessary for adequate analysis of the text (see 'Subheadings' in Chapter 4). They should be meaningful and comprehensible, but not consist of lengthy descriptions or explanations – medicine is not practised from the index. Long sequences of subheadings should be helpfully grouped, not mixed regardless of type (see 'Arrangement of entries' below and 'Subheading order' in Chapter 5).

Proper names

Proper names are a prominent feature of many medical indexes. They include:

- personal names (researchers, clinicians, therapists)
- corporate names – hospitals and other treatment centres, educational establishments, pharmaceuticals manufacturers, government departments, regulatory bodies, professional institutions, patient groups, and information providers
- proprietary names of drugs
- disorders named after the people who first identified them or the place where they were first notified
- genera of infectious organisms

The principal responsibility for ensuring accuracy of names in the text of a document lies with the editor, but the indexer should keep a watchful eye and a handy reference source and should check if in doubt about the way in which any name is presented. Accents should be retained wherever possible, to ensure accuracy and comprehension, to avoid ambiguity, and to avoid offence to named individuals:

Guillain-Barré syndrome

Occasional difficulties with some computer keyboards and printers may mean that accents are not always produced, giving the possibility of confusion of similar terms (see 'Accented letters and special characters' in Chapter 5).

Personal Names

Personal names can provide a valuable trail for tracking the progress of research – pioneering work done on a particular topic by 'Mary North's team', for example, and the career and affiliations of 'Michael South'. Accuracy in the input of personal names is crucial – one omitted or incorrect letter can cause the name to be misfiled and a key bibliographical reference or passage of text overlooked. The international range of medical documentation and indexing generates a large number of indexed surnames (family names), of which the form and entry element may differ from country to country (see 'Personal names' in Chapter 4).

When a prefixed family name becomes part of another term (such as a disorder, treatment or aspect) – the 'von Willebrand factor', for example – the indexer must either discover the conventional form of entry from reputable medical reference sources, or make a decision on the most suitable form. The personal name would, by normal practice, be entered under 'W', but the factor may be more likely to be looked for under 'V'. It is not unknown, of course, for reference sources – in any subject field – to differ in practice. Whatever decisions are taken with regard to name entry, cross-references or general directives are usually necessary to aid users unfamiliar with the treatment of compound and unusual names.

Corporate Names

Many of the corporate names are sometimes represented by initials or short forms, instead of – or as well as – featuring in full:

AIMS = Association for Improvements in the Maternity Services

The indexer should note which forms are used and then select the most suitable one for that particular index, giving cross-references or making additional entries for the others. It does happen that a set of initials may have more than one meaning, even within a single specialism, so the indexer must check the meaning in each case and avoid gathering together references to different organizations.

Proprietary (Brand) Names

Texts normally distinguish brand and generic names by the use of initial capitals for brands:

> aspirin
> Disprin

and the index should follow this style. Some brand names have capital letters within the name, not just at the beginning; these must be retained:

> Beta-Adalat

Generic names for drugs are normally internationally used, but brand names are bestowed by manufacturers for use in specific locations, so can differ from country to country. In a cumulated index to documents from a variety of international sources, the indexer needs to ensure either cross-referencing or double entry for two names for the same drug.

Disorder Names

Only those disorders that contain proper names (of people or places, for example) require initial capital letters:

> Dupuytren's contracture

Organism Names

The scientific (genus and species) names of organisms are conventionally presented in italic, with an initial capital for the first element of the name:

> *Clostridium tetani*
> *Entamoeba histolytica*

Virus names and groups are not italicized:

> Epstein-Barr virus
> myxoviruses

Keyword indexing

Indexing using only the significant words from titles of books, articles and other documents can help to provide a rapid current-awareness service, notifying those in the field of new publications. Titles in medical literature are usually (not always) indicative of their content and so title words are likely to be helpful. However, unless edited – with added cross-references, for example – variant spellings (oestrogen/estrogen) and different terms for the same concept (keratitis/corneal inflammation) will not be matched and so the references will appear in separate alphabetical parts of the index.

Thesauri and classification schemes

Indexers working with journals, abstracting services and bibliographical databases, which often require the consistent use of terms (including cross-references) based on a worked-out structure of the whole subject field, can draw on one of the medical thesauri or classification schemes. The National Library of Medicine (in the US) publishes *Medical subject headings* (MeSH), which covers the whole field, primarily for use with *Index medicus* and the Medline database. When MeSH is used in the UK, modifications to spelling may be required and some terms (such as those representing disorders and treatments) may need replacing by the UK equivalents. Many other lists of terms exist, focusing on specific conditions or areas of study – HIV/AIDS, alcohol and drug abuse, and disability, for example.

Arrangement of entries

The suggestion by Mulvany (1994, pp. 126–127) that word-by-word order may give better groupings in indexes with many related, multipart phrases is relevant to medical indexes (see 'Alphabetical arrangement' in Chapter 5). On the other hand, letter-by-letter order – which ignores spaces and hyphens – is better at handling the variant formations of terms that appear in the medical literature:

    anticoagulants
    anti-coagulants

Hyphens and other punctuation marks which occur in medical terms:

>DNA-protein cross-links
>Jun-N-kinase
>Pott's fracture

must never be omitted from headings, even when ignored in filing (see 'Punctuation marks: their effects on order' in Chapter 5).

In subheading sequences any essential function words that are retained can be either ignored in the filing order, or treated as significant, depending on the desired grouping. The word 'and' is often used in subheadings, in the general sense of 'in relation to', but may sometimes be more usefully replaced by 'effect of', 'caused by', 'result of', or another more specific phrase. This sequence (arranged alphabetically by significant words, ignoring function words):

>obesity:
>>cancer and
>>in children
>>and fatty foods
>>in Germany
>>and heart disease
>>in office workers
>>in Scotland
>>and sugar

could be more usefully arranged (using some function words and substitute phrases) as:

>obesity:
>>children
>>office workers
>>in Germany
>>in Scotland
>>link with fatty foods
>>link with sugar
>>risk of cancer
>>risk of heart disease

Other groupings and phrases are possible – the choice should suit the text being indexed.

References

British Standards Institution (1996) *Information and documentation – guidelines for the content, organization and presentation of indexes* BS ISO 999: 1996. London: British Standards Institution

Mulvany, Nancy C. (1994) *Indexing books*. Chicago: University of Chicago Press

United States National Library of Medicine (2000) *Medical subject headings (MeSH)*, 2000 supplement to *Index medicus*. Pittsburgh, PA: Government Printing Office [Annotated, permuted, and tree structure compilations are also available. Information and a fact sheet are available on the internet at: www.nlm.nih.gov/mesh

Wyman, Pilar (1999) Medical indexes reviewed. *The Indexer*, **21**, 125–126

Further Reading

Blake, Doreen, Clarke, Michèle, McCarthy, Anne, and Morrison, June (1995) *Indexing the medical and biological sciences*. Occasional papers on indexing: no.3. Sheffield: Society of Indexers

Wellisch, Hans H. (1995) *Indexing from A to Z* 2nd edn. New York: H.W. Wilson (pp. 299–313: Medical texts)

Wyman, L. Pilar (1999) *Indexing specialties: medicine*. Medford, NJ: Information Today, Inc

Archaeology

This respected academic subject has produced, and continues to produce, much very detailed and well-researched literature, a large proportion of which is of interest to archaeologists and historians but not normally seen by bookshop customers or library users. In recent years a more general interest in archaeology has been sparked by the creation of 'heritage' sites, radio and TV programmes focusing on the exploration of particular sites and buildings, and by the remodelling of local and national museum displays. As a result, there is now a range of documents requiring indexing, from simple books for children to dense and highly technical reports for professionals.

Knowledge of the subject, at the appropriate level, is necessary. In indexes for professional and academic use, there are certain conventions – affecting entry terms and the grouping of subheadings – which may differ from standard recommended practice and so need explanation in an introductory note.

Materials and readership

The literature of archaeology consists of:

- encyclopaedias and dictionaries
- atlases and maps
- textbooks for students
- archaeological excavation reports
- academic and professional journals
- museum catalogues
- bulletins and newsletters of archaeological societies
- conference proceedings
- reports of meetings
- scientific method handbooks
- collected archaeological records of geographical and administrative areas
- guides to individual sites and buildings
- surveys of archaeological and historical periods
- introductory books for children
- manuals for amateur archaeologists
- archaeological tour itineraries
- guides for the interested layperson

Much information also appears in non-text forms – films, videos, photographic prints and slides – and on internet web sites. Collections of found objects also need an indexer's attention. In the recent past, some lengthy documents have been produced partly in microfiche form, in order to keep costs down. Newer items are more likely to be placed on the internet for consultation, either in full or as abstracts or summaries.

Users of the literature include professional archaeologists, historians, museum curators, antiquarians, excavation index recorders, conservators, social researchers, architects, planning authorities' staff, school teachers and pupils, tourists, amateur archaeologists, and interested laypeople.

Indexable content

Illustrative content is often of equal value to textual matter, and sometimes is the prime medium of information transmission. Photographic reproductions (halftones) in black and white and in colour, diagrams, and other kinds of illustration all need indexing – sometimes in detail. Additional information contained in tables, footnotes, chapter notes, and other supplementary components, such as appendices on microfiche, should not be overlooked.

In a report in the newsletter of the Society of Indexers' Archaeological Group, Lavell (1995) comments on 'the depressing fact that archaeological report writers are either indifferent to indexes or (occasionally) actively hostile to them'. As in other subject fields, some writers (wrongly) consider a detailed contents list to be sufficient.

Number of sequences

For the majority of documents, the most useful index is a single sequence containing all categories of heading. However, multisequence indexes are commonly found, containing separate sequences for categories such as authors of articles, historical people, geographical locations, and everything else (sometimes loosely known as 'subjects'). The marshalling of index entries into separate sequences can sometimes be justified, when it is of clear benefit to users, but it should not be done as a matter of course.

Language

Indexers in this field require familiarity with outdated terminology as well as access to authoritative specialist dictionaries. Many of the terms encountered are archaic; others still exist in modern-day language but have changed their meanings. Spelling variations and errors are another hazard. Fixed spellings for names of people, places and objects are a comparatively modern feature. Name references in older documents, on buildings and on manufactured items frequently differ; some may be in Latin, some in recognizably modern English, and others may use a vernacular rather than an aristocratic or 'educated' form. Norman French and Anglo-Saxon words also occur.

The general recommendation (see 'Grammatical forms' in Chapter 4) that terms representing countable items should be in the plural, and those for non-countables in the singular, gives a suitable result in most cases. However, if there exists a 'one and only' specimen of a type of object, presenting the term in the singular is justified. Definitions of terms in glossaries or within the main texts of documents normally need to be indexed, particularly when the terms are not in everyday language, or have special meanings within the archaeological community.

Access points

Multiple access points are necessary in most archaeological indexes. Users commonly want to look up archaeological periods, place names (individual settlements, counties, regions, countries), buildings (by name and by type), sites (by name and by type), and artefacts (by name and type). Other categories of interest, depending on the kinds of document being indexed, are historical periods and events, archaeological methods and tools, kinship and social groups, and organizations of various kinds.

Generally, direct entry of terms in indexes is considered most useful, with each sought term appearing as a heading:

daggers
spearheads

and with cross-references provided from category headings:

copper alloy objects *see* daggers; spearheads

Combinations of classified and direct entries are sometimes seen in archaeological indexes, in which references to individual types of artefact are gathered under the category heading – such as 'pottery' – and then subdivided chronologically by period (e.g. 'Neolithic'), each period being further subdivided by individual type ('Peterborough ware'). If broad categories of this kind have to be used as the primary means of access, the basis for grouping should be explained in the introductory note, and sought terms should always be accessible through cross-references (see 'Cross-references' in Chapter 4).

Proper names

Proper names feature extensively in the literature. Careful checking is often needed to ensure that older names are uniformly presented in a cumulated index or an index to a collection of documents; different spellings and different styles of a name should be recognized and the best-known or approved form used as a heading, with *see* cross-references from the other forms (see 'Proper names' in Chapter 4). Older editions of reference books, as well as the latest versions, are necessary for tracking down these variations.

Period Names

These names are of paramount importance in archaeology, but nevertheless are capable of different interpretations: 'All these [period] terms are elastic and unstable, and the usage of the text should always be followed' (Lavell, 1998). The broad periods, such as Palaeolithic, Bronze Age, and Romano-British, may be subdivided (according to the convention for the particular period) into Early/Middle/Late, Early/Middle/Upper or Earlier/Later. Other time-related descriptors are common, such as 'Tudor and Stuart', 'Anglo-Saxon', and 'Celtic'. Alternative and overlapping forms appear, too: 'Middle Ages', 'Medieval', and 'Migration', for example. When two or more period names feature as subheadings, they should be listed in chronological, not alphabetical order.

Place Names

Place names can represent all sizes of area and settlement – from individual fields through villages, towns and cities, regions, countries, and groups of countries. Names are frequently not unique. 'Moscow' is in Russia, in Strathclyde (Scotland) and in several locations in the United States. 'Etruria' is a former country in Italy, a district of Stoke-on-Trent in Staffordshire (England), as well as being the name of the factory set up by Josiah Wedgwood. There are twelve places in England called 'Wootton': in Bedfordshire, Hampshire, Humberside, the Isle of Wight, Kent, Northamptonshire, Oxfordshire (two), Shropshire (two), and Staffordshire (two). Except when a text deals with a restricted geographical area, and the place name therefore has no potential for ambiguity, a name needs amplifying with the county name or other relevant addition. Because of boundary changes, places can shift from county to county or region to region – the English town of Slough is now in Berkshire, but was formerly in Buckinghamshire – so the most recent county affiliation may not always be the appropriate one for an index.

Some places are differently classified – according to their purpose and structure – by government departments and agencies, historical and geographical associations, research institutions, public utilities and service providers, retailers and advertising corporations. The English county of Hertfordshire, for instance, has been variously classed in East Anglia, the South Midlands, the Home Counties, and South-East England. Cross-referencing is frequently necessary to ensure that users do not overlook relevant information because of such diverse approaches.

There are different views on the best form of entry for multipart names. Many names begin with an adjective describing their position, size, or importance, in relation to each other: Little Dunmow, Great Dunmow; North Stoke, South Stoke; Higher Ballam, Lower Ballam. Some adjectival elements indicate past ownership of land or historical association: Abbots Ripton, Kings Ripton. All these can be entered in unaltered form, a practice supported by the guideline in the indexing standard BS ISO 999 (British Standards Institution, 1996, subclause 7.2.2.4), which recommends that multiword terms in common usage should be used without inversion:

> Little Dunmow (under L)
> North Stoke (under N)
> Abbots Ripton (under A)

with, when necessary – double/multiple entry or cross-references for any sought terms after the first.

In practice, in cases where it is more useful to bring together the 'Dunmows', 'Stokes', and 'Riptons', etc. – say, in an index for a local area, indexers may prefer to invert the names:

> Dunmow, Great (under D)
> Dunmow, Little
> Stoke, North (under S)
> Stoke, South
> Ripton, Abbots (under R)
> Ripton, Kings

A third method is to reverse the order for size and directional names:

> Dunmow, Great
> Stoke, North

but to leave names such as Abbots Ripton and Kings Ripton uninverted.

It may sometimes be necessary to consult someone with local knowledge or to check local government sources in order to ensure the correct entry. Whichever method is chosen after considering the purpose of the index and its likely usage, *see* cross-references or general directives should be added (see '*See* cross-references' and 'General directives' in Chapter 4). The introductory note (see 'Introductory note' in Chapter 5) can also explain the practice employed.

Personal Names

The usage of given names (forenames, family names (surnames), titles, and epithets has varied over time, and continues to vary. This can make it difficult, with any certainty, to identify some historical personages. For more information on personal names see 'Proper names' in the 'Genealogy and family history' section which follows, and 'Personal names' in Chapter 4.

Thesauri and classification schemes

Several thesauri, such as Lavell (1989), Museum Documentation Association (1997) and Royal Commission on the Historical Monuments of England (1998), have been published for use in the standardized indexing of archaeological documents. Each one aims to meet the specific purposes of the recording or publishing organization, so is suitable for application in a similar environment. All can be useful in suggesting additional terms and cross-references for inclusion in other indexes. Some are available only in print, some only on the internet, and some in both forms. Links to thesauri and guides to terminology resources are provided on the web sites of the Museum Documentation Association (www.mda.org.uk) and English Heritage, National Monuments Record (www.rchme.gov.uk/ nmr.html).

Choice of locators

Locators relating to illustrations, tables and notes within texts need to be enhanced, in the usual way, by typographic styling (bold, italic) or by suitable abbreviations (see 'Indication of illustrations and other material' in Chapter 4). The practice of printing some archaeological reports in double-column format may require locators to include a column indicator, in addition to the usual page or paragraph numbers. Locators for individual frames (pages) on a microfiche normally refer to the row and the number of the frame or page.

Arrangement of entries

The choice between word-by-word and letter-by-letter order for an individual index should be determined, as always, by comparing the results of both methods to see which gives the better sequence (see 'Alphabetical arrangement' in Chapter 5). Letter-by-letter can be useful where there are many multipart place names, because names appearing in forms with varying spacing and hyphenation (perhaps on maps of different dates) are treated as alike:

Iron Bridge
Iron-Bridge
Ironbridge

References

British Standards Institution (1996) *Information and documentation – guidelines for the content, organization and presentation of indexes*. BS ISO 999: 1996. London: British Standards Institution

Lavell, Cherry (1989) *British archaeological thesaurus*. York: Council for British Archaeology.

Lavell, Cherry (1995) Archaeological indexing workshop, SI Norwich Conference, July 1994. *Trial trench: a newsletter for archaeological indexers*, no. 4, 1–2

Lavell, Cherry (1998) General brief for indexing archaeology, with special reference to Britain and Ireland. *Trial trench: a newsletter for archaeological indexers*, no.7, 8–11

Museum Documentation Association (1997) *MDA archaeological objects thesaurus*. Cambridge: Museum Documentation Association

Royal Commission on the Historical Monuments of England, English Heritage
(1998) *Thesaurus of monument types* 2nd edn. Swindon: Royal Commission
on the Historical Monuments of England

Genealogy and Family History

Genealogy – the professional study and investigation of lines of descent –
is often relevant to legal claims for titles and property, and has strong
links with heraldry. The descent traced is often patrilineal (following the
male line) and based on surname, but matrilineal (female line) ancestry is
also studied – some titles of nobility in the UK, for instance, can descend
through the female line. Family history has a wider interest among the
population at large, being concerned with activities like tracing the
ancestry, socio-economic background and life events of an individual,
discovering connections between people having the same surname, and
researching the origins of surnames and their variations. It has close associations with local and social history, being affected by factors such as local
and national events, occupational patterns, migration, and public health.

Materials and readership

Many individual documents and collections of documents are unindexed
or inadequately indexed. Others have indexes that were made for use at
the time, within the institution or establishment that created the documents, but which require amplification and reorganization for present-day
research use. Full-text searching, when available, can be helpful but may
only reveal the term searched for, not necessarily similar word-forms or
related terms. The materials studied for a particular project – a surname
study, for example – may be published in different countries and so use
varying terminology and observe differing conventions.

Most forms of printed and written document can contain information of interest. Some of the most common are:

- textbooks
- biographies
- town and county histories
- historical travel books
- manuals and guides

- introductions for the amateur
- newspapers
- specialist journals and general magazines
- newsletters of local and amateur societies (e.g. historical, archaeological, literary), and surname groups
- census records
- ecclesiastical records, including those of baptisms, marriages, and burials
- registers and certificates of births, marriages, and deaths
- burial ground records
- membership lists of societies and clubs
- court and assize records
- prison records
- shipping records
- business and company archives
- trade directories
- family papers
- photographs and photographers' records
- maps and accompanying documents (e.g. tithe maps with record books)
- diaries
- correspondence
- property deeds
- wills
- county records
- parish records, including those for workhouses (poorhouses) and almshouses
- school records
- charters of towns, guilds, and companies
- bank records
- warrants to supply goods and services
- street directories
- telephone directories
- commercial and trade directories

Objects such as tombstones, war memorials, commemorative statues and plaques can also be significant. An increasing number of genealogical web sites are appearing on the internet.

Users of indexes include professional genealogists and historians, social and historical researchers, amateur family historians, journalists, and members of the general public.

Indexable content

As well as appearing in the main texts of books and journal articles, genealogical information often features in footnotes or chapter notes. These details may be only a side issue as far as the main theme of the text is concerned, but can be of greater significance to genealogists and family historians who are following other trails. Information is frequently in the form of lists of names, with brief amplifications – dates of birth and death, birthplaces, places of residence, and occupations. Diagrammatic representations – such as genealogical tables and family trees – and graphic and photographic images of individuals and groups, are also common.

Number of sequences

As with archaeological indexes (see above), the separation of entries into more than one sequence can sometimes be justified. For example, if there are large numbers of personal name entries, and also entries for places and occupations, and if usage will be primarily based on personal name searching, it can be more helpful to put personal names in one sequence and places and occupations in another.

Language

Archaic terms occurring in older documents should normally feature as headings, and the necessary cross-references should be added so that users searching under modern terms can be directed. These terms may relate, for example, to occupations that no longer exist or which are now known by other terms, or to illnesses and causes of death that have been renamed. Definitions of such terms need indexing, each with an indicator that the locator leads to a definition.

Proper names

Proper names are the core indexing element in this field, particularly personal names, but also those of places and events. The accurate formation of names and the best choice of entry elements are therefore crucial.

Personal Names

Personal names can consist of just one element, or a few or many elements. Their formation and arrangement in indexes is not always straightforward, but published rules and recommendations give detailed guidance (see 'Personal names' in Chapter 4).

Very few personal names are unique, even within a single country. Some people named in older documents may only be known by a single given name (forename) or a nickname. The use of family names (surnames) and multiple forenames can help to distinguish individuals, but further differentiation is sometimes needed. In a large index covering a wide geographical area or a large expanse of time, details such as dates of birth, dates of death, places of residence, occupations, relationships, titles, and epithets are required. Alternative forms of names are common – 'Richard Septimus Fortune' may appear later as 'Dick Fortune'. In older documents, 'Mary' and 'Maria', 'Isabella' and 'Elizabeth', 'William' and 'Gulielmus' (the English and Latin forms) may refer to the same individuals.

Family names may require cross-referencing between related or variant forms of names – as with Rundle, Rundell, Arundel, and Ford, Forde, fforde. The custom of a family name handed on from generation to generation is a feature of some countries and cultures, but not of all. In Iceland, for example, and formerly in Shetland, a person is identified by a forename followed by a patronymic that is usually derived – according to the custom of the region – from the forename of the father, mother, or an ancestor.

Compound surnames and prefixed surnames can require hard thinking, particularly when different practices are observed in different countries, even in different parts of the same country. Compound names can arise as a result of marriage or inheritance, or by the combination of mothers' and fathers' surnames for their children, or by a person deciding to add another name element later in life. With prefixed names, there is often a dilemma: whether to observe the normal practice of the country of origin (and risk users not finding it because they do not know about that practice) or to treat the name in a 'common-sense' way so that it will be found (but does not conform with the custom of its native area). Whichever conventions are followed for these names, the use of cross-references should be considered to guide users from other name elements. The introductory note (see 'Introductory note' in Chapter 5) can contain an explanation of the treatment of such multipart names.

Place Names

The requirements for place names, and their characteristics, are similar to those relating to archaeology (see the previous section). Many surnames originate in a specific place, therefore particular interest centres on investigating links between place names and personal names – Glasgow the place and Glasgow the surname, for example. Similar links exist between place names and events – Battle the place, and the site of a battle. Headings of different types must therefore be clearly distinguished, and cross-references may be necessary to alert the user to related headings beginning with different letters of the alphabet or existing in variant forms.

Arrangement of entries

Comparison of letter-by-letter and word-by-word arrangements will usually confirm which method best suits an individual index (see 'Alphabetical arrangement' in Chapter 5). Letter-by-letter arrangement may be more useful for listing names, if the aim is to collocate different presentations of the same name. On the other hand, the word-by-word method can give more helpful groupings if there are many multipart headings.

Further Reading

Mulvany, Nancy C. (1994) *Indexing books*. Chicago: University of Chicago Press (Chapter 7: Names, names, names)

Science and Technology

The breadth and depth of science and technology engender many opportunities for knowledgeable and competent indexers. As with advances in medicine, developments in some branches take place at a rapid rate, and the terminological resource is huge. Another feature is the emergence of interdisciplinary fields – some combining different branches of science and technology, others amalgamating elements of natural and social science, or of technology and the arts. Considering all these factors, it is clear that no indexer can take on work at all levels or in all branches of such a vast field. Indexers normally work within the speciality for which they are best qualified, and may also do work at the general level of science and technology for the layperson, or for school students.

Materials and readership

The literature of science and technology includes (in print, on CD-ROM and online):

- textbooks at all levels
- periodicals (widely used for publishing descriptions of current work, results of experiments, and reports of new developments)
- conference proceedings (often containing papers from an international range of contributors)
- technical and research reports
- information bulletins
- fact sheets
- operating manuals for hardware and software
- current-awareness publications: abstracting and indexing periodicals
- bibliographical and other databases
- patent specifications
- standards and regulations
- codes of practice
- plans, drawings, and photographs
- specimens, manufactured objects and samples

Information for internal circulation in industrial companies, university departments and government research establishments is usually written and indexed in-house by technical authors on the staff. Some of these items are made available for external use in modified form. Some current-awareness services (published and in-house) are thoroughly and competently indexed, providing multiple access – by author, by topic, by corporate institution; some have no indexes, thereby critically reducing their information value to the scientific and technological community.

Readership groups include practising scientists and engineers, operators of machinery and equipment of all kinds, people with a general interest in science and technology, knowledgeable non-professionals (amateur astronomers, for example), teachers, librarians, school pupils, university students, media professionals, science writers and readers.

Indexable content

Apart from the main text of books, articles, reports, conference papers and so on, highly indexable information is to be found in lists of bibliographical citations, appendices, tables and illustrations of all kinds.

Number of sequences

Separation into category sequences is sometimes justified by the context – as in the case of very large indexes containing more or less equal numbers of disparate types of heading. Authors' names may at times be more useful in their own sequence, allowing quicker location of the names of researchers known to be working in the same field. The same observation applies to names of corporate institutions. Product and component names and numbers, particularly when they contain words from everyday language, can look odd in a combined index and – unless separated – may require typographical distinction or a qualifier such as 'product'. Chemical and other formulae also fit uneasily into an alphabetical sequence, so may be separated. Botanical and zoological names in Latin (see 'Scientific names' below) are sometimes listed in a separate sequence, but it is not essential to do so – their presentation in italic is sufficient to distinguish them.

Each issue of *Abstracts in new technologies and engineering* (Bowker-Saur), for example, which presents abstracts in subject groupings, has three index sequences – authors, subjects and names, and sources (the journal issues from which the abstracts have been written).

Proper names

As in any literature, all kinds of names may appear, but personal, corporate, product and scientific names are the principal ones of interest in this field.

Personal Names

Bibliographical references feature prominently both within texts and in lists of citations. Whether or not all the authors' names are to be indexed depends on the nature and purpose of the index. If they are included, the form and number of personal names can occasion problems. Some indexes give individual authors' names exactly as they appear in the cited reference, others reduce them to surname and initials (see 'Personal names' in Chapter 4).

Journal articles and reports frequently have multiple authorship, but some indexes only enter the first named (who may not always be the most important) with 'and others' or '*et al*' (Latin abbreviation, meaning 'and others'). Another approach is to create a separate entry for each author; alternatively, all the names may be listed in the entry for the first name, with *see* cross-references from the second and successive names. (See 'Cross-references' in Chapter 6, for examples.)

Scientific Names

Individual flora and fauna, and classes of flora and fauna, can be denoted in texts by their common, everyday names – silver birch, swallow, stag beetle, roses (rose family) – or by their scientific, Latin, names – *Betula pendula, Hirundo rustica, Lucanus cervus, Rosaceae*. Both names are often required in indexes; it is conventional to give the scientific names in italic, with an initial capital for the generic name and lower case for the specific name. The common name can be added in parentheses, or a cross-reference made from it. Only a small percentage of known species have common names, and even those names vary regionally, nationally and internationally, so it is not always appropriate to include them.

Keyword indexing

As with medical indexing, described earlier in this chapter, using keywords from titles (and from texts) can be an effective method in the preparation of current-awareness publications and databases for use by people familiar with the terminology. Titles that adequately indicate document contents are the best suited to this approach, while those containing terms that are not to be taken literally (like 'White elephants in the power generation and supply industry') can result in information being misplaced.

Thesauri and classification schemes

Many thesauri and classification schemes have been published (e.g. Petrites and Kleiber (1998), National Aeronautics and Space Administration (1998)), most of them focusing on a branch of science or technology (such as astronomy) or a collection of related fields (like aeronautical technology and space science). Some are used mainly in conjunction with published abstracts, indexes and online databases. They can be helpful to indexers of individual documents by supplying definitions, indicating synonymous terms and alternative spellings, which may require *see* cross-references, and by showing the conceptual hierarchy of the subject. Some thesauri are multilingual, showing the term in two, three or more languages, and some can be consulted online.

Locators

Locators may necessarily be lengthy when they represent articles in periodicals, particularly for indexes covering several titles, in which each article may need to be identified by abbreviated periodical title, date, volume number, part number, and page numbers. Styles of presenting these details vary. For example:

> J. Biol. Chem. 1956 v218, p97–106

and:

> Proc. Natl Acad. Sci. USA (1982) 79, 4123–4127

Arrangement of entries

The comparative advantages of the two methods of alphabetical arrangement (see 'Alphabetical arrangement' in Chapter 5) must be considered for each index. Word-by-word can be better at arranging multipart headings:

> arc and spark photometers
> arc discharges

arc furnaces
arc lamps
arc sprayed coating
arc welded joints
arcades
arch bridges
arch dams
arches
architectures

Letter-by-letter, on the other hand, can more satisfactorily handle variations in the presentation of technical terms (Mulvany, 1994, pp. 126–127). For example, 'time lapse photography', 'timelapse photography' and 'time-lapse photography' might appear in different periodical articles but, if featuring in the same current-awareness index, can be recognized as representing the same concept.

Punctuation can influence the placing of a heading (see 'Punctuation marks: their effects on order' in Chapter 5). Even when letter-by-letter order is being used and insignificant punctuation is being ignored, giving a filing value to a comma which represents a 'natural break' in a heading can give a better result:

Murre, Common
Murre, Thick-billed
Murrelet, Ancient
Murrelet, Craveri's

Entries beginning with alphabetical or numerical prefixes, or containing numerical and other infixes, require the indexer to have contextual knowledge and ready access to up-to-date reference sources. Alphabetical prefixes are usually ignored as the primary elements in filing when they are the first elements of chemical terms (in Roman, Greek or other characters – sometimes italicized):

B
cis-but-2-ene   [not under 'C']
trans-but-2-ene   [not under 'T']

> C
> cadaverine
> E-cadherin　　[not under 'E']
> caffeine
> β-carotene　　[not under 'B']
> calcium

However, in a text where *cis* isomers are discussed in general, the entry '*cis* isomers' files under 'C'.

The guideline for alphanumerical arrangement in BS ISO 999 (British Standards Institution, 1996, subclause 8.3) proposes that, except for chemical names, headings which begin with numerals be either placed separately before the alphabetical sequence or interfiled as though spelled out. Numerical prefixes and infixes in chemical names should be ignored in filing, except to distinguish homographs:

> I
> indole-3-butyric acid
> indole-5-butyric acid
> indole-3-carbinol
> indole-5-carboxylic acid
> indole-3-propionic acid
>
> M
> 2-methylbut-2-ene
> 3-methylbut-1-ene
>
> N
> nitromethane
> 1-nitronaphthalene
> nitroprussides
> 2-nitrotoluene
> nitrous oxide

In practice, the treatment of prefixed terms among chemists, biochemists, microbiologists, and doctors (and, of course, laypeople) can differ. For example, 'gamma-aminobutyric acid' (short form 'GABA') might be looked for under 'gamma-aminobutyric acid', 'aminobutyric acid' or 'GABA'. For this reason, cross-references or double/multiple entry are almost always necessary, to provide for all the alternative approaches.

It must be remembered, too, that some characters can have more than one meaning, dependent on their use. Mulvany (1994, p. 137) highlights four common uses of the Greek letter μ – each requiring different treatment.

References

British Standards Institution (1996) *Information and documentation – guidelines for the content, organization and presentation of indexes* BS ISO 999: 1996. London: British Standards Institution

Petrites, Seyem D. and Kleiber, Michael C. (1998) *ITS thesaurus: a controlled, hierarchical vocabulary for indexing materials relating to intelligent transportation systems.* Berkeley, Cal: University of California, Institute of Transportation Studies

Mulvany, Nancy C. (1994) *Indexing books.* Chicago: University of Chicago Press

National Aeronautics and Space Administration (1998) *NASA thesaurus.* NASA [Details are available on the internet at: www.sti.nasa.gov/thesfrm1.htm]

Further Reading

Wellisch, Hans H. (1995) *Indexing from A to Z* 2nd edn. New York: H.W. Wilson (pp. 465–472: Technical manuals and reports; pp. 463–465: Tables)

Biography

Biography as discussed here is a specialist form of literature, rather than a specialist field of study; a biographical item concerns the life of an individual or a collection of individuals and therefore may refer to whichever specialist subjects are associated with the biographee(s). Biography publishing is an active sector with a sizeable market and, because of the multifarious people, events, places, and activities that can typically feature in even a single book, indexing in this field requires all-round knowledge.

Materials and readership

The most familiar publications, prominent in every bookshop and public library, are biographical and autobiographical books dealing with the life of an individual. Most comprise single volumes, but detailed accounts of the lives of significant figures may run into two or more volumes, each one maybe having its own index, or there may be a single index covering all the volumes. Other published material relating to individuals comes in the form of diaries and memoirs. Some biographies deal with collections of people, such as eminent figures in chemistry, or the members of an artistic group like 'the Impressionists'. Apart from publications that are principally biographical in content, some books and journal articles contain indexable biographical information, sometimes in footnotes, chapter notes or appendices. Collections of correspondence, too, may have a separate section of biographical notes.

The readership for biography is extensive. Depending on the identity of the biographee and the subject background against which the life is presented, readers may be students and teachers of any discipline, members of any occupation, friends and family, or observers of human life in general.

Indexable content

The main text is normally the chief source, but the preliminaries – such as preface, foreword, dedication, and acknowledgements – may also contain significant references. There may be illustrations – of people, places and events – that require inclusion. Items in lists such as bibliographies or appendices are often indexable – for example, the titles of works in a chronological list of plays written by an author, showing for each one the date and location of the first performance, the principal actors and the producer.

Bell (1998) describes the indexing of biography as an unappreciated art, and emphasizes 'the daunting nature of the task of reducing the subtleties of a human life to structured categories'. There is a delicate aspect to biographical indexing, too. Some biographies are of a highly personal nature, and their indexes may seem to highlight references to intimate matters, dreadful crimes, shameful actions, glaring errors, and obscene or scandalous remarks (see 'Sensitive content' in Chapter 3). Not all biographical material is concerned with the critical exposure of private vices, misdemeanours and personal traumata; much relates to the chronicling of individual achievements and activities.

Good indexing practice requires indexers not to reveal their own opinions and prejudices in their indexes; this is particularly applicable to biographical indexing (see 'Neutrality of the indexer' in Chapter 2).

Headings should reflect the attitudes described in the text; the indexer's critical view or bias should not be apparent from the words chosen for headings. Because of concern about some types of content, and reluctance to contribute to the publication and furtherance of ideas or statements of which they disapprove, some indexers are selective about the biographical indexing jobs they undertake.

Number of sequences

A single sequence containing all kinds of heading is normally best. It is sometimes claimed that a few readers of biographies are initially interested only in checking whether their own names, or those of their friends and acquaintances, appear in the indexes. This limited interest does not justify the placing of personal names in a separate sequence.

'Classified' and 'direct' headings

A typical biography contains references to many aspects of an individual's life – birth, marriage, divorce, bereavement, education, career, family and other relationships, social activities, travels, opinions and attitudes, and so on. The representation of these as index terms is a matter of constant debate. Three points in particular need consideration: first, the choice of aspects to be shown as subheadings under the name of the biographee, rather than (or as well as) direct headings; second, the amount of detail to be included in subheadings; third, the best method of arranging the subheadings. There is usually a need for the name of the biographee to appear as a heading, though this is sometimes disputed on the grounds that if a person is the subject of the whole book then a heading for the person's name is superfluous – just as an index to a book on architecture would not normally require a heading 'architecture'. Where a name heading is given for the person, very long subheading sequences (perhaps also including sub-subheadings), within which a user has to conduct a long search, can be tiresome. Some indexers therefore prefer to limit the subheadings to those for major life events (birth, marriage, divorce, death), personal attributes and principal activities. All other matters are then entered under their own headings. Other indexers insist on the value of a detailed analysis under the main name, taking great care to present the subheadings in suitable groups (see 'Arrangement of entries' below). The general recommendation for index headings and subheadings is that they should be meaningful, comprehensible and concise; following this advice should ensure that they do not appear in the form of long phrases extracted unaltered from the text.

Proper names

Proper names may seem to be the stuff of biography, and certainly they often feature prolifically. Wherever they occur, care is needed to index them correctly, recognizably and accessibly.

Personal Names

Individuals can be known by many different names or forms of name during their lives, acquiring and discarding given names, family names, nicknames, pseudonyms, and titles. Indexers are not always responsible for tracking the various names used by an individual, but they do need to make entries for the correct or most suitable forms (not necessarily the fullest possible forms) and to provide cross-references to other sought forms (see 'Personal names' in Chapter 4). In correspondence and diaries, for example, references to 'Miss Collins', 'Mrs MacBride', 'Margaret', and 'Peggy' can all relate to the same person, and so need to be gathered together under one name, with references from other forms. Cross-references may be necessary, too, to guide users from a pet name used familiarly within a family to the formal name used as a heading:

> 'Wol' *see* Grimley, Walter Oliver Leslie

Names with epithets, such as those linking a person with a place or describing a characteristic or attribute, are entered in their normal form, not inverted – Ethelred the Unready, Jack of Newbury. Cross-references or double/multiple entries should be made if relevant; it may be useful, for example, to refer from, or enter under, the place 'Newbury', but to do the same with 'Unready' would be unnecessary (except in an index to epithets).

There may frequently be a need to add words indicating family relationships or occupations, particularly when there are people with the same or very similar names:

> Strong, Eleanor *mother of FP*
> Strong, Eleanor *portrait painter*

Arrangement of entries

The arrangement of proper names, including compound and prefixed surnames and names with epithets, titles, or unusual punctuation, may need special attention (see 'Alphabetical arrangement' in Chapter 5) to ensure that they file in the most suitable order for the index.

The choice of subheading order should be influenced by the nature of the text being indexed and the expected needs of the users of the index (see 'Subheading order' in Chapter 5). Some biographies start at the beginning of a life and follow it through to the finishing point, while some are divided into thematic chapters, and others are a hybrid of chronology and theme. In the first case, arranging subheadings in chronological order will give the same result as arranging them in page order. In the second and third cases, it will not. Bearing in mind that the index acts as a complement to the text, an arrangement giving an alternative 'finding strategy' to that of the text has something to be said for it. If many subheadings are to be entered under the name of the person, the subject-grouped (classified, thematic) method is often the better, providing clear and easily identifiable clusters of associated subheadings, each of which is easily searched.

Introductory note

As well as the usual matters (such as coverage and exclusions, indicators for illustrations and major references – see 'Introductory note' in Chapter 5), any repeated use of abbreviations for people or institutions should be explained, e.g.: 'Angela Carter is referred to throughout as AC'; 'RSC stands for the Royal Shakespeare Company'.

References

Bell, Hazel K. (1998) *Indexing biographies and other stories of human lives* 2nd edn. Occasional papers on indexing: no.2. Sheffield: Society of Indexers

Further Reading

Mulvany, Nancy C. (1994) *Indexing books*. Chicago: University of Chicago Press (Chapter 7: Names, names, names)

Wellisch, Hans H. (1995) *Indexing from A to Z* 2nd edn. New York: H.W. Wilson (pp. 59–60: Biographies)

CHAPTER NINE

Literature for children

The core indexing techniques explained in Chapters 3, 4 and 5 apply to all kinds of indexing. This chapter considers some factors which relate specifically to indexing for children.

Index Awareness

If learning to read – or listening to others read – is the most important experience of anyone's early life, stimulating the imagination and encouraging an interest in words and language, the concept of 'compressing' a text into selected words and phrases for an index may seem to be counterproductive. On the other hand, we may ask, is it ever too soon to introduce a child to an index? Certainly, there may be no need to wait until the child can read fluently. Once there are obvious signs of an interest in looking at pictures and text – in print or on screen – the notion of 'how to find' an item can be ushered in, accompanied by the excitement of discovery.

Most parents read to their children at some time, so using an index can be a complementary activity. Parental examples of the consultation of lists, and the selection and following up of items from the lists, are crucial at an early stage – not only when encouraging and instructing the child in the use of printed and on-screen documents, but when using different kinds of information resources for the parents' own purposes, such as checking addresses and phone numbers in address books and telephone directories, looking up favourite recipes in cookery books, finding words in dictionaries, and picking out and clicking on items in screen lists. Those children who are introduced early to word and spelling games may soon go on to become eager readers and competent users of indexes.

This early familiarity with indexes and lists can stimulate the imagination and establish the idea of 'the index' as a normal, expected and desired component of any information-bearing item. Even from casual observation of the way in which today's adults use books and other materials, it is easy to see that many of them did not even become 'index aware' during their years of formal and informal education, let alone develop the associated information-seeking skills.

At a later stage, alongside index use, children can learn to construct simple indexes, perhaps to individual books that they have been given or – more interestingly – to a selection of books in their collections. Questions formulated by parents or other carers, such as 'Where [in which book or books] is there a picture of a tiger?' and 'How many mentions of the Tower of London can you find?' can be answered by searching the collection and noting down the locations. This kind of exercise – and similar activities staged by the children's sections of public libraries – can also show the child that information comes in different forms – sometimes words alone, sometimes an illustration, sometimes a combination; if computer-held multimedia information is also included, then audio and the moving image can be added to the list.

The National Curriculum (for England and Wales) includes guidelines that specify that pupils should be taught how to find information in documents and use indexes. A valuable study of the provision and quality of indexes in information books for children at National Curriculum Key Stage 2 was carried out by Williams and Bakewell (1997). The children they studied showed a high level of index awareness and understanding of the difference between indexes and contents lists. Dixon (1996), in a paper describing an earlier survey, noted that librarians favoured children's early introduction to indexes and also the idea that books should be used as tools for discovering information. She emphasized that children should be able to find what they want in the index at the first attempt, otherwise they will probably give up.

The children (and grandchildren) of indexers should, of course, be perfectly situated to receive first-class guidance and could have a head start when preparing for life in the 'knowledge society'. Many freelance indexers start their careers on a part-time basis while raising their children and continue this double, and demanding, existence for a number of years. Others, perhaps having moved on from other occupations, may combine freelance indexing with the occasional care of grandchildren.

During the formal schooling years, the development of the child's information-seeking skills should proceed concurrently with the further acquisition of knowledge. To a certain extent, this is a natural and involuntary process. It is always dependent on factors such as the personality and temperament of the child, the physical home environment, family attitudes to learning and knowledge, and the quality and resources of the teaching institution. Whatever the nature and circumstances of the child, however, some organized and structured tuition in information skills, which should include the use and compilation of simple indexes, is essential. The role of teachers and school librarians is pivotal.

Organized education is usually strictly age-related, with all pupils in the same age cohort receiving the same level of instruction. This can be a severe disadvantage for children who – for example – have not had much pre-school or home experience with learning materials. The school library (if there is one) and a good librarian (sometimes performing a dual role of teaching and information provision) can be of great value in helping to compensate for this lack. Friendly tuition and the gradual introduction to resources – including the use of indexes – can give diffident children the boost they need and enable them to take better advantage of what is available. Indexers practising in this field may sometimes be asked (or may themselves offer) to talk with groups of children about 'finding their way in books' and (with older pupils) about how indexes are made.

At the undergraduate level, university and college librarians have often noted a lack of competence among some incoming students; knowledge of the existence of general reference books may be limited, and the ability to consult (successfully) basic sources such as library catalogues is absent. To help fill this gap, first-year library induction and follow-up sessions are organized in many academic institutions, to help familiarize students with the wealth of materials available so that their academic work (and eventual results) can benefit. Freelance indexers could offer professional assistance to their academic acquaintances in this respect, being able to explain the way in which indexes are compiled and constructed and how to use them.

Documentary Forms

Some very young children are using computers, selecting items from pictorial menus in order to produce images and to play games; this experience can be seen as an introduction to a type of index. For many, though, the first form of structured and organized information they encounter is still likely to be a small, easily handleable (but robust) book. The content may be largely in the form of colour illustrations, or outlines to be coloured in, or 'lift-up' and 'pop-up' features, with small amounts of text – perhaps single-word captions to pictures. Topics may be common everyday themes, although – at least in the UK – 'exotic' animals (elephants, lions) tend to be popular subjects. As the child grows, so the material increases in content range, and the language develops, with wider vocabulary and longer phrases. The semantic scope starts to extend, too, with the introduction of examples of words with similar meanings, opposites, and categories of words (denoting colour, shape, and number, for example) – all giving excellent early practice in the kind of identifying, grouping, and relating processes on which indexing and indexes are based.

Children who quickly develop an interest in looking at books and in learning to read are likely not to confine themselves to their own collections, but will explore those belonging to any older children and of adults in the household. The presence, availability and frequent use of a home computer is also likely to prompt a desire to explore electronic resources. Influences from pre-schools and playgroups can further encourage and reinforce a child's interest and abilities. By the time children reach the age of formal education (the legal age for starting school varies from country to country), some may already be able to read, and others may have had their interest in looking at printed and electronic materials stimulated to the extent that they are ready to take full advantage of what the school curriculum has to offer.

As time goes by, the range of documents that the child encounters – at school and at home – widens to encompass not just illustrated items, but fictional tales, accounts of travel and adventure, poetry, reference materials, school textbooks, magazines, maps and atlases, television and radio listings, art originals and reproductions, audiotapes, music CDs, films and videos, slides and transparencies, CD-ROMs, kits, and models. Some of these materials appear more indexable (and index-worthy) than others, but if children have access to a good library and are given instruction in how to identify and locate items through catalogues, their knowledge and understanding of access through indexes can be developed. Older pupils can be introduced to the idea of reading a book's index as an indicator of its content or an analytical tool, not solely as a finding device for a particular topic. Since most of the indexed documents encountered by pupils up to this stage are very likely to be what is generally termed 'non-fiction', it may be appropriate at this stage to highlight the possibilities of indexes to fiction items (see 'Fiction indexing' below).

At the time of writing it is not possible to predict to what extent e-books (electronic books) (see 'Document technology' in Chapter 11) – recently introduced to the market – will replace print-on-paper documents. Full-text searching gives increased accessibility in so far as the location of words is concerned, but does not provide the same level of precision that indexing by concepts (ideas) supplies. As things stand at present, the unique experience of handling and using printed materials – particularly those in book and related forms – cannot be supplanted, and should be emphasized as a counterbalance to the idea that anything and everything of worth is available via the computer (on the internet, on CD-ROM).

The use of computers at the primary level of schooling in the UK has varied, but should level out as a result of National Curriculum requirements and the intention to provide internet links in all schools. The time available, per child, on school computers is limited in infant classes, and some young children have more experience than others because of their domestic environment. Those in whose homes computers are used every day, for recreational or business purposes, are more likely to be conversant with the basic features and operations.

The Indexing Needs and Information Skills of Children

The purposes for which children consult indexes will naturally vary according to factors such as reading age, interests, and educational environment. Children need to be taught how to use indexes, but the tuition need not (and should not) be restricted to a formal teaching situation. The fascination of discovering bits and pieces of information – by reading from cover to cover, dipping in here and there, looking at the illustrations first, scanning and skimming, and all the other ways in which children use texts – fits easily with the idea of trying to remember in which book or on which page something was seen. Recognition of the usefulness of 'making a note' follows from that and lays the foundation for the making and using of indexes.

Simple exercises can include finding a mention of a concrete (physical, 'tangible') topic (such as 'castles' or 'earthquakes') in one or more books, locating an illustration of a particular object (a helicopter, perhaps), and looking up a named person to find basic information (such as place and date of birth). The first two examples require the child to understand that the index is in alphabetical order and that topics are entered under words that specifically denote them; the third needs the additional understanding that personal names are normally indexed with the family name first. Later practice, for older children, can introduce the idea of abstract concepts (like courage, health, and friendship), and different aspects of a subject (silver mining, silver jewellery, silver added in cooking, for example) leading to the use of subheadings in indexes.

The minimum mental capabilities needed for children to be able, unaided, to use the most basic printed indexes are:

- ability to read and understand the relevant fund of words
- understanding and memorization of alphabetical order
- understanding and memorization of numerical order

When first encountering *see* and *see also* cross-references in indexes, most children need explanation and guidance from an adult or older child. Williams and Bakewell (1997) noted that most of the children in their study found cross-references difficult to comprehend.

To be able to start to create simple indexes, they must have – in addition to the abilities listed above – the capacity to:

- identify the main topics of a piece of text
- present the topics as suitable index headings – ensuring that the sought terms come at the beginning, including inverting personal

names; forming nouns in the relevant singular or plural form; making nouns from verbs. It is important at this stage to emphasize the caution that indexing is not just extracting words and spotting names
- assemble the topics into alphabetical order
- add accurate locators (page numbers, for example)

More advanced creative tasks – identification of synonyms and variant spellings and consequent provision of *see* and *see also* cross-references, composition of subheadings, distinction of references to illustrations and other special features – can follow at a later stage.

Characteristics of Indexes for Children

The presence of an index in a book is not usually conspicuous, which is particularly unfortunate in the case of books for children. If there is an index, by convention it is likely to be the last element of the book and listed as the last item in the contents list (if there is one). From one point of view, the index might be better situated at the beginning, along with the preliminary pages – title page, contents list, and list of illustrations – in order to encourage early familiarity with index arrangement and use and to stimulate the young reader to expect indexes to be provided as a matter of course. On the other hand, indexes in adult books are usually at the end, and Williams and Bakewell (1997) record a teacher's comment that if children are taught to look in one place for the index, it is frustrating for them to find that it is somewhere else. Wherever an index is positioned, the publisher should give it due respect; Williams and Bakewell stress the importance of the index having its own page or pages, not just being fitted on the last page of text 'as though an afterthought'.

At present, the level of provision of indexes in children's books is patchy, with some publishers including them whenever they are considered relevant and others rarely doing so. Some of the reasons given to Williams and Bakewell (1997) for lack of indexes in particular books included: not enough space, not enough time, books were small or contained very little text, books were arranged alphabetically, and books were for home rather than school use (it is not clear why the publisher thought that this made a difference). School libraries and local public libraries can influence publishers and other document producers in this regard, if, when assessing and selecting materials for their stock, they favour those containing good indexes. Dixon (1996) was told by a school librarian that she would not buy unindexed books for the library unless they were otherwise exceptional, and schools library service librarians questioned by Williams and Bakewell also recommended that books without indexes should not normally be bought for school use.

It is not just a question of 'having an index'. It is crucial that the index should be of high quality, observing all the canons of good indexing practice: in particular – concise, consistent and comprehensible headings using words from the text and words that children will use for 'look-up'; accurate locators (children will be mystified and deterred if they cannot find information on the indicated page); no long strings of locators without at least an indication of the major references; no sought terms hidden away as subheadings only; correctly constructed and relevant cross-references; clear layout; explanation where needed.

Children learn and develop at different rates, so guidance in index use and preparation for them cannot be provided strictly in relation to specific ages. Much depends on whether children are working independently or with a teacher. In general terms, book index use by younger children is best aided by:

- a short index, displayed at a single opening (one or two pages)
- one A-Z sequence only (names and other kinds of terms not separated)
- headings composed only of single words or short phrases
- 'main' headings only; no subheadings (Dixon (1996) suggests that subheadings should be avoided in books for children below eleven years of age)
- inclusion of all possible 'look-up' terms
- in books containing a description or an illustration for each of a number of single items (a kangaroo, a duck-billed platypus), use of the singular form of these 'countable' nouns is better than the plural – 'giraffes' as a heading may seem odd if leading to a single picture of a lone animal
- illustrations (usually the most important element as far as the young child is concerned) indicated by special forms of locator
- capital letters used only at the beginning of proper names (not for all headings) – to aid discrimination of different meanings. This

practice is in line with the grammatical rules that the children learn from their teachers

- page numbers for locators (not paragraph or figure numbers – though this does depend on the use and prominence of such numbers in the text)
- the word 'pages' displayed at the head of each column of locators
- short locator strings, perhaps no more than 3 locators (see 'Locators' below)
- page ranges given in full form (34–35, not 34–5) (see 'Locators' below)
- limited use of bold and italic type; if used, they must be conspicuous (see 'Typestyles' below)
- absence of abbreviations
- a linespace between each letter sequence, and a display letter (A, B, C . . .) at the beginning of each letter sequence (see 'Signposting and directions' below)
- clearly printed, contrasty and well-spaced type in an easily readable size and font, on good quality paper
- few (if any) cross-references; double entry may be better. If some cross-references are needed, an alternative form of words (rather than the usual 'see . . .') may be advisable (see 'Cross-references' below)
- no general directives such as '*see names of individual animals*'. If essential, the use of *see* and *see also* with the names of specific animals should be used
- use of colour and decoration in the index

Older children are better able to deal with more complex features:

- headings of more than one word, and containing longer words
- headings containing inverted terms, including personal names
- headings for personal names with titles and epithets
- subheadings, which are clearer when presented in the set-out style (see 'Subheading layout' in Chapter 5); sub-subheadings are probably best avoided, except for more advanced specialist works
- more than one index sequence (common names and scientific names, for example)
- longer indexes (covering more than one page opening, arranged in columns, and containing broken sequences with continuation statements)

- more complex locators (containing number of volume as well as of page; using bold and italic type for certain kinds of content; including abbreviations)
- introductory note, clearly explaining the content, form and features of the entries (see 'Introductory note' in Chapter 5)
- cross-references (*see* and *see also*) (see 'Cross-references' below)
- general directives to look also at names of individual items (see 'General directives' in Chapter 4)

They can also understand and practice using indexes of different kinds, such as:

- combined indexes to more than one document
- 'first lines of poems' indexes
- magazine/periodical indexes
- CD-ROMs, multimedia and online forms with full-text searchability and using links
- concordances

Headings – selection of terms, editing, modification and addition

As with adult documents, some children's texts are easier than others to 'mine' for ideas and terms. Most of the index headings are likely to be extracted from the text, but the usual subsequent editing process is necessary in order to harmonize differing word-forms ('sport' and 'sports', 'measuring' and 'measurement'), and to add contextualizing information. Synonyms not used in the text, but which might be looked for by readers, must be identified and then included either as headings in their own right (double/multiple entry) or as *see* cross-references. Dixon (1996) reports one publishing house that preferred the index not to include terms used in the contents list, so as to accentuate the contrast between the two kinds of list; however, to do this, and so omit from the index major terms likely to be looked for, would be bad practice.

Opinions differ concerning the length and components of headings. Dixon (1996) concludes from her survey that phrases, perhaps including synonyms, are better than single words, whereas about two-thirds of the respondents to Williams and Bakewell (1997) preferred words to phrases. It is risky to generalize in relation to all books for all children; indexers should – as with all their work – consider the targets and requirements of each document and act accordingly, using single words or phrases in the most suitable way.

The terms featured in the index are sometimes highlighted in the body of the text, so that the readers can locate them easily on the page. This kind of presentation is for the editor and author to decide and is not the responsibility of the indexer. The indexer needs to know if this is intended, so that index terms can be (as far as possible) made to match the text words.

Glossary and definitions

It is common for an information book for children to contain a glossary – a list of terms and their definitions that the reader needs to know in order to be able to understand the rest of the text. In some cases it precedes the main text, in others it follows it, and occasionally it is combined with the index. With a combined index and glossary, the reader has only one list to consult for information, but may be confused by the two kinds of entry (index entry and definition). Williams and Bakewell (1997) state that reactions to combined indexes were mixed. A separate glossary, on the other hand, can be used as as a quick-access guide to new terms, and – because all glossary terms are highly significant and central to the subject – the terms should be included in the index so that they can be found together with other relevant information.

The signposting of definitions of terms (whether in a glossary or located in the text) is clearly important in indexes for children, particularly those used for finding out about unfamiliar subjects. Many of the terms they look up may not have a clear meaning to them, so the first information they need is a definition. Using the word 'glossary' or 'definition' (or an abbreviation) as a subheading, or adding a symbol to the locator, helps the reader to pick it out easily.

Alphabetical order

The two methods of alphabetizing – word-by-word and letter-by-letter – are both in use in children's literature, as they are in the adult world (see 'Alphabetical order' in Chapter 5). It would be convenient to be able to confirm unreservedly that one of the methods is far and away the best for children, but it cannot be reliably done. There seems to be no instinctive tendency towards one method or the other. Williams and Bakewell (1997) reported that around two-thirds of their respondents (indexers, librarians, teachers, parents, writers, and publishers) favoured the word-by-word system for children's books. The consultation of indexes is not easy to observe or analyse, and users (whether adults or children) may find it difficult to explain the intuitive process. One teacher suggested to Williams and Bakewell (1997) that children may go to the general relevant area of the index and then scan for the desired word, rather than proceed through the first, second and third letters to find it; for this approach, word-by-word order would be better. A librarian, on the other hand, felt that the letter-by-letter system was easier because children are already familiar with the straight alphabetical sequence. An indexer suggested that the rigid application of either system could cause problems, and that a more flexible approach should be taken

Dixon (1996) and Williams and Bakewell (1997) recommend the printing of the alphabet (upper and lower case) on the same page as the index, as an aid to finding. As a further help, the individual letter (display letter, header letter) can be printed in large colourful type at the beginning of each new letter sequence. Indexers who are compiling indexes for use by children are best advised (unless the commissioning publisher has a certain house style) to compare the results of their final indexes using both methods and to select the one which – for that particular document – gives the most helpful order.

Older children who are beginning to encounter multiword index headings will need explanation to enable them to understand and recognize the order used. The indexer's introductory note, set out at the head of the index in clear type and well spaced, should provide this information – with at least one example, to show how the system operates (see 'Introductory note' in Chapter 5).

Subheading order

Williams and Bakewell (1997) recommend that subheadings should be used only when absolutely necessary, so that children do not miss useful words hidden under main headings. Any sought term should, in any case, appear as a heading in its own right. When subheadings are justified, they should be restricted to short sequences and arranged in what the indexer judges to be the most helpful order for the intended young readers. There are several possibilities for ordering subheadings within a sequence (see 'Subheading order' in Chapter 5).

Locators

The full form of page ranges (67–70) is more helpful (see 'Page ranges' in Chapter 4), but Williams and Bakewell (1997) report that some children interpreted the dash as a minus sign, and that others referred only to the first page and the last, and not to those in between. A similar confusion was noted by Weinberg (1996), with some children thinking that the comma between two locators connected page numbers exceeding 1000. Mistaken assumptions like these are easily cleared up by adult explanation, but the cases show the importance of some guided instruction in index use. A range should not be presented as 67, 68, 69, 70; to do so implies that information on the topic is to be found on individual parts of these pages, not continuously from the first page to the last.

Long strings of locators (more than six or seven) are not normally advisable in any index – regardless of the age and ability of the reader. In indexes for younger children, short strings (perhaps a maximum of three) should be the rule. Some older children may enjoy the thrill of the chase by working through longer strings until they find exactly what they want, whereas others may be discouraged by having to spend time discovering which reference is the best. In most cases the indexer should indicate the principal reference(s) leading to the fullest or most important information (see 'Typestyles' below).

Typestyles

The use of italic type for scientific (Latin) names of animals, flowers and other groups is conventional in indexes; it is also sometimes used for headings that are titles of books and other documents. Bold type can be used to distinguish certain headings, particularly when one class of heading is more important than any other, or when a heading represents a major section of the text.

The styling of locators for illustrations is particularly important in documents that children are likely to search for illustrations, in order to indicate exactly where the illustrations are. This may mean that the specification of locators needs to be more complex; an illustration on one page within a multipage sequence of text is more helpfully represented if individually shown: 'eclipses 78–83, *82*' for example. There are several ways in which this information can be presented (see 'Indication of illustrations and other material' in Chapter 4), so the indexer should select whichever is appropriate for the situation. The majority of respondents in the study by Williams and Bakewell (1997) thought that illustrations should be indexed and that their locators should be distinguished from those for text. The use of either bold or italic type was suggested by some, but disapproved by others on the grounds that bold locators could be interpreted as being the important ones and the italic form not understood or even recognized.

In some typefaces, there is not a sufficiently pronounced distinction between the plain roman, italic and bold versions; it is essential, therefore, that typefaces for children's indexes should be chosen for their clarity. The use of colour as a means of distinction was proposed by some of the respondents to Williams and Bakewell – and it can certainly provide an added attraction – but it was recognized that this was unhelpful to children with colour-blindness. The standard abbreviations *illus.* or *ill.* or *i.* can be used; *pic* was suggested by some respondents, and also the use of symbols as part of the index entry. As pointed out by Williams and Bakewell, children are familiar with design features such as symbols and boxes, through the use of CD-ROMs and computers.

Cross-references

The traditional means of directing a reader from a synonym to the equivalent (preferred) term featured as a heading with locators, is the *see* cross-reference. For suggesting additional places to look – the *see also* cross-reference applies (see 'Cross-references' in Chapter 4). Some indexers doubt whether inexperienced index-users understand cross-references when they find them. In the case of children, particularly the younger ones, '*look at*' and '*also look at*', or – as suggested to Williams and Bakewell (1997) – '*look up*' or '*try the word*', may be more easily understood. The 'adult' instructions, though, will have to be learned sooner or later, and there is a case to be made against teaching children things which they have to 'unlearn' at a later stage.

When adding *see* cross-references for synonymous terms that are not used in the text, the indexer should make sure to include the synonym in parentheses after the heading word that does feature in the text, so that the young reader will recognize the piece referred to. The normal indexing convention is to refer from one to the other without specifying locators:

> airships *see* dirigibles
> dirigibles (airships) 43, 55, 67, 112

Some indexers prefer, for young readers, to provide a 'hybrid' cross-reference/heading:

> airships *see* dirigibles 43, 55, 67, 112

This helps by providing all the information at a single look-up, but the hybrid form may cause confusion for children later on when they find *see* cross-references without locators (the normal form).

The position of a *see also* reference (and its equivalents using different words) should also be considered (see 'Location of cross-references' in Chapter 4). It should usually follow the locator for the heading (or subheading) from which it refers:

> queens 123, 201 *see also* empresses

Alternatively, when there is the possibility of the *see also* reference being overlooked – perhaps because there is a long list of subheadings before it – it can be placed in parentheses between the heading (or subheading) and its locators:

> queens (*see also* empresses) 123, 201

An indexer needs to consider carefully the effect of positioning *see also* cross-references and to choose the form that seems most suitable for the age range of the intended reader. Placing words in parentheses in the middle of an entry seems likely to confuse children who are not used to index conventions.

Because the use of cross-references may be new to some of the index users, they should be simply explained – with examples – in the introductory note. Given adequate guidance from teachers, librarians or parents, children can get into the habit of dealing with quite complicated concepts.

Signposting and directions

Indexes – even those for adult use – can sometimes appear stark and uninformative when they are long and dense, with only the gradual succession of alphabet letters and page numbers giving any indication of order. For any explanation of the use of bold, italic and abbreviations, the reader must turn back to the beginning of the index where there should be an introductory note. This can clearly explain coverage, form of locators, typographical features, method of alphabetization, order of subheadings, and anything that the user may need to know. The study by Williams and Bakewell (1997) found that children (like many adult readers) did not read the introductory notes and even at first denied their existence. This situation can be remedied by earlier guidance in index use and by adding information (in boxes, or as running notes, for example) throughout the index, which not only brightens the aspect but helps readers to find what they want more speedily.

Bold letters (A, B, C . . .) should be displayed at the beginning of each sequence. If the index entries are a mixture of proper names (starting with capital letters) and other headings (beginning with small letters), then both forms of the letter should be shown.

If the index can be printed on different coloured paper from that of the text, or in another colour, or if the letter sequences can be thumb-indexed or given coloured edges, this makes it stand out as a different and important component of the book. The increased production cost involved in this kind of provision is just one reason why it is not a common feature of children's books.

Fiction Indexing

Children's fiction, like fiction for adults, is rarely indexed. Most authors and publishers of fiction probably do not even consider the need for indexes. The idea is, in any case, contentious. Bell (1992), writing in relation to adult fiction, points out that more could be made of the 'serious' fiction resource if indexes were provided. However, she has objections to the idea of indexing for children (1999, personal communication), considering that a child's early reading should concentrate on learning to see and appreciate the book as a whole and that the child should be encouraged to persevere with it, not pick and choose or omit sections because they are too long or uninteresting or irrelevant.

An alternative view is that the fun of reading and a desire to explore further can be stimulated through indexes. Characters, objects, events, actions, places, and abstract concepts are all indexable, and children can be encouraged to use indexes by being able to trace their 'favourite bits' in books that they have already read or by looking up interesting historical characters to see if they appear in texts that they have not yet tried. The exploration of children's classics and of myths and legends, for example, can be encouraged through indexes. Following trails and going from text to text – rather like using hypertext links in multimedia sources – can be an exhilarating and knowledge-widening experience.

The Nature and Value of the Work

Indexing has a low profile in the world at large, and the uninformed may suppose that indexing for children is the easiest of all kinds of indexing. This is a mistaken idea. Although the texts may be short in extent and simple in terms of the ideas and vocabulary they contain, the indexer (an adult) has still to 'think like the reader' and so to set aside the impedimenta of mature years. The formation of suitable headings, the indication of illustrative material, the presentation of the entries, and the design of the whole index (in which the indexer should be involved), are influences on readers that can thereafter affect their use of documents and the benefits they gain from them. The financial reward for the work must not be devalued on the grounds that 'it's only for children'. Williams and Bakewell (1997) reported that half of the publishers who responded to their questionnaire never used a professional indexer and that the general tendency was for the index to be compiled by the editor of the book, although some thought that the author was the best person to compile it.

Indexers who are involved with children and who specialize in indexing literature for children (which may also include the provision of indexes, for children, to literature mainly intended for adults) have a significant role in encouraging the use of indexes among children and also in urging the publishers of materials for children to recognize their responsibility for the commissioning of good indexes. A proactive stance is particularly relevant in this sector of indexing, where the knowledge-acquisition and information-processing skills of future generations are at stake. In a knowledge-based society, those who are deprived of access to information suffer a kind of poverty, and indexers have a part to play in its relief.

There are diverse opportunities for 'crusading' indexers to raise awareness of indexes – both in children and in the adults responsible for them – and to promote their services to publishers and other potential customers. Events and campaigns organized by schools, libraries, parent-teacher associations, local administrative authorities, literacy organizations, book clubs, broadcasting organizations, reading clubs, booksellers, publishers, and literary societies, all provide the chance for involvement by indexers. Also of importance are national curricula, national and international projects, programmes and strategies to develop children's reading skills, to encourage them to read recreationally, and to improve their information-handling abilities. Some of the individuals and organizations responsible for managing and resourcing these activities are aware enough to include indexers within their circle of contacts, but – until there is wider enlightenment – the onus is on indexers to make themselves and their valuable work known. Where local schemes are concerned, focusing for example on groups of children with restricted access to literature and information, involvement may be voluntary; indexers carrying out social and community tasks in such an environment can nevertheless find that their professional expertise becomes more widely recognized on a commercial basis, through this work.

References

Bell, Hazel K. (1992) Should fiction be indexed? The indexability of text. *The Indexer*, **18**, 83–86

Dixon, Yvonne (1996) Indexing for children. *The Indexer*, **20**, 8–10

Weinberg, Bella Hass (1996) Page references as locators: it's not all that obvious, or, what do they teach kids about indexes? *Key words: the newsletter of the American Society of Indexers*, **4** (3/4) 23–28

Williams, Paula L. and Bakewell, K.G.B. (1997) *Indexes to children's information books: a study of the provision and quality of book indexes for children at National Curriculum Key Stage 2.* British Library Research and Innovation Report 129. Wetherby: British Library Research and Innovation Centre. [May be purchased as a photocopy or microfiche from the British Library Document Supply Centre, Boston Spa, Wetherby, West Yorkshire, LS23 7BQ. A summary of the report appeared as: Williams, Paula L. and K.G.B. Bakewell (1997) Indexes to children's information books. *The Indexer*, **20**, 193–194]

Further Reading

Williams, Paula L. and Bakewell, K.G.B. (1999) Indexing children's information books. *The Indexer*, **21**, 174–179

CHAPTER TEN

Managing the work

NOTE: The legal and administrative matters mentioned in this chapter refer to the situation in the United Kingdom.

Employment Status

The ways in which people enter the indexing arena, the backgrounds from which they come, the training they receive, and the environments within which they do their work, are dealt with in Chapter 2. Possession of the relevant aptitudes, abilities, skills, and understanding is an indispensable requirement for a successful livelihood, but paid work does not often materialize at the instant that the expectant freelance indexer feels ready for it. People who are employed as indexers on the staff of companies and organizations are fortunate in this respect, knowing that – so long as their work after training is satisfactory – a regular income is guaranteed, at least in the short term. Whether preparing to be employed or self-employed, the indexer's fund of knowledge (general and subject-related) and competencies (professional and technical) must be sufficient for the range of intended work.

318 Indexing: The Manual of Good Practice

The freelance business

The new freelance must first determine the size and range of the business activity, through these questions:

- How much do I want/need to earn each year?
- Do I want to work full-time or part-time? (This takes into account other activities and commitments, the need for preparatory training and continuing professional development (CPD), and how much leisure time is desired.)
- Which subjects am I capable of specializing in (by virtue of knowledge and experience from work, educational courses, and private interests)?
- Which materials, what sort of jobs? (Textbooks, periodicals, children's information books, images, electronic media, other forms; small and medium-sized one-off jobs, larger jobs extending over several months or years, continuing jobs requiring attention once or twice a year.)
- Do I want/need to work at something else as well as indexing? If so, should it be related to indexing (such as proofreading and editing) or something completely different, which is not dependent on the same market conditions as indexing?
- Where is the best market for what I have to offer?
- Have I a unique selling point (USP)? (Something that no-one else is offering, but for which there is a demand.)
- What am I particularly good at and what do I want to avoid?
- Do I want to work entirely at home or will I occasionally take jobs that involve working on a client's premises?

There is no one time of year better than any other for starting as a self-employed indexer. Once the indexer feels confident about the answers to the questions above, possesses the necessary knowledge and skills, has allocated suitable accommodation and provided the required equipment, and knows that there is work available in the chosen field, a start may be made. 'Starting a business' courses and workshops are often run by local adult colleges; they can be invaluable in providing guidance on identifying and researching the market, planning, finance and accounting, legal requirements, and publicity. Working to a strict strategy is essential for some people, while others prefer to proceed on a 'see what turns up' basis. Some simple planning is necessary, to ensure a smooth start and continued operations, problem-free accounting and cash flow, and a high standard of work.

It is possible for people working as employees, in companies or other organizations, also to have self-employed status in relation to freelance indexing work undertaken outside their responsibilities to their employer. The two employments are entirely separate, so the freelance activities conform to the same tax and social security requirements as the full-time self-employed. This is a suitable arrangement when the two employments are equally important, or when the person is aiming to become fully self-employed in due course. An employee who does the odd outside job now and then, but who does not wish to go fully freelance, or aims to go free-lance once sufficient experience and training have been acquired, declares these casual earnings on the standard tax return, not on a 'self-employed' page. Keeping the 'day job' going while doing the occasional indexing job is a way of checking the suitability of indexing as a career and testing the market.

One of the advantages of indexing as a freelance activity is that it does not require a great deal of money in order to start up, particularly if the intending indexer already has an up-to-date computer and access to a basic stock of reference sources. If starting completely from scratch, untrained and with no equipment or resources, a bank loan or other form of credit may be needed. From time to time, there may be government initiatives – such as grants, or allowances for the purchase of equipment – to encourage the setting up of small businesses. If they are eligible, and the terms of acceptance are not onerous, would-be indexers may be able to launch themselves sooner than expected, or at least to feel more secure when they begin. Any institution that provides financial help at the start-up stage will want to see a business plan that describes the service to be offered (including its USP – unique selling point), provides information about the applicant's qualifications and experience, illustrates the market for the service, identifies the existing competition, and estimates the finan-cial income and outgoings over a foreseeable period.

Statutory Requirements

The procedure for setting up as a self-employed person is usually simple, but each indexer should check the requirements of the country of residence. In the UK, the Inland Revenue must be informed by any individual starting work independently (technically known as a sole trader) or in partnership with another self-employed person. The Inland Revenue must be satisfied that the person concerned is, in reality, self-employed – not just working at home for a single employer instead of at the employer's premises. Teleworking by employees (working at home for a single employer, using a computer and other equipment provided by that employer) does not, therefore, normally count as self-employment. Self-employment in the UK involves being responsible for:

- providing the place to work and equipment to do it with
- accepting, processing and delivering work
- deciding when to work
- running the business
- taking work from several different clients
- accepting any losses as well as taking any profits
- bearing the financial and time costs of putting right faulty work

It is not necessary to form a limited company. This is something that may be considered later if the size of the enterprise warrants it, though company status carries with it additional legal obligations. There is no need to have a special business name, either. The indexer's personal name (or a shortened or variant form of it) is sufficient, but if desired a business name can be used – it may be more effective for publicity purposes and can give the impression that the business is more substantial. Some words and expressions may not be used without government department approval ('Royal', for example) and there are rules requiring the name(s) of the person(s) involved to be displayed on business stationery. Full details are available in a leaflet from offices of Companies House (and on web site www.companieshouse.gov.uk).

Insurance companies with which the building and its contents are insured must be informed, because ordinary domestic policies do not usually cover business use and may be completely invalidated by it, so that the companies refuse to pay out in the event of a claim. Existing policies can sometimes be extended to cover business use; alternatively, a special home-working policy may need to be taken out to cover business equipment. Building societies or banks having an interest in the property as mortgagees, and landlords of rented properties, may also need to be informed. Indexing businesses do not create noise or traffic congestion, produce toxic waste or pollution, change the character of the property, create any public nuisance, or ruin the neighbourhood, so there is normally no reason to be concerned about planning permission or environmental regulations. Business rates (UK local taxes) are normally not applicable so long as the primary use of the dwelling is domestic; however, using one part of the home exclusively for the business could cause liability to pay business rates and also – when the property is sold – could generate a demand for capital gains tax. Government attitudes to the self-employed, teleworkers and small businesses can change from year to year, making it essential for those concerned to keep abreast of changes in the tax regime.

Employee indexers

Not everyone wants to venture into the risky and uncertain world of free-lance indexing. Though self-employment and independence have their charms, many people prefer the comparative security of regular employment. For them, having a steady and guaranteed income, being in a workplace where equipment and services are provided, experiencing professional and social contact with (and support from) colleagues, being part of an organization, having access to free training, enjoying paid holidays and the prospect of career advancement, are far more attractive. Indexing in the corporate environment at large can – as with freelancing – provide the opportunity to work with a variety of materials: textbooks, newspapers and periodicals, audio and visual documents, catalogues, and the rest. An employee indexer, though, is likely to work only with the one kind of publication produced by the employer, rather than to move from one type of job to another as freelances do in response to the demands of the market. To obtain experience with other materials, the employee indexer usually needs to move to a different organization. However, long-term work on, say, the indexing of items for an abstracting periodical, the preparation of annual and cumulative indexes to a learned society's journal or the indexing of illustrations for a picture library, can be a satisfying and rewarding experience.

Teleworking by Employees

Some corporate employers permit, even encourage, certain kinds of employee to work at home; their continuous presence on the employers' premises is not essential, so they are provided with the necessary telecommunications equipment and carry out their duties at home, maintaining contact with their managers back at base and receiving and transmitting their work by phone, post, fax and email. The benefits to the employer are that space (very costly in urban areas) can be saved at the workplace, and that productivity is higher; the employee is relieved of commuting, has more control of the way in which the work is done and when it is done, and does not have to bear the stresses and strains of corporate office life. Some kinds of employed indexing work are suitable for teleworking, and the environment is convenient for indexers who need to combine earning with home commitments but who appreciate the corporate support provided by the employer. This is not self-employment or freelancing; the employee may be able to choose the precise hours of work but is still supervised, managed and paid by the employing organization. Employed teleworkers can experience some of the highs and lows felt by freelance workers – on the one hand, choice of working hours, no unwanted interruptions by colleagues, no office politics, but on the other, isolation, no staff canteen or drinks machine, responsibility for own health and safety, and little opportunity for training (with the risk of getting out of date).

The Home Office

The daydream of moving to a favourite (possibly remote) part of the country and working as a freelance or an employed teleworker in a relaxed environment, communicating electronically with customers and colleagues, and enjoying a relaxed and pressure-free lifestyle, is not always achieved. Most freelances and teleworkers make space in their existing homes. The convenience of being near shops, post offices, schools, libraries, leisure and entertainment facilities, and the need for contact (regular or casual) with friends, colleagues, fellow professionals and customers, are major factors in the smooth running of business, domestic and social life.

The office may be a room or a part of a room, or in a separate building – hut, cabin, shed, garage, caravan (trailer), for example. Wherever it is, it should be welcoming and comfortable – the indexer needs to feel good about going there to start work. The desk, table or workstation and other equipment should be placed so that the workspace is well lit and comfortably accessible from the chosen seating position. A good chair is essential – many hours are spent on it, so it must assist good posture. The telephone and other frequently used items can be stationed within arm's reach for convenience, but some workers prefer to have them at a slight distance so that from time to time they have to get up and exercise their leg muscles.

A view through a window to the outside world is essential for some, providing interest during mini-breaks and the opportunity to refocus their eyes. For others, it is an undesirable distraction from their work. Personal taste dictates the nature of the decor, the use of colour, the display of plants, pictures, photos, and ornaments. Very occasionally, in the course of a long career, an indexer may receive a letter from a client expressing appreciation of an index; framed and displayed on the wall or desk, it can give encouragement at times of stress – the new indexer may like to leave space somewhere in anticipation of this rewarding event.

In the UK, if an entire room or building is used solely for business purposes – not shared with domestic use – there may be a capital gains tax liability if the property is sold.

Equipment

The kind of work an indexer intends to do is a primary influence on the equipment needed in the home office. The Society of Indexers advises that the essentials are:

- a computer plus a printer: Most clients now need copy in disk form, or as a file that can be emailed, as well as (or instead of) paper copy. Email is also used for much business correspondence and many commercial transactions, and professional contact groups use it for exchanging information
- a telephone, a fax and an answering machine: These can be separate or combined. It is not essential to have a separate business

phone line, or separate lines for phone and fax, but in a crowded or busy household they can be an advantage

● stationery and small office items: A browse through an office supplies catalogue or a stationery shop can tempt the new freelance into overprovision; the bare necessities should be bought first – such as a stapler (and perhaps a destapler, too), a hole punch, postal scales, clips and fasteners and tags of various kinds and sizes (for keeping papers together), pens with different coloured inks, pencils, and an eraser

● storage equipment (boxes, files, cabinets): It is essential to have plenty of storage space. Jobs in progress, jobs completed, correspondence, publicity material, professional journals and books, work records, stationery, office gadgets, reference books and CD-ROMs – all must have their place.

● accounts records

For some indexers, a photocopier is necessary; a fax machine with a copying facility may be sufficient if only copies of single sheets are required. Scanners – through which paper documents can be copied to computers – are also needed for some kinds of work. Mobile phones, which are increasingly being designed to take on other functions – not just one-to-one voice communication – are vital for indexers on the move, or who work in different places inside and outside the office, and who need to be contacted quickly by customers, colleagues or family. Not all indexers need or want such instant contact, preferring even to unplug, switch off, or turn down the sound on all telephonic devices while they are working, so that they can concentrate totally. An answering machine is essential for collecting messages from potential and actual clients, colleagues and other professional contacts. Detailed information on the features and functions of computer equipment of particular importance to indexers is given in Chapter 11 (see 'Indexing technology (input and output)').

In addition to space and equipment for storage, generous work surfaces are needed – to enable office equipment to be positioned ergonomically, lay out the work in hand, check dictionaries and other sources, make notes, and stand the cup of coffee (herbal tea, pure spring water) safely. The minimum reference sources recommended for the freelance indexer, by the Society of Indexers, are listed in Chapter 2 (see 'The indexer's reference sources').

Health and safety

In the corporate workplace, health and safety are the official responsibility of the designated person or persons in the organization. Freelance indexers and teleworkers must look after themselves. Being ill or just below par can mean delay, even the risk of losing work and income. Taking care and planning ahead (including considering sickness insurance for freelances) is well worth while.

At first sight the home office may appear a harmless enough place, but the typical workplace provides many opportunities for personal damage. A large amount of electrical and electronic equipment is present, objects on shelves can fall off, overloaded shelves can collapse and poorly balanced cabinets topple, cables on the floor can cause a fall, sharp metal objects can wound, mechanical equipment can entrap hair and dangling jewellery, fluids can stain and give off fumes, copiers can emit gases, hot drinks can scald, even the edges of paper can cut fingers. Add to this possible backache, eyestrain, repetitive strain injury (RSI), headache and stuffy nasal passages due to inadequate ventilation, and the general stress of working to deadlines, and it becomes clear that the freelance environment has its hazards. Serious accidents are probably very rare, but solo workers in any occupation need to take care. The planning of the workspace, the siting of equipment and its electrical supplies, the provision of clear space in which to move from one area to another, the safe storage of items, and the careful arrangement of the working surfaces, are crucial. A well-equipped first-aid kit should be maintained and kept within easy reach, and some strategies should be prepared in answer to questions beginning 'What would I do if . . . ?' Thinking beforehand about how to act in the event of a minor accident or a major emergency (and remembering that the first rule is 'Don't panic!') can save valuable time if one occurs.

General health affects performance, so attention to diet (quantity and quality) and exercise (physical and mental) is advisable. A good working posture helps to avoid aches and pains, and regular breaks revive concentration; moving away from the workplace for even a minute – to stretch the limbs and to take in a different view – can be surprisingly reinvigorating. People who experience RSI and other joint and muscle problems as a result of sustained keyboard or 'mouse' work have the option of changing to voice-operated equipment and ball-controlled 'mice'.

The availability of these alternatives should not encourage anyone to work for long sessions; the voice can suffer from overuse, too, and so needs to be nurtured.

Sources of Information

Information and advice on setting up a freelance operation and working at home is not hard to come by. Libraries and bookshops normally have a selection of books, videos and CD-ROMs, published by reputable publishers; banks and finance houses produce free leaflets and may have small business advisers on their staff; government tax departments also distribute leaflets and give information to callers at their local offices and – in some cases – visitors to their internet web sites; professional bodies sell or distribute free literature to their members; newspapers have business and financial advice columns, and television and radio consumer programmes include the self-employed within their compass. Health and medical organizations supply information on general health and hygiene, fitness, and first aid. Leaflets from several of these sources are also available from local Citizens' Advice Bureaux (CABs) and community information centres. Consumer advice magazines (such as *Which?*, Consumers' Association, monthly) regularly include articles on self-employment, tax, pensions, insurance, computer equipment, phones, and service providers of various kinds. Internet sources include news and discussion groups for freelances within particular professions (see 'Internet discussion groups and mailing lists' in Chapter 12). Local colleges run courses on starting up, keeping accounts, choosing and using computers and software, and other related topics. Business advice centres and enterprise agencies, publicly supported, provide information in many forms; everywhere in the UK should have reasonable access to one of these.

Finding Freelance Work

Some starters already have useful contacts – former colleagues and employers, friends and relatives, fellow-members of organizations – through whom the fledgling business can be made known and the first few jobs may come. They may have already done the occasional small job on a casual basis, while still in employment. Others – particularly the self-trained who have reached an adequate level of competence entirely by their own efforts – may feel at first that they have no personal fruitful connections, but it is easy to identify at least one or two possible sources and so to start the ball rolling.

Effort is required to run a business – and it is needed well before the first job is acquired. It can take several months (even two or three years) to build up to full-time working, so groundwork is essential to identify likely sources of information and potential customer sectors. Recommended activities include:

- taking stock of individual strengths and weaknesses; the strengths can perhaps be developed further, and the weaknesses remedied; in publicity materials, strengths can be highlighted and weaknesses played down until they are improved
- checking reference sources (print, CD-ROM and online) for names and addresses of potential clients
- attending events where there is an opportunity to get to know relevant people and to find out what is going on
- making oneself known to other indexers in the field (who may occasionally need a subcontractor or co-operator)

The client categories for any one indexer depend on the subject field chosen and the type of material preferred, but may include:

- book and periodical publishers (firms whose business is entirely or mainly publishing)
- book packagers (firms and individuals with design and graphics expertise, producing books with a high proportion of illustrated content and with international appeal, sometimes subcontracted by book publishers. Some act solely as co-ordinators for the activities involved (on a freelance basis); others cover all editorial and production tasks)
- academic (educational) institutions
- learned and professional societies and institutes
- national government departments and agencies
- international organizations
- broadcasting organizations

- charitable organizations
- freelance editors
- individual authors

Many of these are easily traceable through directories and lists available in libraries and bookshops and on the internet. Authors may be discovered through libraries' and publishers' catalogues, through bookshop browsing, and by reading reviews and profiles in newspapers and magazines.

Local contacts may be worth exploring. Membership of community bodies and special-interest groups, checks of directories prepared and distributed by local administrations and of newsletters and bulletins displayed in public libraries, can identify organizations and situations in which indexing has a part to play and also local writers who may be interested. An indexer who is from the community, has suitable local knowledge, is readily available, and (importantly) can appear in person to discuss a proposal, has a good chance of securing a job or of convincing someone that an index is, after all, needed.

Clients do not have to be based in the same country as the indexer. Fast delivery of packages between countries, and electronic transmission of messages and files, make international work feasible. Indexers with foreign language capabilities or personal knowledge of the culture of other countries therefore have the possibility of extending the range of their work. It is particularly important to clarify the method, currency and form of payment in the agreement covering the work, and to be aware of any significant differences in business and legal practice between the two countries.

Temporary work, especially within the publishing industry, has the benefits of giving an insight into the way the industry functions and how publications are commissioned, produced and marketed, and can provide contacts that may be helpful to the budding freelance. Informal apprenticeship or mentoring arrangements with a practising indexer are similarly advantageous (see 'Training and qualifications in indexing' in Chapter 2).

As mentioned above, self-employment (in the UK at least) involves working for a number of clients. The self-employed status can be jeopardized if work is done on a continuing basis for one client only – the authorities may take the view that the person is an employee, not self-employed. Apart from this risk, another danger for any freelance who works only for one client is that if the particular source of work disappears – through closure, merger, or change of staff, for example – the person is left high and dry, possibly being owed money for work already done, and with no other work immediately available to fill the gap.

The promotional message

Whichever forms of promotion and publicity are selected, the aim should be to make sufficient impact for potential customers to take notice and to understand exactly what is on offer. Statements and descriptions should be clear, factual and unambiguous, and should radiate professionalism. Only those services that the indexer is confident of providing at an adequate level should be offered. Exaggeration can lead to the embarrassment of admitting defeat after overeagerly taking on a job beyond the indexer's capability.

Business Stationery

Starters are sometimes reluctant to pay out for business stationery and publicity before receiving any income, but in the launch of any business activity some initial outlay is essential. Stationery can be home-produced on a computer or ordered through a high street print shop or jobbing printer. However it is produced, it must be smart and clear, so that it makes a good impression on the recipient and stands a chance of being remembered. A small stock of stationery – headed paper (A4 size), compliments slips and business cards is all that is needed at first. All should include the indexer's name, full postal and email addresses, and phone and fax numbers. Additional wording can be included to specify the services offered – but should be brief.

Standard Letters and Mailshots

A straightforward letter (on headed paper) can be sent to the relevant individual staff member (the managing editor, the commissioning editor for humanities, or the production editor, for example) in the companies of the indexer's choice. Email can be used to send promotional material, but may not have the same impact as a well-printed letter (see 'emailing' below). Only those firms and organizations that publish the kind of material and on the subjects that the indexer wants to deal with, should be contacted. Annual directories such as *Writers' and artists' yearbook*, *Benns media UK*, *Willings press guide*, *Literary market place* and *The writer's market*, can be consulted for information relating to publishers and book packagers, and other subject-related directories for details of organizations working in specific subject areas. Browsing in bookshops and libraries helps to identify which publishers produce books in which subject fields. A subject search of the internet will also reveal relevant firms and organizations.

Each letter should address the person by name (this information can be discovered by phoning the company), not just by title, and should describe the services offered and the qualifications and experience of the indexer. A sample of the indexer's work can be included (see 'Sample indexes' below). More detail can be given in a separate leaflet or brochure, but this may be better left until further into the indexer's business career, when the market is more familiar and the information can be more precisely targeted. A CV (curriculum vitae) is usually not needed – much of the information in a 'whole of my life' account of academic qualifications and employment experience is immaterial to clients looking for indexers. The letter should include only those details that are relevant in the context, such as the services and skills being offered, any specialist subjects, and previous experience. A standard letter held on computer can be added to and amended for each addressee, to emphasize the experience and interests that are particularly relevant to the client; this is helped if the indexer puts in some work beforehand and finds out a little about the various companies and their activities (subject fields, target readership, kinds of publication).

Sending letters to authors requires an individual approach; referring to a recently published book by the author, or one reported to be in progress, can give the 'handle' on which to hang whichever of the indexer's services are particularly appropriate. If the indexer already knows that a certain publisher or author regularly produces books without indexes, it is prudent to include in a promotional letter a brief list of points explaining (though without being patronizing) the value of indexes and the benefits to the individual or company of including them (see 'The necessity for indexes' and 'Who should care about indexes' in Chapter 1). For the client's reassurance, the indexer may provide (with the permission of those involved) the names, addresses and phone numbers of previous clients or other people who can vouch for the satisfactory standard of earlier work. Specifying rates of pay is inadvisable at this stage; indexing work varies so much from the short simple job to the longer complex one, that fixed rates can be unhelpful. A new indexer tempted to publicize a low rate in order to get work may well find it difficult to persuade clients to accept a higher, more appropriate, rate later on. It is better to indicate that fees are reasonable or negotiable (see 'Fees' below.) Dates of posting can be influential. Mail arriving in offices just before the Christmas, New Year and Easter breaks may not be attended to promptly or with full attention. Public holidays, customary vacation periods, and major national events can also affect the issue.

The initial response to a mailshot may disappoint. Some recipients may not reply at all, others may say that they already have access to a sufficient number of indexers (in-house or external) or that they have noted the information for future use. There is, though, the possibility of an immediate job – perhaps the regular indexer is on holiday, busy or ill, or the client happens to have a book in preparation whose subject matches the indexer's specialism. Even letters that lie in the clients' files are not necessarily wasted. They can be rediscovered at times of need, or when a new member of staff takes over.

Most newcomers do not want to be deluged with work straight away – one job at a time, with plenty of opportunity to scrutinize the final version of the index, is preferable. The first few jobs are likely to be executed at a slower speed than will become the norm and so the additional pressure of scheduling multiple jobs is something the indexer should try to avoid. It may be best to send out the promotional letters in batches rather than all at once.

Emailing

At the time of writing, it is more common for communications to potential clients to be in the form of letters or mailshots (see above). A good-looking, permanent record, which can be filed and easily referred to later, is likely to have more impact and to make a better impression, and so be more effective in generating enquiries from possible clients. Some freelance workers use email only for brief, informal messages and for urgent matters; others use it for all or most of their communications, including proposals for work, invoices and the dispatch of the finished work itself. The use and acceptability of email seems likely to increase.

Directory Entries

Entries in large classified directories, such as those published by some telephone companies, are not usually relevant for the starter indexer, who may be unwilling to meet the cost and who – as already indicated – is not looking for a large input of work in the early stages. Potential clients looking for indexers are unlikely to check these directories anyway, turning instead to sources specific to the publishing industry. On the other hand, if the indexer has a business telephone line (this is not essential, see 'Equipment' above), the classified directory entry may come free of charge, and some people regard the existence of such an entry as an indication of a 'real' business.

Paying a much smaller amount to be entered in the directory produced by one of the organizations for professional indexers is more to the point (see Chapter 12 'Professional organizations and interest groups'). Each organization has its own rules governing inclusion, which may require entrants to have a certain level or period of experience or one of a range of qualifications. Starters may therefore be excluded, but should aim to qualify for inclusion as soon as possible. Directories that until recently have been issued only in print are now being presented on the organizations' web sites and these may become the habitually consulted form. How quickly anyone procures a job via a directory entry depends on how frequently the list is updated, how large a distribution it has, and how many indexers there are in relation to the size of the market in a particular subject area.

Sample Indexes

Any suitable work that the indexer has already done, perhaps as a practice piece or for personal use, can be sent to a potential client – either with a mailshot or if asked for by the client. A previously unindexed book published by the client can be a useful source; if the indexer has produced an index to it for home use, an extract can be used to demonstrate to the client that the indexer has adequate subject knowledge and the technical competence to index suitably. If interested in periodicals indexing, the indexer can prepare an index to the latest few issues of a chosen title.

Phone Calls ('Cold Calling')

The acceptability of phone calls as the first, or only, contact for publicizing a business varies from client to client. Some indexers feel it inadvisable – few clients are likely to have an immediate indexing need that results in a job straight away. Once the call is completed, the potential client has no permanent record of the indexer's details. The call, coming unexpectedly and perhaps inconveniently, may even annoy and deter the person being called. If making a call, the indexer should have ready a prepared and informative message that can be left, if necessary, on answering machine or voicemail system. If the called person happens to have an immediate indexing need, the indexer may be fortunate enough to be called back. Automated menu-style voicemail systems offer different sets of choices, depending on the company, and the indexer may have to make a swift decision about which option to select in order to leave a message; if there is no obviously correct automatic option, enquiry through the human operator is best.

As a follow-up a few days after sending a letter or a mailshot, or leaving a message, a call can be useful in reinforcing the indexer's information with the client and helping it to be remembered. Good telephone technique is important; voice, manner, message content, and an air of self-assurance should all strengthen the good impression created by the mailshot.

Web Sites

Free web site space is offered by several internet service providers (ISPs). A well-designed and informative web site can be productive of enquiries, but will only be found by a client who has decided to make a search for an indexer, or who already knows the indexer's name. It is therefore more appropriate for an indexer who is already in practice. New indexers need to put their data more positively in front of future clients (for example by mailshot). An alternative to having a personal web site is for an indexer to lodge details on an online directory, or a network which handles information on job opportunities and people available for work. A fee is usually payable for inclusion in the directory and for addition to the network. The success of such enterprises depends on the numbers of clients who use them to find freelance workers. One important advantage of publicity via a web site or network is that it has international reach and so can procure work from outside the indexer's country of residence. The Society of Indexers' annual directory *Indexers available* (see 'Society of Indexers' in Chapter 12) includes the web site addresses of those members who have them.

Professional Memberships and Interest-Group Contacts

Membership of a professional organization (see 'Organizations for indexers' in Chapter 12) is important because it enables indexers to make peer contacts, network with fellow professionals, find out about forthcoming opportunities, gather information about potential customers, and feature in publicity materials (directories, web sites) maintained by the organization. Psychological benefits also result, alleviating the sense of isolation and bolstering self-esteem. Belonging to an interest group – centred round a hobby, a recreational activity, a political or community issue, for example – can also create connections that lead to work opportunities later on; however, joining one of these groups with the express aim of lobbying for work is likely to engender bad feeling and to be counterproductive.

'Stand-alone' indexing

Most freelance indexing is done on the basis of commissions from publishers and other organizations, for works in the course of publication; in most cases the index is published as an integral part of the work. There is, though, the possibility of indexers producing – on their own initiatives – indexes to individual works, or series of works, or collections of works, that have already been published. These are sometimes referred to as 'after-the-fact indexes'.

An index of this type may be created originally for the indexer's own use – perhaps to act as an analytical guide to the writings of a favourite author (Bell, 1998) or the life of a notable person – but can be of value to other enthusiasts and to students, academics, literary critics, and historians. Creation of such an index may be an enjoyable labour of love, but finding a publisher for it may be difficult. The publisher(s) of the works on which the index is based may be interested, though the potential sales may be perceived as low, requiring a discouragingly high price in order to make a profit. A small specialist publisher in the relevant subject field may be more likely to show interest than a large mainstream one. An alternative recently suggested is self-publication, with sales via the internet; this method of distribution can keep costs under control, because copies need only be produced once firm orders (and perhaps payment, or a deposit) have been received. Copyright matters (see 'Copyright' below) need to be carefully checked before embarking on self-publication; an index can be considered to be a work in its own right, but merely extracting pieces of text from another work (or works) and sorting them unaltered into an index sequence can amount to infringement of copyright. It is important to select widely available editions for indexing; an index that refers to page numbers in an out-of-print edition may be useful for scholars and academics, but not for the general reader.

In-house work

Freelance work does not all have to be done in the home office. Occasionally a job may need to be done on the client's premises – because the documents to be indexed are situated there or because the work needs to be done in close co-operation with other members of a team. A short-term arrangement, with the indexer maintaining control of the working schedule and being available to take on jobs from other clients, should not endanger the official freelance status. To be tied to working solely for one client, under conditions and scheduling imposed by the client, is to risk being classed as an employee (albeit a temporary one) – which has implications for tax and social security contributions.

Co-operative work

Large projects, particularly those requiring a wide range of subject specialisms, or needing to be completed very quickly, are sometimes undertaken by freelance indexers working in temporary co-operation. The work may be divided up in equal parts, or allocated by subject or skill to the persons most suited. One of the indexers may be the organizer of the work and responsible for liaison with the client. The number of such projects is not large, but newly qualified indexers could watch out for notices – in professional indexing society periodicals and indexing-related web sites – inviting suitable people to get in touch. Co-operation is not to be seen as a 'sheltered' form of work in which the inexperienced can learn their trade; those involved are equals in status and are expected to be self-reliant. It can, though, provide the new freelance with a supportive environment; the shared responsibility for the project and the opportunity to discuss technical points with fellow-workers can provide both reassurance and stimulus.

Volunteering

This may seem a strange way to start making a career, but some indexers have found it a means of getting themselves known and gaining experience. Small organizations such as community bodies, medical and health support groups and other special-interest associations run by volunteers on a shoestring frequently produce bulletins and information leaflets that – with the passage of time – form a valuable archive. Most are not indexed on a regular basis, not because their editors are not aware of the need but because the financial resources are not available. Editorial appeals for volunteer indexers are therefore sometimes seen in the organizations' publications or on their web sites; though the work is unpaid, it can provide a new indexer with useful experience, and the opportunity to advertise the business and result in a completed index to show to potential clients. Indexers who are already involved with such groups could take the initiative and offer to produce an index for, say, a year's issues, in exchange for some free publicity for their services. Local libraries can often help to identify suitable groups and their publications. Opportunities for volunteer indexing are sometimes snapped up by people who have no great knowledge or experience of indexing, on the basis that 'it will be an interesting thing to do in spare time'. Trained indexers who are eager to get involved should be able to promote themselves successfully in this field by emphasizing their superior qualifications and greater aptitude for the task.

Selectivity

It is particularly important for the confidence and reputation of the indexer that the first completed tasks are of good quality and delivered on time. New indexers need to beware of grasping any and every job that is offered them, without first considering whether it is right for them. Starting with a series of small jobs may be more comfortable, interesting and educative than plunging into a large, long-term project. Anyone who lacks the adequate level of subject knowledge, is doubtful about being able to meet the deadline, finds the specification and requirements of the client too complicated, the terms of the proposed agreement too onerous, or some other aspect of the job unacceptable, should probably decline it – politely and in such a way that the door is not closed to future, more suitable, opportunities with the same client. There are several ways to leave a client, and to turn down an unwanted job: being too busy with other work; quoting an enormous fee that is bound to be rejected; being about to go on holiday, give birth, go into hospital, move house . . .

Financial Aspects of Freelancing

Self-employment involves not just finding jobs and completing them, maintaining good relations with customers and being paid. The financial health of the enterprise has to be monitored and promoted. The individual indexer has responsibility for this and normally there is no-one to whom it can be delegated; there is, though, a great deal of advice available (some of it free of charge).

Keeping records

The freelance indexer should not delay keeping a formal record of financial transactions until the first job is completed. Some outlay (expenditure) is always necessary before any income is received – equipment, stationery and postal charges, for example. Trying to make sense of the first few months' dealings from scrappy notes on separate slips of paper and unsorted receipts is no way to run a business and is a shocking waste of a professional indexer's time. Before the first job is taken on, a system (which need be only a simple one) must be in place for logging outgoings like the purchase of equipment and stationery, the cost of post and telephone, business travel expenses, and also income – principally payments for work done. In the UK, for tax purposes, the self-employed have to keep records for about six years after the end of the tax year to which they apply.

The records should show for each day the amounts spent (expenditure) and the amounts received (income). Expenditure is entered under column headings indicating the category of expenditure, and income may also be columnized if – for example – it arises from different kinds of activity, as is the case where an indexer is also offering proofreading and editorial services. When expenditure columns are individually totalled and the totals added together, this represents the total expenditure over the period. Income is totalled in the same way. Records may be kept manually (in an account book or loose-leaf folder, for instance) or on a computer, using a software accounts package. By ensuring that the columnar amounts are always totalled each time a new transaction is registered, the indexer is able to see at a glance how much has been spent and how much earned and – most importantly, what the difference is.

Some freelance workers find the financial records component of their work tedious, and in complete contrast to the invigoration they experience when indexing. There is no escape from it, however; without it they will have no clear way of monitoring the progress of the business, nor will they able to report precise figures to the tax authorities, with the result that they are likely to be required to pay more in tax than should be the case. An accountant engaged to produce annual accounts and deal with tax matters can only do so efficiently if credible, legible and comprehensible records are supplied by the freelance. The accountant will also charge a fee (at a rate per hour much higher than that earned by the average indexer). A volunteer (or reasonably paid) book-keeper within the indexer's own household, however, is worth considering (See 'Delegation . . . ' below).

Comparison of work records (see 'Work records' below) and invoicing (billing) data (see 'Invoicing' below) gives the indexer useful facts concerning the ease of working for particular clients (whether extra, unexpected work was necessary, whether problems of any kind occurred) and highlights good and bad payers. From this information, it is possible to identify those clients whose custom should be fostered, as well as those whose enquiries can be courteously rejected in future. Other records that should be retained include: bank statements, receipts for purchases and travel expenses, invoices for work done, and paying-in slips for income received. A record of business mileage travelled in the family car is needed. Bills for utilities (electricity, gas, telephone, etc.) can be apportioned according to the level of business use.

Income tax

In the UK it is the responsibility of any taxpayer to inform the Inland Revenue of income received and to pay the necessary tax when asked. Employed teleworkers are normally covered by the PAYE (Pay As You Earn) system, under which tax is deducted by their employers and forwarded to the Inland Revenue. Self-employed people are required, under the self-assessment system, to fill in a tax return form each year and to pay the appropriate tax in two half-yearly instalments, with a balancing payment if necessary. There are plans for submission of self-assessment tax returns over the internet; there may be discounts for people who do this and also pay their due tax, on time, electronically. Sending in a tax return late incurs a financial penalty, as does late payment of the tax (which has interest added). Advice is available from the Inland Revenue, in several forms: in leaflets, 'across the counter' at local tax offices, enquiry centres, and tax clinics, and on the Inland Revenue web site: www.inlandrevenue.gov.uk. Correspondence from the Revenue should never be ignored and should be dealt with promptly to avoid the possibility of an excessive tax demand.

Accountants (charging a fee) can give advice and will also complete the tax return, if desired, on the basis of information supplied by the self-employed person. If choosing an accountant, it is better to select one who has a recognized qualification and deals regularly with small businesses and the self-employed (rather than with very large corporations). The accountant's responsibility is to ensure that the self-employed person pays no more tax than is properly due. Anyone asking a reputable accountant to arrange tax evasion (against the law) will be disappointed. Tax avoidance (the planning of financial matters so that tax is kept to the lowest level) is entirely legal and considered by some to be a mark of good money management – though others consider it immoral.

Expenses and Allowances

Self-employed people can claim certain outgoings as business expenses. These are costs that are wholly and exclusively incurred for the business and can include (amongst others) expenditure on travel and motoring, phone bills, postage, stationery, professional literature, accountants' fees, advertising, and a proportion of costs of heating, lighting, cleaning. Certain training costs, arising from CPD (continuing professional development) activities, such as course study and workshop attendance, may be tax deductible.

The purchase of equipment for use in the business, including a vehicle, can qualify for tax relief under the capital allowances system. Additional allowances for the purchase of certain types of equipment required to start up a business, are announced from time to time in the government's annual budget statement.

VAT (value added tax)

A UK business must register for VAT if the annual turnover (the total income received from the work – not just the profit) exceeds a certain amount; the amount is usually increased each year. Most freelance indexers do not reach the 'VATable' level of income, so are not obliged to register. However, it is possible to register voluntarily even if the income is lower than the specified amount, and some indexers do this because they can then reclaim the VAT that they (in common with every purchaser) pay on business equipment. Another benefit of being VAT-registered is that the VAT registration number is indicated on business stationery and gives the impression of a serious, substantial enterprise. Anyone who is registered must keep separate VAT records, submit regular returns to the Customs and Excise, and be prepared for occasional visits and inspections by Customs and Excise VAT officials. Information is available from Customs and Excise offices and on the web site: www.hmce.gov.uk.

Social security

In the UK, self-employed people must pay National Insurance contributions in two parts. A regular, fixed-rate contribution is payable each quarter, and a further amount – the size of which depends on the individual's annual turnover – is payable along with the income tax demand. The benefits available to the self-employed differ slightly from those applicable to employed people. Freelance workers need to consider taking out separate insurance (with commercial companies) against the risk of long-term unemployment, sickness and accident.

Pensions

On retirement, people who have made sufficient contributions through National Insurance are entitled to the basic State Retirement Pension, and those who have paid in to occupational schemes through their employers can start to draw pensions from them. The self-employed who wish to ensure an additional pension, over and above the state scheme, need to consider taking out private pension plans.

Money management

It is not essential to have a business account at the bank, but it is easier to keep track of business transactions if they are handled in a different account from the one used for household and domestic affairs. Monitoring the cash flow (money received, money spent) in order to maintain a safe and healthy balance is important. Cheques received should be banked as quickly as possible (before they get lost), to ensure that the amount is transferred quickly to the indexer's account. Bank charges should be avoided if possible, or kept to the minimum; in the UK, at the time of writing, it is easy to find accounts that do not incur charges, so long as a specified amount remains in the account. Sums of money that are not likely to be required for immediate spending are best transferred to interest-paying accounts.

The same guidelines apply to the management of business money as to the care of private funds: keeping spending within the necessary limits, taking advantage of tax allowances, accepting bargain offers (but only if they are items that are really needed). A percentage – say 30 per cent – of every sum earned may be set aside in an interest-bearing account to meet tax demands and to pay for the service, repair and replacement of equipment. Nothing should come as a surprise or throw freelances into a panic, so long as they always have at least a general idea of the balance between their income and their outgoings.

Free advice on financial and business matters is available from several sources (see 'Sources of information' above). Professional financial advisers (who may be paid on a commission basis by the providers of the products they sell, or by an agreed fee) can give detailed advice tailored to someone's personal situation and needs – pensions, insurance, investments and so on. To be worthwhile, the advice needs to be relevant, comprehensive and impartial, so anyone aiming to consult an adviser should first consider what is needed and how much can be afforded, and then sift the information provided to make sure that it fits the individual situation.

Keeping Costs Down

Business expenses are a necessary component of the freelance operation – there is a continuing need for stationery and minor equipment, phone calls, postal dispatch, fax and email communication, electricity supplies, and the rest. From time to time major outlay is required – for example on new computers and office furniture.

Without becoming obsessive about saving minute amounts, the freelance can take steps to avoid spending out unnecessarily. Phone (and email and fax) calls can cost less at certain times of day and night and may be cheaper at weekends; phone companies offer special deals at particular times, and long-term deals for regularly called numbers. Internet service providers (ISPs) compete with each other for custom in a fast-changing market, by offering free or reduced-rate email and internet services and free web site space. The small print of such 'free' offers and special deals needs to be checked for drawbacks, such as high minimum charges, costly helplines, slow operation, and email services that require the messages to be composed online (with the phone cost mounting). Individual use and circumstances differ, so what is of benefit to one person may not be the best buy for another. Someone who needs only to send and receive email does not necessarily benefit from using the same ISP as someone else who is a heavy user of internet information sources. It is possible to sign up with more than one provider, relying on the second as a back-up if there are problems with the first one. Some freelance workers feel that it looks unprofessional to use an ISP service that is well known to be 'free'. Others are quite at ease with 'free' services, knowing that any money saved by using them can be applied elsewhere in the business. Changing from one phone company or internet service provider (ISP) to another can be beneficial, but the calculation must take into account the cost (as well as time and inconvenience) of informing colleagues and clients about new numbers and addresses, printing new stationery and so on.

Shopping around for stationery supplies, reference books, CD-ROMs, software, and computer equipment, is worthwhile. Internet shopping can sometimes offer significant savings and a high level of convenience, but only reputable suppliers with recognized systems for protecting personal information should be used. Second-hand shops, auctions and clearance sales are good sources of office furniture and equipment, but checks should be made that electrical and electronic items are in good working condition and completely safe. Recommendations from colleagues, and information in professional society newsletters, can be a great help in finding true bargains.

Fees

Successful freelancing depends on doing good work at rates that clients are willing to pay. There is no 'fixed rate' for indexing work; individual indexers charge what they judge to be reasonable for the job and obtainable from the client. An indexer wants to make a reasonable living and get a fair return for the work, but does not fix prices so high that clients are deterred. Clients who recognize the value of indexes in their documents normally allocate a certain sum (up to a specified maximum) in their budget for each job, for the preparation of an index. In book publishing, either the author or the publisher may be responsible for commissioning and paying for the index; alternatively, the publisher may arrange it but then deduct the sum out of the author's royalties.

There are various ways in which indexing fees can be calculated. All of those discussed below are in use and all have their advocates. It is up to individual indexers to consider the strengths and weaknesses of each method, in relation to the kind of work they expect to do and their target income. A delicate balance has to be struck between the quality of product and a reasonable return from a job. For some jobs one basis may be clearly more suitable than another; indexers can decide which – for the job under discussion – is better. Publishers and other clients sometimes have their own policies for fees. Indexers should always be prepared to negotiate for a fair return – while remembering that to agree to a low rate in order to secure that first job may make it difficult to move to the proper rate later.

Some professional organizations issue recommendations regarding rates for various kinds of work, and indexers can use these as baselines from which to calculate and negotiate their fees. The rates need to be carefully applied, because they are not relevant to each and every indexing job. Indexers are to a certain extent in competition with each other, which keeps prices within a similar band, but – as with other professions – there is variation between the rates charged by individual practitioners. This reflects differing kinds of work, levels of experience, depths of subject knowledge, expenses involved, the need to work long and unsocial hours in situations of urgency, and – in some cases – degrees of entrepreneurial flair. Discussions with experienced indexers – at professional meetings, through online groups, for example – can be helpful for new indexers.

The Society of Indexers recommends, for those who wish to work on that basis, a minimum rate to be charged per hour (see 'Hourly rate' below) but notes that some clients and indexers prefer to agree a set fee for each index (see 'Set fees' below). The Australian Society of Indexers (AusSI) also quotes a minimum rate and says that fees are always open to negotiation. The American Society of Indexers does not cite a rate, but points out that a fee should be commensurate with the type of material, the kind of index, and the experience of the indexer.

A client asking for a firm quotation (a definite price that cannot be changed) for a job, without the indexer having seen any of the material to be indexed, should be given an estimate (an approximate figure) at this stage, based on the information available – the size of the job (approximate number of pages, units or words), which parts of the content are to be indexed and which not, the level of the text, the amount of illustrated material, the kind of copy required, the closeness of deadlines, and any additional services such as proofreading the index. When the indexer receives the material itself (or a representative sample) and can see what kind of document it is, roughly how many indexable elements there are per page or per unit (see 'Index density' in Chapter 3), and whether there are any special features, a firm quotation or a 'between £x and £y' figure can be supplied. Features that make the job more time-consuming or difficult, or that incur extra costs, include: special treatment of illustrations, separate index sequences, special coding or disk formats, inconsistent treatment of proper names (resulting in time spent checking reference sources), and queries requiring higher than usual expenditure on post, phone and stationery (see 'Extra charges' below). If, during the course of the work, the indexer realizes that the job has been significantly under-quoted (because of some unforeseen factor), the fee should be renegotiated.

Occasionally clients need to discuss their indexing needs at greater length and may ask the indexer for advice. A certain amount of information is exchanged over the phone as a normal part of the background to any job, but the indexer should not be drawn into protracted and detailed discussions that include the making of substantial free-of-charge recommendations to the client. The situation may be one in which the indexer can offer a small consultancy, which could involve going to the client's premises for meetings with staff, examining the materials requiring indexing, and looking at past and present work done in-house. Consultancy is normally priced on an hourly or daily basis – at considerably higher rates than those available to indexers. Not all freelances wish to do consultancy, but for those with an interest in it and a talent for it, the work can be engrossing and rewarding.

Some indexers have started their freelance careers by working to one of the rates described, and then – by examining their time records and calculating the financial return for the work done over a suitable period – have devised their own scale of charges for different kinds of work. Low rates (such as the minimum specified by the indexing societies) are only suitable for light indexing of straightforward texts where, for example, simple proper names or the headings of sections of text can be extracted and used, with the minimum of editing, as index terms. Some rates (page rate, for example) are more applicable to print-on-paper texts; electronic texts requiring embedded indexing (see 'Software' in Chapter 11) may be better suited to an hourly rate or a set fee.

Hourly rate
Those societies that suggest rates do so on a rate-per-hour basis; some publishers also quote an hourly rate when they propose a fee. The disadvantage of an hourly rate, for the indexer, is that it only recognizes the time taken to do the work. If linked to the idea that 'x pages can be indexed in an hour' – regardless of the type of material, its academic level, and the density of the indexable content – it gives a false impression of the work involved. Some indexers work faster than others, but time is only one of the factors involved in index preparation – what matters is the quality of the finished product. Clients usually need to have some idea of the eventual fee, so may ask how many hours will be charged for. Indexers working at an hourly rate may feel pressurized to complete their work in the shortest number of hours possible, with the result that the indexes are not as good as they might otherwise be. Others – producing an index to a straightforward publication in a short time – may feel that

their return from the work does not adequately reward them for the value added to the item by the index. If working to an hourly rate, but uncertain about the number of hours that will be required, the fee can be quoted as 'between £x and £y'. This reassures the client about the maximum sum payable while at the same time giving the indexer a guarantee of at least a certain amount.

The Society of Indexers' minimum rate is regularly reviewed and increased from time to time, and is intended to apply to '(a) a standard non-specialist text and (b) the least experienced indexer in any subject at any level of specialism. Experienced indexers, and especially experienced specialist indexers, work faster than the less experienced, and clients should therefore expect this experience and skill to merit a higher hourly rate', though it will not necessarily result in a higher total fee. The Australian Society of Indexers (AusSI) also specifies a minimum rate for freelance, self-supporting, registered book indexers working on short-term contracts. Details of the current recommended minima can be obtained from the offices of the societies (see 'Organizations for indexers' in Chapter 12).

Page rate

Not all the pages in a document contain indexable content, so this rate takes into account only those pages that the indexer and client agree are to be covered by the index. The number of entries generated from a single page varies widely, according to the subject, level, readership, size, and format of the document. A single, fixed, page rate cannot therefore be applied to all jobs. Indexers can work out, from their own experience with certain kinds of text, a range of rates from which they can select the most appropriate for the work in question. Higher rates are applicable to the indexing of academic and learned publications requiring greater levels of knowledge, comprehension and analysis, and containing contributions by different writers, 'difficult' names, alternative terminologies, large amounts of bibliographical data, or other special features.

An advantage of the page rate, as compared with the hourly rate, is that the indexer receives a reasonable return whether a fast or slow worker. Also, as with the set fee (see 'Set fees' below) the client and the indexer both know more or less what the amount will be, before the work is started. It is important, though, to check with the editor what the page format of the text will be – large pages with double-column text in small-sized type will generate more entries per page than small pages with short paragraphs, much white space and many illustrations.

Entry rate
This rate is based on the number of entries in the final index and takes no direct account of the amount of work necessary to produce them – which can vary greatly from one kind of text to another. An indexer regularly producing indexes for a particular publisher, for books that are similar in length, level, content, and style, and which require comparable indexes, may feel safe in accepting a standard entry rate. A single fixed rate is unlikely to be suitable, though, for all kinds of text. Before committing themselves to a rate per entry, it is essential that indexer and client agree on the definition of an entry. The definition given by BS ISO 999 (British Standards Institution, 1996, subclause 3.6) is: 'Single record in an index: it consists of a heading; a qualifier or scope note if required; subheading(s) if required; and either locator(s) or cross-reference(s) or both'. An entry by this definition, therefore, could consist of a single heading and locator on a single line or, alternatively, could occupy several lines – with subheadings, many page numbers, and see *also* cross-references – and could have taken the indexer a considerable time to compile. A better recognition of the indexer's work is achieved by counting as an entry each of the following:

● a heading with locator(s) and/or cross-reference(s)
● a subheading (sub-subheading and so on) with locator(s) and/or cross-reference(s)

Indexing software often counts as an entry any heading (or subheading) with a locator, so that the same heading (or subheading) entered later on with another locator is counted as a second entry, even though the two locators will – in the final version – be merged into a single entry.

One disadvantage about payment by entry is that, if an index has to be reduced in size (because fewer pages are available for it than anticipated), the work of constructing and subsequently removing entries is not paid for.

Per record rate
The indexing of databases (consisting, for example, of bibliographical records) is often charged at a fixed rate per record. The rates vary from job to job, depending on the kind of indexing required and how much work has to be done for each record.

Set fees
Some indexers (including this writer) prefer to quote a fixed sum for most conventional work, such as the indexing of a textbook or a periodical. To be able to do this with confidence requires experience, based on comparison and analysis of jobs done over a reasonable period of time. The figure quoted for any job will take into account factors such as the number of indexable pages, the readability (easy comprehension) of the text, the density of the text (how many entries are likely to be generated from each page), special features of the text (such as illustrations, or bibliographical data) to be indexed, the number of index sequences (author index, subject index, product index, and so on), and whether the indexer is to proof-read the index.

Extra charges
Although most freelances can choose the times at which they work and some of them regard evenings (even nights) and weekends as normal working time, most of them tend to have at least some periods in the week or month or year that they regard as reserved for domestic, social and leisure activities and therefore not available for work. Nevertheless, if they are approached by clients with urgent jobs, they are sometimes willing to set aside their private times and speed the work through, working during the night, over weekends, or at holiday times. If this happens, it is reasonable to make an extra charge; the amount will vary according to the kind of work done – one option is to charge 1½ times the usual rate. If the indexer is asked to make a special journey to deliver urgent work in person as soon as it is ready, the cost should be borne by the client. Extra charges may also be applied to the production of camera-ready copy (CRC), to very complicated work and to the indexing of materials that are in poor condition or difficult to handle. Additional work arising from late amendments to the text – passages removed or inserted, chapter order changed, or illustrations moved around, for example – or

from a request to reduce or extend the size of the index (see 'Making the index shorter or longer' in Chapter 5), will necessitate further charges.

Clients should be informed if extra charges are going to be incurred, and given at least an estimate of the amount, and their agreement should be obtained. It is not usually necessary to itemize the extras in detail on the invoice.

Invoicing

Sending the invoice and receiving the money should be the simplest part of the freelance operation, but some beginning indexers are unsure about the conventions – when to send the invoice, how strongly to react when an invoice remains unpaid well after the due date, what to do if a client contests the amount charged. Trouble-free invoicing is partly dependent on making a satisfactory agreement with the client before a job is started, so that both parties know what work is to be done, how much money is involved, and when and how it should be paid. Once an invoice is dispatched, it must not be forgotten about – the indexer's 'outstanding invoice' file should indicate if it becomes overdue. Good money management implies sending an invoice (bill) with the completed work, or very shortly afterwards. Delay in invoicing means that the payment is held up, with a negative effect on the indexer's cash flow.

Larger jobs that are expected to extend over several months can pose a problem for the indexer if it is necessary to wait until the whole project is completed before an invoice can be sent. Clients are usually agreeable to staged payments, each stage being paid for after it has been completed. Jobs that require the indexer to spend money – say on new equipment or software – before the work even starts, may be appropriate for an advance payment (refundable if the work is not satisfactorily completed).

Documentation

Standard invoice forms may be generated via an accounts program, or the indexer's normal headed paper can be used with 'Invoice' clearly added (perhaps in colour). For ease of reference, invoices should be individually numbered, and each one should contain the name and address of the client, the date, brief details of the work to which it relates, and the total amount due for payment. Any agreed additional expenses should be itemized and included in the total. Any purchase order number, job number, or reference number allocated to the indexer by the client must appear prominently. The period for payment is often stipulated at the bottom; 30 days is the normal commercial period, but freelance workers often agree a shorter period in their contracts – 14 days or 7 days, or payment on receipt. Some companies operate a 'fast-track' system for freelance workers – it is worth asking about this when discussing jobs with new clients.

A copy of every invoice should be kept in an 'Outstanding invoices' file until the payment is received from the client. The file may be a simple notebook, or a loose-leaf file, or a segment of an accounts software system on the computer.

Getting Payment

Indexers are not normally paid in cash. The payment may be received through the post in the form of a cheque, or it may be credited direct to the indexer's bank (or building society) account through the computerized BACS or CHAPS systems. Organizations representing some small businesses in the UK often complain about delays in receiving payment from large companies and organizations (including departments of national and local government), and have lobbied successive governments to take action. Recent legislation obliges public limited companies to declare, in their annual reports, the average time they take to pay their bills, so regular late payers can be identified. There is also now legal backing for small operators in some cases to charge interest on bills not paid by the agreed date; indexers wishing to exercise this provision should stipulate it in their agreements with clients. These measures are helping, but the solo indexer – whose cash flow situation (like that of any freelance) may at times be precarious – bears the principal responsibility for prompt collection of money owed and for pursuing the debtor when necessary. Invoices that remain unpaid after the agreed period must be politely but persistently pursued – with increasing vigour if necessary. There need be no embarrassment about asking for the debt to be paid – the work has been done and accepted according to the agreed terms and conditions, and the client is bound to pay.

Companies sometimes pay all invoices at a particular time of the month, in which case the date of receipt of the invoice is significant. An indexer knowing this may be willing to wait a little longer for the payment, if it is certain to come. If a large job is being carried out, under a 'staged payment' agreement, and one of the payments is delayed, it may be advisable to halt the work until the money for the previous stage is received. A properly worded agreement should provide for this situation.

The formal method of chasing an invoice is to send (by post, fax or email) a reminder, headed 'statement', quoting the invoice number, date and amount owed. Alternatively, if relations between the indexer and the client are suitable, a friendly phone call to the person who commissioned the work, pointing out the difficulty, is often effective. Continued reminders (labelled 'second statement', 'third . . .') can be sent, or further phone calls made – perhaps to increasingly higher people in the hierarchy, until payment is received. The relevant officer of any professional indexing society to which the indexer belongs can also be notified and may be able to exert additional pressure. If interest has been agreed on late payment, it can help to send the client a schedule showing how much will be payable for each day's delay.

The majority of clients do pay within the agreed period or shortly after the due date. Refusal to pay is very rare, so most indexers will never have to take a client to court to enforce payment. The indexer should not rush to law or take a heavy-handed attitude. Polite, persistent reminders, increasing in severity and indicating the intention to take 'the necessary action', are better. One method that has been suggested for ensuring prompt payment is to withhold copyright permission for the index to be used, until the invoice has been paid. (See 'Copyright' below.) Another is to offer a small discount for payment within a small number of days of the invoice date, but it is not advisable to give money away in this fashion (particularly to larger operators) without justification. In the UK, the Small Claims Court handles actions for the recovery of amounts up to a specified amount. If legal action is contemplated, the indexer should consider whether, for the amount in question, it is worth the time and expense involved and the inevitable loss of a client. Clients with poor payment records quickly become known among the indexing community, via professional meetings, discussion groups and by word of mouth, so will find it difficult to engage indexers in future. A policy of working equally for several clients, and not becoming overdependent on one of them, can protect the individual indexer from complete loss of livelihood.

Ways of Working

Freelance workers in general are said to have higher levels of job satisfaction than employed workers, stemming partly from the feeling that they have control of their own work situation. They have choices – what to do, when and how to do it, when to take breaks, how to work and where. If freelancing follows a previous period as an employee under an imposed timetable, this freedom of choice can be exhilarating – but perhaps not for long. Eventually the situation of free choice is taken for granted, and the freelance realizes that self-discipline and organization are needed. The proximity of the home office and the domestic domain – convenient in so many ways – can also endanger the effective and efficient use of working hours. Like any group of freelance workers, indexers vary in personality and temperament; some have always led highly organized lives and so can easily build a framework into which their freelance activities neatly fit. Others who – perhaps without realizing it – have become accustomed to depending on their employers' regimes, have to come to terms with the fact that they are now responsible for organizing everything relating to their work. Negative aspects – several jobs coming at once, periods with little or no work, an occasional sense of isolation – must be accepted as necessary risk and considered worth enduring.

Indexers have some choice over the work they do – a job can always be turned down in favour of something more interesting or lucrative. They can also select the best times for working and arrange their timetables around them – though they may sometimes have to spend long hours on a job with a short deadline. There is marked variation in the 'how' of the work (see 'How they index' in Chapter 2); each person discovers, after processing a few reasonably sized jobs, the preferred way of working.

Some like to do one index at a time, so that they can concentrate totally on the content and maintain continuity of thought throughout. Others prefer to work on two (or more) indexes at the same time, so long as they are different in subject, level or form, or are at different stages of preparation. Working on one job for a few hours, processing it to a certain stage, and then moving to another task on another index, can provide relief and renewed mental stimulus and interest – perhaps enabling the indexer to put in more hours than would otherwise be possible. The indexes may even be stored on different computers in separate rooms, or one on a desktop PC and the other on a laptop for outdoor use (though some people find the external environment too distracting). If another, related, kind of work is also being done – copy-editing or proofreading, for example – to switch from one type of job to another can be a welcome change.

Time management

Much of the advice on time management in books, courses, and videos applies to the corporate environment, but most of the suggestions made are equally relevant to self-employment and are easily implemented.

Working Hours

A certain number of hours per day should generally be regarded as time for work. Others in the household need to be made aware of this and casual visitors must be discouraged. Even if there is no paid work on hand, other small office jobs need to be done regularly. The discipline of attendance at the desk at a certain time each day to deal with post, email, filing, professional reading and other CPD (continuing professional development) activities, following up work opportunities, and general tidying, can bolster the morale and supply the feeling of being in a business environment. Precise time planning for indexing work is not always possible, because anticipated work can be delayed by shifts in publishing schedules and unexpected demands can be received from clients with rush jobs. This is something that indexers have to live with – it 'comes with the territory'; there will be occasions when more than one job has to be processed and others when unforeseen leisure time presents itself. Some book indexers notice increases in demand in the period before Christmas and in the summer.

Individual preference determines the best times for working. There is no single 'best time'. Some people are at their most efficient, productive and creative in the early mornings, others peak later in the day or produce their best work during the quiet of the night. Some work best in short spurts of perhaps 20 to 30 minutes at a time, while others can settle down for an hour or two without flagging. It is unwise to go on working doggedly once fatigue or discomfort sets in; pressure of deadlines can encourage this, but tends to lead to errors and misjudgments that then take up time later when they are discovered and have to be corrected. It is equally important to recognize the worst times for working and – whenever possible – to avoid them. Early afternoon is a common low-efficiency period for corporate workers; some freelance workers suffer the same effect. Some people find their concentration waning after dark and most people slow down after a substantial meal. There may be seasonal effects, too. Short winter days with low light levels can reduce the stimulus for activity for some; others are tempted away from the desk by summer weather. Individual best and worst times may be influenced by any drugs taken for medical or other purposes and by alcohol intake. Whether the influence is beneficial or otherwise depends on the substance, the amount and the individual. Awareness of the effects on concentration and alertness – and taking the necessary action – is entirely the responsibility of the person concerned.

Good health being vital for the freelance, regular breaks for exercise and refreshment must be built in to the timetable. Sitting for long periods at the desk can be uncomfortable and harmful. A break need only last a few minutes (if no more time is available) and involve walking round the house, going outside, eating or drinking, making a social phone call, lying down, meditating, listening to music, or doing a few physical exercises. The beneficial effects (physical and mental) of even a short removal from the workplace are immediate.

Diary

Maintaining a diary of forthcoming events and actions required is one of the most important components of time management. It can be a separate diary for business items only, or one in which domestic, social and business dates are combined. The format is for the individual to select; the 'one week at a view' style is convenient for giving a picture of the whole of the impending week. The main concerns are to avoid taking on too much work at the same time, to maintain alertness about deadlines, to prevent double booking, and to allow space for leisure, family and other commitments. Given the interweaving of work and private events that most freelances have to face, a combined diary can provide a fuller picture of what is expected to happen, and will need to be done, during a particular period.

Watching the Time

Positioning an easily visible clock at the workplace helps to keep track of the passage of time and to maintain accurate records of time spent on particular jobs – an essential part of the freelance activity, providing feedback that helps with job pricing. Digital time displays are usually integrated into computers, fax and answering machines and other electronic computer devices – these are useful, but may not be as noticeable as a big clock on the wall. A small mechanical or battery-operated timer can be set to bleep as a reminder to do an essential task (phone someone, take mail to the post office in time for the last post, collect a family member from school, station or airport, take something out of the oven, take medication). Electronic organizers, combining clock, diary, alarm (bleep), address, phone book, and other functions, in a pocket-sized or palm-sized unit are convenient. However, if lost or stolen, or the data is inaccessible because of a fault, the everyday running of the business can be thrown into confusion. A secure copy of important information should therefore also be kept on paper.

Interruption Control

Much indexing work requires concentration and continuity of approach, which can be easily disturbed by the phone, and by household and external activities. Use of an answering machine, with the ring switched off and the sound turned down, ensures that no important call is lost but that the work is not disrupted. Working in a closed room with a 'Do not disturb, work in progress' notice on the door, facing away from the window, and instructing others in the household that all but the most urgent external noises will be ignored, enables the worker to exclude most nuisances.

Priorities

The setting (and resetting) of priorities is a regular feature of the freelance's working hour, day, week, month and year. Jobs awaiting processing must be allocated a place in the queue, along with office 'housekeeping' tasks (filing, selection and purchase of equipment and stationery, correspondence, professional reading) and promoting and publicizing the business. Incoming post, faxes and emails need to be checked through quickly and those requiring urgent responses should be dealt with straight away; everything else can be sorted into a decreasing order of importance, for later attention. The temptation to keep checking to see if any email has arrived is better resisted, except when something urgent or vital is anticipated; it wastes time, it can be depressing to find repeatedly that there is nothing, and – at least with a dial-up system on which the call is priced – it wastes money, too.

The aim is to have each assignment completed by its due time or date, but not to spend time sooner than necessary on a task less important than another. At times the indexer feels like a juggler, trying to keep several balls in the air at once; success in this is a mark of good planning and organization (plus perhaps a little good luck). The separate set of priorities relating to the indexer's private life has to be taken into account, too.

Delegation (Co-operation), Using Commercial Services, Subcontracting

The art of delegation is bound to come up in any discussion about time management in the corporate environment, but at first sight may seem irrelevant to the solo worker. However, if there are others in the household – and particularly if they are benefiting from the proceeds of the self-employed person's work – they may be able and willing to co-operate by offering occasional support (answering the phone, printing pages, checking that page proofs are complete and legible, taking mail to the post office, buying stationery when out on a shopping trip, making light refreshments, walking the dog, for example). Paying commercially for domestic services such as cleaning, laundry, cooking, and child-minding may be an option for some, but such items are not all deductible as business expenses; the main purpose is to buy time for more profitable work.

Subcontracting parts of the indexing work is not usually necessary for the new freelance, but is something to bear in mind for later periods of heavy workload. Paying a suitably qualified and reliable person to do the more elementary elements of the work, so that the indexer can concentrate on the more advanced components, can make sense. If the indexer has first to train the subcontractor or minutely scrutinize and correct the completed work, the benefit is reduced – careful assessment of the situation is needed before committing to subcontracting. Time also has to be taken to formulate and complete a written agreement (covering specification of the work and the fee) with the subcontractor.

Communication Control and Method

The feeling of isolation sometimes experienced by freelances can tempt them into 'overcommunication', leading to wasted time and effort. It makes sense to organize outgoing phone calls so that several minor matters are dealt with together, rather than making separate calls as soon as the topic comes to mind. Instant 'knee-jerk' replies to communications received – despite giving the satisfaction of having dealt with the matter promptly – often have to be followed up by further information, questions, minor or major amendments, even apologies. Allowing subconscious thinking time may delay the response a little, but usually gives a better result and a reduction in working time.

The method of communication can influence time, cost and effectiveness. The different methods – phone, post, fax, email, face-to-face – have their own suitabilities, so the freelance needs to consider which is better, not just in terms of the preparation time taken and the speed of transmission and response, but also in relation to the impact on the recipient, the creation of a permanent record, the need for copies to be circulated to others for information, any legal requirements, and the cost.

Organization

An organized workplace, in which work can proceed smoothly and in which needed items and information can be quickly found, saves time. Piles of unopened post and unfiled papers, stacks of loose unlabelled disks, rows of disordered box files, a scatter of undated notes and messages on the desk and stuck round the computer screen – all these are obstacles to a smooth flow of work. Anyone who is not naturally well-ordered should try to set aside a particular time each day to tidy up. Others in the household may need to be warned not to try to 'help straighten the office', not to move or touch anything, not to switch off equipment or pull out plugs – and domestic pets with troublesome habits should be kept at a distance.

Scheduling

New indexers should not be alarmed if the first jobs they tackle occupy far more hours than they anticipated – this is common. The most important thing is to produce an index of a good standard, which satisfies the client and meets the deadline, so that other assignments will follow. Extra care and double-checking are worthwhile. Charging at an hourly rate is obviously not suitable in this case – a 'reasonable' figure for the work has to be calculated. The financial return may therefore work out, initially, at rather a low rate, but the knowledge gained will feed back into the next job.

Being able to plan the best use of available time – and to agree sensible deadlines with customers, and to charge realistic fees – means identifying the tasks that make up a typical job and how long each one takes (see 'Work records' below). Because individual indexers work in different ways and with a variety of documentary materials, there are no globally applicable standard times. They need to discover their own productivity levels by measuring (if only roughly) the relevant elements – how long it takes to input entries for the average page of the average book, how much additional time is taken up editing and fine-tuning the final entries, how long to print out, how long to pack and post the finished item, and how much time is taken up by the phone, postal, fax, and email communications that are associated with a job. The total time for a job should be reckoned from the moment the first enquiry is received, up to the point when the finished product has been dispatched and all the related documentation filed away.

Work records

Some indexers keep records of what they do and when they do it. The data from these records are invaluable for calculating fees for prospective jobs, planning timetables and assessing forthcoming workloads. They also enable the indexer to check trends from year to year and to make adjustments in workload, time for leisure and other activities.

Records can be paper or computer-held worksheets on which the job name and the element of the job (input, editing, printing, correspondence, filing) and the times taken (in, say, fifteen-minute spans) are entered. A computer program can produce total and average figures, display the data in chart or diagram form, and recalculate schedules when there is a change to any of the many variables affecting the time taken on an index. The statistical data provided by dedicated indexing programs, too, make a useful contribution to work measurement. Typical information includes the number of entries or lines in an index, the average and maximum length of entries, the number of locators per entry, the average number of entries per page of text, and the number of cross-references. This automatically generated information is helpful to those indexers who decline to spend valuable working time on the compilation of records. The collected data can answer some important questions:

- How long did that job really take (from first enquiry to dispatch and filing?
- Did I charge the right amount (in relation to the time it took)?
- Which part of an indexing job needs most time?
- Which alternative, optional or occasional features add significant time to a job?
- What do I really do in the course of a day (and should I reorganize)?

The indexer dealing mainly with one kind of text soon acquires the ability to assess approximately how long an index is likely to take. Other jobs, perhaps with unusual features, can cause initial uncertainty. In this situation, working through a small sample or doing a dummy run with some similar material, while measuring the time taken, can supply basic data on which to build a provisional proposal. If, over time, the indexer notes down the times taken on any new job elements that occur, a useful reference file can be built up.

Beginning indexers want to know the answers to simple questions like: How many book indexes can I produce in a year? How long does it/should it take to index the average textbook? How many pages an hour can you index? The answers to the questions are anything but simple and have to be prefaced 'It depends. . . . ' It depends on the density of the text, the need for subheading analysis, the readership, the number of sequences, the need to add highlighting for major references and illustrations, the time needed for checking and harmonizing proper names, and so on. One indexer's personal worktime data are not necessarily applicable to any other indexer. They may be dealing with different subjects and different levels of text. They may not be equally fast at inputting entries, they may use different programs, and follow different house styles. Even something as apparently simple as typing personal names can vary in the time taken. If the names are of a familiar type, or if the forenames are initialized, input speed will be high; if they are foreign to the indexer, or have to be given in full, with multiple elements or accents, input speed will be low. Indexers who are working in teams or on co-operative projects, and who want to establish standard production targets for the work, need to compare notes at the start in order to determine the range of times to be taken into account.

Actual and elapsed time
There are two aspects to the time taken to do an indexing (or any other) job; both are relevant in discussions with clients and in scheduling. The estimated actual time spent working on, say, an index to a book may total 24 hours, but this does not mean that the index will be finished 24 hours after starting work. The working time is not (and cannot be) continuous, but is spaced out over a number of days (the elapsed time), with inter-vals for food, relaxation, sleep, and other work. Even when an indexer is not actively engaged on production, the mind is still subconsciously working on the index and ideas can occur for improvement. Once the index has reached the final draft form, it should – if possible – be set aside for a short time and then returned to for a fresh look. High-quality indexing, particularly for advanced texts, needs time for thought; some people, though, feel that they produce their best work when under real pressure.

Elapsed time may sometimes be long, though actual time is short – for example if the material to be indexed arrives in a few small batches several weeks apart. By contrast, on occasion, actual time and elapsed time can be very close; rapid electronic transmission can enable certain very simple jobs to be received and processed extremely quickly.

Receiving the Work

It should be the case that documents received for indexing are in perfect shape and that the indexer can start reading and indexing straight away. It is not always so, and the wise indexer therefore takes a little time to check through what has arrived, perhaps using a checklist of questions. The following are applicable to a document in page-proof format:

- Are all pages (including preliminaries, contents list, etc.) present, legible and in the correct order?
- Are there any unexpected additional chapters, sections, or illustrative matter (i.e. for which the indexing treatment has not been discussed)?
- Are there any proofreader's markings that indicate that pieces of text are to be moved (to another page, back or forward) in the final printing? If so, the indexer must take care to ensure that the exact page number is known, for inclusion in the index.

A preliminary read, usually necessary in order to understand the general direction of the text, and to note its principal themes and messages, may also reveal to a sharp-eyed indexer some very obvious errors – names inconsistently spelled, literals (miskeyed and transposed characters), words duplicated. The correction of errors in the text is not, contractually, the indexer's responsibility, but few indexers feel they have done a proper job if they pass them by. Not all writers check their facts or employ perfect spelling, grammar and punctuation, and their mistakes are not always picked up during the editing process. One set of proof pages is often read by a proofreader at the same time as the indexer is indexing from another set; the proofreader should therefore note any errors. Indexers, because they are reading the text for meaning, often notice mistakes that others overlook – some indexers, in any case, also work as proofreaders. Clearly, any error that affects the index – the inconsistent spelling of an indexable name, for example – must be cleared up. In addition to this, though, most indexers prefer to be associated with a text of high quality and integrity, so if they notice a factual error or an indisputable fault of grammar they will inform the client. Instances have been quoted in which parts of texts have had to be rewritten because of serious errors discovered by indexers. There is normally no additional payment directly received for this extra service, but in perhaps saving the reputation of others, indexers can enhance their own standing and also ensure that more work comes their way. Depending on their number and degree of seriousness, errors can be reported when they are noticed, or listed and sent with the completed index.

While reading, some indexers mark page proofs with highlighting or coloured pens, to indicate obvious indexable elements. This is just a first stage – complete indexing is done only on the basis of a fuller reading and understanding. Marking up is an individualistic process, with colours meaning different things to different indexers – and some indexers do not mark up at all (see 'How they index' in Chapter 2).

Book indexers sometimes have to start creating indexes even before the final pagination has been determined – working from galley proofs (proofs containing all the text in its correct order, but not yet divided into regular pages), or from authors' typescripts. The indexer assigns temporary numbers to the individual sheets, so that the index can be compiled, and then – once the final page proofs are available – replaces the temporary numbers with the permanent ones. Dedicated indexing programs can speed up the process of conversion (see 'Indexing for unknown or changed pagination' in Chapter 11). With embedded indexing, the indexer deals not with page proofs, but with electronic files containing the whole text of the document, into which codes are inserted to indicate index terms; page numbers are added automatically by the client's word-processing system (see 'Software' in Chapter 11). The time available for indexing may be short (whether being done in-house or externally) and the work may be done in sections, perhaps chapter by chapter, as they become ready.

Delivering the Work

Whenever possible, the work should be delivered on or shortly before the agreed date, and in the agreed format. Delivery long before the date (if the work has proceeded much more quickly than expected) may lead the client to expect express service on all future jobs. It is always better to allow for thinking and reviewing time (see 'Actual and elapsed time' above).

At the time of writing, floppy disk (diskette) and email are the two favoured methods of delivery often accompanied (by post or fax) by a hard copy (printout), which shows the client how the index entries should be arranged, and which can be annotated if necessary. Some indexers like to deliver in person, if in the vicinity, so as to get to know the client personally, and perhaps talk about future work. Others like the anonymity of distance. It is prudent, when dealing with a new client who requires email transmission of the index, to send first a short message with a sample file in the agreed format; if the client confirms satisfactory receipt, then the complete file can be dispatched (see 'Index files for emailing' in Chapter 11). Occasionally when the index has been commissioned by an editor, the indexer may be asked to send a copy of the index to the author for comment before dispatching it to the publisher's editor. Normally, though, the editor is responsible for liaison with the author (see 'Contracts' below).

A covering letter (which can be produced from a standard template held on computer) can include (or have attached) any explanatory information for the client regarding, for example, disk format, codes or marginal/textual markings used. The invoice for the work is usually sent at the same time; any exceptional delivery charges that have been agreed – such as the cost of express mail, courier, or travel to deliver in person – may be included either in the main invoice or in a separate one sent shortly afterwards (see 'Invoicing' above). Proof of collection and delivery can be arranged if needed.

If the indexer is to proofread the printed index (as agreed in the contract), the client may send the proofs by post, fax or email; the indexer needs to be able to check and return them quickly, with clear notes of any amendments required. The fee for proofreading may be included in the main invoice – either as a separate item, or consolidated into the whole fee – or another invoice can be sent once the work has been done.

Proof pages are not normally returned to the client; they are often heavily marked and annotated by the indexer and so are not in suitable condition for further work on them. The indexer needs to keep them, anyway, in case there are queries about the content or coverage of the index. It can also be useful later on, for comparison, if the indexer is asked to index a second edition. In the case of a book index, the indexer needs also to check the published copy of the book against the proof copy, to ensure that the pagination of the text has not been changed since the index was made. Late changes are sometimes made in the publishing house – to incorporate a new section of text, for example, or to change the positions of illustrations, or to set the text in a different size. What should happen, in this case, is that the editor immediately contacts the indexer to find out what changes need to be made to the index; if the text has been completely reset – in which case most of the locators in the index will need changing – a new set of proofs should be provided. Sometimes, however, the resulting effects on the index are not realized by the publisher and so an indexer finds out only after the book has been published, that the index supplied is no longer accurate. The users of the index, finding that it does not seem to work, may well assume that the errors were made by the indexer, whose reputation suffers. Indexers are right to feel aggrieved about this, particularly if their names appear with their indexes, and should take up the matter with the publishers straight away; if the effects of the alterations are serious, they may wish to ask that the authors be notified of the cause of the problem and of the indexer's blamelessness, and that a printed slip with suitable wording be inserted at the beginning of the index in all copies of the book. They may wish also to offer to produce (for a suitable fee) an adjusted index for inclusion if the book is reprinted.

Client Relations

The relationship with a customer may begin before the question of a specific job arises. Any promotional material sent out by the indexer sets the scene and makes an impression. Poor-quality material – low in informative content, slipshod in appearance – will almost certainly not result in any enquiries. Smartly presented, comprehensive but concise information inspires confidence and the expectation of good work. To find reliable indexers, some clients act on recommendations received from colleagues or others in their particular business, some consult the directory put out by the relevant professional society in their country, and others follow up publicity materials sent to them by individual indexers. In order to be satisfied that a particular indexer is suitable, a client may ask to be supplied with a reference from a previous client, or a copy of some earlier work. If the new client's work has some special features, the indexer may be asked to produce a 'test sample' – an index for a small extract from the indexable material.

The first direct, job-oriented, contact between client and indexer is often by phone, to discover whether the indexer is able to take on an urgent job immediately, or will be able to do one at a later (specified) time, or is interested in being added to the client's list of freelance indexers, or is willing to join a team of indexers working on a long-term, part-time project. During this conversation, the client is looking for signs that the indexer sounds professional and capable. Hesitation and uncertainty are particularly obvious in phone conversations. Indexers who are not entirely at ease when on the phone, or who are not sure that they sound confident, can add polish to their presentations by practising typical dialogues (with friends, family or fellow-indexers), recording them, listening and then revising them – or by attending workshops on communication skills at local colleges. Alternatively, the enquiry may come by post – usually an indication that the document to be indexed is in preparation and not expected to be in its final, indexable, form for a while. Email is used for enquiries, but – at present – more by clients who already know their indexers from previous jobs undertaken. The responses to postal and email communications can be in like form or by phone.

Exchange of information

Before concluding any kind of agreement (oral or written) the two parties (indexer and client) must be sure that they have a mutual understanding about the content of the job, its technical specification and the terms and conditions under which the work is to be done. Getting the details straight at the very beginning cannot guarantee that nothing will go wrong later, but it goes a long way towards ensuring a smooth passage. The indexer and the client take an equal part in the discussions preceding the agreement. The client, if experienced at commissioning indexes, may have all the relevant information ready to pass on to the indexer. Otherwise, the indexer needs to proceed through a list of questions (copies of which can be kept by the telephone) in order to get a full picture of the job and its demands. The first things the indexer needs to know concerning a book requiring an index are:

- How long is the text (number of indexable pages)?
- What is the subject (at what level, and for which readership)?
- Is there anything unusual about the physical format and content type (anything which affects the making of an index)?
- When will the final, complete proofs be available?
- When is the finished index required?
- Who will proofread the index?

Having received answers to these questions, the indexer can decide whether the job is feasible and of interest. Other matters that indexer and client need to discuss before the job is started – though not necessarily during their first conversation – include:

- the method by which the proofs will be sent to the indexer (post, express courier . . .)

- the amount of space available for the index (number of pages or lines)
- which content is to be indexed, which not. The indexing of features such as bibliographical matter, appendices, illustrations, chapter notes, etc.
- a need for separate index sequences
- the format in which the index is to be delivered (paper copy, disk, email file); if disk or email copy is required, the kind of file (ASCII, Word RTF, etc.)
- client's house style regarding capitalization, spacing and punctuation, typestyles (use of italic and bold), subheading layout, form of locators, use of display letters, alphabetical arrangement

The business aspects must also be considered:

- the fee – how much (how calculated), when and how it will be paid; refund of special expenses
- the acknowledgement of the indexer's work/crediting of the indexer's name in the book (if the indexer wishes to assert moral rights)
- the supply of a complimentary copy of the book when published
- ownership of copyright of the index

Contracts

Business contracts are governed by the law of the country. In the UK at least, a contract does not have to be in written form to be legal – an oral agreement (over the phone, for example) is equally valid. Indexers who have built up a good relationship of trust with certain clients may feel quite safe in coming to an agreement on the phone – particularly when the job is urgent – and may know from experience that problems are unlikely. However, if matters do go wrong and there is no written agreement to consult for clarification, and if – as is usually the case – the client is a company or organization, the indexer can be comparatively powerless. For the protection of both the indexer and the client a written agreement, which can be formulated by either party, is strongly recommended; misunderstandings are much less likely to arise and develop into disputes if the job content, specification, terms and conditions are recorded in a mutually acceptable document at the start. A straightforward letter (from client to indexer, or indexer to client) in plain English, containing the relevant information, and a simple confirmation by the other party, is usually all that is needed. Most small and medium-sized jobs do not require a complex contractual document phrased in technical legal language, whereas larger, long-term, projects – particularly with government departments and agencies – often do. A formal contract is normally produced in two copies, both of which are signed by each party.

A publisher's contract with an author may require the author to supply an index (either self-compiled or commissioned from an indexer), but usually offers the alternative of having the publisher commission it – the cost being deducted from the author's royalties on the book. An indexer may, therefore, be contacted either by the author or by the publisher. An author who is experienced in dealing direct with indexers should already be aware of indexers' needs, ways of working, and styles of presentation, but one who is engaging an indexer for the first time may have little idea of what is involved, what is feasible and what is not. Setting out the ground rules and relevant information at the beginning contributes to a smooth relationship between the two creative individuals. Some indexers prefer not to accept commissions from authors, but favour – as they see it – the assurance of greater security of working with publishers' editors. Others are content to work directly with authors, though some make it a condition that they receive an advance payment of part of the fee (say a third or a half).

Where contact with authors is handled by the editors, they act – where necessary – as intermediaries between authors and indexers. Some authors make it a condition that they see and approve any index commissioned by the publisher, and the publisher may wish to include this condition in the agreement with the indexer. An indexer faced with this condition should only agree to it if confident that there will be no haphazard or uninformed interference with the index. Some indexers welcome the opportunity to have a discussion with authors before – and sometimes during – the making of the index. The interchange can be valuable, assisting the indexer to formulate headings containing specialist vocabulary, for example, and helping the author to appreciate the creativity and technical skill of the indexer. If an author has little understanding of index compilation and structure, though, a perfectly adequate index could be rejected or unsuitably amended. Refusal to pay part or all of the fee could follow, or – if the fee is paid to the indexer before the author's adverse comments are received – the publisher may suggest that rates for future work should be reduced; such practices are unacceptable and any clause to permit reduced rates should be excluded from the agreement. Any changes that the editor or author feels should be made to the index should be discussed with the indexer (see 'Degree of autonomy of the indexer' in Chapter 5).

Some clients have a standard contract for all freelance operators with whom they work, specifying rates of pay and other terms and conditions; indexers should read these through carefully (particularly those relating to payment and criteria for approval of the index) and if there is anything to which they cannot agree, should cross out or amend, and sign alongside. Contracts with excessively severe clauses, for example any that seek to limit an indexer's freedom to accept work from other clients or that provide for the fee to be withheld (or refunded if already paid) if the author is not satisfied with it, should be returned to the client unsigned and then renegotiated.

A typical proposal for a contract to index a printed document may refer to:

- delivery date
- index specification: coverage, length, layout, style (BS ISO 999 or house style), form of copy (disk, printout, camera-ready, email file)
- any special features or requirements
- responsibility for proofreading
- fee (and expenses if relevant)
- copyright

Other matters (see 'Exchange of information' above) may be included as deemed necessary. It is important to know whom to contact within the organization – who can solve a problem and who will authorize the bill. If in doubt about a company or organization, indexers can consult fellow-professionals and indexing societies and check official sources for information concerning clients' reputability.

From time to time, the idea of a cancellation or postponement clause is floated. Under such a clause, if a client should cancel or drastically postpone a job shortly before an indexer expects to start, a penalty fee would become payable. This would provide at least some compensation for an indexer who has timetabled the necessary period – and perhaps turned down other jobs in order to keep it clear – and then finds the time completely barren of work. The idea has not so far met with wide approval from indexers; it is unreasonable to expect client's schedules always to turn out to the day as planned. A more accommodating approach is usually preferred, so that indexers know that work will continue to come from their regular sources and that if they themselves experience unexpected delays, because of illness, family crisis, or equipment failure, for example, the client will be equally flexible. A penalty clause in the contract is probably best reserved for those clients whom the indexer knows from past experience, or from information from other professionals, to be unreliable. Alternatively, it can be included in every contract, just in case, but not enforced unless the indexer finds it absolutely necessary.

Copyright

Copyright, broadly speaking as it relates to literary works, is the legal right to print and publish a work for a certain number of years. The law concerning copyright differs from country to country and is affected by certain international conventions. In the UK, under European law, the period of copyright is 75 years after the death of the author. Copyright in an original work exists automatically as soon as it is in a fixed form (for example, written down, printed, or electronically recorded); it does not have to be registered or asserted. It belongs, initially at least, to the person who created the work. The owner of the copyright can assign it to another party, by selling it to that party, or may keep the ownership but licence another party to use the right. If indexes are original, created works (which they usually are), then (in the UK at least) copyright in the index belongs initially to the freelance indexer. The copyright in indexes prepared by employees of a company or other organization normally belongs to the employer.

Copyright seems rarely to have been covered specifically in contracts between freelance indexers and their clients, and many indexers are not concerned about it. Both parties have probably assumed that the client has purchased the copyright to the index on payment of the agreed fee and that, anyway, the value to the indexer of ownership of copyright may not be great. The matter has potential importance, though, if the index concerned is a large or continuing one and if electronic rights also enter the frame. Indexers need to consider the inclusion of a suitable clause in their contracts; permanent retention of copyright may not be of interest, but it can be worth deferring the assignment of copyright until the agreed fee for preparing the index has been paid. Some indexers assign the copyright but obtain agreement to produce copies of the index for publicity purposes, as samples of their work. Others may prefer to keep ownership of their work, but licence the client to use it. Mulvany (1994, pp. 28–34) and Wellisch (1995, pp. 31–41, pp. 97–102), referring to the situation in the US, discuss the question in relation to 'work done for hire' and the index as a 'supplementary work'; much turns on the legal definition of terms, and some people dispute that freelance indexing is 'work done for hire'. This book cannot provide legal advice or interpret the law as it applies under various jurisdictions. There are differing opinions about the copyright status of indexes, and the law varies between countries. If in doubt about the inclusion or phrasing of a copyright clause in their contracts, indexers should obtain advice from their professional indexing societies (see 'Organizations for indexers' in Chapter 12).

Moral rights

In the UK there now exist, in addition to copyright, moral rights for authors (and other creators) of copyright works. Moral rights remain with the author/creator for life and cannot be assigned to anyone else during that time. There are four rights, two of which are particularly relevant to indexers:

● right of 'paternity': the right of the author to be identified as the author of the work. To take effect, this right must be asserted by the author/creator/originator – a suitable statement should appear in all copies of the work, such as:
'The right of A.N. Indexer to be identified as author of this work has been asserted by [her/him] in accordance with the Copyright, Designs and Patents Act, 1988.'
● right of 'integrity': this protects the work against derogatory treatment (such as additions, amendments and adaptations that distort or mutilate the work and impugn the author's reputation). It does not have to be asserted.

The other two rights protect authors against having work falsely attributed to them, and give the commissioner of a private photograph privacy against copies being published without permission.

Indexers who are concerned about copyright and moral rights should make sure that nothing in their contracts disturbs them. Those wishing to be identified as the creators of their work can assert their right, while remembering the possible downside of this if work is published with unsuitable alterations (see 'The indexer's name' in Chapter 5). Amicable agreements, acknowledging the professional status and reputation of both parties, and maintaining good relations between them (see 'Keeping the relationship sweet' below) are best. Contesting a situation after an index has been published is unproductive and there is no joy to be had from protracted arguments about inappropriate amendments made to the index.

Keeping the relationship sweet

Harmonious working relationships between freelance indexers and their clients are much more common than discordant ones, and unforeseen problems that occur are more often settled by discussion and adjustment than by legal means. Any indexer who is discontented with any aspect of the job, either while the work is being done or afterwards (having viewed the published results) should take up the matter with the client and try to resolve it as quickly as possible. Advice and, if necessary, support, can be sought from the professional indexing society. Taking a client to law should be seen as a last resort.

The freelance should consider setting aside a certain amount of time for keeping in touch with clients. It may at first sight seem like unproductive and unpaid labour, but maintaining goodwill can bring rewards in the longer term. Clients need to be informed that indexers are still available, that a new service is on offer, that rush jobs are a speciality, and must be told about new addresses and phone numbers. Changes of address (post, email) and phone number should be widely (and repeatedly) publicized. Old addresses continue to appear in directories and in clients' contact lists for a long time; if clients are unable to get in touch, work may be lost, so arrangements for forwarding mail and messages from previous addresses need to be made. The value of publicity on a web site is that information can be quickly updated.

Ethics and Professional Responsibilities

The importance of professionalism, both in indexing practice and in handling business matters, should be recognized. The Society of Indexers' annual directory *Indexers available*, lists the responsibilities that its indexer members should bear in mind in accepting and processing work from clients. They concern:

- attaining and maintaining indexing competence
- keeping up to date with subject knowledge [see CPD below]
- indexing only within chosen subject fields and relevant levels of text
- discussing with clients at the start, agreeing specifications
- handling of problems
- delivering on time
- agreeing fair and suitable fees

CPD (continuing professional development)

One of the risks of solo working is the failure to recognize the gradual change that takes place in all sectors of life. The indexer needs to be quickly made aware of new indexing styles and standards, changes in business practice, technological innovations, revisions in the legal situation, and developments on the cultural scene. General and specialist subject knowledge must be maintained at a level adequate for the indexing work being accepted. When selecting an indexer, a client is only interested in engaging one with current knowledge and everyday familiarity. Members of professional groups of all kinds are therefore being encouraged to involve themselves in CPD in order to keep themselves up to date. Under orga-nized schemes, the time used for professional reading, attending conferences and meetings, participating in workshops and other kinds of training event, maintaining individual professional contacts (face-to-face, on the phone, via the internet, and so on) is recorded and notified to the professional body concerned.

Professional recognition, as well as inclusion in publicity materials, may increasingly depend on evidence of CPD activity. Attention to self-development, as to all other aspects of managing the work, can not only benefit the individual indexer and the profession as a whole, but can also improve the quality of the indexes produced and the documents that they support.

Data protection

The Data Protection Act (1998) in the UK requires data controllers (collectors and users of personal data) to process that data fairly and lawfully. Broadly, they must not process (obtain, record, retrieve, consult, hold, disclose, or use) personal data (whether held on paper or in a computer) without the permission of the individuals concerned or unless the processing is necessary for purposes defined by the law. In the circumstances within which most freelance indexers normally operate, the holding of personal names in a file for the purpose of making an index to a document is perfectly in order. It could be unlawful, though, for an indexer to use for another purpose any 'sensitive', unpublished, personal data gathered, say, for an in-house index. The processing of personal information received over the internet may also be against the law if the data controller is not registered with the Office of Data Protection. Full information on data protection law is available on the web site of the Office of the Data Protection Commissioner: www.dataprotection.gov.uk.

References

Bell, Hazel K. (1998) Thirty-nine to one: indexing the novels of Angela Thirkell. *The Indexer*, **21**, 6–10

Benns media – UK. Tonbridge: Miller Freeman UK

British Standards Institution (1996) *Information and documentation – guidelines for the content, organization and presentation of indexes*. BS ISO 999: 1996. London: British Standards Institution

Literary market place. New Providence, NJ: Bowker

Mulvany, Nancy C. (1994) *Indexing books*. Chicago: University of Chicago Press

Wellisch, Hans H. (1995) *Indexing from A to Z* 2nd edn. New York: H.W. Wilson

Willings press guide. Teddington, Middlesex: Hollis

Writers' and artists' yearbook. London: Black

The writer's market. Cincinatti, OH: F & W Publications

Further Reading

Brittney, Lynn (1999) *The Which? guide to working from home* 2nd edn London: Which?

Golzen, Godfrey and Kogan, Helen (1999) *'Daily Telegraph' guide to working for yourself.* London: Kogan Page

Reynard, Keith W. and Reynard, Jeremy M.E. (1998) (ed.) *The Aslib directory of information sources in the United Kingdom* 10th edn. London: Aslib

Vass, Jane (1998) (ed.) *The Which? guide to starting your own business.* London: Which?

CHAPTER ELEVEN

Technology

There are no predictions in this chapter. It aims to give a snapshot of current document and indexing technology and of those developments in electronic and telecommunications technology that may be particularly significant for indexers, altering the range and nature of their work. Any indexer's strategy for CPD (continuing professional development) needs to include maintaining awareness of new technical devices and gaining familiarity with them.

It is not only indexers who are involved in developments in indexing technology; other professionals – as librarians, IT (information technology) specialists, and computer programmers – are vital contributors. Such a mix, with people having different perspectives and aiming at a variety of needs, can result in a high level of innovation, to the benefit of all. The downside, if the groups are not working together, is that each group establishes its own vocabulary – sometimes using the same words but with different meanings, as well as having different words for the same concepts. Not even the words 'index', 'indexer' and 'indexing' have common meanings for all the groups. It can also happen that an idea, thought to be new, is named by one group, only for them to discover that another group has been implementing it for some time but under a different name. Increased co-operation should help to avoid hold-ups of this kind.

Document Technology

A document can be produced in a variety of physical formats. The enduring use of paper may seem extraordinary to people who long ago became convinced that the personal electronic library and the paperless office would take over well before the beginning of the 21st century. It is no surprise at all to those who recognize the numerous qualities – in terms of function and convenience – of 'the book'. Paper documents are still being produced, therefore, and are used independently or alongside other forms. Ideally, every document should be produced in the form most suited to its intended users, its purpose and its type. If possible, it should be produced in more than one form, to make it available through wide distribution to a larger readership. In practice, cost and time factors often intrude, with the result that some documents may be available to only a comparatively small number of people. In industrialized countries most people can get access (though not always conveniently) to the necessary equipment for viewing documents online, on CD-ROM, in video and audio forms, and in microform. This may be at work, at home, in public libraries, community centres, and in specialist service points such as cybercafés.

At the time of writing, four of the developments that have particular implications for indexers are:

- on-demand publishing
- mobile telephone access to the internet and other electronic information sources, through WAP (Wireless Application Protocol)
- digital interactive television,
- e-books (electronic books)

On-demand publishing, with the texts held by the publisher in digital form only, reduces the publisher's production costs (including the expense of storage space). It enables older texts that have gone out of print and out of copyright to be produced – by the most rapid and convenient electronic means – whenever a consumer asks for a copy. It should therefore be possible for texts that were originally published without indexes, or with inadequate indexes, to be provided with them; it is up to indexers, individually and collectively, to convince the producers of the added value.

The broadened use of mobile telephones ('third-generation', WAP, mobiles) is expected to enable anyone – whether at home, at work, on holiday, or on the move – to send and receive emails, manage finances, check facts, find information, keep up with the news as it breaks, consult a health professional, browse job advertisements, play games, listen to radio, take part in video conferences, and do many of the other things that form part of the normal daily round. Digital interactive television is more static, but – as with the mobile phone – the user needs no personal computer to gain access to the internet and other information sources.

It is not yet clear whether large numbers of people will want to manage their information requirements (and their lives) through mobile phones and TV sets and so whether there will be a sufficient demand for the apparatus and the services. Similarly, e-books are available for use on portable, compact, battery-operated readers, but it is too early to say in which sectors of people's lives they will become most popular. Calling up news and business information on a TV screen may be satisfactory, and reading limited portions of scrolling text on the small display of a mobile phone may be appealing for leisure purposes, but people involved in lengthy research and consultation may prefer other methods using older forms of document. Changes in the preparation, production and use of documents are dependent not only on the available technology, the costs of production and the financial returns required by the producers, but on psychological factors concerning the users of documents (almost the whole population in some countries).

It may be that in the not-too-distant future, all indexes will be compiled by marking and annotating electronic forms of text, rather than by keyboarding entries while examining printed page proofs. The 'death of the book' has been foretold for many years, but has not yet occurred. 'The book' in its printed form is a superb design, highly adaptable to use in very different situations and circumstances, usable by all with sufficient sight, durable and resilient to wear and tear, and can still be used even when damaged and beginning to disintegrate. It shows no signs at present of falling into disuse, so indexers are likely to be working with paper for quite a while yet, alongside electronic forms. In any case, happily, as far as the indexer's role is concerned, the form of the document is largely irrelevant. We can suppose that, even if electronic chips carrying immense libraries were implanted in the brains of humans, indexers' intellectual skills would still be needed at the preparation stage in order to make the information retrievable.

Almost all documents require indexing in order to make them fully usable and useful, and the principles of indexing are the same whatever the documentary form. Differences in information need and document usage affect the scale and level of indexing – for example, accessing the latest economic statistics via the display on a mobile phone does not call for the same indexing provision as searching the century-old paper archives of a scientific research institute. The way in which the index terms are generated and displayed may differ considerably, but the underlying principle is the same. People need information on a topic and they want to locate the information without having to scan the whole document or collection of documents; the key in each case is provided by an indexer. Indexing involves the handling of large amounts of coherent text, not just bits of data and facts, sometimes also images and other presentations; it requires intellectual processing, concentration, attention to detail – as well as physical space and a conducive work environment. Not all indexers wish to deal with all forms of document. Most concentrate on one or two major forms and therefore can match their equipment to the needs of those forms.

Electronic media

The electronic medium is, then, just another document format. The purpose of indexing is the same as for non-electronic media – to enable people to find the information they need. The same principles of indexing apply, too, but the methods and detail may differ. There is no single method of 'electronic indexing'.

In print documents the index normally leads the user from headings to locators (page number, paragraph number, line number, or some such). In electronic documents – such as whole texts available online, or data-bases and encyclopaedias on CD-ROM – the text may be 'continuous', or divided into linked sections each with its own title, but with no locators. Selecting an index heading should bring up on screen the relevant portion of text. Within the text, codes can be added to make immediate links with other parts of the document, images, sounds, other indexes, related web sites, and email addresses.

The increasing availability of documents in multiple forms has yet again underlined the desirability and possibility of recording information only once and then making available for use in a variety of contexts and in different styles – simplified, amplified, or customized according to need.

There is nothing new about this idea. Decades ago, librarians began pooling and exchanging catalogue entries so that the same publication did not have to be separately catalogued in many individual libraries. Now, catalogue records in electronic form are available for most published items, from central cataloguing agencies. The records are easily incorporated into an individual library's own catalogue, with 'local' information – such as the shelf-mark or location of the item – added. Additionally, records of several libraries can be merged, to enable locations over a large geographical area to be shown.

Metadata and Mark-up Languages

'Metadata' is a word used for machine-understandable information that describes or represents the content of any kind of document. As pointed out by Milstead and Feldman (1999), librarians and indexers have been producing metadata – in the form of catalogue entries and index headings – for a very long time, but have not used that term. With the development of electronic documents, it has become possible to store very large amounts of information; but storage is not of much use without the capability to retrieve, convert, transfer and reuse the information. To enable the identification and retrieval of only that information which is needed for a particular purpose, it is therefore necessary to know what each document is about and, even better, what each part of the document is about.

All kinds of creators, users and processors of electronic content need to use metadata. Uniformity in the description and representation of electronic and Web resources is therefore important for accessibility. Standards for different levels of metadata are being developed, and information sources set up. The Dublin Core [web site: purl.org/DC] is a simple metadata element set providing an alternative to the very detailed MARC (MAchine-Readable Catalogue) used in many libraries. A project group of the World Wide Web Consortium (W3C) [web site: www.w3.org/Metadata] is working on the Resource Description Framework (RDF), designed to meet a variety of metadata needs. The Association of American Publishers (AAP) has initiated the Metadata Information Clearinghouse (Interactive) (MICI) [web site: www.wileynpt.com/mici], to gather information about projects, standards and initiatives.

The identity of the documentary parts is also important, so mark-up languages such as SGML (Standard Generalized Mark-up Language),

HTML (HyperText Mark-up Language) and XML (Extensible Mark-up Language) are used for tagging the different kinds of content within a document. This idea is familiar to librarians and others who have been using the MARC format for catalogue entries, where a set of fields and codes identifies the different elements (title, statement of responsibility, physical description, series, and so on) in each record.

Monographic Texts

Some monographs (non-serial items such as textbooks, technical manuals, government reports, information and consultation papers) are published in both print and electronic form so as to reach as many different categories of user as possible. Others, originally produced in print only, can be converted to electronic format for viewing on screen, complete with their 'back-of-the-book' indexes originally created by indexers working from printed proofs. This may apply to some of the out-of-print and out-of-copyright texts that are now being made available commercially as downloaded e-books for use on personal reading devices. The existing index headings, including subheadings and cross-references, can continue to serve their original purpose – with or without locators. With locators, such as decimal paragraph numbers, users are taken to the start of the relevant numbered part of the text; without locators, they are taken to the point in the sentence where the indexed terms (or linked synonymous terms) occur. Keyword searches can also be made in the text for any word that the user thinks relevant – these pick up any occurrences of the specified words, but without regard to their level of significance or existence of multiple meanings – so searching for 'feet' may pick up text on leg extremities and also on units of length.

Monographs composed uniquely for electronic use and not appearing in any print form – online technical manuals, 'self-published' e-books, reports, training materials, for example – should, of course, be properly indexed. Some writers of these documents use the limited indexing facilities of whichever word-processing software they have, to mark or select the words or phrases that they wish to place in an index, together with any cross-references that they think may be needed (see 'Software' below). Because readers for e-books can store more than one book, the interesting possibility arises of being able to merge the indexes of the different books so that a single search could reveal relevant items in them all. This would not be entirely successful, because the headings would not be harmonized – different word-forms, varying forms of name, for example – but so long as the user could tolerate the raggedness, the combined index could still be useful for searches by names and word stems.

Reference Sources

Many reference sources – such as encyclopaedias, directories, bibliographies, and current-awareness lists – are now produced in CD-ROM form or are available online; some are available in both forms. The same level of detailed analysis is required for electronically held reference sources as for the printed versions. Full-text searching, on its own, does not provide the same subtle representation and precise retrieval as a good whole-document index does.

Like 'the book', 'the CD-ROM' is considered by some to be unlikely to remain in use for much longer – both of them being inevitably superseded by 'the online product'. However, the current usefulness of the CD-ROM is undeniable and it may well continue as a suitable carrier for the more 'static' kind of information, which does not need updating day by day (retrospective bibliographies and encyclopaedias, for example), but which has to be easily searchable using different points of access. Online provision is clearly essential for those sources that have to be frequently renewed – those containing news, business data, current awareness (bibliographical and other items) lists, and catalogues, for example. Facilities for advanced searches are needed here, so that several search terms – author's name plus keywords, but with certain aspects specifically excluded, for instance – can be combined in order to locate the desired information quickly and without any additional unwanted items.

What is often needed in an encyclopaedic document, whether on CD-ROM or online, is the possibility of going first to the article on a specified subject – such as 'volcanoes' – and to see also pictures, with other keywords in highlighted text providing links to elsewhere. In the 'volcanoes' article there may be links to other pieces of text on specific volcanoes – 'Ngauruhoe' and 'Etna', for example.

Help Indexes

Screen-displayed indexes (online and offline) aiming to lead program users to guidance on problems they are encountering need to be straightforward and compact. They can usually be consulted in two ways: the user can either specify a word to be searched for or can browse through the list in alphabetical order. Too often these indexes are merely untidy lists of paragraph and section headings extracted from the text of the user guide or manual and presented in alphabetical order without any change of wording or order. As a result, some headings start with unsought terms:

> about links
> about URLs
> looking up addresses

There is often a great deal of repetition, with a heading being listed over and over again, on its own (maybe in both singular and plural forms) and in phrases, then with its individual (poorly worded) subheadings:

> page
> page colours
> pages
> pages, how to create
> pages, file commands on
> pages, using links to
> pages, opening and viewing
> pages, creating URL links to

To be effective and efficient, each heading in a help index should (as in any other index) begin with a word that a user is likely to look up, and the structure and display of the headings and subheadings should give a clear indication of the information available.

With some online systems, a benefit for the indexer is that feedback from users can be received and – if appropriate – acted on in order to improve the index.

Web Site Indexes

It is estimated that there are now a few million active web sites on the internet. Finding the relevant ones for a user's enquiry is largely the function of the various search engines, each of which covers only a fraction of all the existing sites. With sites variously coming into existence, enlarging, becoming out of date, and closing, keeping a totally accurate record of them is impossible. Individuals, libraries and organizations with special interests can provide a valuable service by gathering information on pertinent sites and making it available on the Web, through newspapers and the specialist press, through user groups and relevant organizations. Several of these already exist and are using a variety of methods for grouping and indexing; some, for example, employ the Dewey Decimal Classification, others have constructed their own subject headings lists. The Cooperative Online Resource Catalog (CORC), for example, under development by OCLC in partnership with several hundred volunteer libraries, is designed to assist libraries in providing their users with well-guided access to Web resources (information at: www.oclc.org/oclc/corc).

Individual sites often include 'indexes', though many of these are no more than contents lists – sometimes diagrammatically displayed. Others provide a display of the alphabet, inviting the user to select the letter sequence in which their search term is expected to appear; the user then browses through the list looking for the term, clicks on it and is taken to the relevant part of the site. As in the help indexes described above, the search words are often very limited and may use only the words that appear in the section headings of the text. Indexers can therefore play an important part at the macrolevel (sites relevant to particular subjects) and at the microlevel (the content of individual sites), by identifying the sought topics and showing how information can be best grouped, represented and displayed. The Australian Society of Indexers (AusSI) awards an annual prize for Web indexing (Walker, 1999). Coverage includes not only site indexes, but also databases, and online book indexes.

Indexing Technology (Input and Output)

When Collison (1972) and Knight (1979) wrote about indexing, the predominant method involved typing or writing index entries on individual cards or slips of paper sorted into alphabetical order. When complete, the entries were edited – subheadings made, major references marked, similar headings harmonized and so on – and then all were copy-typed, double-spaced, onto paper sheets that the indexer proofread against the cards or slips. Small errors might be corrected by hand on the typed sheets; more extensive amendments could require a whole sheet to be retyped. The finished sheets were sent to the client, whose typesetter then rekeyed the whole index to produce the printed version. Easier input methods came with electronic typewriters, then simple word processors, followed by PCs (personal computers) using dedicated indexing programs, word-processing programs and desktop publishing (dtp) packages with indexing facilities.

It is still, of course, possible to produce a full, well-structured and effective index using the simplest of methods. Some people develop an interest in indexing and get their first experience by making a card index relating to their personal files, or to information relating to a recreation or hobby. It is the intellectual input that determines the quality of the content, regardless of the mechanical aspects of recording the entries and presenting and displaying the finished index. Card indexes constructed long ago remain in use in offices, archives, libraries and resource centres – many of them containing information relating only to past years, but some still being augmented. Formerly, a clear distinction could be drawn between 'manual' and 'electronic' input methods, but this is no longer the case. What can be seen is that there are three major ways of creating index entries:

- they can be freely typed (keyed in) by the indexer, who chooses the exact form of words
- they can be generated by codes placed against words and phrases that exist in the text of the document on screen (embedded indexing)
- headings can be 'automatically' extracted from other (related) indexes and databases and from electronically held thesauri, with locators being keyed in by the indexer

Any method relying on entry via a keyboard is at risk of error, even when the indexer is an accomplished operator. Characters can be omitted, duplicated and transposed, spelling errors may be made, and incorrect locators entered. With embedded and extractive methods, it may be thought that there is no chance of error, because the index terms are copied exactly and have the relevant locators attached. However, many of the terms picked out are not in a suitable form for use as index headings – phrases may need the order of words changed, to bring the sought term to the front, personal names may need reversing, adjectival and verbal forms may need changing to noun forms, additional words may be needed, and so on. The time saved at the input stage is therefore taken up at the editing stage in the production of usable, helpful entries. A combination of methods offers advantages, enabling rekeying of data to be avoided as much as possible, while preserving the indexer's freedom to create the best entries for the purpose.

From the user's point of view, output is the only concern – what the index contains, how it is structured and arranged, and what can be found in it. One advantage of an on-screen indexed document is that the user can search not only by index headings provided by the indexer, but also for the occurrence of any word or phrase in the full text of the document – whether or not that word or phrase has been selected as an index heading. In a well-indexed document, this facility may not add much value, but it could help to locate an unusual reference that the indexer has judged below the relevant level of significance. Another advantage is that the user – whether selecting an index heading or a word at random – is automatically shown the relevant text in the document.

'The machinery'

Practising indexers need to equip themselves suitably for current requirements of the world of work and the demands of the market, where speed of production is ever more important. People entering indexing now expect to take advantage of the latest electronic and communications technology for the input of raw data and the generation of index copy, including in some cases the production of camera-ready copy (CRC), which requires little or no further processing before final reproduction. They should also expect frequently to change, upgrade or add to their equipment, in order to keep pace with their clients' systems and to maintain or extend the range of work they do.

Development in the field of electronic communications is rapid; there are not only improved models of existing devices, but new ones that combine the functions of previously separate items. Anyone considering making a purchase should make certain of checking the very latest information available before risking acquiring something that will shortly be out of date. The physical life of a piece of equipment may far exceed its useful working life; the pressure to upgrade generally arises from the need for faster working, greater storage capacity, more flexible operations, extra facilities, and greater convenience. Being unable to receive, process and transmit certain data or formats, or to respond to messages with sufficient speed, can mean that an indexer is unable to take on certain jobs. It is not, of course, necessary to upgrade computer equipment every time a new model appears.

It is normally better to buy new electronic equipment (such as a computer), with the proper guarantees, than to acquire second-hand machines – except from the most trustworthy of sources and with help close at hand if things go wrong. A new computer can be set up with software that exactly fits the indexer's needs and with no remnants of old files or viruses lurking on the hard disk waiting to cause trouble.

The temptation to discard old, but still functioning, equipment as soon as the new model is installed, should be resisted. The new machine may have minor faults; even if it does not, the indexer may take a while to get used to its operation and functions and so prefer to continue doing work on the older one until thoroughly familiarized. Even after that, the old one may still be worth keeping as a secondary or back-up machine. Busy indexers sometimes want to keep two jobs going at the same time, on different machines, perhaps using different software. Lastly, clients may not always have the latest technology and may be looking for indexers who can still handle earlier formats.

Indexing programs (of whichever kind – see 'Software' below) need to be easy to use, flexible, able to do the mechanical tasks, capable of handling large amounts of data without losing or corrupting any, formatting it in different ways, enabling its reuse, saving the indexer time and presenting the final copy in good order. Indexers with more than one computer can link them into a network, in order to provide more capacity and enable swift backing-up of files, as well as to allow sharing of files and the use of a single printer – both useful for team working.

Input devices and sources

Most regularly working indexers need a computer with suitable indexing software and a printer attached. A scanner (see 'Scanners' below) is also needed if the content of paper versions of earlier indexes, lists of keywords, or text documents are to be transferred to the computer without the indexer having to rekey them. Indexers using dedicated indexing software generally type their entries (headings and locators) through the keyboard while observing them taking shape on the screen. Entries with identical headings are merged, with the locators automatically placed in the correct order (usually ascending numerical order), and all entries are automatically sorted (usually into alphabetical order). Those using embedding systems look at the text of the document on the screen and identify and code the words and phrases that are to be included; the locators are automatically 'attached' to the headings to make entries in the index.

Keyboards

Most keyboards used in English-speaking countries are of the 'QWERTY' type (those keys being the first five in the top line of letters); even so, from country to country there may be small variations in the provision and position of keys – to allow, for instance, for easy keying of £ or $ symbols, or accented letters. Other layouts exist (such as the French 'AZERTY') and these may be more useful for indexers working regularly with foreign-language material. All indexers need a full range of characters, including upper-case (capital) and lower-case (small) letters, numerals, punctuation marks, accents and other diacritics. Italic and bold styles and underlining are also part of the indexer's 'palette' and so must be easily available. Other alphabets, mathematical symbols and other special characters may be needed, too. The extent to which these are provided and the methods by which they are produced on screen depend on the particular software installed on the computer. Ergonomic keyboards (shaped to make operation more efficient and comfortable) and wrist-rests may be helpful.

Scanners

Indexers are frequently contracted to produce indexes to second editions of books that they indexed the first time around, or to produce a cumulation of the separate indexes they made for the annual volumes of a periodical. They may have the data still stored on disk, but otherwise only the print-on-paper copies may be available. To avoid copy-typing from the printed sheets, which is tedious and carries the possibility of introducing errors (by omission, duplication or misfingering), the sheets may be electronically copied into the computer via a scanner using OCR (optical character recognition) software. Similarly, terms from headings lists and thesauri can be imported (see 'Terms from electronic thesauri' below). Errors are still likely to occur, particularly if the paper copies are not of good quality with clear and reasonably sized print, because the scanner may not always be able to distinguish two different characters that look rather alike ('I' and 'l', '0' and 'O', for example) and because of the irregular shape (and often columnar layout) of indexes. The word-processing program that receives the text after scanning may, if not sufficiently advanced, lose some or all of the formatting information. The scanned text needs to be visually checked, possibly character by character, to ensure that it has been correctly transferred; a spell-checking program will not necessarily find all faults. Once in good shape, the file containing the index can be incorporated into the new index file using the available software.

Rather than buying scanners for their own use, some indexers prefer to take the material to specialist scanning services.

Mouse Input

Depending on the software in use, a mouse may be used mostly for selecting options and making commands, or for flagging those terms within a text which are to be entered in the 'automatically' generated index. Varied designs of mouse are available, so the most comfortable form should be chosen.

Voice Input

Input is possible using voice-recognition software – very useful for anyone whose manual dexterity becomes impaired and helpful for someone needing occasional relief from keyboarding and mouse-clicking, or wanting to use a combination of input methods such as keyboard for entries and voice for commands.

Importing Other Index Files

An index to a document like the first edition of a textbook is started from a blank screen or page and is compiled exclusively from the textual concepts as represented by the indexer. Other situations can benefit from, and sometimes positively need, input from other indexes. Someone indexing a second edition or a cumulation, for example, could make use of at least some of the full entries or just the headings from the earlier index.

If the files are on disk they can often be rapidly imported to form the basis of the new index file, avoiding the necessity to copy entries manually via the keyboard or electronically, but more slowly and with the risk of error, by scanner (see 'Scanners' above). The file to be input must be compatible with the indexing program in use.

Terms from Electronic Thesauri

Thesauri and subject headings lists – standard lists of words and phrases, usually relating to a particular subject field or a cluster of related topics – are often used for the indexing of periodical articles, books, reports, and conference papers, when they appear in regular indexing/abstracting publications. Many exist in print form only, but may be scannable (see 'Scanners' above. Others are held electronically, in which case the indexer can highlight the required terms in the thesaurus file and copy them as index headings without having to rekey them. Whatever the form, this kind of copying can only be done when it does not infringe copyright.

An advantage of using a thesaurus or subject headings list for serial types of publication (see Chapter 6: Serial publications) is that topics can be indexed consistently and with built-in cross-references from synonyms and between related terms. Contexts differ, though, so what is suitable for one index may not be so for another. For some subject areas, several thesauri exist, each one compiled from the perspective of a particular group of users or set of needs (see Chapter 8: Subject specialisms). A single vocabulary set, therefore, cannot serve everyone's purpose. If used, a thesaurus must be kept up to date with technical developments in the field, new words, and changes of meaning.

Input features and aids

To be of real service during the input stage, an indexing program must be able to accommodate as many entries as the indexer finds necessary and of whatever length is needed. It must also provide a range of features – commands and key combinations, for example – which can save the indexer time and enable style instructions to be included and special characters to be indicated. A good indexing program can offer the following:

Repeats and Reversals

Complete headings, parts of headings, and locators should be repeatable, as a basis for other entries, without the indexer needing to retype them. In addition, headings consisting of two elements separated by punctuation, should be convertible to reverse order, to provide an entry under each element – 'museums, air conditioning' into 'air conditioning, museums'.

Special Characters

Letters with accents and other diacritics, mathematical symbols, superscript and subscript numbers and letters, dashes, and other characters with special contextual meanings, should be able to be included in entries in a straightforward way and with the assurance that they will appear correctly in the printout and in the file sent to the client.

Incorporation of Pieces of Word-processed Text

If the indexer has the right combination of software, it should be possible to copy pieces of text from a separate word-processed file into an index entry, avoiding retyping. This is particularly helpful if the index needs to contain elements such as lengthy, unfamiliar names or foreign-language phrases – a situation where the risk of introducing errors during retyping is increased.

Keywords for Common Terms

Instead of repeatedly keying in the same word or phrase when the topic occurs in many places, it should be possible to designate a brief 'keyword' – a single character or combination of characters that is not used in the index for any other purpose – which can be input instead, but which will convert to the full wording when displayed.

Macros

Macros are another form of short cut enabling speedier input. Each one contains a whole series of commands and can be executed by a simple keyboard action (such as pressing two specific keys together). A program should allow an indexer to select or formulate macros as needed for particular circumstances.

Spell-checking

Spell-checkers containing specialized words suited to an indexer's subject needs can be useful, but must not be totally relied upon for automatic correction (see 'Spelling errors and literals' in Chapter 5).

Multiple Indexes (Parallel Indexes)

It is often necessary (and it can make the work more interesting) to compile more than one index, or sequence of entries, at a time. Several indexes may be available on screen at one time, in separate windows. It is also possible to add a unique prefix to each entry for, say, the index of authors' names, and then to separate it ('split it off') from the subject sequence at the output stage. Several sequences can be created in this way, using different prefixes.

New Locators for an Old Index

As indicated earlier (see 'Importing other index files'), a file containing the index of an earlier edition or separate volumes can be imported and used as a basis for the revised version or cumulation. The indexing program should be able to strip off the old locators and leave just the headings ready for reuse. In the case of a cumulation, the locators may be retained but require volume numbers or dates to be inserted. Some indexers prefer to import whole entries, including locators, as aids to finding the new position of the information referred to; in this case it is vital to distinguish old locators from new ones, so that all the old ones can be gradually replaced. This can be done by styling all the old locators in, say, italic or bold and the new ones in plain type. Identifying the page numbers to be changed can be helped by either a locator order file (page number order file) or a grouping procedure, followed by search and replace instructions.

Locators for Unknown or Changed Pagination

Most indexes compiled from proofs are prepared after the text has been completed and the final order of chapters or sections, the layout, and the page breaks or numerical paragraphing are determined; the locators are therefore fixed and can be used with confidence in the index entries. Occasionally, though, indexing has to start before the final locators are known – usually when schedules are getting tight or last-minute decisions are being made about which pieces of text should be included, and in which order they should appear. This problem does not arise with document-processing systems where the index can be generated directly from the text. Because each term flagged for inclusion in the index carries its page or paragraph number with it as long as it stays in the system, locators are automatically adjusted whenever the text shifts position.

With proof-based indexes there are three possible situations, all of which should be provided for by an indexing program:

Printed proofs: page breaks determined, but order of chapters/sections not yet decided
Because the final page numbers cannot be known until the chapter or section order is fixed, each page should be entered as a combined and temporary chapter/section and page number (to indicate page 3 of section 12, for example). When the order of the text has finally been decided and the fixed locators are known, the program should be able to substitute them for the temporary numbers.

Typescript or manuscript copy: chapter/section order known, pagination not yet known
A program should enable each entry to be identified by a unique number – rather than referring to a page or paragraph number – and, once the final pagination is known, the entry numbers relating to a particular page should be converted to that page number.

Changed locators: from addition or removal of whole pages of text
Occasionally, after an index has been compiled, a new chapter is inserted into the text or an existing one is removed. In that case all page numbers after the new or excised part need to be adjusted by a fixed amount – plus 20 or minus 35, say. The program should be able to do this automatically once it has been informed of the amount, saving the indexer the bother of searching for and retyping each number.

Checking Cross-references

A cross-reference that points to a term not appearing in the index, or that leads to a term only to be referred back to the original term, is a highly visible fault when it occurs (see 'Checking cross-reference connections' in Chapter 4). A program should be able to check whether the cross-references in a completed index are valid and accurate.

Finding, Grouping, Searching and Replacing

In a long index, certain words are likely to occur again and again, within different entries. Because indexing is a creative process, an indexer is quite likely to have second thoughts about wording and phraseology. It is essential, therefore, that the program can enable the rapid finding of entries containing a particular word or combination of words, group them and present them on the screen to let the indexer review the situation and come to a decision, and then replace the terms – if so desired – with the new ones. Similarly, if the entries on a particular page need all to be changed or even removed, it should be possible to identify swiftly all the entries containing that locator.

A search and replace instruction can operate on a one-by-one basis, where each occurrence is found and only replaced when confirmed by the indexer, or by automatically (globally) changing all the instances found.

Caution is needed when using the automatic mode; all occurrences of the specified letter combinations will be changed, including some that are not relevant – changing 'realis' to 'realiz' (for word-forms based on 'realize') will also change 'aurora borealis' to ' . . . borealiz'.

Index Measurements and Statistics

Book indexers frequently work to strict space requirements and need to monitor the size of the growing index, so as to keep within the necessary limit (see 'Index density' in Chapter 3 and 'Work records' in Chapter 10). Size may be measured in terms of the number of characters (including punctuation and spaces), the number of entries, or the number of lines that the index takes up when printed out or displayed. Other data that can be useful in the planning and pricing of subsequent jobs include the number of pages indexed, the average number of indexed items per page, and the most, least and average number of locators per entry. The more of these figures that can be computed by the program, the better.

'Tidying Up'

The use of 'opening and closing' marks is common in entries of all kinds. Some appear as integral parts of headings – such as single and double quotation marks, parentheses (round brackets, curves), square brackets, and angle brackets – and must be printed out or displayed with the headings. Other symbols and codes are inserted in order to influence the sorting or appearance of entries and are not printed out or displayed. It can be easy to forget to type the closing mark, so the program should alert the indexer to any 'unpaired' instances.

Query Listing

Provision should be made for accumulating any queried entries – such as headings for which the indexer needs to check spelling or best-known form. These can form part of the index file, but need to be collected together for attention later.

Output devices

High quality of output is important, both for the indexer while working and for the client in terms of the finished product.

Screen Display

The screen is the indexer's 'visual workspace' and so must provide not only all the requisite functions and features, but also convenience and comfort. It is up to the individual indexer to decide the preferred size of screen and the backgrounds, colours and contrasts used for the display of index entries. The combination of these should give each indexer the optimum screen appearance. Older monitors displaying only black and white, green and white or a similar 'monochrome' combination can be acceptable, though the indexer misses out on the benefits of colour distinction for certain entries, elements of entries and sequences of entries.

Back-up Files

Index entries being the essence of the job, the loss of any data may have serious consequences. The disappearance of even a small number of entries can add extra time to a job while they are replaced, and perhaps endanger a deadline. Backing up (making copies of index files on a separate medium) during and after compilation is a worthwhile precaution. Back-up files can be made on floppy disks, tape-based systems, writable CDs, or the hard disks of other (networked) computers.

Printers

A printer attached to a computer is a necessity for most indexers. Not all clients ask for hard copy (printout) as well as disk or emailed copy, but many do. In any case, indexers often prefer to check and edit their indexes in printout form. Correspondence, mailshots and other items also need to be produced. Colour printing may not be relevant for many indexers, but is usually available.

The principal requirements are:

- reasonable speed of printing with all the programs used
- clarity of print (faint print is not only tiresome to read, but can lead to comprehension and copying errors)

- accurate printing of not just the normal range of characters, in a variety of styles and sizes, but also the special ones required in the indexing of some special subjects, such as mathematics, chemistry, and linguistics
- use of ordinary paper (no smudging, no unwanted spots or lines, no paper jams, no need for expensive special paper)
- quiet operation
- no fumes or smells

Output features and aids

Output is not just a matter of displaying and printing, but of organizing the material in a suitable way.

Sort and Merge

The final index must contain properly merged and sorted entries. Entries containing identical headings and different locators must be merged into a single entry with the locators in ascending order and suitably punctuated. Each entry must be in its correct alphabetical (or other relevant) position, and subentries (if present) must be sequenced in the desired way. Ranges of locators must be shown in a consistent style. The program should offer all the recognized options for merging and sorting, enable the indexer to see the sorted and merged entries during compilation, and implement the features selected by the indexer for each index. These features can include:

Alphabetization

Both methods of alphabetical arrangement – word-by-word and letter-by-letter (see 'Alphabetical arrangement' in Chapter 5) – must be available so that the indexer can select whichever is appropriate for a particular index. Options must also be provided for:

- handling of headings containing hyphens or beginning with numerals or characters from non-Roman alphabets
- subheading order, ignoring or recognizing common function words (conjunctions, articles, prepositions)

- different treatments of abbreviated elements – such as Mac, Mc and M', and St, Ste and S
- alternative positions for cross-references

Form of locators in ranges
Full and minimum ('squashed') styles should be easily available: 123–124; 123–4 (see 'Page ranges' in Chapter 4).

Complex locators
Locators consisting of more than one element – such as volume number, issue number or date, and pages – must be merged in an unambiguous way (see 'Complex locators' in Chapter 4). This may involve showing the volume number in each locator rather than only in the first locator in the string. It must be possible to prevent the merge order being disturbed by punctuation within the locators – such as slashes, hyphens, full stops (periods), and colons – and abbreviations attached to locators – like '*illus.*' and '*n*'.

Locator Number Order Files (Page Number Order Files)

The facility to produce a file in locator order (a page number order file) is an important aid to checking the accuracy of entries, revealing imbalances in coverage, assessing the number of entries per page or section, and identifying omissions.

Reproduction of Special Characters

When input with the right codes or character combinations, special characters – such as accented letters, and signs and symbols with special meanings – should reproduce correctly on screen and printout. They also need to appear accurately when the index file is converted for use with another program, say by clients or colleagues. In particular, characters that are not in the basic ASCII set may not reproduce correctly when the file is converted to a typesetting program. Merely being able to see such a character on screen does not guarantee that it will still appear when printed out or when the file has been converted.

Styling and Restyling

Some styling is normally set up during the input of individual entries – such as for capitalization of the initial letters of proper names, italicization of locators referring to illustrations, and emboldening of major locators – and all must print correctly. Additional style features and alterations are often needed prior to printing. Rapid restyling of all the entries should therefore be available for changes such as lower-case (small) letters to upper-case (capitals), upright type to italic, roman numbers to arabic, emboldening, and vice versa.

Layout

A variety of layouts should be available, with options for individual features, from which the indexer can select for each index, as required.

Single-column and two-column printing
Most index copy produced by indexers is printed out or placed on screen or disk in a single column, running from one page or screen to the next. The client's typesetter usually produces the version for publication in two or more columns. Some indexers need to produce two-column layout – this is particularly relevant when camera-ready copy (see 'Camera-ready copy (CRC)' below) is required by a client.

Set-out and run-on subheadings
Both styles are in regular use (see 'Subheading layout' in Chapter 5). Indexers sometimes decide only at a late stage which style they will use – the choice must therefore be available immediately before printout or display. Shortage of space commonly causes a change from set-out to run-on style.

Turnover (continuation) lines
It should be possible to specify the indention of these (long lines that run over) as desired for a particular index; the recommended practice is one space (one em in typesetters' language) further in than the deepest subheading, but circumstances sometimes require other treatment (see 'Turnover lines (continuation lines) in Chapter 5).

Punctuation, spacing, length of line
The indexer should be able to specify the punctuation and spacing to be inserted – between heading and first locator, between locators, before cross-references, between lines, between entries, and between letter sequences (see 'Spacing' in Chapter 5) – and to designate the maximum number of characters per line.

Display letters (header letters)
The option of automatically displaying the individual letters of the alphabet at the beginning of their respective sequences, to provide greater clarity where needed, and where there is space, should be provided (see 'Display letters (header letters)' in Chapter 5).

'Continued' statements and page breaks
Index copy sent elsewhere for typesetting does not normally need 'continued' statements or any consideration of page breaks, because only the typesetter can insert them in the appropriate places for the finished version (see *'Continued* statements' in Chapter 5). Those indexes produced in final form by the indexer, though – camera-ready copy, for example – do need to have page breaks automatically entered in suitable places and, if broken sequences of subheadings are unavoidable, 'continued' statements must be added.

Introductory note
Adequate space must be provided for the insertion of an introductory note, of any length, at the top of the index (see 'Introductory note' in Chapter 5).

Camera-ready Copy (CRC)

CRC in paper form must be faultlessly printed and laid out. The clarity, sharpness and quality of the print depends largely on printer and paper used, but the program must provide a professional standard of layout. CRC on disk, to be reproduced elsewhere, must similarly have all the necessary coding and formatting included so that no further input is required, except possibly the addition of page numbers.

Conversion to Other Formats

Instead of editing the index file within the indexing program and printing directly from it, some indexers needing to add other style or design features – such as headers and footers – prefer to transfer the data to a word-processing program and carry out the editing and printing functions there. Files produced on disk or sent by email should enable clients to print the index directly with no rekeying of entries. Formatting into columns and inserting page breaks and 'continued' statements are normally carried out by the typesetters or by document-processing systems. Indexes that are to be imported into databases also require conversion to suitable formats. Clients' requirements for disk formats vary, so the indexing program should be able to produce all of the most common – such as ASCII, Word-RTF, WordPerfect, Quark Xpress, TeX and Xywrite. Index files are also sometimes required for processing by desktop publishing (dtp) programs such as PageMaker and Framemaker. Cautious indexers send their index files in two formats, say ASCII and another, so that typesetters can work with whichever best suits their systems.

Mark-up for SGML, HTML and XML

The use of an indexing program that can insert index entry tags for use with mark-up languages enables the indexer to provide additional services to both print and electronic publishers (see 'Metadata and mark-up languages' earlier in this chapter).

Index Files for Emailing

Increasingly, indexers are emailing their indexes, as attachments to messages, instead of sending them on floppy disks. This improves turn-round times, but can only work satisfactorily when the index files are in a suitable format and there is a level of compatibility between the email systems used by the indexer and the client, and the word-processing or desktop publishing software employed by the client. If not correctly handled, files may be unreadable by the client, or may be corrupted, losing characters and omitting codes relating to styling and layout. Some indexers find that ordinary ASCII files are processed successfully, others rely on RTF (Rich Text Format) files. There may be a need also to compress the file (using suitable software) before sending it. The indexing program used by the indexer should be able to produce a variety of formats, so that the indexer can provide a small test file to send to the client early on.

Software

The principal distinctions to be drawn are those between:

- dedicated programs designed specifically for indexing documents, with the multiple needs of indexers in mind
- index-generation or embedding programs that are modules within word-processing, document-preparation or desktop publishing packages
- database programs, which typically hold large numbers of records, with each record containing specified categories of indexable element

None of these types is to be described as 'fully automatic indexing software', which involves the assignment, identification and extraction of terms by computer, with no direct participation by an indexer. What the programs described here do is to carry out certain mechanical tasks, leaving the indexer to provide the intellectual input.

Working with dedicated indexing programs, indexers produce entries (headings and locators) of their own choosing, using one or more input methods, as described earlier. The full sweep of an indexer's creativity can influence the entries, and terms can be incorporated from other files. What is from one point of view an advantage – being able to enter the best possible form of words to represent each indexable element – is from another point of view a disadvantage – each of these 'free-form' headings has to be typed (keyed in). Input is eased by the provision of a range of sophisticated facilities for:

- repeating, rotating, merging, sorting, and styling, of the individual entries
- reviewing and amending the index during compilation
- checking the effectiveness of cross-references
- displaying (laying out) and producing the final index in the required format – hard copy, disk, camera-ready copy, files for emailing, marked-up files for electronic transfer

Many of the features and options described earlier, under 'Input features and aids' and 'Output features and aids', are provided in these programs, allowing the indexer plenty of choices during the compilation and production of each index – form of entries, filing orders, subheading layouts and so on. Any method that relies considerably on keyboard input runs the risk of error, so careful checking is necessary at the editing stage.

Index-generation and embedding programs are used 'face-to-face' with the text of the document to be indexed. The simplest file generated is one that lists – as a concordance – every occurrence of any word or phrase specified by the indexer, regardless of its level of significance and without harmonizing similar terms, so cannot be relied on to produce a proper index, but it can be useful as an aid to checking comprehensiveness, or as a very basic indicator. More structured files can be produced by selecting words either as headings or subheadings. In an embedding program the document text is displayed on the screen, so that the indexer can go through the text, identifying each term within the text which represents an indexable element, and inserting codes (tags) to show the start and finish of the relevant portions of text. The index is generated from the coded (tagged) terms, with locators automatically attached – if any piece of text is subsequently moved to another part of the document, the locators are therefore adjusted without any action being required of the indexer. The 'automatic' copying of terms and the attachment of locators should eliminate the possibility of error – assuming that the terms and locators themselves have been correctly presented in the text. The initial result, though, does require editing – to harmonize the word-forms, identify major references, analyse into subheadings, add synonym entries, and insert cross-references – and the edited entries have to be re-embedded in the text. It is possible, too, that errors may be introduced during editing, so careful checking is still needed.

Features and options in some index-generation and embedding programs are limited. It may not be possible to indicate the extent of a piece of text (where it starts and where it ends), because a system only allows for the first page number to be entered, rather than a range of pages. There may be no choice of filing order and layout. In some cases, only information in the main body of text can be indexed – so any matter enclosed in a display box in the margin, for example, may be excluded from indexing. The better programs allow the inclusion of words and phrases of the indexer's choosing, the insertion of cross-references, and the construction of various levels of subentry. Authors using word-processing programs sometimes index while they write, using the index-generation facility; this is probably most common in in-house technical writing environments where speed of production is important. This indexing of keywords can make useful contributions to the final index, but is very unlikely alone to result in a harmonized, well-structured index. Mulvany (1999), after comparing the features and performance of four embedding programs and one dedicated program, concluded that, while embedding programs in general had improved since her previous survey in 1989, they remained crude tools when compared with dedicated indexing programs.

Database programs are designed primarily to process records of individual items – persons, events, publications, products, or organizations, for example – and to retrieve them in response to requests based on elements such as names, dates, titles, departments, functions, or keywords relevant to the purpose of the organization to which the database belongs. The information relating to each individual item is coded on the record – each perhaps having its own tagged 'field'. Each coded element or important field is searchable; it is thus possible to retrieve all items having common information in the same field – all publications by Mary Brown, or all members who registered in the year 2000, for example. Database programs are not indexing programs, but they provide for limited indexing of certain kinds of record. Records that need subject indexing information (such as those that relate to documents) can be given either classification numbers or subject headings (selected from a published scheme or a customized one) or keywords chosen from the titles and perhaps the texts. This method helps to identify a document that may be of interest to the enquirer, but does not pinpoint the position of the information within the document itself. These programs are therefore more suitable for collection indexing – where each document is represented by an index term or terms indicating its subject(s) as a whole – rather than for detailed whole-document (page-by-page) indexing.

Troubleshooting and Support

No technology is trouble-free, but wise buying, good maintenance and prompt access to advice and support can help to keep problems to the minimum. Before buying equipment (including software) the indexer should identify exactly what tasks it is required to perform, get recommendations from others working in similar fields, and read for information – computer magazines, consumer surveys, and professional newsletters. Bargains are at first sight attractive, but reliability, range of functions, good instructions, and efficient (and not too costly) helplines and technical support are more important.

When the equipment is up and running, membership of user groups and online and email discussion groups, and participation at training events and workshop sessions at professional conferences, are all helpful. The usual advice, when something goes wrong, is first to read the manual (which, it is hoped, has a good index and a 'troubleshooting' section). Panic and aggression are not normally useful emotions when dealing with a hardware or software problem – recourse to a helpline, support group or another professional is better. Any new equipment that fails to do what it is supposed to do should be taken or sent back to the supplier.

Even the thought of software viruses can cause unnecessary alarm. Precautions against them include checking any disks and files received from other people, using virus protection software, and taking account of reliable warnings about viruses (many warnings, fortunately and unfortunately, are hoaxes).

References

Collison, Robert L. (1972) *Indexes and indexing* 4th edn. London: Ernest Benn

Knight, G. Norman (1979) *Indexing, the art of: a guide to the indexing of books and periodicals*. London: George Allen & Unwin

Milstead, Jessica and Feldman, Susan (1999) Metadata: cataloging by any other name. ONLINE, January [Online at: www.onlineinc.com/onlinemag/metadata]

Mulvany, Nancy C. (1999) Software tools for indexing: revisited. *The Indexer*, **21**, 160–163

Walker, Dwight (1999) AusSI Web Indexing Prize 1998. *The Indexer*, **21**, 108–110

Further Reading

Brenner, Diane and Rowland, Marilyn (2000) (eds.) *Beyond book indexing: how to get started in Web indexing, embedded indexing, and other computer-based media.* Medford, NJ: Information Today, Inc

Cawkell, Tony (1999) Electronic books. *Aslib proceedings,* **51**, 54–58

Henninger, Maureen (1999) What makes a good Web index? *The Indexer,* **21**, 182–183

Mulvany, Nancy C. (1994) *Indexing books.* Chicago: University of Chicago Press (Ch.10: Tools for indexing)

Wellisch, Hans H. (1995) *Indexing from A to Z* 2nd edn. New York: H.W. Wilson (pp.168–174: Equipment)

Dedicated Indexing Software: Producers

CINDEX:
> Indexing Research
> 100 Allens Creek Road
> P.O. Box 18609
> Rochester
> New York 14618–0609
> USA
> Phone: +1 716 461–5530
> Fax: +1 716 442–3924
> email: info@indexres.com
> Web site: www.indexres.com

MACREX:
> MACREX Indexing Services
> Beech House
> Blaydon Burn
> Tyne & Wear
> NE21 6JR
> UK
> Phone: +44 (0)191 414 2595
> Fax: +44 (0)191 414 1893
> email: sales@macrex.com
> Web site: www.macrex.com

For North America:
    MACREX Support Office
    c/o Wise Bytes
    P.O. Box 3051
    Daly City
    CA 94015
    USA
    Phone: +1 650 756–0821
    Fax: +1 650 757–1567
    email: macrex@aol.com

For Australasia and South-East Asia:
    Master Indexing
    44 Rothesay Avenue
    East Malvern
    Vic.3145
    Australia
    Phone/fax: +61 (03) 9571 6341
    email: mindexer@interconnect.com.au

SKY:
    SKY Software
    350 Montgomery Circle
    Stephens City
    VA 22655
    USA
    Phone: +1 800 776–0137
    Fax: +1 540 869–6581
    email: info@sky-software.com
    Web site: www.sky-software.com

CHAPTER TWELVE

Professional organizations and interest groups

Professionalism in Indexing

The practice of indexing is not protected or regulated at national, regional or local level; anyone can claim to be a competent indexer and offer indexing services to the world at large. From the point of view of freedom of opportunity this is fair and just, allowing suitably experienced people from related backgrounds to change their occupations and add their talents to the professional indexing pool. On the other hand, it may lead the ill-equipped and the incompetent to believe that indexing is a routine, straightforward activity that anyone with a reasonable standard of education can carry out (see 'Myths about indexing' in Chapter 1); their careless, erroneous output can then tarnish the reputation of indexers in general. There is concern, therefore, in those countries with an active indexing community, that indexers should have relevant qualifications and that good indexing should be recognizable when evaluated by agreed criteria. Even if all practising indexers were competent and provided good services, there would still be variations in practice, relating to factors such as layout and order of index entries and subentries, formation of headings and locators, capitalization, punctuation, and styling. Practitioners need to discuss continually the alternative forms and styles, and to identify best practice for all kinds of indexing application.

Indexing is clearly established as a profession, though some indexers prefer to call it an art, craft or trade. It meets all the criteria by which professions tend to be described, being an occupation that:

- provides services that spread technical knowledge for the general benefit of the public
- involves theoretically based skills for which education and training are necessary
- requires the competence of the practitioners to be assessed
- sets and maintain standards of conduct for practitioners
- has professional associations that promote the activity, organize and represent members, and foster the interests of those members

People and Groups

Bearing in mind the tendency for people of like mind and common interests to associate and form groups for mutual reinforcement and reassurance, it is understandable that in the indexing world several professional organizations have been created and nurtured, mostly based on a single country or neighbouring countries, and most of them having similar aims. Several organizations in related fields – such as publishing, editing, library and information management, journalism, proofreading, and technical writing – also have an interest in indexing and may provide relevant information and guidance to their members.

In addition to the established professional organizations, there are informal groups, which have no organized structure or precise membership and are often based on the internet. Internet discussion groups and mailing lists provide a more informal and international means of exchanging information and of raising, discussing and solving indexing problems. The fact that the participants are in different countries, even different continents, is often irrelevant and unnoticed. Communication is enabled between indexers who do not otherwise have the possibility of contact with each other, and information can be transferred swiftly between interested individuals and then find its way into the professional canon and the literature. Beginners can find out about indexing as a career and seek guidance and training; practitioners can debate technical complexities, suggest improvements in the life of the solo worker, give their opinions about new software and publications, and have 'virtual' meetings. These informal groups complement the professional organizations rather than threaten them. The need and desire to meet in person (not just electronically) and to organize for development, representation and protection, act as safeguards to the existence of the professional bodies.

The membership of any one professional organization may never be large, but if one of its permanent elements is a significant number of practitioners who are committed to the establishment, maintenance and promotion of good practice, it can have the potential to influence other activities in different spheres – the arts and humanities, science and technology, medicine, education, government, business, industry, and communication. Being a member involves a two-way process – the service to members depends on the health and continuance of the organizations, which can only be assured if the members, in return, make useful contributions by participating in voluntary administrative, decision-making, advisory and other activities. Belonging to a professional organization is especially helpful to indexers working on their own account (self-employed), or as lone indexers within large organizations, any of whom can experience feelings of isolation from fellow indexers. The benefits include:

- dissemination and refreshment of knowledge through regular publications and meetings
- access to information resources
- assessment and recognition of competence
- legal protection, representation, and advice
- status
- promotion of practitioners' services
- recommendations for work
- establishment of suitable remuneration rates
- feeling of professional community and strength in numbers
- holding office
- recognized qualifications
- special-interest groups
- participation in setting standards and reinforcing ethics
- contact with professionals in other fields
- occasional grants, bursaries and concessions
- discounts on the organization's publications
- social contact

Individual members' levels of participation vary considerably. Some people take an entirely instrumental view, regarding membership as a means of acquiring information, qualifications, recognition, and the contacts that they need to carry on a successful career. They read the relevant parts of any publications that come as part of their subscription (but may never contribute articles or letters to them), attend those meetings that are relevant to their work, and may or may not vote in society elections. Their measure of a society's success is based on what it can do for them, and each year they weigh the cost of the subscription against its perceived value in relation to their own interests. At the other end of the scale are those who – as well as being current practitioners – are voluntarily involved in the long-term running of the organization. They serve as unpaid officers or as members of permanent committees (setting policy and taking decisions), organize meetings, set up local and specialist groups, write articles, represent the society in discussions with other organizations, speak at society conferences, and engage in earnest and lively debate using various communications media. For most of them, active membership is regarded as an enjoyable duty or responsibility – part of the give-and-take of being a professional. In between are those members – perhaps the majority – who try to balance the demands of an active working life with their social and domestic commitments but who are able and willing to contribute to society activities from time to time. Some write an occasional article for a periodical or write letters to the editor, others take part in ad hoc committees or temporary working groups, help to run conferences or annual general meetings when held in their local areas, advise trainees, and make themselves available for phone or email discussions on matters relating to their special fields. There is usually also a short-term membership element, including people who are temporarily doing work in the field, beginners who try out indexing as a possibility and who then move on to something more suitable, as well as practitioners who belong for a short time to get information or to make contacts.

Professional organizations have to change with the times, reflecting developments in national and international organization and administration, technological innovations, communication methods, educational levels and objectives, and social trends. At the same time, they sometimes need to lead, taking a proactive stance on behalf of the membership as a whole.

The information which follows was drawn mostly from official publications and web sites, during March and April 2000.

Indexing Societies

There are six indexing societies working in affiliation under the terms of a 1999 international agreement, which is based on reciprocal relationships and the strengthening of international links. They provide services to indexers, publishers and authors in Britain and Ireland, the United States of America, Canada, Australia, Southern Africa, and China. Some of them have strong connections with the publishing and communications industry, some maintain a stronger link with professional organizations in the field of library and information management, others relate more to the academic environment. The periodical *The Indexer* is published in the UK by the Society of Indexers on behalf of all the affiliated societies. Some of the societies have their own qualification systems for the recognition of indexing competence and also provide training. Most of them promote the services of members through directories that are distributed to publishers and other relevant bodies. The majority of the societies are run mainly by volunteers.

Society of Indexers (SI)

Address: The Globe Centre, Penistone Road, Sheffield, S6 3AE
Tel: +44 (0)114 281 3060
Fax: +44 (0)114 281 3061
email: admin@socind.demon.co.uk
Web site: www.socind.demon.co.uk

The Society of Indexers is the British and Irish professional body for indexing. A non-profit organization, it was founded in 1957, has about 900 members, and provides services to indexers, publishers and authors. Membership is open to individuals and to organizations. Its purpose is to promote indexing, the quality of indexes and the profession of indexing, through specific objectives:

● promotion of improved standards and techniques in all forms of indexing
● provision, promotion and recognition of facilities for the initial training of new indexers and for further training at more advanced levels

- establishment of criteria for assessment of conformity of indexes to recognized standards
- establishment of procedures for conferring upon members recognized professional status
- conduct and promotion of research into indexing and related matters
- publishing and dissemination of guidance, information and ideas concerning indexing
- promotion among indexers, authors, publishers and other interested persons and organizations, of relationships conducive to the advancement of good indexing and the professional status and well-being of indexers
- enhancement of awareness and recognition of the role of indexers in the analysis, organization and accessibility of recorded knowledge and ideas

Promotion and External Relations

SI actively promotes to potential clients the services offered by qualified indexer members and publicizes indexing as an significant activity, by means of:

- its web site: www.socind.demon.co.uk
- its annual directory *Indexers available* (see 'Publications' below)
- its periodicals, booklets, information sheets, and occasional papers (see 'Publications' below)
- the Register of qualified indexers, from which the Registrar provides clients with the names of indexers suitable for specific kinds of work and in particular subject fields
- its local and special-interest groups (see 'Regional groups' and 'Special-interest groups' below)
- advertisements in relevant periodicals and at events staged by other bodies
- representation on the committees of other related organizations
- recommendation of a minimum remuneration rate for the most straightforward indexing work (see 'Fees' in Chapter 10)
- participation in the annual award of the Wheatley Medal (see 'Awards' below)
- regular updating of entries in directories and databases

Publications

For SI, as for most professional organizations, its regular periodical publications are a significant and valuable feature, providing information on indexing and raising its profile to a wide readership, enabling practising indexers to pass on their wisdom in relation to indexing and business practice, encouraging discussion on technical matters, publicizing forthcoming events, and highlighting topical items in related fields. *The Indexer* is the professional journal for all the affiliated societies, circulates in more than sixty countries, and is published twice a year. It contains articles about indexing and indexers, current-awareness bibliographies on indexing, reviews of published indexes, reviews of books on indexing and related subjects, society news, and letters to the editor. *SIdelights* is the newsletter of SI, available only to SI members. It appears four times a year, giving information on SI and other events, policy, training and qualifications, group activities, publications, practical and technical matters, and 'people' news, as well as providing (via letters to the editor) a forum for lively discussion of topical concerns.

SI also publishes an 'Occasional Papers' series, each one of which is devoted to the requirements of indexing a particular subject field or type of document and is written by indexers specializing in the field. At the time of writing, the subjects covered so far are biography, law, medical and biological sciences, newspapers and periodicals, and children's books.

Once a year the directory *Indexers available* is updated and dispatched (free of charge) to a large distribution list of publishers' editors, project managers, editorial agencies, and others who may wish to find indexers for particular work. It consists of a list of members of SI who meet certain criteria relating to qualifications and experience and who are available to take on indexing work; details are shown of their qualifications and their subject specialisms and document/media types. The directory, which is also available on the SI web site, includes indexes by subject specialism, materials and media specialism, other related skills (such as abstracting and proofreading), and postcode; an editor or author looking for an indexer can therefore quickly locate those relevant to a particular need. The directory also contains a statement of recommended practice and moral rights of indexers. The Scottish Group of SI produces, every two years, *Indexers available in Scotland* – a list of SI members resident in Scotland and available for indexing work. SI's Irish Group has produced

Indexers available 2000, its first directory of indexers available in Ireland, for free distribution to publishers; publication is intended to be annual.

A range of information leaflets is produced, dealing with topics such as indexing as a career, training and qualifications, running a freelance business, and buying a computer for indexing. The booklet *Last but not least: a guide for editors commissioning indexes*, the text of which is also available on the internet (at www.socind.demon.co.uk/commiss.htm), helps publishers and others who require the services of indexers.

Qualifications

There are two levels of SI qualification: Accreditation and Registration. Any member of the Society who buys and successfully completes the formal test papers based on the Society's *Training in indexing* open learning units (see 'Training and development' below), and thereby shows theoretical competence in indexing, is entitled to the status of Accredited Indexer (AI) while in membership of the Society. It is not a requirement that the member should have studied indexing by means of the SI units; training may be acquired from any source (formal or informal). Anyone may buy a sample set of self-administered tests (taken from the units), so that they can assess readiness for formal tests, whether or not they have bought the units.

To become a Registered Indexer (RI), a member must show experience and mastery of indexing skills in the practical indexing of books, periodicals, or other publications by submitting an index (published or unpublished) together with answers to a searching questionnaire, answering a short test paper (which includes creating an index to a short set text), and providing references from publishers or other clients. An applicant for Registration must be an SI member and must either:

- have satisfactorily completed an indexing course followed by at least two years' practical indexing experience

or:

- have no formal qualification but at least four years' practical indexing experience

Applications are examined by the Board of Assessors, made up of Registered Indexers with experience of index assessment and/or training. A larger panel of subject specialists is available to judge subject competence when necessary.

Training and Development

Training publications and programmes have been designed for indexers at all levels. The principal components are open learning units, workshops and a CPD (continuing professional development) scheme.

Open learning units

The *Training in indexing* units are based on the principle of open learning and are aimed at giving trainees a thorough grounding in the principles of indexing. Each unit contains a self-administered test (with answers) by which trainees can check their readiness to proceed to the assessed test papers (one per unit) which can be bought from the Society of Indexers. Units, tutorial support and formal tests are all available separately so that individuals can learn in their own way and at their own pace. Successful completion of the formal tests entitles an SI member to the status of Accredited Indexer of the Society (see 'Qualifications' above). Study by means of the units is not the only way in which trainees can prepare themselves for the formal test papers and become Accredited Indexers. The units are revised as and when necessary. At the time of writing, the current (2nd) edition consists of units covering:

- basic terminology, the documentary process, the ways in which documents can be categorized, the functional and mutual relationships of authors, users and indexers, and how indexes are made
- the selection of concepts for indexing, the choice of terminology, the form of headings (including names) and locators, and the use of cross-references
- the principal rules for arrangement of entries (filing order), the case for multiple sequences, the requirements of team and cumulative indexing, the procedures involved in book and journal production, the presentation of copy for setting, and how the finished index may be presented

- the advice and guidance available in standards, textbooks and peri- odicals, guides to specialist aspects of indexing and to indexing software, reference sources, the use and construction of thesauri, and how to make the most of libraries and databases through under- standing of classification schemes and use of catalogues and online searching
- good practice in establishing and running an indexing business: start-up, finance and taxation, commissions and contracts, customer relations, time and records management, legal matters, developing the business, and the activities and services of the Society of Indexers

Workshops
An annual programme of workshops is provided, led by qualified and expe- rienced indexers. Some are aimed at indexers at specific levels (beginners, in training, newly qualified, experienced/advanced) and others deal with particular indexing concerns (such as business aspects), indexing in a certain subject field (law, for example), indexing a certain type of mate- rial (e.g. periodicals), and preparing to apply for Registration.

Continuing professional development
SI emphasizes the importance of continuing professional development (CPD) for its members, in order that the overall level of indexing compe- tence is maintained and where necessary improved. Many indexers have long working lives, during which styles, customs, techniques, and formats change repeatedly. Like the members of any other profession, but partic- ularly because many of them are lone workers with a tendency to isolation, they need constantly to monitor their work and to keep in touch with technical, documentary, social, commercial, and political changes, and to implement whatever is required of them.

SI has carried out an audit of its members to discover the extent to which they were individually involved in CPD, and now has a subcom- mittee that is exploring possible schemes for CPD. Members are encouraged to become involved in group activities such as workshops, conferences, and meetings of local and subject groups, but also – as indi- viduals – to enhance their development by private reading of professional books and journals, writing articles for relevant periodicals, discussing technical matters with colleagues, and participating in indexing-related discussions on the internet (see 'internet discussion groups and mailing lists' later in this chapter).

Grants and bursaries
Small grants are occasionally made for research, and bursaries are available to assist indexing trainees to attend the annual conference.

Structure and Control

The Society is administered from its office in Sheffield, South Yorkshire, and managed by an elected Council, with the support of a number of committees covering specific tasks such as finance, training and qualifications, marketing, publications, research, and the constitution. Most council and committee work is carried out on a voluntary (expenses paid) basis; honoraria are paid to officers. A distinguished person in the field of indexing is elected as president for a period of from two to four years.

Regional Groups

SI members are widely spread around Britain and Ireland (and a few are in other countries), so local groups help to keep those in particular geographical areas in touch with each other and enable them to meet for discussions and training events. Because they are dependent on the number of members living in each area, and particularly on those members who are able and willing to organize meetings and other events, some of the groups are strong and permanent, whereas others tend to come and go. At the time of writing, there are groups for these areas:

England:
- Hereford and Worcester, Gloucestershire, Shropshire, the West Midlands (the Three Choirs Local Group – a musical allusion to the famous Three Choirs Festival)
- London
- North West
- North East
- Sussex
- West Country
- Yorkshire

Ireland
Scotland

Special-interest Groups

Individual indexers tend to specialize in the subject areas in which they
have been educated or trained, or of which they have particular experience or knowledge. The groups so far formed, focusing on the needs of
certain subjects, include:

- Archaeology
- Genealogy
- Law

Conferences

Conferences are normally held every year, sometimes incorporating the
annual general meeting. The venue changes from year to year, moving to
a different location in Britain or Ireland (in recent years, for example,
Canterbury, Tynemouth, Dublin, and Cambridge) so that indexers in the
locality have the chance to attend. Speakers are drawn from the indexing
and publishing world (including some from other countries), and there are
discussion groups, workshops, demonstrations, trips to local places of
interest, and other entertainments.

Awards

The Wheatley Medal – inaugurated in 1960 and named in honour of Henry
B. Wheatley (the nineteenth century author of books on indexing), and
sponsored by Whitaker, is awarded each year by the Society of Indexers
and the Library Association for an outstanding index published in the
United Kingdom in the two years preceding the date of submission.
Indexes are judged on their clarity and comprehensiveness, the choice of
index terms and their formation into suitable headings, the appropriate
use of cross-references, helpful presentation of locators (page or paragraph references), the layout, presentation and overall impact of the index,
and its relevance to the text. In addition to the medal, winners also receive
a cash prize. Winners in recent years include:

- Barbara Hird, for *The Cambridge history of medieval English literature*, published by Cambridge University Press, 1999
- Caroline Sheard, for *Textbook of dermatology* 6th edn., published by Blackwell Science, 1998
- Janine Ross, for *Rheumatology*, published by Mosby International, 1997
- Gillian Northcott and Ruth Levitt, for *Dictionary of art* , published by Macmillan, 1996
- Ruth Richardson and Robert Thorne, for *'The Builder' illustrations index 1843–1883* , published by Hutton and Rostron, 1995
- H.C.G. Matthew, for *The Gladstone diaries*, edited by H.C.G. Matthew, published by Oxford University Press, 1994
- Janine Ross, for *Encyclopaedia of food science, food technology and nutrition*, by R. Macrae and others, published by Academic Press, 1993
- Paul Nash, for *The world environment 1972–1992*, published by Chapman and Hall, 1992
- Elizabeth Moys, for *The British tax encyclopedia*, published by Sweet and Maxwell, 1991

The Carey Award, first presented in 1977 in memory of SI's first President, Gordon V. Carey, is conferred from time to time on individuals who have performed outstanding services to indexing. The Bernard Levin Award, first presented in 2000, is named in honour of *The Times* columnist Bernard Levin, for his promotion of the cause of indexes and indexing.

Library

The Society's Library, consisting of books and pamphlets on indexing and related subjects, is housed at its office in Sheffield, South Yorkshire.

American Society of Indexers (ASI)

Address: ASI Administrative Support Office
11250 Roger Bacon Drive, Suite 8
Reston, VA 20190–5202
Tel: +1 703–234–4147
Fax: +1 703–435–4390
email: info@asindexing.org
Web site: www.asindexing.org

ASI was founded in 1968 'to promote excellence in indexing and increase awareness of the value of well-written and well-designed indexes', and is the only professional organization in the United States solely devoted to the advancement of indexing, abstracting and database construction. It is a non-profit educational and charitable organization, serving indexers, librarians, abstractors, editors, publishers, database producers, data searchers, product developers, technical writers, academic professionals, researchers, readers, and others concerned with indexing. It has members from around the world. It works to improve the quality of indexing and to serve the needs of indexers by:

- increasing awareness of the value of high-quality indexes and indexing
- offering members access to educational resources that enable them to strengthen their indexing performance
- keeping members up to date on advances in indexing technology and the expanding role of indexing through conferences, workshops and publications
- providing members with a variety of means of communication – through meetings, directories, publications, and electronic communication – with each other and related professionals
- defending and safeguarding the professional interests of indexers
- promoting index standards for indexers, editors and abstractors
- co-operating with other professional organizations in information science

Promotion and External Relations

ASI publicizes its activities and its members' services centrally through:

- its web site: www.asindexing.org
- its directory *Indexer locator*
- its local chapters
- its special-interest groups
- its newsletter, books, and booklets
- contact with related organizations
- awards

Through its affiliation with the indexing societies of other countries it liaises about technical and commercial matters, and it co-operates with other professional bodies in the field of information and library science.

The society does not publish a scale of recommended remuneration for indexing work, but gives general advice to indexer members about price-setting and charging for services.

Publications

The newsletter *Key words*, issued six times per year, is free to members and can be bought by non-members. A separate publication, *Key words index* is an index to past issues of *Key words* and its predecessor *ASI newsletter*; a hypertext version of the index is also available. *Indexer locator*, a directory of freelance indexers available to take on work, gives details of special expertise and experience. Indexers are listed by subject and language speciality, by types of material indexed and by geographical location. It is distributed free to publishers. *Working with freelance indexers*, a guide for publishers and others considering engaging an indexer, is available on the internet (www.asindexing.org/editorsguide.shtml).

Qualifications

ASI does not set its own qualifications. Members have received training and acquired experience by several different routes. (See 'Training and development' below.)

Training and Development

Training courses are not centrally provided by ASI. The annual meeting includes workshops, round tables and presentations, and individual Chapters also include workshops and presentations in their regular meetings.

Structure and Control

The ASI's administrative support office is operated from Reston, Virginia. Management is the responsibility of the elected Board of Directors. Numerous committees attend to particular concerns, such as: archives, chapter relations, conference planning, editorial, awards, indexer services, long-range planning, membership, professional development, publications, publicity, special-interest groups, and the web site.

Chapters

The spread of the membership throughout the United States gives great significance to the formation of state-based or regional chapters, which enable members to meet and co-operate more easily. Some are more active than others, depending – as usual – on the number of people involved and their availability and their willingness to become involved. Some have installed local directories of their indexer members on their own web sites. At the time of writing, chapters exist in:

- Arizona
- Carolina
- Chicago/Great Lakes
- Colorado
- Golden Gate
- Indiana-Heartland
- Massachusetts
- New Mexico
- New York
- Pacific Northwest
- South Central
- Southern California
- Twin Cities
- Washington
- Western New York
- Wisconsin

Special-interest Groups (SIGs)

These groups, focused on the indexing of particular subject areas or certain types of document, provide networking and marketing possibilities for ASI members through the use of email lists, newsletters, brochures, and meetings. At the time of writing, the groups are:

- Culinary
- Gardening/environmental
- Genealogy/transcription
- History/archaeology
- Psychology/sociology
- Scholarly indexing
- Science/medicine
- Sport/fitness/travel
- Web indexing

Annual Meetings

The annual meeting takes place in a different location in the United States each year – including, in recent times, Indianapolis (Indiana), Seattle (Washington), Winston-Salem (North Carolina), and Denver (Colorado) – and includes talks by indexing experts, speakers from the world of literature and publishing, a variety of focused sessions and panels, educational and professional development sessions, and social events.

Awards

The ASI/H.W. Wilson Award, established in 1978, honours excellence in the indexing of an English language monograph or other non-serial publication published during the previous year. Its existence provides and publicizes models of excellence in indexing and encourages greater recognition, among publishers, of the importance of quality in book indexing. The indexes submitted are assessed on content, structure and accuracy of entries, physical format, typography and style. The award comprises a citation and a cash prize for the indexer, and a citation for the publisher. Winners in recent years include:

- Richard Genova, for *Brownfields law and practice* by Michael B. Gerrard, published by Matthew Bender & Co., Inc
- Laura Moss Gottlieb, for *Dead wrong: a Death Row lawyer speaks out against capital punishment*, by Michael Mello, published by University of Wisconsin Press
- Gillian Northcott and Ruth Levitt, for *Dictionary of art*, edited by Joan Shoaf Turner, published by Grove's Dictionaries. (This index also

won the Wheatley Medal in the UK, where the book was published by Macmillan; see 'Society of Indexer: Awards' above.)

- Martin L. White, for *The promise of pragmatism* by John Patrick Diggins, published by University of Chicago Press
- Patricia Deminna, for *Carnal Israel: reading sex in Talmudic culture*, by Daniel Boyarin, published by University of California Press
- Rachel Jo Johnson, for *The American law of real property*, by Arthur Gaudio, published by Matthew Bender
- Nancy L. Daniels, for *Beyond public architecture: strategies for design evaluation*, by Hamid Shirvani, published by Van Nostrand Reinhold
- Marcia Carlson, for *Strategic nuclear arms & arms control debates*, by Lynn Eden and Steven Miller, published by Cornell University Press
- Philips James, for *Medicine for the practicing physician* 2nd edn., by John Willis Hurst, published by Butterworths

The Ted C. Hines Award – named after one of the founders of ASI – was established in 1993 and is presented to members who are judged to have provided exceptional service to ASI.

Australian Society of Indexers (AusSI)

Address: PO Box R598, Royal Exchange, NSW 1225, Australia
Tel/fax: +61 500 525 005
email: memsec@aussi.org
Web site: www.aussi.org

AusSI is open to any individual and institution engaged in indexing or interested in promoting the objects of the Society. Its members are based in all the states and territories of Australia and in New Zealand. It was founded in Melbourne in 1976, succeeding the Society of Indexers in Australia. Its objectives are:

- to improve the quality of indexing in Australia
- to promote the training, continuing professional development, status and interest of indexers in Australia
- to act as an advisory body on indexing to which authors, editors, publishers and others may apply for guidance

- to provide opportunities for those interested in and connected with indexing to meet and exchange information, ideas and experience relating to all aspects of indexing
- to establish and maintain relationships between the Society and other bodies with related interests
- to publish information in accord with the foregoing objectives

Promotion and External Relations

The services of practising indexers are promoted by the Society by way of:

- its web site: www.aussi.org
- its directory *Indexers available* (see 'Publications' below)
- its newsletter (see 'Publications' below)
- the Register of Indexers, which lists those members whose practical ability in the compilation of indexes has been assessed and formally recognized by the Society as of professional standard
- its branches
- recommendation of a minimum remuneration rate for freelance back-of-the-book indexers
- the award of an annual medal for an outstanding index
- a prize for an outstanding Web index

Publications

Indexers available aims to help publishers and authors to find an indexer. It is maintained on the AusSI web site and published in print. Entries relate to indexers who are AusSI members and who expect to be available to take commissions. It includes Registered Indexers, as well as other indexers with training and/or experience whose competence has not yet been established. The *Newsletter* appears in print and on the web site.

Qualifications

A Register of Indexers is maintained. To become a Registered Indexer, a member must produce an index of sufficient quality to meet the professional standards of the Society. The index should provide efficient and effective access to all sources of information relevant to the work's readership, and should display the indexer's understanding of indexing practices and processes, modified as required by external publishing requirements. The indexes submitted are judged by a Panel of Assessors.

Training and Development

AusSI members conduct courses on book indexing and on indexing and abstracting for databases and thesaurus construction. Other opportunities for continuing professional development are provided through meetings, courses and workshops, at national and branch level and through the newsletter.

Structure and Control

AusSI's executive base is in Sydney, New South Wales. The elected Committee is responsible for management. State branches have their own officers.

Branches and Groups

Branches and groups have been formed in:

- Victoria
- New South Wales
- Australian Capital Territory
- South Australia
- Queensland

Special-interest Group

A special interest group has been formed for indexers interested in genealogy.

Conferences and Meetings

Annual meetings and occasional international conferences are staged in different locations; branch meetings are held in the local areas.

Awards

The Society bestows an annual medal for an outstanding index to a book or periodical compiled in Australia or New Zealand. An index submitted must be of substantial size and contain complex subject matter. The indexer's expertise must be revealed through the language, form and structure of the index and it must serve the needs of the text and the reader. Recent winners are:

- Lynnette Peel, for *The Henty journals: a record of farming, whaling and shipping in Portland Bay, 1834–1839*, edited by Lynnette Peel, published by Miegunyah Press with the State Library of Victoria, 1996
- Barry Howarth, for *Portrait of the family within the total economy*, by G.D. Snooks, published by Cambridge University Press, 1994
- Max McMaster, for *Chemistry and biology of 1–3 beta-glucans*, edited by A.D. Clarke and B.A. Stone, published by La Trobe University Press, 1993
- Max McMaster, for *Infectious disease in pregnancy and the newborn infant*, by G.L. Gilbert, published by Harwood Academic, 1991
- Margery Price, for *Law handbook*, published by Fitzroy Legal Service, 1992
- Geraldine Suter, for *The Argus, 1860* [newspaper], published by the State Library of Victoria, 1990

Since 1996 an award has been made for an outstanding Web index (from anyone anywhere in the world), judged on content and layout. Winners include:

- Tasmania Online, State Library of Tasmania, Hobart, www. tas.gov.au. Lloyd Sokvitne (manager and metadata developer), Liz Holliday (editor of the subject index and business guide's Javascript) and Elizabeth Louden (cataloguer)
- Christabel Wescombe, Faculty of Education internet Guide. www. library.usyd.edu.au/Guides/Education
- Alan Wilson, Australian Parliamentary Library Index. www.aph.gov. au/library/parlindx.html

Library

The AusSI collection of books and periodicals on indexing and related topics is housed in the Library of the University of New South Wales.

Indexing and Abstracting Society of Canada (IASC) / Société Canadienne pour l'Analyse de Documents (SCAD)

Address: IASC/SCAD, PO Box 744, Station F, Toronto, Ontario, Canada M4Y 2N6
Web site: www.indexingsociety.ca
The Society was founded in 1977, with these objectives:

- to encourage the production and use of indexes and abstracts
- to promote the recognition of indexers and abstractors
- to improve indexing and abstracting techniques
- to provide a means of communication among individual indexers and abstractors across Canada

Any individual or institution interested in the promotion of these objectives may become a member.

Promotion and External Relations

IASC/SCAD promotes its members' services, and a better understanding of indexing, through:

- its web site: tornade.ere.umontreal.ca/~turner/iasc/home.html
- its *Register of indexers available/Répertoire des indexeurs* (see 'Publications' below).
- its bulletin, thematic reviews and bibliographies (see 'Publications' below)
- liaison with other, related, organizations

Publications

The *IASC Bulletin/Bulletin de la SCAD* is published four times a year. The *Register of indexers available/Répertoire des indexeurs*, a bilingual (English and

French) list of indexers who are available for work on a part-time or contractual basis, is produced annually and mailed to Canadian publishers; it is also installed on the IASC/SCAD web site. All the indexers listed are members of IASC/SCAD, but inclusion in the list does not carry any warranty or accreditation. Indexers are listed alphabetically by family name (surname), and indexes are included leading from name, language (other than English and French), major cities, skills, materials, and subject. Apart from these regular publications, occasional thematic reviews and bibliographies are produced.

Qualifications

IASC/SCAD does not have an accreditation system.

Training and Development

Members have acquired their training by various means, including library/information and publishing courses at tertiary institutions, correspondence courses, and 'learning while doing'.

Structure and Control

The society is run by the Executive.

Conferences and Meetings

Annual and local meetings are held, plus the occasional joint meeting with other, related, organizations.

Association of Southern African Indexers and Bibliographers (ASAIB)

email: jkalley@eisa.org.za
Web site: www.asaib.org.za (under construction, at time of writing)

ASAIB, now having around 80 members throughout South Africa, Namibia and Botswana, was established in 1994 to serve the interests of indexers and bibliographers in Southern Africa and to promote all aspects of indexing and bibliographical activity. Membership is open to anyone engaged in indexing or bibliographical work, or interested in ASAIB's objectives, which are:

- compilation and maintenance of a register of freelance indexers and bibliographers, which is disseminated to the publishing industry
- liaison with the publishing industry to ensure the maintenance of standards, and the negotiation of appropriate fees for indexers and bibliographers
- organization of short courses, meetings and workshops
- functioning as an advisory bureau and information clearing centre, including information on recommended books, computerized indexing programs, and university and other courses in indexing and bibliography offered in Southern Africa
- publication of guides (e.g. basic manuals) and information booklets for its members

Promotion and External Relations

The status of indexing in general and the indexing services offered by members, are fostered through:

- its *Directory of indexers and bibliographers in South Africa* (see 'Publications' below)
- its periodicals and booklets (see 'Publications' below)
- contact with the publishing industry in relation to indexing standards and fee negotiation

Publications

The *Newsletter* is distributed to members three times a year. The *Directory of indexers and bibliographers in South Africa* gives details of indexers' qualifications, experience and specialist subjects, and includes geographical and subject specialization indexes. Monographic publications include guides dealing with various aspects of indexing and bibliography, and an information series of pamphlets.

Training and Development:

Training and professional development events organized by ASAIB include short courses, meetings and workshops in indexing and bibliography.

Structure and Control

ASAIB is run by the National Executive Committee.

China Society of Indexers (CSI)

Address: Mr Ge, East China Normal University, 3663 Zhongshan Road
(North), Shanghai, China 200062
Tel: +86 (21) 6223 2317
Fax: +86 (21) 6257 9196
email: indsoc@libserver.lib.ecnu.edu.cn
Web site: www.yp.online.sh.cn/suoyin/sy-sy.htm

The Society, an independent non-profit academic organization, was founded in 1991 and now has over 1000 members. It is involved in uniting indexers throughout China, and overseas colleagues, in order to extend the range of indexing services using modern advanced methods and to use indexing in the cause of modernization and socialization. Its aims are:

* to promote the research and study of index theory
* to encourage index compilation and publication
* to train professional indexers
* to strengthen academic exchange at home and abroad

Promotion and External Relations

Information about the Society and about indexing is disseminated by means of:

* its web site: www.yp.online.sh.cn/suoyin/sy-sy.htm
* its publications (see 'Publications' below)

Publications

A membership directory and a newsletter are published.

Training and Development

Academic seminars are held.

Structure and Control

The Society is based in Shanghai. Its departments include: Secretariat, Compilation, Research and Study, Propaganda, Liaison, and Editorial.

Conferences

Conferences are held biennially.

Internet Discussion Groups and Mailing Lists

'Subscription' to these groups is normally free; all that an intending partic-ipant usually has to do is to send an email message to the group address; from then on all messages received from the groups' members are emailed to the new participant, who can take part by replying to existing messages and by raising new topics. Some subscribers are content just to 'lurk' – to receive and look at the messages and note useful information, but not to correspond. Others join in with enthusiasm, giving accounts of their indexing experiences and suggesting solutions to problems identified by others. Some groups are concerned with any indexing-related topic, some are primarily for students/trainees, others are focused on the use of a particular indexing program. The groups tend to come and go, to spawn new ones, extend and limit their subject range. Some of them are moder-ated (the content of messages received is informally checked, before dissemination to group participants); others receive and forward messages as received, without checking or review. Some of those active at the time of writing are:

aliaINDEXERS

An Australian discussion list for people involved in all aspects of indexing activity. Information at: www.alia.org.au/e-lists/subscribe.htm

ASI-L

A forum for discussion of the administration of the American Society of Indexers (ASI); limited to ASI members.

Information at: www.asindexing.org/asi-l.html

CindexUsers

A forum for discussing the CINDEX professional indexing program – exchanging tips, tricks and techniques among CINDEX users.

Information at: www.onelist.com/community/cindexusers and at: www.egroups.com.community/cindexusers

The Indexer's WebRing

Provides contact points for people interested in indexing – indexers, authors, publishers, publications managers.

Information at: www.geocities.com/Athens/4537/indxr.html

INDEX-L

A discussion group aimed at promoting good indexing practice by providing a forum for the sharing of information and ideas relating to all aspects of index preparation; open to aspiring and professional indexers and others interested in indexing. Participants include, but are not limited to, members of professional indexers' organizations, librarians, library school faculty, and editors.

Information at: www.asindexing.org/discgrps.shtml

INDEX-L Archives

A facility for looking at the archives of INDEX-L (see above).

Information at: www.asindexing.org/discgrps.shtml

Index-NW

A list for the discussion of topics relevant to experienced or aspiring indexers, index users, and publishers of indexed materials, in the Pacific Northwest of North America.

Information at: www.asindexing.org/discgrps.shtml

Indexstudents

A discussion list for issues related to learning about indexing books, magazines, databases, and the Web. Focused primarily on the concerns of people doing the USDA (United States Department of Agriculture) Graduate School courses in indexing (about which information can be found on the internet at grad.usda.gov/programs_services/corres/edit_coursedes.cfm). Topics also include other methods of education, and starting a freelance indexing business. Membership is open to beginners, experienced indexers and course instructors.

Information at: www.egroups.com/group/skyindexusers

MACREX List

A forum for discussion on all issues related to indexing with the MACREX dedicated indexing program, and to air and share tricks, tips, problems and solutions.

Information at: www.macrex.cix.co.uk/discuss.htm

SIdeline

Open to members of the Society of Indexers, for discussion of indexing, the business side of indexing, and Society matters.

Information at: www.socind.demon.co.uk/Sideline.htm

SKYIndexUsers

A mailing list for users of the Sky indexing program to exchange tips, tricks and techniques

Information at: www.egroups.com/group/SKYIndexUsers

WINDMAIL (Web Indexers' Mailing List)

A discussion list for Web indexers

Information at: windmail.listbot.com

Related Organizations in the UK

Because indexing has a wide range of applications, other organizations in many fields – such as publishing, library and information work, research, archives, records management, writing, history (local, regional, national, and international), genealogy, medicine, law, national and international standards – also have an interest in indexing. Some have indexing subgroups; others have a representative who maintains liaison with the relevant indexing organization.

Professional organizations

Aslib (the Association for Information Management)

Staple Hall
Stone House Court
London EC3A 7PB
Tel: +44 (0)20 7903 0000
Fax: +44 (0)20 7903 0011
email: aslib@aslib.com
Web site: www.aslib.com

Association for companies and organizations concerned with the efficient management of information resources. Promotes best practice in the management of information resources.

Association of Learned and Professional Society Publishers (ALPSP)

> South House
> The Street
> Clapham
> Worthing
> West Sussex
> BN13 3UU
> Tel: +44 (0)1903 871 686
> Fax: +44 (0)1903 871 457
> email: sec-gen@alpsp.org.uk
> Web site: www.alpsp.org.uk

> Represents the interests of all those involved in the publication of academic and professional information in all media.

Business Archives Council

> 101 Whitechapel High Street
> London E1 7RE
> Tel: +44 (0)20 7247 0024
> Fax: +44 (0)20 7422 0026
> email: bac@archives.gla.ac.uk
> Web site: www.archives.gla.ac.uk/bac

> Objectives: to encourage the preservation of British business records, to advise on the administration and management of archives and current records, to promote the use of business records.

Business Archives Council of Scotland

> BACS Surveying Officer
> Archives & Business Records Centre
> University of Glasgow
> 77–87 Dumbarton Road
> Glasgow G11 6PW
> Tel: +44 (0)141 330 4159
> Fax: +44 (0)141 330 4158
> email: bacs@archives.gla.ac.uk
> Web site: www.archives.gla.ac.uk/bacs

Concerned with the active preservation of Scottish business records.

European Association of Science Editors (EASE)

Secretary-Treasurer, Mrs Jennifer T. Gretton
PO Box 426
Guildford
GU4 7ZH
Tel/fax: +44 (0)1483 211056
email: secretary@ease.org.uk
Web site: www.ease.org.uk

Non-governmental organization aiming to promote improved communication in science by providing efficient means for co-operation among editors, and to assist in the efficient operation of publications in the sciences.

Institute of Information Scientists

39–41 North Road
London N7 9DP
Tel: +44 (0)20 7619 0624
Fax: +44 (0)20 7619 0626
email: iis@dial.pipex.com
Web site: www.iis.org.uk

Association for people involved in creating, retrieving, organizing or disseminating information. Planning to form a unified professional body with the Library Association (see below).

Institute of Publishing

7–8 Kendrick Mews
London SW7 3HG
Tel/fax: +44 (0)1905 613869
email: rosiethom@compuserve.com
Web site: www.instpublishing.org.uk

Aim: to foster excellence in publishing, through the provision of services, products and benefits (including education, training and development) for individuals in the publishing industry.

Institute of Scientific and Technical Communicators

Blackhorse Road
Letchworth
Herts
SG6 1YY
Tel: +44 (0)1462 486825
Fax: +44 (0)1462 674777
email: istc@istc.org.uk
Web site: www.istc.org.uk

Offers opportunities to exchange views and information with other professional communicators, subsidized training for members, recognition of professional status, magazine, and special-interest groups.

Library Association

7 Ridgmount Street
London WC1E 7AE
Tel: +44 (0)20 7255 0500
Fax: +44 (0)20 7255 0501
email: info@la-hq.org.uk
Web site: www.la-hq.org.uk

Association for librarians and information managers in business and industry, further and higher education, schools, local and central government departments and agencies, the health service, the voluntary sector and national public libraries. Planning to form a unified professional body with the Institute of Information Scientists (see above).

Library Association: Cataloguing and Indexing Group

> Hon. Sec: John Scott Cree
> Tel: +44 (0)20 7972 5928
> Fax: +44 (0)20 7972 1609
>
> For LA members engaged or interested in the organization and retrieval of information and in the planning, production, maintenance and exploitation of library catalogues, bibliographies and indexes.

Publishers' Association

> 1 Kingsway
> London WC2B 6XF
> Tel: +44 (0)20 7565 7474
> Fax: +44 (0)20 7836 4543
> email: mail@publishers.org.uk
> Web site: www.publishers.org.uk
>
> Association for book, journal and electronic publishers in the UK.

Records Management Society of Great Britain

> Woodside
> Coleheath Bottom
> Speen
> Princes Risborough
> Bucks.
> HP27 0SZ
> Tel: +44 (0)1494 488599
> Fax: +44 (0)1494 488590
> email: rms@rms-gb.org.uk
> Web site: www.rms-gb.org.uk
>
> For all concerned with records and information management, regardless of their professional or organizational status or ualifications, and for organizations wishing to develop records or information systems and those providing services in these fields.

Society of Archivists

Executive Secretary: Patrick Cleary
40 Northampton Road
London ECIR 0HB
Tel: +44 (0)20 7278 8630
Fax: +44 (0)20 7278 2107
email: societyofarchivists@archives.org.uk
Web site: www.archives.org.uk

Exists to promote the care and preservation of archives and the better administration of archive repositories, to advance the training of its members and to encourage relevant research and publication.

Society of Authors

84 Drayton Gardens
London SW10 9SB
Tel: +44 (0)20 7373 6642
Fax: +44 (0)20 7373 5768
email: authorsoc@writers.org.uk
Web site:www.writers.org.uk/society

Founded to protect the rights and further the interests of authors. An independent trade union, with members working in all media.

Society of Freelance Editors and Proofreaders (SFEP)

Mermaid House
I Mermaid Court
London SEI IHR
Tel: +44 (0)20 7403 5141
Web site: www.sfep.demon.co.uk

Aims to promote high editorial standards and to achieve recognition of the professional status of its members.

Writers' Guild of Great Britain

> 430 Edgware Road
> London W2 1EH
> Tel: +44 (0)20 7723 8074
> Fax: +44 (0)20 7706 2413
> email: postie@wggb.demon.co.uk
> Web site: www.writers.org.uk/guild

> Mission: to ensure that writers of all media are properly represented, paid and accredited.

Standards organizations

The International Standards Organization (ISO), based in Geneva, Switzerland, is a non-governmental federation of national standards bodies from around 130 countries, including the British Standards Institution (see below). It promotes the development of standardization and related activities in the world, with a view to facilitating the international exchange of goods and services and developing co-operation in the spheres of intellectual, scientific, technological and economic activity. The international indexing standard ISO 999: 1996 (published in UK as British Standard BS ISO 999) was prepared by one of its technical committees.

British Standards Institution (BSI)

> 389 Chiswick High Road
> London W4 4AL
> Tel: +44 (0)20 8996 9000
> Fax: +44 (0)20 8996 7400
> email: info@bsi.org.uk
> Web site: www.bsi.org.uk

> Standards and quality services organization serving the public and private sectors, and working to facilitate the production of British, European and international standards.

The Society of Indexers takes an active interest in the development of published standards relating to indexing, and is represented on the relevant technical committees of the British Standards Institution. For instance, the technical committee for indexes, filing and thesauri, which was responsible for the UK contribution to the international standard published in the UK as BS ISO 999: 1996 *Information and documentation – guidelines for the content, organization and presentation of indexes* and in Australia (under the same title) as AS/NZS 999:1999. Janet Shuter, an SI member, was project leader of the international working group that compiled the standard and herself compiled its index. The standard offers guidelines – applicable to all kinds of print, non-print and electronic materials – for the content, organization and presentation of indexes, with illustrative examples. Basic principles and practice, on which indexers can build, are its main concern, therefore it does not deal with detailed indexing procedures or with the totally mechanized generation of indexes. British Standards are reviewed periodically, and it is at this stage that individual members of participating organizations may offer suggestions collectively via their organizations.

Organizations providing training in the UK

Because indexing varies considerably in its applications – depending on the material being indexed, the purpose and intended use of the index, so the training for it differs. Several kinds of organization (academic, commercial, professional) provide training, often aiming at particular target groups, though some provision overlaps. The methods used include open day courses, workshops and seminars focusing on specific levels of indexer and subjects, in-house day courses customized for the needs of particular organizations, modules in academic and vocational courses (e.g. for librarians, editors, technical writers), correspondence courses and other types of distance learning. Aside from these 'institutional' methods, there are the possibilities of private study – learning by reading about indexing, examining indexes, compiling indexes for personal use, talking to working indexers, and thereby building up a body of knowledge and technique – and of one-to-one tuition by a practising indexer. Some of the best-known organizations are listed below; other institutions (such as academic institutions) and individual practising indexers also provide training. Details of current opportunities are available from the professional organizations for indexers and on the internet.

Society of Indexers (see 'Indexing societies' above)

> Open learning units, providing a route to Accreditation. Workshops and seminars.

Aslib (the Association for Information Management) (see 'Professional organizations' above)

> Open and in-house courses in information management, including cataloguing and indexing.

Book Indexing Postal Tutorials (BIPT)

> Ann Hall
> The Lodge
> Sidmount Avenue
> Moffat
> DG10 9BS
> Tel/fax: +44 (0)1683 220440
> email: bipt@lodge-moffat.co.uk
> Web site: www.lodge-moffat.co.uk

> Individual postal or residential tuition in back-of-the-book indexing.

Indexing Research

> 100 Allens Creek Road
> P.O.Box 18609
> Rochester
> New York 14618–0609
> USA
> Tel: +1 716 461–5530
> Fax: +1 716 442–3924
> email: info@indexres.com
> Web site: www.indexres.com

> Training in the use of the CINDEX dedicated indexing program (in the UK as well as the US).

Indexing Specialists

> 202 Church Road
> Hove
> East Sussex
> BN3 2DJ
> Tel: +44 (0)1273 738299
> Fax: +44 (0)1273 323309
> email: info@indexing.co.uk
> Web site: www.indexing.co.uk

> Mainly a producer of indexes, providing training in-house for its staff and, on request, for other organizations.

Library Association (see 'Professional organizations' above)

> Seminars, conferences and workshops.

MACREX Indexing Services

> Beech House
> Blaydon Burn
> Tyne & Wear
> NE 21 6JR
> Tel: +44 (0)191 414 2595
> Fax: +44 (0)191 414 1893
> email: D.Calvert@macrex.com
> Web site: www.macrex.com

> Workshops on the use of the MACREX dedicated indexing program.

> North America:
>> MACREX Support Office
>> c/o Wise Bytes
>> P.O. Box 3051
>> Daly City
>> CA 94015–0051
>> USA
>> Tel: +1 650 756 0821
>> Fax: +1 650 757 1567
>> email: macrex@aol.com

Australia and South-East Asia:
    Master Indexing
    44 Rothesay Avenue
    East Malvern
    Vic. 3145
    Australia
    Tel/fax: +61 (03) 9571 6341
    email: mindexer@interconnect.com.au

Paul Hamlyn Foundation

    18 Queen Anne's Gate
    London SW1H 9AA
    Tel: +44 (0)207 227 3500
    Fax: +44 (0)207 222 0601
    email: phf@globalnet.co.uk
    Web site: www.phf.org.uk

    Not a training provider, but operates a support scheme for training,
    for freelance workers in publishing.

Peterborough Technical Communication

    8 Whitewater
    Orton Whistow
    Peterborough
    PE2 6FB
    Tel: +44 (0)1733 237037
    Fax: +44 (0)1733 239933
    email: help@petecom.co.uk
    Web site: www.petecom.co.uk

    Training courses in technical communication techniques and tools,
    including indexing.

Publishing Training Centre at Book House

> 45 East Hill
> Wandsworth
> London SW18 2QZ
> Tel: +44 (0)208 874 2718
> Fax: +44 (0)208 870 8985
> email: publishing.training@bookhouse.co.uk
> Web site: www.train4publishing.co.uk

> Open and in-house courses in a wide range of publishing and management skills, including indexing.

Records Management Society of Great Britain (see 'Professional organizations' above)

> Training programmes being developed.

TFPL Ltd

> 17–18 Britton Street
> London EC1M 5TL
> Tel: +44 (0)207 251 5522
> Fax: +44 (0)207 251 8318
> email: central@tfpl.com
> Web site: www.tfpl.com

> Information management company offering training, consultancy, recruitment and executive search, conferences and seminars to the information market.

Further Reading

Wellisch, Hans H. (1995) *Indexing from A to Z* 2nd edn. New York: H.W. Wilson (pp. 432–439: Societies of indexers)

Index

Jane A. Horton asserts her moral rights as the creator of this index (July 2000)

NOTE: The index is alphabetized in word-by-word order, for example *data protection* is filed before *databases*. Numbers in headings are filed as though spelled out, for example *W3C* is filed as *WthreeC*. Prepositions in subheadings are ignored in filing. Page numbers are given in full form, e.g. 124–125. Page numbers followed by *bib* refer to bibliographical references. Where more than one page number is listed against a heading, page numbers in bold indicate major treatment of a subject. The following abbreviations are used in headings in the index: ASI for American Society of Indexers; AusSI for Australian Society of Indexers; SI for Society of Indexers.

Beare, Geraldine   222*bib*, 244*bib*
Bell, Hazel K.:
  biography indexes   294, 297*bib*
  fiction indexes   334, 373*bib*
    for children   313–314, 315*bib*
Benns media UK   330, 373*bib*
Berger, John   232, 243*bib*
Bernard Levin Award   419
bias in indexing   36, 62, 138,
    294–295
Bible   102–103, 149
biblical allusions   53
bibliographical citations:
  form of citations   59, 194
  as indexable elements   48, 59
  indexing and abstracting journals
    194
  indication in locators   141
  as locators   212
  science and technology materials
    289
  see also cited authors
bibliographies:
  annotated: limit on number of
    terms   64
  index sequences   18
  indexable parts   44, 294
billing clients   338, **349–351**, 363
biography indexes   293–297
  abbreviations in headings   76,
    297
  biographee's entry   295
  chronological subheadings
    147–148
  indexable content   41
  maintaining neutrality   106,
    294–295
  medical indexes   263
biological terms   165, 219, 271, 289
BIPT (Book Indexing Postal Tutorials)
    443

bis (locator suffix)   117
Blake, Doreen   222*bib*
'blind' cross-references   125
bold type:
  in index:
    categories of headings   174–175,
      209
    children's book indexes   306,
      310, 311, 313
    italic   175
    locators to major references
      133, 141, 174, 183
  in text: defined terms   61
Book Indexing Postal Tutorials (BIPT)
    443
book packagers   327
book reviews:
  comment on indexes   9, 30
  as indexable elements in serials
    indexes   194, 213
book-keeping   337–338
books:
  design advantages   376, 377
  see also documents; e-books
Booth, Pat F.   37–38, 39*bib*, 54,
    65*bib*
botanical names   82, 288
braces (curly brackets)   394
brackets:
  dates in law indexes   258,
    259
  illustration locators   111
  unpaired   394
  see also parentheses
brand names   208, 266, 269, 271,
    288
breaks in working hours   325, 354
Brenner, Diane   405*bib*
briefing for indexes   19–20, 180,
    365–366, 368
British humanities index (BHI)   179